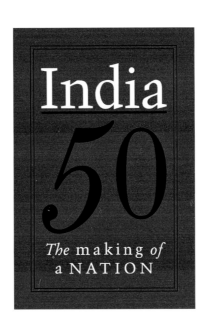

India
50
The making *of* a NATION

Oberoi Hotels
MUMBAI

First published in India in August 1997 by
Ayaz Memon and Book Quest Publishers

Book Quest Publishers
21 Rajgir Chambers, 2nd Floor
12/14 Shahid Bhagat Singh Road
Bombay 400 023
India
fax: (91 22) 2663281

Cover Design: Sunil Mahadik
Book Design: FX Designs, *Mumbai*
Processing: Jasra Graphics Pvt Ltd, *Mumbai*
Printed and Bound by: Pragati Art Printers, *Hyderabad*
Cover sculpture: Jaidev Baghel
Cover photograph: Israr Qureshi

Price: Rs 2,000, US $ 60, £ 40 sterling

ISBN: 81-86025-06-5

CONTENTS

FRIENDS UNLIMITED

A book of this nature would have been difficult to complete without assistance from innumerable people and institutions. We have to thank:

All our contributors, especially former Prime Minister V P Singh who corresponded from a hospital bed in London, noted poet Ali Sardar Jafri who wrote in spite of family troubles, Farooq Abdullah who took time off from a busy chief minister's schedule and former Supreme Court Chief Justice A H Ahmadi, who wrote between hectic travelling. Also, Vir Sanghvi and Janardan Thakur who responded unhesitatingly even though the request went to them at the 11th hour.

Clayton Murzello, Nirmal Mishra, Subuhi Saiyed, Sujata Hardikar, Ajit Nambiar, Shubha Sharma, Naushi Begum for inestimable help in research and putting up with impatience and extraordinary demands. The Bombay University Library from where large volumes of information were gathered, Mohini Bhullar for letting us use the India Today library in Mumbai.

Vitusha Oberoi, Narendra Kaushik and Sanjay Austa for vital help in Delhi, chasing contributors and digging out pictures. Mukhtar Ahmed, Bhagwan Singh, M S Shankar, Sanjay Suri, Michael Gonsalves, Sandhya Mendonca, Russell Murray and Narendra Kusnur for pitching in with critical information and help on call. Sandeep Patil for working long hours, often through the night, to provide clinching graphics.

Arun Katiyar and Vivek Sharma of Syndications Today were a godsend doing a rapid picture search in their archives and providing not only the bulk of the photographs used in this book, but doing this with a smile.

Arun Arora and Pradeep Guha for throwing open the Times of India archives, even if belatedly, and Anita Pujari and Zulekha Pancha for assisting in finding the pictures and getting prints made in double-quick time. Sajida Momin and Samarjit Guha of *The Statesman* (Calcutta) for devoting valuable time in a frantic last-minute picture search without which this book would have been incomplete. *The Hindu* for pitching in with a couple of key pictures in almost a stop-press situation. The Press Information Bureau, the staff of the Nehru Memorial Museum at Teen Murti, at Gandhi Smriti and the Defence Public Relations Department at Pune for allowing us to access their archives and then providing prints promptly. Basheer Ahmed, the additional secretary to the Chief Minister of Jammu & Kashmir for following up our request diligently. Also our photographer friends — Mukesh Parpiani, Sherwin Crasto, Gautam Patole, Jagdish Agarwal of Dinodia Picture Agency and Namas Bhojani — who came forward unhesitatingly, often to impossible deadlines. A special thanks to Ustad Alla Rakha for sharing his personal photo collection. And to Varini Trivedi for rifling through the Mid-Day library to fill in the gaps.

We would also like to thank Natwar Singh, Jasjit Singh, Rahul Singh, Sujit Podar, Abdul Ahad Saaz and Susan Abraham for giving us their invaluable advice in editorial matters and using their influence whenever required. Also Dr Vibhuti Patel for sharing her expertise on law matters.

At the production stage, all the typesetters in Mid-Day who punched in enormous amounts of copy. Pramod Kadegaonkar, Shubha Samant, Sudhendu Pratape and Dharmendra Rane and everyone else at Flagship Advertising who worked tirelessly and put up with hysteria and neurotic behaviour without complaint. Winston Albuquerque for painstaking precision in proofing the manuscript to minimise errors. U Menon and the technicians at Jasra Graphics and Pragati Printers who went hell for leather to finish the book in time. Israr Qureshi for his creative photography on the publicity folder and the cover. Pravin Kale and Vijay Kumar for helping in an emergency.

It would have been impossible to complete this book without our colleagues at Mid-Day being understanding of the enormity and urgency of our task. Excellent secretarial assistance by Philomena Lokare and Selwyn Vaz of Mid-Day in Mumbai who provided yeoman service, sending faxes, receiving messages, following up on commissioned articles with a touching willingness. Plus, Rajendran for ferrying people and material all over the city. In Calcutta, Churi Sundar and Nergish Pestonjee put their shoulder to the wheel, too.

A very special thanks to Arijit and Bulan Banerji for not only providing important books and vital tips but being a constant sounding board over intricate matters of history.

Finally

None of this would have been possible without Ayaz Memon. My debt to him is unrepayable. For coming up with a stupendous idea, as always, and then constantly enhancing it. For giving me the opportunity of a lifetime and then trusting me to do justice to it. For providing infinite patience, tolerance, encouragement and succour.

Thanks also to Ashok Chabria for his support, to Bunny Gulab for lending a sympathetic ear on demand, Sunil Mahadik for plunging in on request. And my family for giving me the wherewithal to rush in where angels fear to tread.

Ranjona Banerji

It would have been impossible to finish this work without the support of Amberin Memon who showed not only her expertise as a computer whiz in retrieving, converting and transferring data from thousands of sources into hundreds of floppies, but also exemplary patience and forbearance in enduring an agonising husband-turned-author-cum-co-publisher for almost a year without losing her sanity.

Ayaz Memon

MAKING OF INDIA 50

ALMOST a year to the day, I sprang up from my seat in the editor's cabin in Mid-Day's swank new office, walked across the room to where senior assistant editor Ranjona Banerji was holding forth in her usual compelling manner to a transfixed audience, broke up this durbar, took her aside and told her about an idea I had of doing a book which took a contemporary look at 50 years of India's independence. As is her wont, Banerji sniffed a challenge, deserted her captive audience, and wanted to hear some more.

Over the next month, *India 50: The Making of a Nation* was fleshed out from a mere grain into a full-fledged project of such seemingly overwhelming dimensions that established publishers got fatigued after the first quiver of excitement itself. Great idea, they said, but thanks no thanks. There was not enough time to complete such a book, and perhaps more pertinently (though unsaid) not enough return on the huge investment that seemed imperative.

By mid-September, there was despair. Time was running out furiously. The next such opportunity would come only 50 years later. Much as some irregular sessions of yoga and squash have helped me face the mirror and weighing machine without great embarrassment as yet, I could hardly delude myself into believing there was another chance for doing such a book. Then one day Ashok Chabria of Book Channel walked into the office wanting to negotiate a special discount scheme for Mid-Day readers and I played the gamble of my life.

Over his third rum and cola at a restaurant a few days later, Ashok Chabria, having willy-nilly become the butt of my hard-sell about the book, put up a hand to stall the monologue and delivered one stunning word — "Done'".

For the next 10 months Ashok used that word frequently as a monosyllabic affirmation of his support and approval of the project. In this period, the cost of the book spiralled more dramatically than did the BSE Sensex during Harshad Mehta's bull run, but Ashok remained unfazed. "Done" he said to every demand, every request. Such tacit approval of the project and such implicit trust in his writers made the passage of this book less turbulent than it would otherwise have been. Naturally for me, Ashok Chabria is a great publisher. But more importantly, he is a splendid man.

The key to the lock found as it were, the book no longer a dream, frenetic action to meet the crunching deadline followed. An assemblage of top class professionals fell rapidly into place, almost in a cascade.

Ranjona Banerji suddenly remembered a friend who was a graphic designer. But Sunil Mahadik was much more than just that. Multiple award winner for his advertising work, Sunil's creative genius exploded magnificently, first in determining the radical concept for the cover, then drawing mock visuals for each chapter on small brown paper envelopes which finally translated into magnificent page lay-outs and colour schemes that have brought the book alive.

Through Sunil Mahadik arrived Ravi Jasra of Jasra Graphics and P Narendra of Pragati Art Printers. Ravi Jasra, always nattily dressed, always gung-ho, was also always accommodating us out of turn at his scanning and process establishment. Putting a premium on quality, he pulled out all the stops nevertheless as the countdown to the deadly deadline began.

The last link in this chain was at Hyderabad where the cucumber-cool Narendrabhai masterminds the growth of Pragati Art Printers into becoming the best printing house in the country. Technology-savvy, deadline conscious and acutely committed to the project from the start, Narendrabhai printed, bound and delivered the book in an outrageously short period of time. Now I know why Ravi Jasra had kept referring to Narendrabhai as the 'miracle man'.

Meanwhile, I still had my job as editor of Mid-Day. I still have it, thanks to Tariq Ansari, managing director of Mid-Day Publications, who lent me explicit support in completing the project, even though this took so much of the time he was actually paying for. He also permitted me to utilise the technology and communication facilities at Mid-Day with the rider that while the book was obviously poaching on my time, I should not neglect the newspapers. I hope that I was able to do justice to both tasks. A less understanding boss would have seen this book as inimical to his interests.

And so to the fulcrum of the project. When I took over as editor of Mid-Day in 1993, Ranjona Banerji was the noted feature writer and irrepressible newsroom gag-bag. Over the next couple of years, however, I discovered she was extremely erudite, was a keen student of contemporary events and also had political thought. From a lifestyle specialist, as it were, to a leader comment writer, she made the transition with such amazing felicity that I had to look not far beyond my cabin to find a co-author. As it transpired, she wrote far more than she had bargained for.

Her versatile interests, scintillating way with words and grim determination in the face of many seemingly insurmountable problems have helped bring this project to fruition.

MAKING OF A NATION

HISTORY is too serious to be left to historians, remarked British Parliamentarian Iain Mcleod somewhere. This seemingly facetious statement was taken seriously in determining the nature and scope of this book.

Let it be stated upfront. This is not a comprehensive recount of India's 50 years since 1947. That would have been too exhaustive and impossible to achieve within the time available. Also, this would have required a level of expertise which neither of the authors possess.

In the vantage position of being an editor of a newspaper, however, one has been wtiness to the ignorance of so many people about India's history — and so often in oneself — that this book posed a unique challenge. It had to be done, but also differently, almost as a seduction for the authors and through them the readers, to probe further into their own lives, their own history.

The idea was not to get unduly academic — there are many better qualified people doing this job already — but provide a more contemporary approach in understanding the phenomena of India at the half-century mark. Which did not imply that a subject as fascinating and as significant as this was to be treated with frolicsome disdain. The search was for an interesting, yet balanced and stimulating perspective of Indian history.

To achieve this, we chose to narrow down the focus on events, people and issues — 50 of these spread over five decades— that have shaped our lives since that memorable mid-August day in 1947. That's where our story begins, the first decade ending in 1956 and so on. We chose to tread an unconventional path by going beyond politics and including business, sports, lifestyles, social issues — anything that we believed had had a strong impact on the Indian mind and the making of the nation.

For the narration of events, the active voice and direct speech style has been adopted. The attempt is to bring alive the events and issues as they may have unfolded in this 50-year passage. To provide a historical, social or political perspective, we sought renowned commentators, analysts or actual participants in the making of such events to contribute their points of view and enlarge the scope of the book. Wherever possible, we have also included statistics to detail or highlight an issue. In our narrative, we have tried to be factual to the extent possible, relying on acknowledged sources for information. Every commentator was given a working editorial brief but no more, allowing for expression without constraint or directive. The editorial policy was simply `let's be objective'.

The selection of subjects represented here will obviously be contentious. The nature of the book does not permit all choices, however popular or seemingly important. There might also be dispute over the treatment of events. But some of this may have been deliberate. There are no detailed assessments, for instance, of former prime ministers V P Singh and Narasimha Rao simply because we decided not to analyse those leaders who are still alive and where the verdict of history has not been hardened to any great degree as yet. Rajiv Gandhi is an exception to this clause and only because after the reopening of the Bofors case last year, his leadership is being reassessed. A small profile is included of how he came into the national reckoning instead.

Yes, there will be many disputes, but if we have succeeded in generating some interest in understanding contemporary India, the effort in bringing out this book will have been worthwhile.

Beyond that, we take full responsibility for any errors of omission and commission. With the plea that we tried our best.

Ayaz Memon
August 10, 1997

AWAKENINGS
1857 - 1905

Rani Lakshmibai of Jhansi in the forefront of the Revolt of 1857. She died in battle defending Gwalior in 1858

Dayanand Saraswati, religious reformer

Bahadur Shah Zafar II, the last Mughal Emperor, surrenders to the British. He died in exile in Rangoon in 1862

Iswar Chandra Vidyasagar, educationist

Bal Gangadhar Tilak, social and religious reformer

Swami Vivekananda, religious reformer

Sir Sy[...]

THE decline of the Mughal Empire makes Britain's rule over India complete. But dissent against such subjugation is never far away from the surface. Mutinies abound, though mainly as sporadic outbursts. Then, in 1857, comes the major outbreak of open and armed defiance. The sepoys in the army revolt, ostensibly because they might be compelled to bite cartridges soaked in cow and pork fat. But preserving the sanctity of caste and religion is only a cloak for more complex and deep-seated dissatisfactions. The most basic of this is the need for freedom from the threat of alien rule.

The desire for this freedom comes not only from political compulsions, but also from the social reforms that have been taking

Raja Rammohun Roy, social reformer, founder of Brahmo Samaj

Rabindranath Tagore, writer, philosopher and strong influence on India

...med Khan, educationist

Bankim Chandra Chatterjee's Ananda Math aroused patriotic fervour

Jyotiba Phule, social reformer and educationist

THE SIXTEENTH OCTOBER.

PARTITION OF BENGAL.

FEELING OF THE PEOPLE.

CALCUTTA IN MOURNING.

A Unique Sight.

Yesterday was one of the most memorable ays in the history of the British administration of India. It being the day on which the lengal partition scheme took effect, the ay on which our unsympathetic government orced a measure by a proclamation in the fficial gazette against the wishes of the hole population, the day on which our ulers tried to separate the Bengoli speaking cople of the East Bengal from those of the est Bengal, the people of Calcutta, irrespec ive of nationality, social position, creed and ex, observed it as a day of mourning. The aders of the Bengali community—Hindus nd Mahomedans—did not however silently iourn and weep. They did something more hey as a legacy to posterity and as a land iark to British administration laid the iendation of the Federation Hall. They lso took a practical step towards the furierance of the Swadeshi movement by pening the National Fund.

Amrita Bazar Patrika reports on the Partition of Bengal

1857	The Revolt of 1857
1858	The Queen's Proclamation, Government of India Act
1869	Birth of M K Gandhi
1875	Theosophical Society started by Madame Blavatsky and Olcott.
•	Arya Samaj started by Dayanand Saraswati
1877	Lord Ripon holds Durbar where Queen Victoria is proclaimed Empress of India
1878	Vernacular Press Act passed by Lord Lytton, putting stringent restrictions on the freedom of the Press, except journals published in English. Lytton is provoked by the severe criticism of his foreign policy
1882	Lord Ripon issues his resolution on local self-government
•	Decentralisation of finance under Lord Ripon
1883	C P Ilbert, law member of Lord Ripon's council, proposes a bill where Europeans can be tried by Indian magistrates and judges. Ripon becomes unpopular with the British in India and has to bow before public pressure. The Ilbert Bill is withdrawn
1886	First session of Indian National Conference held on December 28 in Bombay
1891	Proposal to transfer Lushai Hills and Chittagong Division from Bengal to Assam
1893	Dr Annie Besant arrives in India. The Central National Muslims Association submits a memorial for the due representation of Muslims in the Viceroy's Legislative Council in August
1896	Ramakrishna Mission started
1897	B G Tilak arrested and sentenced
•	Famine in the Deccan
1899	Official Secrets Act passed
1904	Treaty of Lhasa imposed on Dalai Lama by Government of India
1905	Shyamji Krishnavarma founds the India Home Rule Society in London
•	Partition of Bengal agreed on. Over 50,000 people sign anti-partition memorial. Adoption of a resolution to boycott British goods at a meeting in Bagerhat and then adoption of swadeshi in Calcutta. Partition comes into force on October 16

The making of a NATION

place in the country for some years now. Pernicious as the British presence may be, it brings with it the thoughts and philosophies of the Age of Reason, of 19th century ideals of self-determination. The popular support that the Rani of Jhansi, that the sepoys across India, that even Bahadur Shah Zafar finds, comes from a combination of these factors.

Although the Revolt means that the British Empire takes over from the East India Company as ruler of India, it cannot be seen as a defeat. Rather, this First War of Independence lays the groundwork for India's future struggles against British Rule. When the Partition of Bengal is imposed in 1905, the country rises in anger. The seeds of the struggle for freedom have taken firm root.

DISAGREEMENT, DISSENT, DEFIANCE
1906 - 1942

Dr Annie Besant, leading the Home Rule Movement with Tilak, 1916

The Leader protests the arrest of Home Rule League leaders, 1917

The wall of Jallianwala Bagh showing bullet marks after the massacre, 1919

Foreign goods being burnt, 1921

PUBLIC MEETING
AND
BONFIRE OF FOREIGN CLOTHES

Will take place at the Maidan near Elphinstone Mills
. . . Opp. Elphinstone Road Station . . .

On SUNDAY the 9th Inst. at 6-30 P. M.

When the Resolution of the Karachi Khilafat Conference and
another Congratulating Ali Brothers and others will be passed.

The Bombay Chronicle announces a bonfire of foreign goods, 1921

Mahatma
Winston
Bagh incident,

Sardar Bhag
martyr

Leaders of the Indian National Congress

Gandhi with Khan Abdul Gaffar Khan, the Frontier Gandhi

The launch o

THE arrival of M K Gandhi from South Africa gives the freedom struggle focus and direction. His experiments with civil disobedience in South Africa are brought to fruition in India, as he channelises nationalistic fervour towards non-violent protest. Hot-headed revolutionaries remain, and they have their uses, but the bulk of the country stands behind this charismatic and persuasive leader.

Gandhi tries to bring all threads of Indian society together — castes, religions, communities, classes. But the insidious British policy of divide and rule shows and spreads its tentacles. Although the country is united in the desire to be free, it is also divided by religion. In communal clashes between 1922 and 1927, over 450 people are killed, and 5,000 injured. In spite of Gandhi's support of the Pan-Islamic Khilafat Movement, he cannot, ultimately, stop Mohammed Ali Jinnah and the Mulsim League from seeking

re until the crowd dispersed.
amount of firing which would
ed widespread effect it was
justify my action. If more
casualties would have been
o longer a question of merely
f producing a sufficient moral
view not only on those who
ally throughout the Punjab.
undue severity.'

General Dyer

N JALLIANWALA BAGH
.CRE

0 persons and the wounding
s as many, at the Jallianwala
an episode which appears to
parallel in the modern history
event of an entirely different
into collision with the civil
ary occurrences which take
far and sinister isolation.'
the House of Commons, on

AGAINST WHIPPING
ECRETARY TO VICEROY

*Bombay
April 21, 1919*

wire dated 19th saying per-
ders issued under martial law
streets. Understand orders
ops. If press wire correct,
hipping would rouse gravest
in any case I would like to
has been given to general
v operations, to whip people
s described above.

*Shaukat and Mohammed Ali with Dr Kitchlew
and the Shankaracharya of Shandapeeth, 1921*

Chandrashekhar Azad, fiery revolutionary

The Independent

Vol. II—No. 67.   ALLAHABAD TUESDAY APRIL 15 1919.   One Anna.

GANDHI'S MESSAGE TO PEOPLE.

"BE SATYAGRAHI NOT DURAGRAHI".

Mr. Gandhi on arriving in Bombay on Friday afternoon sent a message to the citizens of Bombay not to create disturbance of any sort.

"GOOD OUT OF EVIL."

HINDUS ADMITTED FOR THE FIRST TIME IN
NAKHODA MOSQUE.

PRUSSIANISM IN PUNJAB.

PUBLICATION OF ACCOUNTS OF DISTURBANCES
PROHIBITED.

SHOOTING IN CALCUTTA.

SEVERAL KILLED AND WOUNDED.

Gandhi exhorts people to non-violence, 1919

gh, revolutionary and

A young Mohammed Ali Jinnah

andhi, General Dyer and
urchill on the Jallianwala
19

GANDHI ON HIS RETURN FROM THE INDIA

MR. GANDHI AT THE CLOSE OF HIS DAY OF SILENCE : THE MAHATMA AT THE MICROPHONE—ADDRESSING
THE GREAT CROWD AT THE MEETING ON THE MAIDAN, BOMBAY, ON DECEMBER 28.

IEN GANDHI SAID THAT IF THE FIGHT WERE RESUMED THERE WOULD BE NO RETRACING OF STE
INTO A MICROP

*Gandhi meets India on his return from the Round Table
Conference, 1932*

Quit India Movement in Bombay, 1942

*The making of
a NATION*

separate political representation for Muslims, leading eventually to the demand for Pakistan.

The momentum of the freedom struggle becomes furious with the launch of satyagraha, and the Civil Disobedience Movement. Over 60,000 Indians are arrested in 1930 alone for their role in the movement. Sporadic incidents of violence notwithstanding, Gandhi's methods prove difficult to combat. Inexorably, the British are made to realise that their days in India are numbered, strengthened by the outbreak of World War II. A series of reluctant constitutional reform measures follow, which will lay the base for the political future of the subcontinent.

The message to the British is now clear: Quit India.

THE CLIMAX
1942 - 1947

Nehru, Gandhi and Acharya Kripalani at the Quit India meet, Bombay, 1942

Sardar Patel and Maulana Abul Kalam Azad, Bombay 1942

Gandhi with Lord Wavell

Gandhi and Jinnah confer, only to differ

THE long march to freedom approaches its climax. Disobedient, uncooperative, even occasionally violent, the Indian people will have their birthright. World War II has taken its toll. Britain is a tired power. Freedom for India is not just an ideological imperative. It is now an administrative necessity.

By the end of the War, the process for transferring power to India has begun. But the glow of impending freedom is dimmed by communal clashes. The Muslim League led by Jinnah is adamant. First in wanting a greater stake in power, which is not acceptable to the Congress, then in not sharing power at all but wanting another country. India is forced to accept the idea of fragmentation. Reluctantly, then resignedly.

Subhas Chandra Bose in the Andamans

The making *of*
a NATION

Gandhi addresses a mammoth meeting in Calcutta

Only one man stands against the idea of a truncated India, torn from limb to limb. But even Mahatma Gandhi's famed powers of persuasion cannot stop this unholy juggernaut. His vision of an India where all communities live freely is tainted forever by the blood of Partition. Gandhi's disillusionment is real. Some of India feels his sorrow.

Still, there is the joy of breaking fetters. Of release from years of foreign domination. Journey's end comes only after paying a heavy price, but...

Look, there's a rainbow in the mid-August sky

COURAGE, CONVICTION, CHARISMA

1869-1948

By Dr Rudrangshu Mukherjee

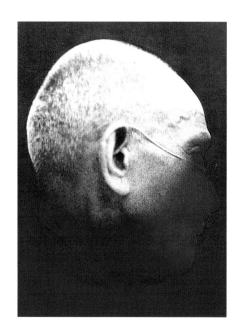

MOHANDAS Karamchand Gandhi undertook a journey from South Africa to India in 1915. He was coming back to rid his motherland of the colonial yoke, the first stirrings of this rebellion having already taken place in his clashes with the white supremacist South African government.

But M K Gandhi was also undertaking another journey, an internal voyage with international implications. One that would take him from being a mere man to a Mahatma, from a freedom fighter like so many to a great soul, from a family man to the father of a nation. At the end of India's struggle for Independence, the man once dismissed as a naked fakir, would tower over the 20th century as its greatest visionary.

In Gandhi's case, however, some of the most poignant betrayals came from within those whom he had nurtured and encouraged. The last year of the freedom struggle saw him sidelined in the fight for political power and he felt with his people the anguish of a country divided on religious lines.

Yet, even in his isolation, Gandhi stood tall over India, as he had for 30 years, skilfully, sensibly, sensationally, taking the country to nationhood. Unlike those he left behind him, he never forgot that power lies with the people. It is there that he found his strength. It is there that a nation must find its answers. And so Gandhi lives.

With Rabindranath Tagore in Santiniketan

With Jawaharlal Nehru and Maulana Abul Kalam Azad

THE name of Mohandas Karamchand Gandhi is inextricably linked to India's national movement. But the first of what he himself was to call his "experiments with truth" was carried out in South Africa. Trained as a barrister-at-law at the Inner Temple, Gandhi was not very successful as a lawyer in India. He moved to South Africa in 1893 at the age of 24 in search of a career. He decided to resist the rampant racism which was in vogue there by peacefully violating certain laws, courting arrests collectively, by organising hartals and spectacular marches. This experiment was to serve as a model of Gandhi's involvements in mass movements in India. But even before he had emerged as a major figure in Indian politics, Gandhi had worked out some of his fundamental ideas in a tract called *Hind Swaraj*. According to Gandhi, this text represented "the views... held by many Indians not touched by what is known as civilisation."

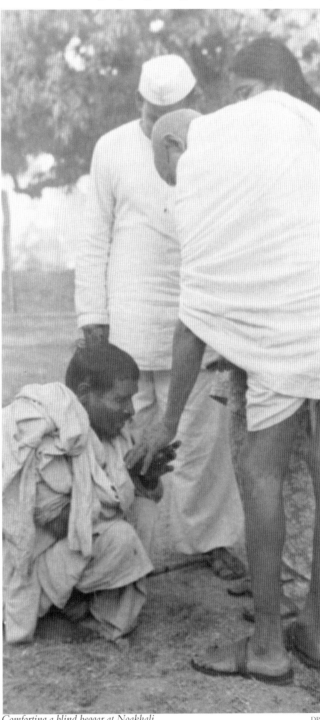

The tract is a forthright and total critique of modern civilisation. Gandhi was emphatic about the superiority of Indian civilisation. He attacked all aspects of the "modern philosophy of life" and he drew from the writings of Edward Carpenter, John Ruskin and Leo Tolstoy. But Gandhi's attack was more comprehensive since he did not exclude any aspect of Western civilisation. He rejected the entire project of modernity and therefore of its complete intellectual apparatus including Reason and Science. He asserted that the scientific mode of knowledge was applicable only to very limited areas of human living. The assumption that rationality and science could provide solutions to all problems led

Comforting a blind beggar at Noakhali   DPA

to insanity and impotence. Only faith could be man's saviour. Similarly, Gandhi was not willing to accept arguments based on history. "To believe that what has not occurred in history will not occur at all is to argue disbelief in the dignity of man." Neither science nor

Gandhi in South Africa

history had any privileged access to Truth. Truth lay in morality, in one's own conscience and in the performance of one's duty.

The alternative that Gandhi posed to modern civilisation had to be located outside the influences of modernity. India was uniquely placed to provide this alternative since millions of Indians lived in the villages and were therefore uncontaminated by modern civilisation. "Real civilisation", Gandhi said, existed in the villages of India. Life there was organised on principles which were antithetical to the individualism which was the governing premise of civil society. In the villages life was held together by a communal morality where each member performed his duty. It was to the "common people" living "independently" that Gandhi turned: India, to him, "meant its teeming millions on whom depends the existence of its princes and our own." The Indian peasant represented the hope of real civilisation.

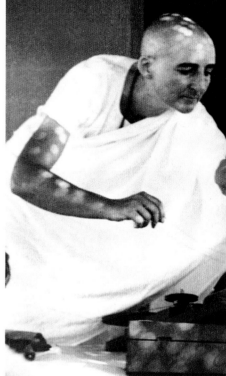

Mirabehn with Gandhi

If the challenge to modern civilisation whose epitome was British rule in India was to come from the peasantry then that challenge had to be non-violent since, according to Gandhi, the Indian peasant had never been violent. Non-violent resistance he called satyagraha and argued that complete non-cooperation would lead to the collapse of government and force the British to leave India. But the end of British rule would not usher in swaraj. Swaraj would come with the end of all tyranny and exploitation and when every individual became independent and self-regulating. Passive resistance was the only road to swaraj. The latter had to be "experienced by each one for himself". Every satyagrahi would learn to regulate his own life by observing perfect chastity, adopting poverty, following truth and cultivating fearlessness. A moral life on the part of every individual was the *sine qua non* for swaraj. A community of self-regulated individuals each performing his moral duty would bring forth a system of complete reciprocity among and participation by every member of society. He called this society Ram Rajya. Society would be held together by equal and self-regulating individuals each performing his duty. Indian civilisation had as its foundation this kind of a system that is why it was more long-lasting than and superior to western civilisation. "Indian civilisation," Gandhi said, "is the best and the European is a nine days' wonder."

In political terms it was clear in Gandhi's ideas that if the Indian national movement had to be successful against British rule then the peasantry had to be its agency, and its principal and only idiom had to be non-violence. His experiments with mass politics in India would show the power of political movements whose mass base was the peasantry, whose principal modality was non-violence and whose direction from its inception was to be regulated by Gandhi. He was often greeted by noisy boisterous crowds eager to pay their homage to the Mahatma. He wrote against such behaviour again and again and described it as mobocracy. The masses would be mobilised but with discipline. He wrote: "[Such demonstrations] cannot procure swaraj for India unless regulated and harnessed for national good. The great task before the nation today is to discipline its demonstration if they are to serve any useful purpose... The nation must be disciplined to handle mass movements in a sober and methodical manner... Workers must either organise these demonstrations in a methodical manner or not have them at all. We can do no effective work unless we can pass instructions to the crowd and expect implicit

Kasturba washes Gandhi's feet

DPA

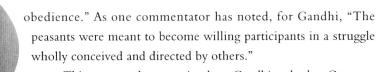

With a young Indira Priyadarshini Nehru   Nehru Library

obedience." As one commentator has noted, for Gandhi, "The peasants were meant to become willing participants in a struggle wholly conceived and directed by others."

This was not always as simple as Gandhi and other Congress leaders expected. Indian peasants read and interpreted the message of the Mahatma in their own terms and within their own network of beliefs and customs. When Gandhi came to Gorakhpur in February 1921, the nationalist leadership there made it clear that the reception of Gandhi would be the work of the local elite. The common people would come, have their darshan and return to their villages. The local elite did not reckon with the fact that coming to seek darshan involved an act of defiance of the landlord's power. This defiance also involved the villagers' own decoding of Gandhi's message. Gandhi's name came to be associated with boons and curses. He was thus deified and he came to represent an alternative source of authority. His name lent itself as a label to all kinds of meetings, pamphlets and to swaraj. Gandhi papers and Gandhi notes came to be circulated. All this took place independently of the district leadership of the Congress. The people of Gorakhpur used the name of Gandhi to legitimise actions not sanctioned by the Congress. They could thus even be violent with the name of Gandhi on their lips. When this happened as in Chauri Chaura and led to the death of 22 policemen, Gandhi called it a crime and withdrew the Non-Cooperation Movement. Gandhi disowned an act carried out in his name since it was not controlled by him.

During the three great mass upsurges associated with the name of Gandhi, the Non Co-operation Movement (1920-22), the Civil Disobedience Movement (1930-33) and the Quit India Movement (1942) the common people responded to Gandhi but they did so on their own terms and often on their own initiative. Recent research is emphasising the people's own initiative and how they adapted the message of the Mahatma to their own codes of behaviour. One result of this was that again and again the mass movements crossed the limits imposed by Gandhi who then withdrew the movement. Another result of keeping the movement controlled and non-violent was that the mass movements did not snowball into a social revolution threatening the entire social structure and the propertied. This guarantee made Gandhian mobilisation attractive not only to rich and dominant peasants but also to Indian business groups. The latter mounted pressure on Gandhi to call off the Civil Disobedience Movement.

The making *of* a NATION

This leverage of the burgeoning India capitalist class had profound consequences. In the 1940s

DPA it became clear that the British wanted to pull out of India. The Indian capitalists and sections of the Congress leadership engaged themselves in ensuring a negotiated transfer of power. There were many mass movements which were all outside Congress control. In the circumstances, a mass confrontation seemed risky to the Congress leadership. A negotiated transfer of power would ensure that the Congress would have control over the independent Indian state. For this end, the Congress leadership, including Jawaharlal Nehru, was willing to agree to the partition of the country along religious lines. Gandhi could not accept this compromise. For him partition was the betrayal of one of his most cherished beliefs. But he found himself increasingly isolated, considered irrelevant by his own chosen disciples. Thus when freedom came and the country seethed with excitement, Gandhi was not in Delhi. He was not a part of Nehru's tryst with destiny. Gandhi fasted and prayed in a slum in Calcutta on August 15, 1947.

THE GREAT DIVIDE

1947

By Khushwant Singh

THE Partition of the subcontinent in 1947 cast a long and bloody shadow over the celebration of Independence for India. Lost in this unholy mélee were hordes of countrymen, large tracts of land, lamentably large numbers of human lives.

The roots of Partition, however, did not just lie in the divide and rule policy of the British. Part of the responsibility for the cleft between Hindu and Muslim in India lies with the people themselves. A history of conquest and aggression carries some of the onus, still much of that is often overcome by proximity. But when the flames of 'otherness' are fanned by selfish opportunists, the consequences can be disastrous. At some stage in India, idealism gave way to political expediency, the desire for power rode roughshod over the need to do right for the future and a foreign ruler was in too much of a hurry to care overmuch.

 The outcome was a wound that has not healed in 50 years, that has bled again and again across three subcontinental borders. What has to be saved is the dream of India as a land, secular and free.

Mountbatten, Jinnah and Nehru decide on India's Partition

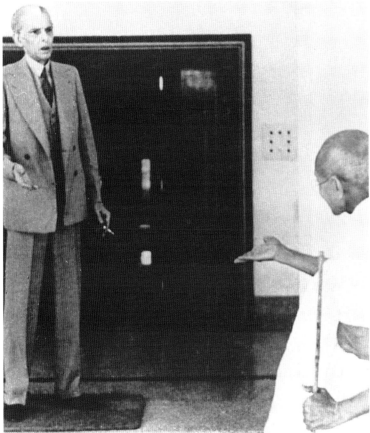

Mohammed Ali Jinnah and Gandhi before they part ways

IT is generally assumed that Hindus and Muslims lived peacefully like brothers till the British arrived on the scene and practised their 'divide and rule' policy in order to keep their hold on the country. This is an over-simplification bordering on falsehood. Maulana Mohammad Ali was closer to the truth, when he said "we divide and they rule".

The Hindu-Muslim divide came soon after Muslims began to enter the country as conquerers. There was no friction between the two communities when Arabs, who had been coming to our West coast to trade from times immemorial converted to Islam. They were welcomed as ever before. They were allowed to marry local girls, build mosques and propagate their faith. We have living proof of this peaceful assimilation in the Moplah Muslim community of Malabar (present-day Kerala). The word Moplah derives from *mapilla* – son-in-law of Hindus of Kerala. The scene underwent a dramatic change with the armed invasion of Mohammed Bin Qasim. He overran Sindhu. The local Hindu rajas fought him at every step till they were overcome. Bin Qasim's foray did not leave much impact on the country. But when tribes from Central Asia, Turkey and Afghanistan entered India through passes in the Hindu Kush and Suleiman ranges, defeated Hindu rajas,

destroyed Hindu temples and tried to force Islam down the throats of the local population, Hindus fought back with all the means at their command. They called for a complete boycott of Muslims and denigrated them as *mlecchas* – untouchables. Those who converted to Islam were likewise ostracised as traitors. They refused to inter-marry or break bread with Muslims. There were many exceptions to the rule of non-cooperation. Muslim rulers fought each other employing Hindu soldiers and generals. They made alliances with Hindu princes to resist fresh invasions of Muslim tribes. By the time the Mughals imposed their hegemony over most of Northern India, a certain amount of give and take had begun to take place. A large number of Hindus had converted to Islam — not in fear of being killed but by peaceful persuasion of Sufi saints like Farid Shakarganj, Mueenuddin Chishti and Nizamuddin Aulya. There were upwards of 12 Sufi *silsilas* spreading the gospel of communal harmony all over the country. Emperor Akbar tried to give this growing closeness formal recognition through his Deen-e-Ilahi. It proved a flop. Mutual suspicion had taken deep roots. Hindus refused to eat with Muslims or give them their daughters in marriage. The divide continued. In regions where a ruler of one community or the other was able to impose his will, there was little inter-religious violence; people swallowed their grievances rather than earn the displeasure of their Nawab or Maharajah. This created the illusion in the minds of many people that there were no Hindu-Muslim riots before the British took over the country.

The British were a neutral power and largely unconcerned with Hindu-Muslim relations except as rulers expected to maintain law and order. They did side with one or the other community as circumstances compelled them. Since Hindus more readily accepted their ways and Muslims sulked over the loss of Muslim rulers and refused to cooperate, for many years Hindus were the favoured community. This was accentuated by the uprising in 1857 and attempt to restore Mughal rule. Though members of both the communities rose in revolt, Muslims predominated and earned the ire of their British victors.

The British soon realised that they could not rule the country showing marked bias against one or the other community. Besides that, they found it much easier to get on with Muslims than with the Hindus who, though their subjects, refused to eat with them. For the Hindu, the Englishman was as much a *mleccha* as the Muslim. Muslims, particularly under the leadership of Sir Syed Ahmed Khan, founder of the Aligarh Muslim University, expressed loyalty to the British, and became the favoured community. They were granted separate electorates, reservation of seats in legislative bodies and the Services.

The early beginnings of the Indian freedom movement was almost entirely Hindu. *Anusilan samitis* of terrorists took their oaths on goddess Kali or Durga and did not admit Muslims. In Maharashtra leaders like Tilak used Ganapati festivals, in which Muslims took no part to rouse patriotic fervour. When Viceroy Curzon announced the partition of Bengal, in 1905, Muslims who formed the minority in East Bengal welcomed the move. Hindus opposed it bitterly by non-cooperation as well as by terrorist activities. The partition had to be annulled because of Hindu pressure. (It is ironic that East Bengal which Lord Curzon had created became East Pakistan in 1947 and Bangladesh in 1971.)

If Hindus had not been as shortsighted on their opposition to Lord Curzon's move, the history of the subcontinent may have been different.

Hindus and Muslims did not share the same concept of free India. Hindus formed the majority of the population and looked forward to carry out their heritage when the British left the country. This was not acceptable to the Muslims. Unfortunately many top leaders of the Indian National Congress were also leading members of Hindu communal organisations. Among them were Tilak, Savarkar, Lala Lajpat Rai, Pandit Madan Mohan Malaviya, founder of the Benaras Hindu University. For the Hindus the national anthems were *Vande Mataram* and *Jana Gana Mana* and not Allama Iqbal's *Sare Jahan Se Accha Hindustan Hamara*. It is not surprising that the Muslim masses kept aloof from the Indian National Congress

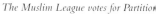
The Muslim League votes for Partition

and gradually leant more and more support to the Muslim League which ultimately asked for a separate Muslim State, Pakistan. During World War II, it became apparent that India could not continue to remain as one country. Muslim leaders in the National Congress lost ground, leaders of the Muslim League gathered strength. During these critical years Maulana Abul Kalam Azad who was a respected leader of the Muslim masses became a drawing room politician. Mohammed Ali Jinnah who had been a drawing room politician became a leader of the Muslim masses — the Qaid-e-Azam.

Jawaharlal Nehru and Jinnah, looking for power   Nehru Library

THE hamlet in which I was born fairly represented relationships between the three religious communities. Hadali, about 40 miles west of the river Jhelum had no more than 150 families living in it. Well over 100 of them were Muslims of different tribes: Tiwanas Noons, Janjuas, Awans, Waddhals, and Mastials. Most of them were land-owning or serving in the army. Sikhs and Hindus were Kirars – tradesmen and moneylenders. There were several mosques but only one gurudwara where both Hindus and Sikhs worshipped. My grandfather, Sujan Singh, was the wealthiest man in Hadali living in the largest haveli. He had extensive trade selling salt taken by the Khewra mines. He hired camels owned by Muslims to take rock salt to distant cities like Lahore and Amritsar and bring back tea, cooking oil, spices and textiles. He was much respected in the hamlet. After he moved to Delhi, men from Hadali, including Muslims – there were quite a few in the Viceroy's bodyguard - came to visit him and some even stayed with him. In Hadali we lived in harmony with each other. Every one of my father's age was *chacha* — uncle. Every woman of my mother's age was *maasi* — aunt. But no more. We never entered homes of Muslims except to attend marriages or funerals. They never came to ours. The only time I ate with my Muslim fellow villagers was 40 years after Independence when I went to visit Hadali. Muslims of Hadali gave me a hero's welcome and laid out a feast for me.

The communal situation in Lahore where I lived from 1940-47 was not very different from the one in Hadali. On the surface it looked as if Lahorians were a unified lot. As a matter of fact the city

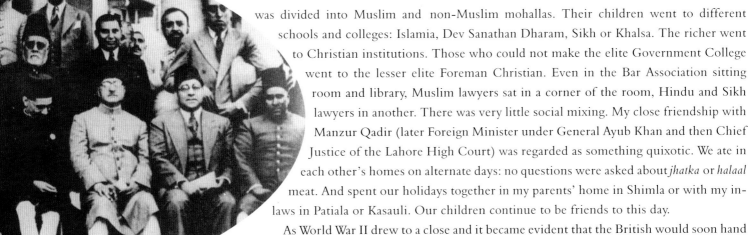

was divided into Muslim and non-Muslim mohallas. Their children went to different schools and colleges: Islamia, Dev Sanathan Dharam, Sikh or Khalsa. The richer went to Christian institutions. Those who could not make the elite Government College went to the lesser elite Foreman Christian. Even in the Bar Association sitting room and library, Muslim lawyers sat in a corner of the room, Hindu and Sikh lawyers in another. There was very little social mixing. My close friendship with Manzur Qadir (later Foreign Minister under General Ayub Khan and then Chief Justice of the Lahore High Court) was regarded as something quixotic. We ate in each other's homes on alternate days: no questions were asked about *jhatka* or *halaal* meat. And spent our holidays together in my parents' home in Shimla or with my in-laws in Patiala or Kasauli. Our children continue to be friends to this day.

As World War II drew to a close and it became evident that the British would soon hand over power to the Indians, the Hindu-Muslim divide became sharper. The Muslim demand for Pakistan gathered support and became more strident day by day. Punjab continued to be governed by the Unionist Party led first by Sikandar Hayat and after him by Nawab Khizar Hayat Tiwana. It was a composite party comprising Muslims, Hindus and Sikhs. Its Sikh components were Sir Sunder Singh Majithia followed by Dasvindha Singh. Hindus were represented by Sir Chotu Ram and Sir Manohar Lal. They were able to make a united front against the onslaught of the Muslim League.

The situation began to change drastically following the 'Direct Action Day' (August 16, 1946) called by the Muslim League in Calcutta. Savage Hindu-Muslim riots broke out in the metropolis. They were followed by rioting in Bihar, where Hindus massacred Muslims and in Noakhali where Muslims butchered Hindus. As news of these killings spread northwards,

tensions between Muslims and non-Muslims in the Punjab and NWFP came to a breaking point. By March 1947, sporadic killings of Hindus and Sikhs began in the north-western regions of Hazara (NWFP), Rawalpindi and Campbellpur districts. A stream of Hindu and Sikh refugees began to flow into Lahore and onwards to Amritsar and Eastern Punjab. The Muslim League organised mass demonstrations in Lahore. Every other afternoon long processions of Muslims marched down the Mall towards the Government House chanting slogans:

Gandhi with Lord Pethick Lawrence, 1946, as Partition becomes a reality

The making *of* a NATION

Pakistan Ka Naara Kya? La ilaha illâllah

Since Khizar Hayat's Unionist Government was the main stumbling block in the realisation of their dreams, he was their chief target:

Taazee Khabar / Mar Gaya Khizar

On March 2, 1947 outside the Punjab legislative assembly building a large crowd gathered to see the outcome of the debate on Pakistan. Pakistanis carried the day. Tiwana threw in the towel and resigned. Outside the House, Master Tara Singh, the Akali leader, drew his kirpan out of his scabbard and yelled: *"Pakistan Murdabad"*.

Muslim crowds jubilated. Their new slogan was: *Taazee Khabar Aiyee hai / Khizar Hamara Bhai Hai.* The fat was in the fire. Communal riots broke out in Lahore. Our nights were disturbed by yells from one side, *"Allah-o-Akbar"*, replied to from the other with *"Har, Har Mahadev"* and *"Sat Sri Akal"*. Hindus and Sikhs took a terrible beating at the hands of Muslim goondas. The Punjab police was predominantly Muslim and by no means even-handed in dealing with rioters. Sikhs suffered more loss of lives than

People flee on either side of the borders of India and Pakistan

Hindus because Sikhs were easily identifiable. They were picked up out of trains and stabbed, knocked down from bicycles and done to death. Every morning's papers reported numbers of casualties of every community. Every evening we sat in our clubs drinking Scotch whisky and comparing these figures as if they were scores in a cricket match. Muslims were winning hands down.

Hindu and Sikh resistance began to build up. The only organisation which did so was the RSS. Stung by taunts that Sikhs had lost their manhood, students of the Sikh National College went round Sikh homes collecting arms and ammunition. They managed to waylay a few innocent Muslim villagers going along the Grand Trunk road and slew them. I recall vividly about a dozen young Sikhs being brought in handcuffs to the Lahore High Court. The Sessions Judge, a Muslim, had rejected their application for bail. They were produced before the only Sikh judge of the High Court, Justice Teja Singh. He ordered their release. Among the boys was Ganga Singh Dhillon, later the most vociferous in demanding an independent Khalistan, now living in considerable comfort in Washington.

One very hot afternoon of June 1947 I was woken up by the shouting of hundreds of people. I went up on my roof to see what was going on.

From the centre of the city billowed a huge black cloud of smoke, I did not have much difficulty

Partition takes a heavy toll of lives and spirit

in spotting that it was Shahalami Gate Bazar which was almost entirely a Hindu-Sikh mohalla. Muslim goondas had succeeded in setting fire to the entire locality. The large-scale arson finally broke the back of Hindu-Sikh resistance to Muslim dominance of the city. I recall Begum Shah Nawaz remarking in the club that evening: "This is nothing. We will make you people recall the days of Halaku and Changez Khan."

Hindus and Sikhs began to pull out of Lahore taking with them whatever they could salvage. One morning I saw my neighbours on either side paint in huge letters on their front wall, *"Parsi ka makaan"* in Urdu. On the other side the occupants had drawn huge crosses to indicate it was a Christian household.

We were within easy walking distance of Mozang, a largely Muslim locality famous for its *pehelwans* (wrestlers) and toughs. I went to see Justice Teja Singh who lived close by to seek his advice. *"Datey raho* — hang on", he told me. Two days later when I went to see him again, I found his house locked and deserted.

He had left for Delhi.

Among my regular visitors was an Englishman Chris Everett who had been with me in college in London. He was then head of the Punjab CID. He advised me to go away for a few days till the situation in Lahore returned to normal. I had already sent my children to Kasauli to stay with their grandparents. A few days later, escorted by half-a-dozen Baluch policemen sent by Everett, my wife and I boarded the train for Kalka. As arranged on the phone at Dharampur we met Manzur Qadir who was coming down from Simla and handed him keys of my house. This was sometime in the first week of August 1947. (We did go back some years after Partition and stayed in what was our house as guests of the Manzur Qadirs.)

After staying a few days in Kasauli I decided to drive down to Delhi to see what I could do to rehabilitate myself. It was the most eerie 200 mile drive. There was not a soul to be seen on the road. Not a sign of life in the towns and villages through which I passed. Only about 30 miles short of Delhi I saw a jeep standing in the centre of the road. I pulled up at a safe distance. When I saw Sikhs step out of the jeep. I drive up to them. There were four of them all armed with rifles. What they said sent a chill down my spine. They had been on a killing spree shooting everyone they could identify as a Muslim.

I was one of the throng outside Parliament House on the night of 14/15th August. I heard Sucheta Kripalani's voice come over the microphone singing *Vande Mataram*. I heard Pandit Nehru make his Tryst with Destiny speech. I joined the crowd in yelling *Bharat Mata Ki Jai*; *Mahatma Gandhi Ki Jai*; *Inquilab Zindabad*. The tragedy of Partition was drowned in the euphoria of Independence.

Next morning I was one of the crowd outside the Red Fort. I saw Lord Mountbatten lower the Union Jack and Pandit Nehru raise the tricolour. It took me some days to comprehend that Partition had meant the uprooting of 10 million people from their hearths and homes on either side of the new border. Over a million were slain in the worst holocaust known to history.

I looked for a job as I realised I would not be able to return to Lahore to resume my law practice. I got one with the External Affairs Ministry and was posted to London. On our first reception in India House I happened to have a few minutes alone with Lord Mountbatten who had arrived half an hour early and had to sit in my office. With great diffidence I asked him, "Lord Mountbatten was there no way out to create the new dominions of India and Pakistan to avoid the enormous loss of life and hardship on the people?" After a pause he replied: "I don't care what people say about me today; I will be judged at the bar of history."

DPA

The end of the Second World War in 1945 heralds the beginning of a New World Order. Adolf Hitler's self-aggrandising onslaught in Europe brings down with it the last remnants of the feudalism, colonialism and enslavement of the 19th century. In China, which did not take part in the War, the Peoples' Revolution has broken with centuries of tradition. The same revolutionary wind is blowing through the rest of the world.

Social changes will mean that women are seen differently, industry will take the initiative away from agriculture and, most exciting of all, the balance of power will realign itself. Europe is no longer the global headquarters. Instead, it becomes a new battleground as loyalties are divided between the United States of America and capitalism on one side and the Union of Soviet Socialist Republics and Communism on the other. Hot winds of trouble blow across Europe. The Cold War has begun.

It is into this exciting, fresh turbulence that India is reborn as a nation state. The British Empire becomes unsustainable at the end of World War II, and Free India is at the vanguard of nations in Asia and Africa, who break loose from imperialism's yokes. The experiment with democracy is fraught with nascent tensions, yet the past has been rejected forthwith. It could be no other way. The voice of the people has spoken, and it could well be the voice of god. In spite of the pain of Partition, of losing friends and property, India's hopes for the future are exuberant, effervescent, incandescent. The task of nation-building is now at hand, and India rises to the challenge.

A new dawn has broken.

1947
1
1956

FREE!

August 14-15 1947

The sun sets on the British Empire.
And India wakes to a new dawn

Life and freedom: *Prime Minister Jawaharlal Nehru at Red Fort*

A UGUST 14, 1947. Close to midnight. A thin quavering voice rises across the darkness. "Long years ago," it says, "we made a tryst with destiny..."

Jawaharlal Nehru is addressing the midnight session of the Consituent Assembly in Delhi. When the dawn breaks tomorrow morning, it will be over a free India.

"... and now the time comes when we shall redeem our pledge, not wholly or in full measure, but very substantially. At the stroke of the midnight hour, when the world sleeps, India will awake to life and freedom. A moment comes, which comes but rarely in history, when we step out from the old to the new, when an age ends, and when the soul of a nation, long suppressed, finds utterance."

The words of the first Prime Minister of India, impromptu, unrehearsed, will echo through the ages. But now, they reverberate through a nation, long deserved of utterance. Battles have been fought, physical and psychological, mistakes have been made, tragedy has been wrought, but the end has come. And with it, a new beginning.

As the clock strikes midnight, India awakes to life and freedom. Outside, in New Delhi, the monsoon clouds burst

with thunder and rain. Inside, Members of the Constituent Assembly take a pledge: "At this solemn moment when the people of India, through suffering and sacrifice, have secured freedom, I, a member of the Constituent Assembly of India, do dedicate myself in all humility to the service of India and her people to the end that this ancient land attain her rightful place in the world and make her full contribution to the promotion of

While the world sleeps: *The midnight session of the Constituent Assembly*   PIB

Unbounded joy: *The people of India*   PIB

world peace and the welfare of mankind."

The pledge is made. There is no turning back.

On the evening of August 14, for the last time, hundreds of Union Jacks come down flag poles all over the country. Tomorrow, their place will be taken by a new flag. The British Raj is over. After the Battle of Plassey, the Mutiny of 1857, the Jallianwala Bagh massacre, India is free. Across the country, there are scenes of joy and exuberation as people break the shackles of a lifetime as colonial slaves. To bars, restaurants, clubs, once reserved for the British, where Indians and dogs were not allowed, the natives throng, secure in their newfound power. *"Azad hai!"* they shout. "We are free."

But where India celebrates, she also burns. On the border,

The Raj salutes: *Lord and Lady Mountbatten with Nehru*   PIB

there is murder and bloodshed. For Independence has brought with it the deadly blade of Partition. Unsheathed, it carries hatred and vengeance.

In Calcutta, the violence is off-set by a small group of Hindus and Muslims standing guard, silently, outside a dilapidated house in a central slum. Inside sleeps the architect of India's freedom. This is not the destiny that Mahatma Gandhi had worked for, dreamt of, lived for. To keep his promise to his nation, he must try and stem the tide of anger and hatred that is dividing his people. "You wish to do me ill. And so I am coming to you," he tells a crowd of angry Hindus. "I have come to serve Hindus and Muslims alike." There is still power in his words, though he may be frail and old. "I have nearly reached the end of life's journey. I have not much further to go. But if you again go mad, I will not be living witness to it."

And so he was not.

August 15, 1947.

The streets of Delhi are streets no longer. They are one mass. Of people. Congregating from all over to share in one moment of joy. The raising of the first Indian flag over the Red Fort. There are too many people to carry out any elaborate ceremony. There are too many people to carry out any ceremony at all. The whole of India's 300 million, it seems, are there to witness Nehru unfurl the flag.

As he walks to the halyard, accompanied by Defence Minister Sardar Baldev Singh and senior Servicemen, India holds her breath. The flag rises up and the sky brightens. As the saffron, white and green cloth, with a blue wheel in the centre, reaches the top of the pole and flutters, a huge roar goes up. The rainbow that flashes across the sky is no illusion.

India is free.   ■

HE RAM!

January 30, 1948

The apostle of peace falls to an assassin's bullets. And the world mourns

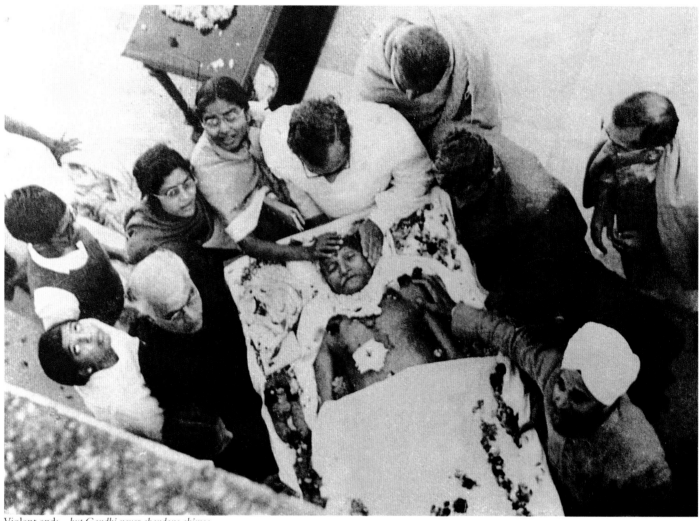

Violent end: *...but Gandhi never abandons ahimsa*

PIB

"My life is dedicated to service of India through the religion of non-violence which I believe to be the root of Hinduism."
— *Mahatma Gandhi*

JANUARY 30, 1948, 5.10 pm. Mahatma Gandhi is rushing for his prayer meeting. He is late, having been delayed by a vital conference with Vallabhbhai Patel.

He does not like to be late. "It is your fault I am 10 minutes late," he laughingly tells his two young companions, his walking sticks. "It is the duty of nurses to carry on their work even if God himself should be present there. If it is time to give medicine to a patient and you hesitate, the poor patient may die. I hate it if I am late for prayers even by a minute."

The three rush down the path at Birla House towards the prayer ground. People are waiting. Gandhi brings his hands together in greeting. From the crowd, a stout young man dressed in khaki bursts out. Mani thinks he wants to touch Gandhi's feet. She tries to hold him back, saying they are already late for their meeting. The young man pushes her aside, and takes out a black Beretta automatic pistol. He aims at Gandhi and fires three shots.

The reasons for the act of this shooting lie in the direction of the freedom struggle itself, in the creation of Pakistan and perhaps even in Gandhi's stubborn refusal to let expediency win over what he thinks is right. On the night of August 14, 1947, Gandhi was in Calcutta trying to stop the communal carnage caused by Partition. When he went on a fast there to appeal to people's hearts, they responded, Hindus and Muslims alike, with that inestimable mix of awe, reverence and love that made him a Mahatma. His next destination was to be the Punjab, on the Pakistan side of the border. His mission is to convince Hindus and Muslims that they have to live together.

"There was a time when India listened to me. Today I am a back number. I have been told I have no place in the new order... Pakistan can never destroy Hinduism. The Hindus alone can destroy themselves and their faith. Similarly, if Islam is destroyed, it will be destroyed by the Muslims in Pakistan, not by the Hindus in Hindustan," he said on September 26, 1947.

But in Gandhi's brand of Hindu-Muslim amity, the onus lay on the Hindu to assuage the fears of his Muslim sibling. Deeply religious he may have been, but his thought was inimical, anathema to fundamentalist Hindus. Gandhi was well aware of this, "I know what some people are saying: 'The

He Ram!

32

Love for a father: *India's masses gather at Gandhi's funeral pyre* Dunodia Picture Agency

Congress has surrendered its soul to the Muslims.. Gandhi? Let him rave as he will. He is a washout...' But violent rowdyism will not save either Hinduism or Sikhism... Hinduism cannot be saved by orgies of murder."

January 13, 1948. Gandhi goes on an indefinite fast to force the Government of India to pay back the Rs 55 crore it owes Pakistan. The Government is adamant that it cannot pay the money. It will be used for bullets in Kashmir, argues Patel. Gandhi points out that the money belongs to Pakistan. The wrangling continues. Gandhi is 78 and frail. A diet of a glass of warm water and soda bircarbonate a day will not go very far. Inititally, reactions are harsh. Let Gandhi die, shout the crowds in Delhi, still smarting with the sores of Partition, displaying their wounds with anger and hatred. Gandhi is unrelenting.

Grateful homage: *Maulana Azad and Jawaharlal Nehru pay their respects* Nehru Library

In darkness: *Nehru announces Gandhi's death*   Nehru Library

As he gets frailer, however, the mood of the nation turns. Gandhi must live, shout the crowds across India. Soon, hard, indifferent Delhi follows suit. Thousands of people stream past his bed to convince him to stop. His kidneys are failing. He is in danger of slipping into a coma. The government relents about the money on January 14, but it is not enough for the Mahatma. He wants the two dominions to promise to solve their differences, heal the wounds. And he wants all India's political leaders to attest to this vow.

January 18, 1948. Political leaders from all parties, including the Hindu Mahasabha and the Rashtriya Swayamsevak Sangh, flanked by the Pakistan High Commissioner, are at Gandhi's bedside.

12.25 pm, he reaches out for a glass of orange juice from the hands of Maulana Azad. The fast is broken.

Not everyone in the RSS is happy, however. Seven young men in Pune, ostensibly inspired by Veer Savarkar, have conspired to kill Gandhi for his perfidy to India's Hindus, his partiality to Muslims.

January 20 is the day. The method will be bombs and hand grenades. But the mission fails, as some lose their nerve. Madanlal Pawha, who threw the first bomb, is led away by the police. Gandhi thinks it was army shooting practice at first, later, was it just a prank?

But Nathuram Godse, Narayan Apte and the others know that their purpose is more serious. They also know that Pahwa's arrest means they must act fast before their conspiracy is found out. The first task is to buy a gun. A Gwalior homoeopath has what they need.

The date is fixed for January 30.

Let me die with the name of god on my lips, Gandhi has said, almost jokingly, after the last attempt.

But he knew the seriousness of it too. The meeting with Patel which made him late for his January 30 meeting was to stop the Iron Man from resigning as Home Minister, for failing to provide Gandhi with enough security.

January 30, 1948.

Three shots ring out. Two in the chest, one in the stomach...

"He Ram!" cries the greatest man of the 20th century as he sinks to the ground, red blood staining his white clothes...

The time on the watch he had forgotten to look at earlier is 5.17 pm.

India loses a father.

Postscript

January 30, 1948, evening.

"Friends and comrades, the light has gone out of our lives and there is darkness everywhere. I do not know what to tell you and how to say it. Our beloved leader, Bapu, as we called him, the Father of the Nation, is no more. Perhaps I am wrong to say that. Nevertheless, we will not see him again as we have seen him for so many years...

The light has gone out, I said, and yet I was wrong. For the light that shone in this country was no ordinary light. The light that has illumined this country for these many many years will illumine this country for many more years, and a thousand years later, that light will be seen in this country and the world will see it and it will give solace to innumerable hearts."

Prime Minister Jawaharlal Nehru can hardly control his tears as he talks to the nation on All India Radio.

Nor yet is any solace forthcoming. From across the world, condolence messages pour in.

January 31. From across India, the multitudes start pouring into Delhi. As they had five months earlier to mark India's freedom, now they come to accompany Bapu on his last journey to the banks of the Jamuna where he will be cremated.   ■

The last word: *A page from Nehru's diary*   Nehru Library

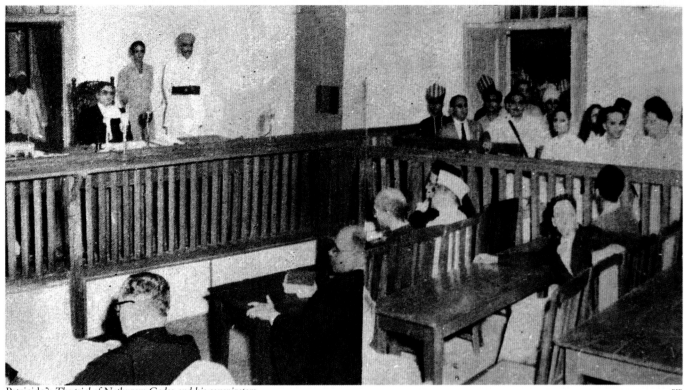

Patricide?: *The trial of Nathuram Godse and his conspirators*   PIB

NATHURAM GODSE'S CONVICTION
A brother looks back
By Gopal Godse

ALTHOUGH he has been called a mad man, a *sarfira* and a *mathaphiru* for killing Gandhiji, Nathuram Godse was sane and intelligent when he pulled that trigger for political reasons.

Justice Acharu Ram of the Simla High Court had said: "Nathuram V Godse has not challenged his conviction under section 304 of the Indian Penal Code for murdering Mahatma Gandhi on 30 January 1948 nor has he appealed against the death sentence ordered. He has confined his appeal and also his arguments at the bar. He personally argued his appeal, I must say with conspicuous ability evidencing a mastery over the facts which would have done credit to any counsel."

Even though Nathuram was not even a matriculate, he had argued his case before the Special Court, Red Fort, in Delhi for two days. And in the Simla High Court he had argued his case for seven days. It was all in English. The judgment observed: "Although he had failed in his matriculate examination, Nathuram Godse is a widely read man. While arguing his appeal he showed a a fair knowledge of the English language and a remarkable capacity for clear thinking."

It was common for us convicts to talk about the events often. Nathuram and I were locked in one room in the Red Fort prison. As for the actual act of shooting he had explained, "Pulling the trigger does not require any force worth mentioning. It is not like moving some heavy stone nor like piercing a dagger. The bullets move automatically and it is all mechanical. But one's mind should be straight, steady and firm. If that is so then your body also remains steady and firm."

Nathuram was firm and steady in his thinking and executing what he thought was right for the country. He was firm about his action even as he marched to face the gallows. The words, "Akhand Bharat Amar Rahe, Vande Mataram" uttered from the platform of death were as steady as from the dias of some of the meetings he addressed.

Nathuram used to seriously talk of life and death with his close friends and associates. He used to explain, "What is sleep? It is a surrender of our body to the gravitation of Mother Earth. Every particle of the body desires surrender. Therefore, sleep in a sitting position like in a train or bus is not comfortable. We get satisfaction only when our body lies parallel to the ground. When the particles of our brain too surrender to the gravitation, we experience dreamlessness.

"What is death then? It is the advanced stage of surrender. Therefore it is called *'chira-nitra'* or permanent sleep, never to be awakened again. I shall be entering my 'chiranitra' through the gallows soon"

Nathuram even as a boy was a serious thinker. During his school days and later in his life he was always fond of books dealing with history and philosophy. He also read detective books and watched Charlie Chaplin films.

He wrote poems on patriotism: "Give up slavery, get away from the shackles of dependence", in Marathi.

Nathuram admired Veer Vinayak Damodar Savarkar and was very influenced by his thinking and philosophy. Even though 50 years have passed since Independence, every year on November 15, the day Nathuram was hanged at Ambala Jail, a gathering is held at the Pune residence of Godses to reaffirm the ultimate wish in Nathuram's will "to immerse the ashes in the holy river Sindhu only when she flows back freely into Akhand Bharat."

BAD NEIGHBOURS
1948

In a newly divided subcontinent, Kashmir's accession to India becomes a recurring bone of contention. And drives Pakistan to war against India

1948. Uncharted mountainous territory, 23,000 feet above sea level. An air-strip constructed by a Ladakhi engineer at 11,554 feet. Yet had Air-Commodore Mehar Singh not flown Major-General K S Thimmayya across to Leh, would India have been able to drive the 'raiders' out of Leh and the Ladakh Valley?

Daring, enthusiasm, keenness and impatience — without these characteristics, the Indian Army would have been at a loss in Kashmir, when it arrived there on October 27, 1947, the day after Maharajah Hari Singh acceded to India. The first unit at hand is a Sikh battalion, under the command of Lt-Colonel Dewan Ranjit Rai. He must secure the airfield at Srinagar, help the Government of Kashmir in restoring law and order to the capital and drive away tribesmen, if any. Rai has no information on enemy strength. He takes the airfield and sets his sights on Baramula. The transport to this vital spot that holds the key to Srinagar's defence is provided by Bakshi Ghulam Mohammed of the National Conference.

The Sikh battalion finds that the raiders are an organised group of men with machine guns and mortars, with commanders trained in modern tactics and ground use. The Indians fight, but realise they are outnumbered by far. They withdraw to Patan, having stopped the advance to Srinagar.

Rai is killed in action.

The Indian Army takes Baramula on November 8: "The sight that greeted us in Baramula is one that no period of time can erase from the memory — everywhere one looked, there were signs of pillage, arson and wanton destruction, patients in hospitals had been slaughtered in their beds. Out of a population of 14,000 at least 3,000 had been slain. These included six Europeans and fourteen nuns. The women, including the wife of a retired army officer, had also been raped."

Brigadier L P Sen, Commander of the Indian troops, is only one of many officers who works to rout the tribal raiders from Kashmir. But his experiences are echoed across that state. Indeed, incidents of outrage and plunder have never been far from Kashmir's modern history.

But these are the days between October 1947 and January 1, 1949. Two countries, newly formed, filled with both the joys of freedom and the sorrows of division. And, within months of birth, at war with each other. These are the days which will set the backdrop against which all future India-Pakistan relations will be enacted.

It takes the Indian troops all this time to rid Kashmir of rampaging tribesmen, trained and abetted by the Pakistan Army. India loses land to Pakistan, known variously as Azad Kashmir and Pakistan Occupied Kashmir; Pakistan does not gain Kashmir, except some rugged mountainous areas in the Northwest.

But while the Indian Army fights against a combination of tribal warriors and trained soldiers, her political masters in Delhi and their counterparts in

A war too soon: *Indian soldiers in Kashmir*   Ministry of Defence

Pakistan, play out a game of advance and retreat, parry and thrust. Yet, all their fencing is inconclusive. A sad and inconsistent set of moves, filled with flurry and fury, signifying chaos. Watch the seeds of the future being sown in Babar's favourite garden.

The Maharajah invites Sheikh Abdullah of the National Conference to form a government. The Sheikh

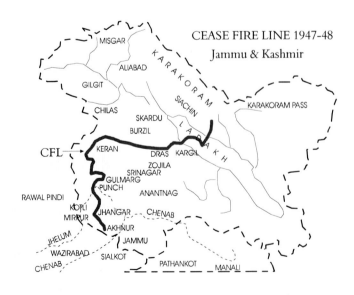

Occupation!: *Map showing battle areas and line of actual control*   Ministry of Defence

accepts. The National Conference is seen by many to be the Kashmiri equivalent of the Indian Congress or Pakistan's Muslim League. Abdullah and the Maharajah are old enemies, now working to a common cause. When the subcontinent's cry in 1942 was "Quit India", Abdullah's was "Quit Kashmir"; now they are apparent allies.

Muslim he may be, but Abdullah has no love for Pakistan's Quaid-e-Azam, Mohammed Ali Jinnah. He has great admiration for Mahatma Gandhi, he and Nehru are friends. He declares that his party's thinking is more in line with India and affirms that Kashmir has acceded to India. Abdullah will later, however, look for Kashmiri independence.

Jinnah wants to send Pakistani troops in. The British Supreme Commander of the Armed Forces, Field Marshal Auchinleck, flies to Lahore: Kashmir is now part of India, legally. If Jinnah goes ahead, every British officer in the Pakistan army would automatically be withdrawn.

Lord Mountbatten offers Jinnah a plebiscite if the raiders stop. Jinnah says that no plebiscite will be fair as long as Sheikh Abdullah is in charge — the people will be too frightened to vote against the National Conference.

Says Jawaharlal Nehru, India's first prime minister, on November 2, 1947, "Not to have taken these steps (military action in Kashmir) would have been a betrayal of trust and cowardly submission to the law of the sword with its accompaniment of arson, rape and slaughter."

Liaqat Ali Khan, Pakistan's first prime minister says, on November 4: "The ownership of Kashmir (by India) is immoral and illegal".

November 11, 1947. The Indian Army reaches Uri. The tribesmen surrender Tangmarg and Gulmarg without firing a shot.

Liaqat Ali Khan and Nehru meet again and again. Nehru demands that the tribesmen withdraw. Khan points out that they might not listen to him. Worse, the prestige of a young Pakistan would suffer if that happens. Let India withdraw first and let a neutral administrator take over from Abdullah.

And so it goes. December 31, 1947. Nehru, on Mountbatten's advice, appeals to the United Nations. Plebiscite is the logical response — where the people of Kashmir will choose between India, Pakistan and independent rule. But the atmosphere and conditions are never right. Not for India. Not for Pakistan. Not for Abdullah. Not for the Security Council, which looks not at the issue at hand but at the history of the problem. Nehru is amazed, says Mountbatten, that "power politics and not ethics were ruling the UNO and was convinced that the UNO was being completely run by the Americans".

So a young, inexperienced India meets the international community, itself regrouping after a long and debilitating war. The idea of India's foreign policy starts germinating in Nehru's mind.

As for Kashmir, some territory lies with Pakistan. But India, through Abdullah, controls the rest. The UN suggests a ceasefire on the last day of 1948. January 1, 1949, ceasefire accepted. It was only the first. ∎

KING-SIZED ERROR
Kashmir's troubles stem from Maharaja Hari Singh's indecisiveness
By Mulk Raj Anand

SEVERAL reasons have been given for Kashmir Maharaja Hari Singh's indecisiveness in joining India. Maybe, it was the inheritance of the large area of strategic importance in North India from his great-grandfather, Maharaja Gulab Singh, who had been sold Jammu and Kashmir for a relatively paltry sum by the British after the death of Maharaja Ranjit Singh of Patiala, that made the Maharaja nostalgic.

But the consequences of his indecision were to be tragic.

Because, after Hari Singh signed the Instrument of Accession, the leaders of Pakistan got occasion to fish in the troubled waters of the Dal and Wular lakes, as also the land where the river Jhelum flowed down from Anant Nag. They wanted this to become part of the theocratic Muslim Pakistan state.

In the months that followed the accession, it became evident that Pakistani authorities had harboured the ambition to include Kashmir as part of their Islamic State. They seemed to ignore the fact that, apart from the dominant Muslim population of Kashmir Valley, the Jammu and Ladakh parts of the state were mostly Hindus and Buddhists. Also, that the whole area had been, for generations, integrated, so as to inspire urges of the people of various religions to live amicably together. The idea of a Muslim theocracy in Kashmir Valley had not found many followers. The Kashmir National Conference headed by Sheikh Abdullah, with Hindu and Sikh Colleagues, had been part of the Indian Freedom Movement

One case of indecision by the then Maharaja of Jammu and Kashmir, was to be used by Pakistan for the next 50 years, as an excuse to infiltrate into Jammu and Kashmir from year to year. And the Pakistan army has waged three wars, as also Pakistan has continued, despite defeat in those wars, to send armed terrorists across the long frontier into Jammu and Kashmir.

Even after reaching agreement at the 1965 Tashkent Treaty to stop such intrusions by Pakistan, Inter-Services Intelligence, the Pakistan army's secret wing, continued to send hired gangs of terrorists, of various fundamentalist aspirations, into Jammu and Kashmir.

The Pakistan army had captured a fairly large segment of Jammu and Kashmir, and a provincial set-up was imposed in the so-called Azad Kashmir. And from that area infiltration of terrorists has been organised, in spite of the United Nation's vigilance, through devious paths in the line of control.

The Indian state is thus confronting not only irregular infiltration by armed guerillas across the western frontier, but also up against attempts to capture by Pakistan decisive areas for future intrusion into Jammu and Kashmir.

Currently, the undeclared war is going on even though there have been three democratic elections in Jammu and Kashmir. And though India has had, perforce, to organise defence against infiltration, and to fight the war on the Siachen glacier, the situation remains unresolved.

WE, THE PEOPLE

January 26, 1950

*India's Constitution draws from the best in the world and Dr B R Ambedkar
constructs a document that will stand the test of time*

Equality above all: *Dr B R Ambedkar*

PERHAPS it all starts in 1913, when Bhimrao Ramji Ambedkar joins the Baroda State Forces as a lieutenant and felt the weight of his untouchability. Or perhaps it is a little later, when he finishes his studies abroad and returns to Baroda to face more discrimination because he was born to the lowly caste of Mahars.

But perhaps the story of the architect of the Indian Constitution takes its first positive turn when Ambedkar speaks out against the injustice of the caste system that strangled Indian society — regardless of religion as a simple study will show — for thousands of years.

On January 27, 1919, this barrister-at-law, with an MA in Economics and a PhD from New York's Columbia University, an MSc and DSc from the London School of Economics, gives evidence before the Southborough Committee on Franchise and strongly recommends a separate electorate with reserved seats in the Legislature for Depressed Classes. A year later, on January 31, he starts *Mook Naik*, a Marathi fortnightly so that India's untouchables could have a voice.

Ambedkar's is an incredible journey, of a man who worked against the odds to build a future for himself in a country where men gained position from birth and not ability.

Burning the *Manusmriti* — the ancient document that set up the social structure that held that some men and all women were less important than others — at Mahad in 1927 is a symbolic action of freedom for a section of society that is still trying to break completely free of the shackles of the past.

Although under British law the demarcations of caste had no legal standing, it is not until the arrival of Ambedkar that the Dalit consciousness moved from the peaceful to the confrontational. He calls upon his people to "educate, agitate and organise". The move is not just for social justice but economic liberation as well.

British law may have been just, but the strength of the Brahmins and other high caste Hindus could not be underestimated — and the country's colonial rulers preferred peace and status quo to social upheaval. It is hardly suprising that so many untouchables converted to other religions — Islam and Christianity primarily — to escape from the tyranny of Brahmanical Hinduism. Yet many found that even religions that preached equality were not immune to the pressures of casteism, and discrimination continued. Ambedkar himself, a trenchant critic of Hinduism, in his later years veers towards Buddhism.

It is clear to him, however, that social change and conversion are not the complete answers. Thunders Ambedkar, "The problem of the Depressed Classes will never be solved unless they get political power in their own hands. If this be true, and I do not think that the contrary can be maintained, then the problem of the Depressed Classes is, I submit eminently, a political problem and must be treated as such."

When the British stop recruiting Mahars into the army, Ambedkar protests, and in 1941, the Mahar Regiment comes into being. Military service was seen as the first avenue of participation in the power structure.

Ambedkar's demand for separate electoral representation for Dalits only wavers when he came across Gandhiji. The Father of the Nation had his own soft spot for India's untouchables — he called them Harijans, or the people of God. The Poona Pact of 1932 found Ambedkar agreeing to a joint electorate in the face of Gandhi's desire to stop the increasing fragmentation of Indian society on caste and communal lines.

Ambedkar's hour of glory comes, undoubtedly, when he is elected to the Constituent Assembly by the Congress from the Bombay Legislature. He is then elected as Chairman of the Drafting Committee and drafts the Constitution. Would that revered document have been framed any differently if Bhimrao Ramji Ambedkar had not been its architect? In his words, "On January 26, 1950 India will become an independent country. What would happen to her independence? Will she maintain her independence or will she lose it again?... Will history (of division and treachery) repeat itself?.. We must make our political democracy a social democracy as well. Political democracy cannot last unless there lies at the base of it social democracy. What does social democracy mean? It means a way of life which recognises liberty, equality and fraternity as the principles of life.

"These principles of liberty, equality and fraternity are

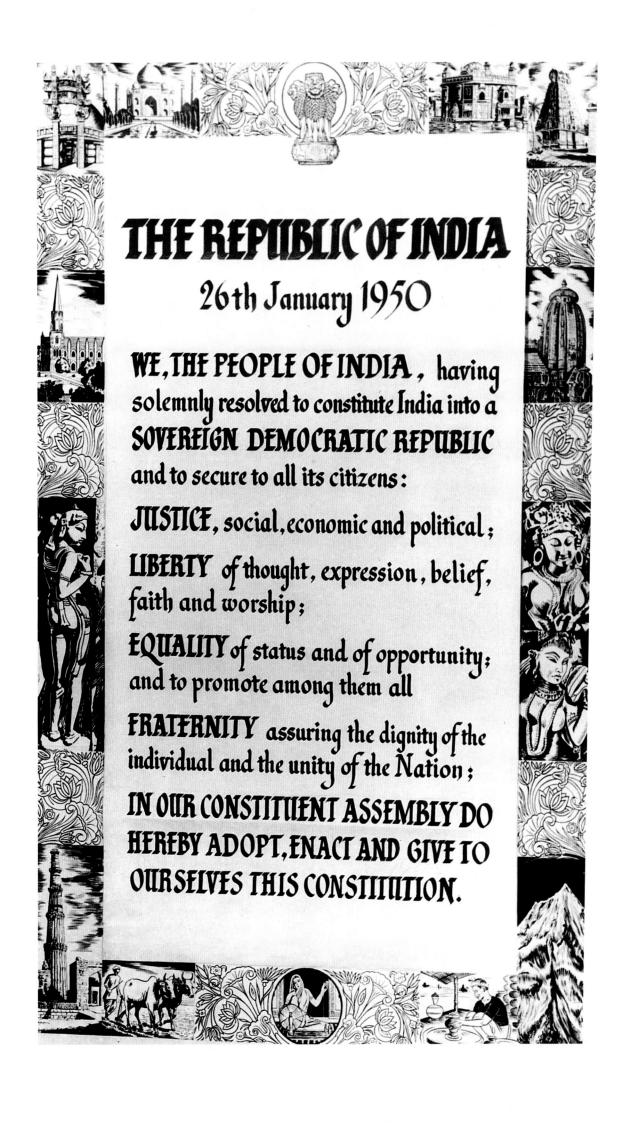

THE REPUBLIC OF INDIA

26th January 1950

WE, THE PEOPLE OF INDIA, having solemnly resolved to constitute India into a **SOVEREIGN DEMOCRATIC REPUBLIC** and to secure to all its citizens:

JUSTICE, social, economic and political;

LIBERTY of thought, expression, belief, faith and worship;

EQUALITY of status and of opportunity; and to promote among them all

FRATERNITY assuring the dignity of the individual and the unity of the Nation;

IN OUR CONSTITUENT ASSEMBLY DO HEREBY ADOPT, ENACT AND GIVE TO OURSELVES THIS CONSTITUTION.

not to be treated as separate items in a trinity. They form a union of trinity in the sense that to divorce one from the other is to defeat the very purpose of democracy."

So Ambedkar, on November 26, 1949, echoes the words of Thomas Jefferson's Declaration of American Independence, 1776: "We hold these truths to be self-evident: that all men are created equal; that they are endowed by their Creator with certain unalienable rights; that among these are life, liberty and the pursuit of happiness." Just over 10 years later, the French revolution would echo Jefferson with its rattling and unforgettable cry of *'Liberte! Egalite! Fraternite!'*

The Constituent Assembly, which looks upon a new world with courage and passion, is born in the same quagmire of religious, political and personality differences that contributed to Partition. The failure of the Cabinet Mission to secure for India one Constituent Assembly that ably and fairly reflects all sections of Indian society falls by the wayside in the overwhelming demand for Pakistan by the Muslim League.

Yet, the Constituent Assembly, which first meets on December 9, 1946, is curiously and thankfully untainted by the horrors of the labour pains which gave it life. Ambedkar and his colleagues take three years to draft the Constitution which gave Independent India a strong central character, from which a sovereign, democratic India would emerge, and they draw freely from the American example, as well as from the traditions of the unwritten British Constitution. A Parliamentary government, with two houses to represent both the people and the states, and a strong Judiciary with a Supreme Court that had the sole right to interpret the Constitution. The checks and balances of the American Constitution are modified and implemented.

For Dalits today, Ambedkar is revered as a godlike figure. His dream of upliftment of the Depressed Classes may not have come completely true, but he has made the laws to ensure total equality. To the country at large, however, he is also a man of tremendous intellectual strength and ability. Whatever faults may be perceived in the Constitution, it cannot be doubted on its foundations of liberty, equality and fraternity. Those who try and weaken those attributes, do so at their own peril. ∎

A republic at last: *Prime Minister Jawaharlal Nehru signs the Constitution*

MERGERS AND ACQUISITIONS

1947-48

The integration of India's princely states into the union is deftly achieved by Vallabhbhai Patel.
And almost scuttled by the rulers of Junagadh, Hyderabad and Kashmir

AUGUST 15, 1947. The country divided. Pandit Jawaharlal Nehru has given his historic speech to the Constituent Assembly at the stroke of the midnight hour. Mahatma Gandhi is in Calcutta. The country awakes to new beginnings.

But, there is some vital, unfinished business to take care of. For the most part, the States Department, Lord Louis Mountbatten and Sardar Vallabhbhai Patel have done their job, and done it well. The 554 states, whose treaties with the Paramount Power of Great Britain has lapsed, who hold two-fifths of the country's land and a large measure of her population in their rule, have signed the Instrument of Accession, ready to become a part of Independent India when she becomes a republic.

Did we say all? Only three states stood out, at Independence. Three states vital for their geographic location, their size and their place in the balance of Hindu-Muslim relations. Because it cannot be forgotten that India was divided along communal lines, and morally and practically, the state must accede where the people want the state to go. The mid-twentieth century has done with feudalism — the Second World War has seen to that. The winds of democracy have reached India.

Junagadh. Hyderabad. Kashmir. Sir Mahabatkhan Rasulkhani, Nawab of Junagadh, was ever an eccentric man. When he flees his palace in late October 1947, he takes to Karachi all the cash balances of his state, all the shares and securities in the treasury, most of his beloved dogs, most of the family jewellery,

and most of his wives. The begum he leaves behind discovered too late she had forgotten a child, and the Nawab has no time to wait. His plane takes off for Karachi without her.

He leaves in his stead a kingdom that has collapsed in law and order and administration, an angry people and a state of confusion. As befits an Indian prince lost in a time-warp, the Nawab has played with several ideas. A strong state of Kathiawar was one, together with his neighbouring principalities. India was the chosen country for accession at the time, and rulers like the Jam Saheb of Nawanagar had worked hard for it.

But then his Dewan changed from Nabi Baksh to Sir Shah Nawaz Bhutto of the Muslim League. Pakistan was much more attractive, then. After all, the Nawab was a Muslim ruler, would he not want to go to Pakistan? It did not matter, surely, that his kingdom was largely Hindu. Junagadh accedes to Pakistan on August 15, informs India a month later. But the Nawab reckons without the will of the people. And the opposition of the Kathiawar princes.

As violence breaks out, and the state administration cannot cope, the Nawab appeals to Pakistan for help — never stopping negotiations with the Indian States Department. But help from Pakistan is not enough. The Nawab flees. Within a month, Sir Shah Nawaz Bhutto hands over the administration of Junagadh to India and leaves for Pakistan himself. A referendum is held on February 20, 1948. Of the almost two lakh people who exercise their franchise, 91 opt for Pakistan.

Coming to terms: *Vallabhbhai Patel with the reluctant Nizam of Hyderabad*

It has been brought to my notice and I have also seen in the foreign press that statements have been made to the effect that I am acting under duress and that I am not allowed free movement, in short, that I am not a free agent in any matter.

(2)   This is absolutely incorrect. On the contrary, my relations with the Indian Union and the Military Administration are extremely cordial and no pressure of any kind is being brought on me; in fact, I am paid all the respect and the courtesy due to the high position I hold as Head of the State

5th October 1948.   *Nizam VII*

Flip flop: *The Nizam dithers between India and Pakistan*   PIB

Of the abandoned begum? She takes a land route to Karachi through the Portuguese settlement of Diu. The dogs that are left behind cost the exchequer Rs 16,000 a month in upkeep.

But compared to the Nizam of Hyderabad, the Nawab of Junagadh is something of a puppydog. Here is His Exalted Highness — the only Indian ruler to be called thus. He rules a very rich state and his land cuts a wide swathe across middle India, practically separating North from South. He has his own currency and stamps. Mir Usman Ali Khan Bahadur is a Muslim ruler, with predominantly Hindu subjects.

Not surprisingly, the Nizam primarily wants recognition of his exalted status. Why can Hyderabad not be independent? Unfortunately for him, that goes outside the terms of the Instrument of Accession and the British policy very clearly ends all treaties with Indian States on August 15. The instrument only requires that the ruler hand over defence, foreign affairs and communication to the Government of India. He continues to rule the state as a Rajpramukh — until India becomes a republic.

But the Nizam wants more. In spite of a Standstill Agreement with India, he gives a loan of Rs 20 crore to Pakistan, even though that is breaking the arrangement. He is also under the influence of the Itehad-ul-Muslimin, an organisation led by the bloodthirsty Kasim Razvi, who wants the waters of the Bay of Bengal to lap at his sovereign's feet. And there is also the option of Pakistan. It was not in the nature of most Indian rulers to pay too much attention to the wishes of their subjects. What the ruler thought right ought to be good enough for them.

The result is a battle of wits between an indomitable Patel and an intractable Nizam. Much as Mountbatten and others involved in negotiations try to convince Patel that they are making headway, the Sardar seriously doubts the bona fides of Hyderabad. As his department's white paper on the issue points out, "An independent state completely landlocked in the heart of another is an unheard-of proposition."

Rioting and looting by Razvi's Razakars start at the borders of Hyderabad, helped by the Communists who see that their own cause can so progress. Reports of Hindus being massacred within Hyderabad start filtering out of the state. Trains leaving and entering the state are attacked and innocent people butchered. But the Nizam cannot tolerate the stationing of Indian troops at the borders to stop these raids into Indian territories. He prepares for war with India.

By January 1948, all negotiations break down. The Nizam appeals to the United Nations. Patel advises military action. The Nizam appeals to Nehru and India again, but Patel prevails over his Cabinet colleagues and Indian troops enter Hyderabad on September 13. Within 24 hours, there is peace, the Nizam surrenders, the Razakars are disbanded, Razvi is arrested.

The dream is over. The Nizam, by turning his back on his own people, brought his own ruin upon himself.

Jammu and Kashmir turns all these arguments on their heads. A beautiful and luscious state at the head of India. The Dogra Maharajah Hari Singh rules over a largely Muslim populace. Kashmir has borders with Tibet, China, Afghanistan. The state could go to India, to Pakistan and, Singh's own idea, remain independent. Certainly, Sheikh Abdullah's National Conference, the most important political organisation in the state would have preferred that. On religious considerations alone, however, Pakistan is the obvious choice.

But events in Kashmir play a strange game, and their repercussions reverberate across the subcontinent to this day. Before August 15, 1947, the Maharajah entered into a Standstill Agreement with Pakistan. Not surprisingly, Mohammed Ali Jinnah is very glad to have Kashmir as part of Pakistan. His eagerness, however, can be said to have exceeded its bounds when food and petrol supplies are cut off to Kashmir followed by some very unfortunate military pressure.

As the tribals in the Northwest — apparently instigated by Pakistan — start raiding, looting and burning their way to Srinagar, the Maharajah panics. Jinnah's attempt to force his hand backfires. Hari Singh flees his capital, his army unable to cope with the tribal warriors. Indeed, many in his army desert and change sides. The raiders cut off electric supply to Srinagar and promise to be there on October 26 for Id celebrations.

The Maharajah, now in Jammu, is desperate for help. V P Menon, secretary of the States Department flies from Srinagar to Delhi, and presents the plight of the state to Nehru and Patel. He then flies to Jammu with the Instrument of Accession — India's terms for military aid. He wakes the unnerved and helpless Maharajah from a troubled sleep. Hari Singh signs immediately. He tells Menon that he had instructed his ADC that if Menon came back he was not to be disturbed, as that meant that India would help. If Menon did not return, he should be shot in his sleep by his aide-de-camp.

On October 27, in an unprecedented military operation, India airlifts troops to Kashmir and stops the tribal invasion,

Friendly ties: *The Jam of Nawanagar with General Cariappa*   PIB

CAST-IRON INTEGRITY
The Life and Times of
Sardar Vallabhbhai Patel
By S Ramakrishnan

A FTER Sardar Vallabhbhai Patel's death, the *Manchester Guardian* wrote on December 30, 1950: "Patel was not only the organiser of the fight for India's freedom but also the architect of the new State when the fight was over. The same man is seldom successful as a rebel and a statesman. Sardar Patel was the exception."

In a moving homage in Parliament on December 19, 1950, Prime Minister Jawaharlal Nehru, with his deep insight into history, thus succinctly summed up the Sardar's work: "History will record his achievements in many pages and call him the builder and consolidator of the new India and say many other things about him. By many of us, he will perhaps be remembered as a great captain of our forces in the struggle for freedom and as one who gave us sound advice both in times of trouble and in moments of victory, a friend and a colleague and comrade on whom one could invariably rely, as a tower of strength which revived wavering hearts when we were in trouble."

The Sardar's "conquests of peace and democracy" are in no way less glorious than the "conquests of war" of Caesar and Napoleon. Indeed, they are worthy of greater respect in world history.

The swift, skilful, thorough and non-violent manner in which the thorny, complex problem of the accession and integration of the 542 anachronistic princely states, many with their own flags, currency, police, railways, posts and telegraphs and other insignia of nation-states, was accomplished is unparalleled. Nikita Khrushchev, during his visit to India in 1956, as chief of Communist Russia remarked: "You Indians are a remarkable people. How did you manage to liquidate the princely states without liquidating the princes!"

Unfortunately the saga of the Sardar's incredible achievements had not been given due recognition by the successive Union Governments, until recently.

The Sardar's life-long colleague and co-worker, Dr. Rajendra Prasad, Free India's first President, noted in his diary on May 13, 1959: "That there is today an India to think and talk about is very largely due to Sardar Patel's statesmanship and firm administration." He added in anguish: "Yet we are apt to ignore him."

Like Gandhi, his master, the Sardar practised complete accord between his thoughts, words and deeds. To him work was worship. But unlike Gandhiji, he did not care so much for niceties of expression and called a spade a spade.

The Sardar's dictum was: "Let words pass; let deeds speak."

Gandhi used to compare Sardar and Nehru to two

The making *of* a NATION

with full help from the National Conference.

The third troublesome state is now part of the new India. But this is a deal that Pakistan would never accept. India, even if it acknowledged that on moral grounds owing to its Muslim majority Kashmir should have gone to Pakistan, had the legal right.

Nehru, to whom Kashmir was no less dear than it was to Jinnah, promises a referendum when peace returns to the Valley. That day has still not come.

But, the blot of Kashmir — if that is what it is — offsets the tremendous achievement of Patel and the States Department that in a few weeks, all states had peacefully and happily become part of the Indian Union.

We can leave the rest to the Nawab of Bhopal, who had once refused to attend a meeting of the rulers and States' representatives, saying they were being invited "like the Oysters to attend the tea party with the Walrus and the Carpenter".

He wrote to Patel in July 1947, "I now wish to tell you that so long as you maintain your present firm stand against the disruptive forces in the country and continue to be a friend of the States, as you have shown you are, you will find in me a loyal and faithful ally."

Patel's reply said that what had happened was a triumph of right and propriety. Perhaps, then, it was. ■

bullocks yoked to a cart. How strong their ties of mutual affection was demonstrated on the occasion of the public meeting in Delhi to observe Gandhiji's 78th birthday on October 11, 1947. It proved to be the Mahatma's last birthday celebration. Gandhiji was extremely unwell and yet he attended the public meeting held to present him with a purse.

The Sardar philosophy was "Work is worship but laughter is life". Speaking on the occasion, he smilingly told Bapu "There is no end to your greed! To collect a purse, you will leave even your death-bed!" Turning to the audience, he added: "Is it my birthday that I should speak? He is to receive the purse and I am to do the speaking — this is most unfair!" He went on to make fun of Gandhiji with superlative good humour: "See how quickly the old man has recovered his strength to relieve you of your money in spite of his illness!" The Mahatma outdid his lieutenant: "The Sardar," he declared, "will not miss a laugh even at the foot of the gallows!"

In 1948, there were persistent rumours that Prime Minister Nehru and Deputy Prime Minister Patel were unable to pull together. At a public meeting, Nehru characterised this whispering campaign as "dishonourable". He emphasised that on all major matters there was unanimity in the Union Cabinet, especially between himself and the Sardar.

In a memorable speech at the same meeting, the Sardar feelingly recalled that both Pandit Nehru and himself had sat at the feet of Gandhiji, their common master for over half a century, and no irreconcilable divergence of opinion existed between them on any major national issue. The Sardar added that as "a disciplined Congressman and self-respecting national servant, I would not think of remaining in office 'even for a minute' if I had the least suspicion that I did not enjoy my leader's confidence."

Once again, on October 2, 1950 he declared, "Our leader is Pandit Jawaharlal Nehru... I am not a disloyal soldier".

On December 11, 1950, four days prior to breathing his last in Bombay on December 15, 1950, the Sardar summoned Shri M V Gadgil, the veteran Congress leader of Maharashtra, a member of the Union Cabinet and took a solemn pledge from him that "no matter how serious your differences are with Nehru, you will not leave the Prime Minister on any account."

That was Sardar Patel, bound by bonds of affection to Gandhi, his master; a pillar of strength to his comrade and Prime Minister Nehru; a disciplined and selfless soldier of freedom; a constructive nation builder; an implacable foe of all "assassins of nationalism" – who included all hues of linguistic and regional zealots, vote-hungry pseudo-champions of endemic reservations on the basis of communities, castes and sub-castes; hypocritical sloganeers of 'garibi hatao' and the like; a man of action, a great and ideal administrator; a statesman of far-seeing vision. Above all, an Indian first, Indian last and Indian always.

The Sardar: *Vallabhbhai Patel*

LAW AND ORDER

1955

The Hindu Code Bill attempts to rationalise a 5,000-year-old system of laws.
But in the process, India loses Dr B R Ambedkar as Law Minister

Justice for all: *Dr Ambedkar tries to push the Hindu Code Bill through*

"The State shall endeavour to secure for its citizens a uniform civil code throughout the territory of India."
— *Article 44, Directive Principles of State Policy, Constitution of India*

"What is more, the Government is committed to this thing (Hindu Code Bill). It is going through with it."
— *Prime Minister Jawaharlal Nehru, November 28, 1949*

"The Hindu Code Bill was the greatest social reform ever undertaken by the Legislature of this country."
— *Union Law Minister Dr B R Ambedkar, in his resignation letter, October 10, 1951*

THE Hindu Code Bill is first introduced in the Constituent Assembly by Dr B R Ambedkar on April 11, 1947. The Bill is ambitious in its scope. It attempts to codify and modernise 5,000 years of Hindu personal law. The Bill is to be a precursor of Article 44 of the Constitution. Derived from principles and precedents scattered across judgments of the High Courts and rulings of the Privy Council, apart from custom and practice in Indian society, codifying Hindu law represents a substantial challenge. The British found it prudent to meddle little in the various personal laws existing in Indian society. Apart from abolishing practices like sati — on the insistence of Raja Rammohun Roy — they only applied the principles of "justice, equity and good conscience" when there was no existing Hindu law. Further confusing the issue is the slightly contemptuous Western attitude towards ancient Hindu texts.

Yet, it is to Western codes of law and jurisprudence, of fairness and reason, that Indian law-makers turn when they take on the gargantuan task of codifying Hindu systems. Dr Ambedkar himself could have said to have suffered from the inequities of Hindu law, the Manu Smriti in particular, which laid down that high caste Hindus were considerably more equal than low-caste Hindus and infinitely superior to those outside the caste system. Apart from the unfairness to untouchables, Hindu law was also patently unfair to women, who were seen as goods and chattel under the Manu Smriti.

Not surprisingly, the attempt to bring Hindu law up-to-date with the 20th century, found many opponents. Religious identity and religious differences, always under the surface of Indian society, gained tremendous impetus from the years leading to Partition, both positive and negative. Secular as the Indian Constitution is in spirit, it does not mention the word. It just points out that all castes, creeds and genders are equal before the law. Codifying Hindu law is one step in that direction.

After being introduced in the Constituent Assembly, the Bill is moved to the Select Commitee of jurists and Parliamentarians on April 8, 1948. Members include Sir Alladi Krishnaswami Aiyar, Dr Bakshi Tek Chand, H V Kamat, G Durgabai. Talks begin here and then don't seem to end. For four years, the bill is discussed, dissected, debated. Hindu customs of marriage, divorce, property, inheritance, succession, adoption, guardianship, maintenance must all be simplified and modernised. The Hindu Code Bill, which includes Jains, Buddhists and Sikhs in its fold, will then act as the basis for a uniform code.

The Bill is a bone of contention, within Parliament as much as among Hindu fundamentalists. Prime Minister Nehru is keen to get the Bill through, but he is also torn apart by the various interests who have reservations about it. But he is certainly not keen enough for the law minister. Ambedkar feels he is forced to resign as Law Minister because of the delays over the passing of the Bill. He resigns on September 27, 1951 but is persuaded to stay on for the Parliamentary debates. However, he finally hands in his letter on October 10, 1951.

Ambedkar's resignation puts forward his anguish very plainly: "The Bill was introduced in this House on the 11th of April 1947. After a life of four years, it was killed and died unwept and unsung, after 4 clauses of it were passed... In regard to this Bill I have been made to go through the greatest mental torture... It has been said that the Bill had to be dropped because the opposition was strong. How strong was the opposition? The Bill has been discussed several times in the Party and was carried to division by the opponents. Every time the opponents were routed... I was therefore, quite unable to accept the Prime Minister's decision to abandon the Bill on the ground of time. I have been obliged to give this elaborate explanation for my resignation because some people have suggested that I am going because of my illness. I wish to repudiate any such suggestion. I am the last man to abandon my duty because of illness."

However, the Hindu Code Bill does see the light of day. It is broken up into a series of acts, but ultimately it does make Hindu law current with the 20th century's ideas of equality and justice. Just under four years after Ambedkar's resignation, on May 5, 1955, the Lok Sabha passes the Hindu Marriage Act, a precursor to the Bill. The Hindu Succession Act is passed in 1956, along with the Hindu Minority and Guardianship Act and the Hindu Adoptions and Maintenance Act.

Through all these, Hindus — which for the purposes of the Bill includes Jains, Buddhists and Sikhs — find themselves in a new era. Child marriages, widow remarriage, sati all saw reform before Independence. Now, women and men are put on an equal footing in terms of marriage, divorce and property settlements. The Hindu Code Bill also introduces a law for civil marriages, which does not involve religions or religious ceremonies.

Over the years, the issue of a common civil code will re-emerge. Few will be as exercised as Ambedkar over the issue. But Indians of various religions seem reluctant to relinquish their personal laws to the state. Changing social perceptions may take longer, but that is only to be expected. ∎

RULING BY RELIGION
How various personal laws in India act

Marriage

Hindu: The Hindu Marriage Act, 1955

Marriage, according to Hindu law, is a holy *sanskar* (sacrament), and not a contract. The Act applies to a Hindu, Buddhist, Jain or Sikh. A traditional marriage is recognised even if it is not registered.

A marriage is said to be solemnised if:

Neither party has a spouse living at the time of marriage; the bridegroom has completed 21 years of age and the bride, 18; and at the time of marriage, and neither party:

a) is incapable of giving valid consent due to unsoundness of mind, or though capable of giving valid consent, has been suffering from mental disorder as to be unfit for marriage and procreation.

b) Has been subject to recurrent attacks of insanity or epilepsy.

Muslim: The Muslim Personal Law (Shariat) Act of 1937 and the Dissolution of Muslim Marriage Act of 1939

The Muslim marriage is a civil contract between a man and a woman. Polyandry is prohibited, but having up to four wives is allowed. Marriage with a fifth wife can be made valid by divorcing one of the wives.

Sunni Muslims can marry a Christian, Jew or Parsi woman. Shia males can do the same as a *muta* marriage (temporary marriage of fixed duration and dower).

A woman, whether Shia or Sunni, can only marry a Muslim.

Muslim women have the right to dower or *mehr*, payable to the wife by the husband in consideration of marriage and recoverable at any time, at the time of dissolution of marriage by death or divorce.

Christian: Indian Divorce Act (1869)

The Christian marriage is considered a sacrament and a civil contract. The reliefs provided under the Act are divorce, nullity, judicial separation, restitution of conjugal rights, maintenance, alimony and custody of children.

A marriage celebrated according to the Roman Catholic religious rites is held valid in law without registration.

Parsi: The Parsi Marriage and Divorce Act (1936) and Chapter III, Part V of the Indian Succession Act (1925)

There are three conditions for validity of marriage:

Avoidance of 33 degrees of prohibited relationships, 'Ashirvad' ceremony by a Parsi priest with two Parsi witnesses and the consent of a guardian.

Parsi marriages are registered.

Divorce

Hindu: Hindu Marriage Act (1955)

Grounds for divorce for both husband and wife are adultery, virulent or venereal disease, conversion to another religion, renouncing the world, disappearance for seven years or more or failure to resume cohabitation for two years after a degree of restitution of conjugal rights and insanity.

The wife has two additional grounds: bigamy on part of the husband, and rape, sodomy and bestiality. Mutual consent is also recognised.

Muslim: The Dissolution of Muslim Marriage Act (1939), Muslim Shariat Laws Application Act (1937), Muslim Women (Protection of Rights on Divorce) Act and customs.

A Muslim husband can divorce his wife without assigning any cause. *Talaq* (divorce) is extra-judicial, and valid without a *talaqnama* or any particular form of word — even under jest, compulsion or intoxication, as in the case of Sunnis.

It can be pronounced in the absence of a wife and the presence of a *kazi*, in various forms.

The *ahsan* is where a repudiation takes place at a single pronouncement of divorce to a wife when she is not in menstruation: subsequently, there being no sexual intercourse.

The *bidat* form has a single declaration of talaq, showing a clear intention to divorce, immediately and irrevocably.

Under the *khula* form, the woman can initiate divorce, but must pay compensation to the husband.

The *mubarat* form involves mutual consent.

Talaq-e-tawfeez is when a wife has the right to pronounce *talaq*, upon delegation of the right by the husband.

In the *faskh*, dissolution by judicial decree can be sought by husband or wife.

Christian: The Indian Divorce Act (1869)

Grounds for divorce are different for men and women. For a husband, it is adultery alone.

But for a wife, adultery must be coupled with incest, bigamy, rape, sodomy, bestiality, cruelty or desertion for two years. Without proving adultery, none of the other grounds are sufficient.

The wife can also present a petition on grounds that the husband has changed his religion and married another woman.

Parsi: Parsi Marriage and Divorce Act (1936)

Grounds for divorce are lunacy, bigamy, rape or any other unnatural offence, causing grievous hurt, infection with venereal disease, seven years' imprisonment, desertion for three years or more, three years' judicial separation, failure to comply with a restitution decree for one year and conversion from Zoroastrianism.

The husband can resort to divorce if the wife is pregnant by another man at the time of marriage, and the wife can do so for being forced into prostitution. Cruelty is also a ground.

Adoption

Hindus: Hindu Adoptions and Maintenance Act (1956)

The father is the natural guardian, and the mother, the second. While mutual consent of husband and wife is recognised by court, only the husband can apply for adoption.

A woman can adopt if she is single, a divorcee, a widow or has 'renounced the world'.

Muslim: Orthodox Muslims say there is no provision for adoption in their personal law.

Christian: There is no provision for adoption in Christian Personal Law. The father is the natural guardian.

Parsis and *Jews* disallow adoption on grounds of their religion not allowing conversions.

Succession

Hindu: The Hindu Succession Act (1956)

Daughters and sons are entitled to succession. A daughter does not have equal share in the parental home with her brother, but only the right of residence if she is unmarried, deserted, divorced or widowed.

A widow shares her husband's intestate property equally with the children, children of predeceased children, mother of husband, and children of predeceased son's predeceased son.

A widower shares property only with children and if they are deceased, with grandchildren.

In the distribution of property, agnates (relatives through males) are preferred to cognates (relatives not wholly through males).

Muslim: Shariat law

The wife's share in husband's property is half that of the husband's share in the wife's property. The daughter's share in the father's property is half that of the son's property.

Christian: Indian Divorce Act (1869)

The husband has control over his wife's property.

In the event of divorce or judicial separation on account of adultery committed by the wife, the court may order the settlement of the woman's property for the benefit of the husband and/or her children.

There is no such provision in respect of the husband's property if he is found guilty of adultery.

A deserted or judicially separated wife must explicitly apply for a court order to prevent her husband or his creditors from claiming right over the property that she acquired after separation.

Parsis: Marriage and Divorce Act and Chapter III, Part V of the Indian Succession Act (1925)

A widow shares the husband's intestate property with children, his father and mother. Her share of ancestral property is equal to her brother's.

A widower and all the children share equally in a woman's intestate property. In the sharing of residual property (in the absence of lineal descendants), each male takes double the woman's share of the same degree of claim.

ON OUR OWN TERMS

1955

Jawaharlal Nehru's Non-Aligned Movement sets a new international order
for countries emerging out of colonialism

Ground-breaking meet: *Nehru, Nkrumah, Nasser, Soekarno and Tito at the Bandung Conference*   Nehru Library

"We are not citizens of a weak or mean country, and I think it is foolish for us to get frightened, even from a military point of view, of the greatest of the Powers today. Not that I delude myself about what can happen to us if a great Power in a military sense goes against us; I have no doubt it can injure us. But after all in the past, as a national movement, we opposed one of the greatest of World Powers. We opposed it in a particular way and in a large measure succeeded in that way, and I have no doubt that if the worst comes to the worst — and in a military sense we cannot meet these great Powers — it is far better for us to fight in our own way than submit to them and lose the ideals that we have. Therefore, let us not be frightened too much of the military might of this group or that group. I am not frightened and I want to tell the world on behalf of this country that we are not frightened of the military might of this Power or that. Our policy is not a passive policy or a negative policy."

— *Jawaharlal Nehru, Prime Minister of India, March 1948*

THUS Jawaharlal Nehru sets the agenda for India's foreign policy, within Asia and in the world in general. India will align herself with no Great Powers, but will stand for herself at all times. Soon, the world will know this as Non-Alignment, a policy closely associated with Nehru as he strives to carve a place for a new country on a new world map.

Cartographers are having a tough time, as it is. The end of the Second World War has changed loyalties and abilities. The power of Great Britain is great no longer and soon the world will be polarised between the United States of America and the Union of Soviet Socialist Republics. For a new Asia, breaking out of its colonial bonds, the idea of non-alignment is very attractive. It speaks of national pride, still a new and shiny commodity untouched by the cynicism of wasted development or scurrilous politicians. It is also an anti-colonialism that is more emphatically anti-Western, than anti-colonialism *per se*. It is this distinction that will taint non-alignment forever, yet at the same time imprint it with a deeply Asian character.

Fine words, national pride and non-alignment. Nehru speaks out strongly against the Dutch occupation of Indonesia and the presence of the French in Southeast Asia. Both European nations will give up their former colonies. Nehru will take this same line in Africa, as more and more nascent nations make their bid for self-governance.

War breaks out in Korea in June 1950. It is a clear sign of the aggravation of the Cold War. North Korea, under Soviet

Friends for now: *Chou-en-lai and Nehru working on Panchshila*

control since WWII, walks across the 38th parallel into South Korea, under the United States. The division is artificial — yet the two countries cannot now resolve their differences amicably. The UN declares Korea's invasion an act of aggression — at a Security Council from which the USSR is voluntarily absent. Nehru sends a mobile army unit to Korea, but cannot agree with the UN military action under General MacArthur. He earns no friends in the United States. But he does raise some admiration in China and the USSR.

And further West in Egypt, where in 1952, General Abdul Gamel Nasser takes over, after the decadent monarchy is overthrown. When Nasser nationalises the Suez Canal in 1956, Britain is outraged. Did it not belong to the British-owned Suez Canal Company. When British and French troops move in to take Suez, the UN intervenes and Nasser finds an invaluable ally in Nehru. Was not the British act one more brutal example of imperial arrogance? Nehru has now antagonised both the US and Britain.

Up North in Yugoslavia, Marshal Josip Broz Tito, breaking away from the Russian stranglehold and unwilling to surrender totally to the West, also finds answers in Nehru's non-alignment. The forces are gathering towards the Bandung conference.

Delhi, June 1954. The crowning glory of Nehru's peaceful foreign policy. Chou-en-lai of China arrives in India. He has recently been insulted by the US, which still does not recognise Communist China as a country, preferring the island of Formosa. Nehru is one of the few champions of China in the world. Cries of '*Hindi-Chin bhai bhai*' rent the air of Delhi. Despite problems of Tibet and the Sino-Indian border along the Macmohan Line, Asia's two greatest powers come together. Later, this will be seen as Nehru's naivete and ultimately disastrous idealism. But not yet. Definitely not yet.

The principles of peaceful co-existence which made their appearance in a trade pact between the two Asian giants are now sanctified. Panchshila, or the five principles of peaceful co-existence may have their roots in Buddhism but they are to be the panacea for a new Asia. Nehru's Fabian background, his gleanings from the lap of Mahatma Gandhi

Facing the world: *Nehru with Krishna Menon*   Nehru Library

NAM OR NOTHING
The Non-Aligned Movement is vital for India
By Natwar Singh

"The Non-Aligned Movement is the largest peace Movement in history."
— *Indira Gandhi*

IN Volume 7 of the *Encyclopaedia Britannica* (Micropaedia Section) on page 380, there is an entry which is most revealing of the mind-set of the West. The word non-alignment is no doubt mentioned. However, the reader is directed to "see, neutralism". And that is that.

Non-alignment is not a dogma. It is not a doctrine. It is not neutrality. It is a state of mind, an attitude if you please. It is a need, not a creed. The documents and declarations of NAM may not be marked by a fluid facility of expression (not easy in five languages) nor do these always succeed in condensing wisdom into impressive brevity. These declarations do, nonetheless, reflect the aspirations, faith and hopes of a very large number of human beings.

The essence of non-alignment is the pursuit of an independent foreign policy, bearing in mind one's vital national interests. No two situations are alike. So each issue is to be judged on its merits. Don't all sovereign states do so? Not quite. Till quite recently capitalist and Communist countries looked at the same problem differently. Invented theology was matched by opportunistic ideology. India strenously opposed both attitudes and hegemonistic pressures by each.

That the hegemonistic mind set exists (even though the Soviet Union has disappeared) is dramatically illuminated by Professor Samuel P Huntington in his now famous article published in the journal *Foreign Affairs*, in 1993. The choice of the title was probably not an entirely happy one — 'The Clash of Civilisations'— and it carried the message of doom with it. The learned professor wrote:

"Global politics and security issues are effectively settled by a directorate of the United States, Britain and France, world economic issues by a directorate of the United States, Germany and Japan, all of which maintain extraordinarily close relations with each other... The West in effect is using international institutions, military power and economic resources to run the world in ways that will maintain western dominance, protect western economic interests and promote western political and economic values."

Those revisionist pundits who pooh-pooh non-alignment should ponder over what Samuel P Huntington has written. So should today's foreign ministers of non-aligned countries. The non-aligned either hang together, otherwise each will be hanged separately. The superficial and the supercilious ask — is non-alignment relevant now that the Cold War is over? We are entitled to answer in equally

have found fine expression.

★ Mutual respect for each other's territorial integrity and sovereignty
   ★ Mutual non-aggression
   ★ Mutual non-interference in each other's internal affairs
   ★ Equality and mutual benefit
   ★ Peaceful coexistence

Asia and Africa now have a viable option to the US in the West and Russia in the East. Colonial yokes can be overthrown and there is a friendly camaraderie to draw strength from. Western domination now has no chance.

April 18, 1955, Bandung. President Soekarno of Indonesia inaugurates the conference, "I think it is generally recognised that the activity of Prime Ministers of the sponsoring countries which invited you here had a not unimportant role to play in ending the fighting in Indo-China. Look, the people of Asia raised their voices and the world listened. It was no small victory and no small precedent."

There are 29 countries attending the conference — including China, India, Japan, the Philippines, Egypt, Ethiopia, Laos. There are great names like Nehru, Chou-en-lai, Nasser, Soekarno, Prince Wan of Thailand.

The Bandung Peace Declaration of Ten Principles incorporates Panchshila.

The hope is that despite Korea, Tibet, Suez, Asia and Africa could still be an area of peace.

History has its own way of playing out events. Whatever history may say later, it cannot deny that Jawaharlal Nehru had a vision and he tried to give it a name. Or, NAM. ■

simplistic terms — is NATO relevant now that the Cold War is over? This is no way to approach profoundly serious questions involving the peace and security of humankind. It really is extraordinary to suggest that NAM should be wound up and NATO extended and expanded. Only NAM stands between the hegemonistic domination by a few over the many.

Conventional wisdom has it that non-alignment was a response to the Cold War. Not as far as India was concerned. Bandung, Brioni and Belgrade are important landmarks, but the beginning goes back to the Haripura Session of the AICC in early 1938. Jawaharlal Nehru drafted the resolution, which stated that independent India would keep aloof from both imperialism and fascism. It further stated that:

India was resolved to maintain friendly and cooperative relations with all nations and similar alliances which divide up the world in rival groups and thus India was resolved to maintain friendly and cooperative relations with all who endanger peace.

In September 1946, as Vice-President of the Interim Government, Nehru said:

We propose, as far as possible, to keep away from the power politics of groups aligned against one another, which have led in the past to world wars and which may again lead to disasters on an even vaster scale. We believe that peace and freedom are indivisible and the denial of freedom anywhere must endanger freedom elsewhere and lead to conflict and war.

India's independent, non-aligned policy was first tested during the Korean War and immediately after that in Indo-China in 1954. On both occasions, we earned kudos from the world community.

India's vision was shared by most newly independent countries in Asia, Africa and Latin America. The movement was fortunate to have at its first Summit in 1961 towering leaders like Nehru, Tito, Nasser, Soekarno and Nkrumah to guide and inspire. Countries queued up to join. Today NAM has 113 members and nearly 35 observers and guests, including Germany, Canada, Australia, China, Russia, Italy. NAM is no longer considered "immoral" by the United States. But numbers are not enough. NAM must do some confessing that its failures are as spectacular as they are tragic. Why did the movement fail to purposefully contribute solutions during the Iran-Iraq war? Why is it helpless in Afghanistan, Rwanda, Burundi, Bosnia, Somalia? Why had a Norwegian diplomat to make a break-through to get the PLO and Israel to talk? What was the movement doing?

I K Gujral put forward eminently wise proposals before the 12th meeting of NAM Foreign Ministers held in Delhi in 1997. He highlighted the sinister re-emergence of the new imperialism of the west. The G7 are writing the global agenda, new labour laws, social clauses, selective global investment regimes, preaching human rights, environmental conditionalities, protectionism and so on. The P5 are unwilling to give up the veto. Democratisation of the UN Security Council is blocked. Why? Because NAM is divided. Too many NAM countries are living on western dole. In several, treasured concepts of civilised behaviour have been abandoned. NAM must deplore the fundamentalisms of globalisation and the market and not remain silent on the fundamentalism being preached and practised in Kabul and Algiers, where civil strife is rampant.

In most NAM countries, poverty remains acute. Over a billion people struggle to live on less than $ one a day. Two hundred million children die each year from poverty-related causes. Private capital is not flowing to sub-Saharan Africa. It is a cruel joke in such circumstances for developing countries to spend vast amounts on weaponry, to have huge defence budgets. The distortion of democracy, the lack of concern for human dignity, the increase in violence leading to human suffering, are all causes for alarm. NAM must reform itself before it can reform the world. The ethical and moral cutting edge is missing in its discussions and deliberations.

Human rights is the new mantra discovered by the G7 countries. The historical human rights of these countries is so shocking that instead of preaching human rights to India and China, they should be atoning for their sins for the next hundred years. The G7 countries should not mix human rights with civic rights. The civil laws of India, China and Pakistan cannot be subject to western whims. The NAM countries must with one voice condemn and resist western interference in such matters.

The time has now come for NAM to have a professionally run secretariat to coordinate its plans, programmes and policies, to keep the movement from slipping into deep slumber between summits, to coordinate its activities. All other organisations have their secretariats. Why not NAM? The movement should not shy away from seriously discussing the establishment of an administrative instrumentality to make NAM an effective organisation. And let not NAM quibble for five years on where the secretariat is to have its headquarters.

The making *of* a NATION

Going strong: *The Seventh NAM Summit in New Delhi, 1983*   India Today

TEMPLES OF NEW INDIA?

1950s onwards

Jawaharlal Nehru's dream of large dams and factories and ground-breaking scientific research to lead India into modernity produces mixed results

"I like big plants, I like the feel of machinery, I like the look of it. I feel it is essential for the planned development of the country."

— Prime Minister Jawaharlal Nehru

HE called them the Temples of New India. They were not to be worshipped perhaps, but these giant dams and factories were certainly to set India's development and industrial base. For Jawaharlal Nehru, if India was to take on the challenge of the world, it had to be from a strong infrastructure. With the power of big machinery.

August 4, 1956. Apsara becomes critical. India enters the nuclear age. With the commissioning of the Apsara reactor, built by the Atomic Energy Establishment at Trombay, Prime Minister Jawaharlal Nehru's dream of an India streaming full power into the world with a scientific temper and modern outlook had one more bulwark. Of course, India's efforts in

this direction had already been set in place. Dr Homi Bhabha, under whose direction the Apsara was built, had already started his seminal work in cosmic rays at the Indian Institute of Science in Bangalore in the '30s which was continued at the Tata Institute of Fundamental Research which he set up in Bombay in 1945.

1954. Bhabha continues to be at the forefront of research in nuclear physics in India, as he heads the just-commissioned Atomic Energy Establishment.

June 10, 1960. India's first nuclear power plant is established at Tarapur, near Bombay, when Circus, built with Canadian help, goes critical.

The discussions over the suitability of nuclear power research is still nascent. All over the world, giant atomic power plants are being constructed, as nuclear physics pushes at the frontiers of modern science. The dangers and feasibility of mammoth atomic institutions will only come up for scrutiny

Big dreams, big dams: *Jawaharlal Nehru opens the Bhakra dam*

Dinodia Picture Agency

Space capsule: *Aryabhatta, India's first satellite*   PIB

1951, precursor of the others, and the Birla Institute of Technology and Science in 1965, means that India has an edge in the pursuit of higher education.

But it was, perhaps, in space, that Sarabhai gives India its biggest impetus. Appointed Scientific Chairman of the UN Conference on Exploration and Peaceful Uses of Outer Space, Sarabhai establishes the Department of Space and the Space Commission in 1972. On April 19, 1975, the first Indian satellite, Aryabhatta — named after an ancient mathematician — is launched by a Soviet rocket carrier. Sarabhai dies in 1974, but the launch of Aryabhatta is a fulfilment of his vision.

much later, as will the arguments over the use of nuclear energy for peace and war.

May 18, 1974, 0.05 am. Pokhran, in the Rajasthan desert. Under the direction of Dr H N Sethna, the first underground nuclear explosion for peaceful purposes takes place. India enters into the global argument about atomic energy.

When Bhabha dies in a plane crash over Mont Blanc in Switzerland in 1966, his mantle passes to Dr Vikram Sarabhai. Apart from setting up the Physical Research Laboratory and the High Altitude Research Laboratory, Sarabhai concentrates on pharmaceutical research and norms for the industry. In 1962, he also establishes the Indian Institute of Management and Business Administration at Ahmedabad. The first Indian Institute of Technology had already started in Kharagpur in

Walking in step with India's strides into modern science, is the fulfilment of the other half of Nehru's dream — large factories and dams. The norm followed across the world becomes a reality in India as well, as bigger is very clearly perceived as better. Under the first Five-Year Plan, (1951-56), the focus is on agriculture, irrigation and power projects. In the East, it is the Damodar Valley Scheme and the Hirakud Dam, in the North, the Bhakra-Nangal project and in the South, the Nagarjuna Sagar river valley project. India's problems of water, irrigation and power are all going to be met at these one-stop shops. "It can hardly be challenged that in the context of the modern world, no country can be politically and economically independent, even within the framework of international interdependence, unless it is highly industrialised and has developed its power resources to the utmost. Nor can it achieve and maintain high standards of living and liquidate poverty without the aid of modern technology in almost every walk of life. An industrially backward country will continually upset the world equilibrium and encourage aggressive tendencies of more developed countries." — so Nehru set the agenda for India's growth in Discovery of India.

The making *of* a NATION

The First Five-Year Plan concentrates on agriculture, and small and big irrigation and power projects, but it does not

Atomic energy: *Dr. Homi Sethna and (right) the blast at Pokhran*   PIB

SPACE CENTRES & UNITS IN INDIA

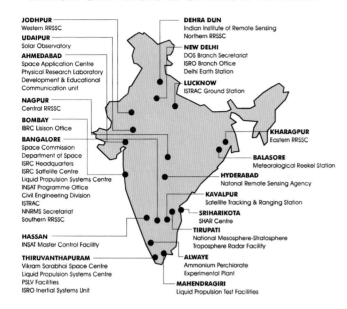

JODHPUR
Western RRSSC

UDAIPUR
Solar Observatory

AHMEDABAD
Space Application Centre
Physical Research Laboratory
Development & Educational
Communication unit

NAGPUR
Central RRSSC

BOMBAY
IBRC Lisison Office

BANGALORE
Space Commission
Department of Space
ISRC Headquarters
ISRC Satfelite Centre
Liquid Propulsion Systems Centre
INSAT Programme Office
Civil Engineering Division
ISTRAC
NNRMS Secretariat
Southern RRSSC

HASSAN
INSAT Master Control Facility

THIRUVANTHAPURAM
Vikram Sarabhai Space Centre
Liquid Propulsion Systems Centre
PSLV Facilities
ISRO Inertial Systems Unit

DEHRA DUN
Indian Institute of Remote Sensing
Northern RRSSC

NEW DELHI
DOS Branch Secretariat
ISRO Branch Office
Delhi Earth Station

LUCKNOW
ISTRAC Ground Station

KHARAGPUR
Eastern RRSSC

BALASORE
Meteorological Reekel Station

HYDERABAD
National Remote Sensing Agency

KAVALPUR
Satellite Tracking & Ranging Station

SRIHARIKOTA
SHAR Centre

TIRUPATI
National Mesosphere-Stratosphere
Troposphere Radar Facility

ALWAYE
Ammonium Perchlorate
Experimental Plant

MAHENDRAGIRI
Liquid Propulsion Test Facilities

India in space: *Units all over the country*

ignore industry. The Chittaranjan workshop for locomotives, a fertiliser factory in Sindri in Bihar start production under the plan. In 1956, plans for the Durgapur Steel Plan are set into motion and the government decides to take over the Rourkela steel plant. The public sector has started its long roll into heavy industrialisation. Private sector investments also rise, and India becomes the world's second largest producer of cotton cloth; cement, paper and steel also see increases in output.

By the end of the First Plan, the industrial index rises from an over-all 105 in 1951 to 157.9 for the first quarter of 1955; the price index drops from 399.6 at the end of 1954 to 358.6 by August 1955. Development expenditure in the public sector totals $ 1.1 billion at the end of 1955. The dream of living by big machinery is fast becoming a reality.

The Second Five Year Plan moves even faster into industrialisation. But gradually, the euphoria is crinkling at the edges. The human face of India is still poor, unemployed, downtrodden. Per capita income stands at $ 58 per annum at the end of the first plan; finance minister C D Deshmukh places India's fully unemployable at 15,000,000. Figures are hard to come by and unreliable, but frightening nonetheless. India's population is growing at the rate of 5,000,000 a year, translating to 1.5 to 2 million people seeking employment every year. This dichotomy between economic growth and social welfare development has always existed. Industrialisation, at best, "cannot absorb more than a small part of the population of this country", admits Nehru in a speech to Parliament in December 1952.

There seems to be only one answer — to go back to Nehru's mentor and the Indian village. Nehru and Mahatma Gandhi had never fully agreed on the question of India's economic development. Gandhi favoured the village and the small scale approach over Nehru's gigantic vision of enormous machineries changing the face of India. But both approached the same problem from different sides of the fence, and both

conceded that the other's idea had its points. Gandhi was all for concentrating on electricity and power if it brought convenient implements closer to the small farmer. Nehru was all for small-scale and cottage industries provided there is also provision for heavy industrialisation.

Going back to India's villages, however, is not easy. As much as water and power, what is required most urgently is in land reform, in squaring the balance between the landed and the landless, between the peasant and the zamindar. This is a problem that requires more than five-year plans to solve. It requires the entire might of a nation reworking its social structure. It is a problem that will recur, time and again, in India's development history.

The industrial and scientific juggernaut, however, rolls on. Years later, when Nehru's vision of economic development is discarded, no one denies that whatever was lost, India has gained tremendously from having a heavy industrial base, from having a modern approach to life, from trying to progress, to whatever extent, in every aspect of development. Perhaps, concentration should have been on primary rather than higher education, maybe land reforms should have preceded large irrigation projects, perhaps the private sector should have been allowed to develop faster. In 1955, all these questions are very far away. The job at hand is tough and the country is still enthusiastic enough to put in the great toil the prime minister says is required. ∎

Where Big is not Better
Controversial developmental projects

Chilka
One of India's three wetlands protected by the Ramsar Convention. However, this salt water lake is being ravaged both by local prawn barons as well as a Tata project which, according to environmentalists, is killing all but a handful of indigenous acquatic species. The case is under trial.

Dahanu
Inhabited by tribals and fruit orchards, Dahanu's peace has been invaded by a World Bank aided thermal power plant being put up by the Bombay Suburban Electric Supply Company. The project will drastically change the eco-system that exists in this green area through the resultant pollution. Already, the project is violating the 500 metre high tide rule that prohibits construction close to the shoreline in India. Fish catch, fruit harvest and output of tribal farms is expected to fall when the power plant is ready.

Sardar Sarovar Project
India has built 1,554 dams since Independence, but the country still suffers droughts and floods. Access to fresh water is half what it was in pre-Independence India. The dam project along the length of the 1,312 km Narmada river will drown 3,500 sq km of forest, 2,500 sq km of fertile fields and the homes of 1.5 million people. Environmentalists are still waging a battle against this World Bank aided project, pointing out that it is not likely to benefit water-starved Kutch and Saurashtra, as claimed.

Tehri Dam
Situated close to a fault-line, the Tehri Hydro-development Corporation dam has the potential to wipe out Hrishikesh, Hardwar and New Delhi if it bursts. Geologists and geophysicists are at loggerheads with the government over this project, which, at a cost of Rs 5,000 crore, is expected to provide 2,400 MW of electricity to Uttar Pradesh. However, funds have been drying up after the collapse of the Soviet Union.

BUILDING FOR PROFIT

1950s onwards

*India's private sector works hard to give the country a strong and viable industrial base.
And two names tower over the rest. G D Birla and J R D Tata*

On the wings of growth: *J R D Tata*

Jitendra Arya

"I am interested in anything that creates more wealth, more employment. I am a capitalist, but I believe in a socialism which means equal opportunity, more employment and a fairer standard of living for everyone. Socialism does not mean socialising poverty, but raising the quality of life."

— *G D Birla*

"The wealth gathered by Jamsetji Tata and his sons in half a century of industrial pioneering formed but a minute fraction of the amount by which they enriched the nation. The whole of that wealth is held in trust for the people and used exclusively for their benefit. The cycle is thus complete; what came from the people has gone back to the people many times over."

— *J R D Tata*

AUGUST 25, 1919, a man of 25 wants to make his own way in the business world. He has already moved away from the family home in Pilani, Rajasthan, and set up a brokerage house in Calcutta. But now he wants to build, not trade. Ghanshyam Das Birla starts Birla Jute Mills.

In October 1932, a 28-year-old pilot flies a Puss Moth from Karachi to Bombay, carrying a cargo of mail. Tata Airlines is born, with an investment of Rs 200,000. The pilot is Jehangir R D Tata.

From then on, two names will dominate India's business world. Born 10 years apart, G D Birla and J R D Tata will nevertheless stand together as the stalwarts of Indian industry, the men who will shape the nation as much as India's political and social leaders. It might be said, however, that Tata has the advantage. His father is a cousin of Sir Jamsetji Tata, the founder of the Tata Iron and Steel Company at Jamshedpur and of the Tata Empire. Birla is more the self-made man, or more rightly, the man who wanted to make himself. But they are both driven by similar urges — to marry their growth with the growth of the country. A fierce feeling of Indian-ness characterises their actions and beliefs. They live in deeply patriotic times, and all of that percolates into them.

Tata takes Tata Airlines to the heights of success, till it becomes Air-India, India's first commercial airline. His maiden flight lays the ground for efficiency and reputation, and setting the stage for his takeover of Tata Sons. Birla takes one jute mill and on that base builds an enormous empire, one that will eventually span almost every aspect of Indian life. Both will also work hard to give back to the community.

Birla gives a loan of Rs 22,000 to an impoverished Indian scientist who promises him that he will win the Nobel Prize. And so C V Raman does. Tata listens to Dr Homi Bhabha's fears that lack of resources and research facilities will dry up Indian scientific talent and so the Tata Institute of Fundamental Research is born. Neither has had much of a formal education, but the importance of education is not lost on them. Schools, colleges, hospitals all follow where Tata and Birla go. The Indian Institute of Science in Bangalore is started by the Tatas, the Indian Institutes of Technology are helped by them. Birla transforms the town of Pilani, and the Birla Institute of Technology and Science is its jewel.

The freedom movement carries them along in its sway. Tata is almost tempted to chuck it all away, so inspired is he by Jawaharlal Nehru. But he sees that his place is elsewhere. Birla forges a close friendship with Gandhiji — it is at Birla House in Delhi that Gandhi attends his last prayer meeting and meets that fatal bullet. In the shadow of the Mahatma, that is how Birla tells the story of his life.

But these are also visionary entrepreneurs, farseeing capitalists, the builders of a nation. Tata takes charge of Tata Sons

The making *of* a NATION

Building for Profit
....
55

in 1938, when he is 34. Birla started out on his quest of building an industrial base for India when he was just 23. They would come together in the 1940s for the creation of the Bombay Plan, a blueprint for India's economic success. Tata invites Birla, Kasturbhai Lalbhai, the textile mill owner from Ahmedabad, Sir Purshottamdas Thakurdas and Sir Shri Ram from Delhi to map out the future. Three technocrats from the Tatas are also part of the group — Sir Ardeshir Dalal, A D Shroff and John Matthai, later to be minister in Nehru's Cabinet. The Plan, published, in 1943 and '44 is the first time that Indian industrialists speak about their plans for the nation. Tata would say of Birla later, "G D Birla was a man of high intelligence and knowledge. When we were floundering to find a structure in the first few meetings, it was he who suggested: 'It is difficult to forecast what India should do after being free... So let's do it this way — first estimate to get the people the kind of standard of living they want. What is needed? So many calories of food requiring so many millions of tons of grain, so many metres of cloth, housing — how many cubic feet of housing, so many schools, etc.' The concept of quantifying made it easy and it was on that basis that Dr Matthai wrote the Plan."

It is perhaps India's loss that such contributions from some of the country's best minds were ignored in the large thrust of government-sponsored socialism. Nehru, somewhat wary of the profit word, was not friendly towards big business. From then on started a system of controlling money-making till the liberalisation of the 1990s. But these were men who were not just making money. They were taking the country forward with as much enthusiasm and commitment and financial strength as Nehru's temples of New India. Steel, aluminium, trucks, automobiles, locomotives, chemicals, fertilisers, cement, textiles, all these and more became company strongholds for both Birla and Tata.

Both men watch with pain as business becomes a dirty word in India, and corruption in business the norm. But it does not move them away from their chosen path. The growth of the country is in both their interests and so it must be. Other Indian industrialists who started with them also move ahead — the Godrejs, the Walchand Hirachands, the Wadias of Bombay Dyeing, the Lalbhais, the Shri Rams. Others cannot deal with the change of pace. Either they have not diversified enough, or they have been profligate in their spending habits. Others will come up later, and sparkle with the their seeming brilliance.

Still, these two names endure.

G D Birla and J R D Tata will die within 10 years of each other, Birla in 1983, Tata in 1993. They will each leave behind them some measure of confusion for their heirs and successors, as without their presence, strength and comfort and leadership are gone. What they built is enduring, however. Whatever is wrong with Indian industry, the economy, business practices did not stem from them. They tried to live by principles, perhaps even those set down by a man who inspired them both.

"We do not claim to be more unselfish, more generous or more philanthropic than other people. But we think we started on sound and straightforward business principles, considering the interests of the shareholders our own, and the health and welfare of the employees the sure foundation of our prosperity."

— *Jamsetji Tata, 1895*   ∎

WORKING WITH NEHRU
How Birla and Tata grew against all odds
By Dr Gita Piramal

A common characteristic in almost every country whose standard of living has risen over the past half century — be it a democracy such as Japan, a kingdom like Thailand, or a neo-colony like Taiwan -- is a collaboration between business and politics. In India on the other hand, the past 50 years has seen an erosion of confidence between the two camps. The concept of partnership gradually whittled away to be replaced by an eyeball-to-eyeball confrontation between businessmen and politicians resulting in what came to be derisively described as the 'Hindu' rate of growth (about 3 per cent) of the Indian economy.

When the British left India, we were among the top 20 most industrialised nations in the world, often with state-of-the-art factories. Fifty years after Independence, we are almost at the bottom of the pile, ahead of countries such as Bangladesh and Ethiopia. What went wrong?

One explanation for the disastrous breakdown in the nexus between business and politics lies in the attitude of the Nehru dynasty towards businessmen which was primarily one of distrust and hostility. And one way to understand this attitude is to see it through the relationship Jawaharlal Nehru and Indira Gandhi had with India's two most important businessmen, G D Birla and J R D Tata.

Inspite of their deep-rooted differences with Nehru and Gandhi, officially both Birla and Tata supported the Congress Party and the Nehru dynasty before and after Independence. Yet in private both businessmen frequently railed at the way Nehru and Gandhi treated them.

The changing situation was more painful for JRD than GD for until Nehru nationalised Air India in 1953, Tata and Nehru were close friends. As JRD once said, "Jawaharlal was the heroic knight in armour who awakened some of the passion and fire that burned within him. While the love and loyalty I had for him remained undimmed to the end, I soon found myself increasingly out of tune with him once he came to power. He knew I disagreed with most of his economic and international policies."

GD was far more blunt. "I received affection, honour and confidence from Nehru in the last decade of his life but nothing positive can be said with regard to Nehru on any subject whatsoever," he once remarked. More diplomatic than the outspoken Marwari, Nehru suavely described Birla as "a curious combination of a buccaneer and a very generous man".

Certainly Nehru didn't dislike Tata and Birla. Not personally at least. But the genesis for Nehru's hostility lay in his general distrust of wealthy men and the business of making money. Intrinsically he was a more committed Communist than, say, Jyoti Basu. JRD once recalled a particularly sharp exchange of words. "Nehru told me,

Mahatma and the merchant: *Gandhi with G D Birla*

'I hate the mention of the very word profit.' I replied, 'Jawaharlal, I am talking about the need of the public sector making a profit!' Jawaharlal came back, 'Never talk to me about the word profit, it is a dirty word".'

Unfortunately, few of Jawaharlal's family shared his legendary integrity. In 1954 the chairman of the Income Tax Investigation Commission privately informed Nehru that the accounts of two large Birla concerns showed that substantial sums had been paid to his sister, Vijaya Lakshmi Pandit. Later GD confirmed the report, adding that only one national leader hadn't taken money from him, "and that is Panditji. All others, including Mrs Pandit, have". And he reeled out all the important names from Mahatma Gandhi and Sardar Patel downwards. Jayaprakash Narayan was shown as GD's private secretary in his ledgers and paid a monthly salary for years.

This investigation formed part of a larger examination into war profits made by all the major business houses. This in turn was followed in the early '60s by the introduction of a slew of draconian legislations which branded business families as 'monopoly houses' and sought to curtail their growth. As Tata and Birla tried to expand their corporate empires in an increasingly hostile environment, their frustration with Nehru swelled.

GD had frequently argued with Mahatma Gandhi and their differences increased over time but they remained close to the end. GD's relationship with Nehru was far more complicated. A practical businessman, GD couldn't appreciate Nehru's ideological flights. "Nehru was an emotional man Sentimental people like him have never become efficient administrators, nor have they been right evaluators of others," declared the pragmatist. Their ambivalent feelings for each other were fully reciprocated. If Nehru didn't care for GD's brand of capitalism, the same could be said for GD's attitude towards Nehruvian socialism.

Though GD was convinced that Nehru's policies were dragging India down the wrong path, he nonetheless respected Nehru. But not his daughter nor his grandson. Asked once what he thought about Sanjay Gandhi, Birla replied "Stupid."

And Mrs Gandhi? "Wicked and stupid." Yet when Indira Gandhi declared the Emergency in 1975, there was deafening silence in both Industry House (Birla's headquarters) and Bombay House (Tata's).

The declaration of Emergency in India was a direct fallout of a case in the Allahabad High Court filed in 1971 where Indira Gandhi's election to Parliament had been challenged and the decision had gone against the prime minister. She appealed to the Supreme Court and asked Nani A Palkhivala, India's foremost constitutional lawyer and a senior Tata director, to take her brief. The night before the day the judgment was to be pronounced, Gandhi declared a state of Emergency.

It unleashed a furious debate in Bombay House with JRD and Palkhivala on opposite sides of a divide. Palkhivala was so outraged that he wanted to return the brief that very day. "This move caused panic among the directors," he recalled, "as they felt it would invite the wrath of Mrs Gandhi on the House of Tata." JRD called an emergency meeting of Tata directors and they urged Palkhivala not to return the brief. JRD did not express his view. Privately JRD had already told Palkhivala that he disapproved of his returning the brief but did not feel it morally right to prevent a valued colleague from following his conscience. After the meeting Palkhivala went straight to his office, drafted a single sentence and sent it to the press. He was withdrawing his brief.

JRD tried to soften the blow on Gandhi. He told a New York paper that the "Emergency was good for India" and that now "trains ran on time". Wherever he could, he lauded the Emergency's "refreshingly pragmatic and result-orientated approach" which had led to "conditions of discipline, productivity, industrial peace, (and) price stability necessary to achieve rapid economic growth". Given the Indian situation, democracy "was not in the interests of 600 million people for whom no freedom of right matters more than freedom from want and the right to work and earn a decent living," said JRD.

Indira Gandhi lifted the Emergency two years later and in March 1977, after she had lost the elections and her seat in Parliament, JRD sent her a hand-written note: "You have been much in my thoughts these last few days. I can imagine the physical and emotional strain to which you have been subjected and my heart and Thelly's go out to you in your ordeal and distress." Soon it was Gandhi's turn to console JRD. Morarji Desai, the next prime minister, dismissed JRD as Air-India chairman. One of Gandhi's first acts after returning to power in 1979 was to re-appoint JRD to the Air-India board. But she didn't make him chairman.

JRD must have felt it. A couple of years after Gandhi's death, JRD lifted the veil on their relationship. "She would doodle or pointedly ignore me while I spoke, cutting open envelopes and pulling out letters. Some people think I have been influential. In all these years, I have never once been asked by Mrs Gandhi, 'Jeh, what do you think?' Never, never, never even once. There was no common ground on which there could have been a relationship as we didn't pay under the table... the principle was quite clear earlier. You paid money to the Congress and you were in. You got everything you wanted. Licences. Growth. The support of the party. That was the policy."

The making *of* a NATION

CULTURAL DIVIDES

1947 onwards

India's languages do not just segregate states, they deprive a people of living heritage.
Indian art, though, goes from frame to good fortune

"Novel taken. Graham Greene responsible."
— *Telegram from Kitta Purna to R K Narayan, 1935*

AND so with the publication of *Swami and Friends* by Hamish Hamilton begins a relationship which is to help R K Narayan get an international audience and weave the magical spell of his Malgudi world to countless audiences. "Narayan is the novelist I most admire in the English language," says Graham Greene, no mean novelist himself, many years later.

October 1956. R K Narayan leaves India for the United States, taking up a fellowship from the Rockefeller Foundation. Going with him is a germ of an idea, a story about "someone suffering enforced sainthood". Narayan travels across America and the idea crystallises in his mind. Finally, he rents a hotel room for $ 75 a month for three months and writes. But while *Guide* is received well enough as a story, *Guide* as a film is another matter. With Pearl Buck as co-producer with actor Dev Anand, who also stars, the film, released in 1964, bears little resemblance to Narayan's story and does not find any audiences.

But Narayan stands head and shoulders above many other Indian writers, in terms of both skill and good fortune. He also has the singular talent of being able to write lucid, charming stories in English. Because much as Indians write, profusely and prolifically, few regional languages can cross state borders and translating facilities are woefully inadequate. History may provide some answers.

In 1947, India did not get just gain Independence from the British. Tucked away into the euphoria of that year are two movements that moved for freedom in other directions. The Progressive Writers Group forged a left-of-centre association that sought to break from the shackles of the past with revolutionary ideas and fiery prose. This was an attempt to find the Indian ethos, explore the Indian sensibility, shake up Indian complacency. The talents at hand were formidable — Ali Sardar Jafri, Ismat Chugtai, Mulk Raj Anand, Balraj Sahni. The Indian People's Theatre Association boasts such names as Shombhu Mitra and Kaifi Azmi, but still the question of words remained unanswered. Across the country, from the stories of Vaikom Mohammed Basheer in South to the poems of Suryakant Tripathi 'Nirala' in the North (celebrating his birth centenary in 1997, unsung), from the novels of Mahasweta Devi in the East to those of P L Deshpande in the West, talent springs up from every imagined source.

But while visual art and music need no artificial device for deeper comprehension, writing is not so lucky. Those writers who break all bounds and reach nation-wide success do so against great odds. the Sahitya Akademi, set up in 1954, tries to encourage writers but fails in one basic aspect. As do the Jnanpith Awards, the publishers and the Universities. The Indian art of translation languishes and in that failure lies a wealth of words lost to a nation. Money is not easily forthcoming either. It is not till a novel in English written by an Indo-Pakistani writer settled abroad is published in 1981 that money enters the stakes. Salman Rushdie's *Midnight's Children* breaks all

M F Husain: *Portrait of the artist as a young man*

the rules, but the trickledown effect is painfully slow.

The other movement born in 1947 is kissed by a generous fairy. The Progressive Artists Group breaks away from the

Writer's bloc: *Graham Greene and R K Narayan at the BBC*

traditions of Indian folk art and the romanticism of the Bengal School to strike out for individual expression in art. M F Husain, F N Souza, S H Raza, K H Ara, S K Bakre, H A Gade travel from all over Bombay to meet at the Bombay Art Society office or even just sit by the sea at Marine Drive and discuss their imperatives. People would later say that they were formulating the Indian modern. But for now, they are exploring themselves, imbibing influences and then putting it all together in their expressions.

The door had been opened by artists like Raja Ravi Varma, who was later tagged the father of calendar art, perhaps somewhat unfairly, and the ebullient Amrita Shergil, who married Western forms with Indian themes. In Bengal, Rabindranath, Abanindranath Tagore and others created a romantic realism that was given a folk feel by artists like Jamini Roy and called the Bengal School. Freedom for India also meant freedom from the past and the chance to make new discoveries.

Contemporary Indian art grows from strength to strength. Walter Langhammer at the *Times of India*, Kekoo Gandhy at Chemould Art Gallery, provide critical and gallery support. Buyers are enthralled by this new, fresh vision, so different from traditional Indian art forms. Of course, there were failures, as the romantic idea of a struggling artist starving in a garret persist. But at the J J School of Art in Bombay, the Fine Arts faculty at Baroda's MS University, the Calcutta Art School and Santiniketan, enthusiastic painters and sculptors find their inner calling. The government helps with limited success with the Lalit Kala Akademis.

By the time the 1980s arrive, contemporary Indian art is big business. Thousands of rupees easily translate into lakhs as corporate buying increase along with disposable income. Progressive, forward-looking and now, money-making, Indian art is established as a strong form. Indian writing has strengths which go back longer and stronger perhaps, but it needs to find a common voice and common expression in an uncommon style. ∎

SIGNIFICANT OTHERS

Writers in Indian languages	Indian Writers in English	Artists
Mahasweta Devi	Anita Desai	Tyeb Mehta
Nirmal Verma	Atia Hosain	Lakshman Shreshtra
Vaikom M Basheer	Vikram Seth	Ganesh Pyne
Amrita Pritam	Amitav Ghosh	Satish Gujral
Sadat Hasan Manto	Arundhuti Roy	Anjolie Ela Menon
P L Deshpande	Firdaus Kanga	N S Bendre

Jitendra Arya

HAPPENINGS

1947-1956

Mahatma Gandhi

January 13
Mahatma Gandhi starts his last fast

March 5
C Rajagopalachari is appointed as the
first Indian Governor-General, to
succeed Lord Mountbatten on June 21

June 8
The Government of
India decides not to
allow Muslims who
had migrated to
Pakistan to return to
India for permanent
settlement. The influx of
such Muslims would be
regulated under a permit
system

June 20
Lord Mountbatten
leaves India

January 15
Lieutenant-General K M Cariappa takes
over as Chief of Army Staff and
Commander-in-Chief of the Indian
Army, the first Indian to be appointed to
the post

January 1
India is elected to the United Nations Security
Council for two years

January 24
Dr Rajendra Prasad is elected the first
President of India

January 28
Finance Minister Dr John Matthai announces
the setting up of a Planning Commission,
with Jawaharlal Nehru as chairman and
Gulzari Lal Nanda as deputy chairman

March 1
The population of India is
347,340,000.

March 26-28
Prime Minister Nehru visits Karachi
for talks with Liaqat Ali Khan,
covering the entire field of Indo-
Pakistani relations

Dr Rajendra Prasad

March 1
India rejects UK and US plan for
settlement of the Kashmir issue

1947   1948   1949   1950   1951

September 1
Mahatma Gandhi starts a
fast in Calcutta for
Hindu-Muslim unity,
which is broken four days
later after peace is restored

November 12
The Government of India
announces the formation of
Air-India International Ltd, with
an authorised capital of Rs 7 crore
and an initial paid-up capital of
Rs 2 crore

November 13
Education Minister Maulana Abul
Kalam Azad advises Muslims to
join Indian National Congress

November 17
Dr. Rajendra Prasad is elected
President of the Indian National
Congress

December 12
The financial agreement between India
and Pakistan is announced by Sardar
Patel. Pakistan is to get Rs 75 crore
from the balance of the cash
of undivided India

August 8
The All-India Hindu
Mahasabha decides to
resume political activity

October 1
Prohibition comes
into force in
Madras Province

July 12
The ban on the Rashtriya
Swayamsevak Sangh is
withdrawn after it assures
the government that it has
abjured violence

November 15
Nathuram Vinayak Godse and Narayan
Apte are hanged in Ambala Jail for the
assassination of Mahatma Gandhi

August 15
An earthquake in Assam
causes widespread damage
and loss of life

October 26
India sends a protest note to China
on the Chinese invasion of Tibet

July 27
Pakistan Prime
Minister Liaqat Ali
Khan suggests a five-
point plan to ease the
tension between India
and Pakistan; Nehru is
invited for talks in
Karachi.

October 21
The Jan Sangh is launched
with Dr Shyama Prasad
Mukherjee as president

October 23
Tax evasion reaches Rs 41 crore

Iftekhar Ali Khan

C Rajagopalachari

January 29
The Indian National Academy of Dance, Drama and Music is inaugurated in New Delhi

February 2
The All-India Khadi and Village Industries Board is inaugurated in Delhi

March 5
Dr S P Mukherjee announces the launching of a civil disobedience movement in Delhi by the Jan Sangh, Hindu Mahasabha and Ram Rajaya Parishad to demand the complete accession of Kashmir to India

March 17
The Lok Sabha rejects, by 278 votes to 49, a motion demanding India's withdrawal from the Commonwealth

March 18
The Backward Classes Commission is inaugurated

May 11
Dr S P Mukherjee is arrested at Lakhinpur for unauthorised entry into Kashmir

May 28
Prime Minister Jawaharlal Nehru leaves India to attend the Coronation of Queen Elizabeth II in London

June 23
Dr S P Mukherjee dies in jail in Srinagar

January 5
Iftekhar Ali Khan, erstwhile Nawab of Pataudi, 42, dies while playing polo. He played cricket for England and then captained India in 1946

April 28
State of war between Japan and India ends

January 1
Prime Minister Nehru lays the foundation-stone of the Tata Institute of Fundamental Research

February 3
A stampede at the Hindu religious festival of Kumbh Mela, held at the confluence of the Ganges and Jamuna rivers in Allahabad leads to the deaths of 500 pilgrims with 2,000 injured

March 12
Sahitya Akademi inaugurated

March 26
C Rajagopalachari resigns as leader of the Congress Party and Chief Minister of Madras

April 2
Prime Minister Jawaharlal Nehru urges the suspension of H-Bomb tests

May 14
The Lok Sabha fixes the monthly salary of MPs at Rs 400 and the daily allowance at Rs. 21

May 19
The Government constitutes a National Film Board and decides to establish a Film Production Bureau and a Film Institute

January 26
Dr Bhagwan Das of Banaras and M Visvesvaraya of Mysore are awarded Bharat Ratnas

February 26
Dr Helen Keller lays the foundation stone of the first sheltered Industrial Workshop for the Blind in Bombay

March 25
Prime Minister Jawaharlal Nehru announces that the Commanders-in-Chief of the Army, Navy and Air Force would now be known as Chief of Staff

April 1
First Class accommodation in the present form is completely eliminated from all trains on the Indian Railways

April 18
Sewagram Ashram, famous when Mahatma Gandhi lived in it, is closed

April 27
India is elected to the Human Rights Commission of the United Nations

April 30
N M Joshi, one of the founders of the trade union movement in India, dies in Bombay

June 7
Government bans the import of horror publications with immediate effect

June 25
Two IAF Dakotas collided in mid-air near Agra killing 19 people

January 7
Government of India extends the Bombay Prohibition Act of 1949 to Kutch

January 11
India win the 'Rubber' against New Zealand. In the Madras Test, Vinoo Mankad and Pankaj Roy put on a world record of 413 runs for the first wicket

January 18
The Companies Act, 1956, restricts contribution by companies for charitable and other purposes, including political, to Rs 25,000 or five per cent of the net profits of the company during the three preceding financial years

January 18
The publication of the States Reorganisation Commission report causes serious riots in Bombay. Police open fire, 860 persons are killed

February 15
Dr Meghnad Saha, eminent scientist and MP, dies

February 16
The Shah and Queen of Iran arrive in Delhi

March 14
Lord Louis Mountbatten and Countess Mountbatten arrive in New Delhi on a week's visit to India

March 21
One person is killed and 6 injured when an Indian Airlines Corporation Dakota crashes on the runway and catches fire in Tezpur, Assam.

April 12
G B Pant announces an increase of Rs 5 in the starting basic salary of Class III employees of the Government of India

May 15
14 persons are killed and 8 injured when an Indian Airlines Corporations' passenger aircraft crashes on the runway at Khatmandu

June 30
The Governments of India and the United Kingdom agree to avoid double taxation with respect to estate duty

1953   1954   1955   1956

September 29
The Central Planning Commission approves the expenditure of Rs 100 crore on a five-year economic development plan for Kashmir

December 19
Jawaharlal Nehru announces the Government decision to establish the state of Andhra Pradesh on the Telugu-speaking areas of Madras State, excluding the city of Madras

Vinoo Mankad and Pankaj Roy

August 1
State Air Corporations inaugurated

September 15
Shrimati Vijayalakshmi Pandit is elected President of the eighth session of the UN General Assembly

October 8
T T Krishnamachari, deputy chairman of the Planning Commission, announces that the scope of the Five-Year Plan would be extended at a cost of Rs 150 crore to Rs 175 crore to include unemployment reduction schemes

October 22
The Government decides that former princes must pay taxes on incomes derived from sources other than privy purses and investments in Government securities

November 9
An interim University Grants Commission is announced with Dr S S Bhatnagar as chairman

August 25
Dr Ram Manohar Lohia and 2,000 satyagrahis released in Uttar Pradesh

September 25
Acharya Kripalani is the leader of the new Union of Socialists and Progressives, formed with 14 members of the Lok Sabha

October 6
Prime Minister Nehru declares a National Health Scheme

October 24
Rafi Ahmed Kidwai, Union Minister of Food, dies

October 29
Dr Rajendra Prasad lays the foundation stone of the Supreme Court building in New Delhi.

July 1
State Bank of India inaugurated

August 1
Direct rail service between Calcutta and Lahore resumed after eight years

August 25
Notorious dacoit Man Singh shot dead after a gun-battle between his gang and the police at Kakekapura, about three miles from Bhind in Madhya Pradesh

September 8
Uttar Pradesh Vidhan Sabha unanimously passes the Anti-Cow Slaughter Bill with four amendments

October 24
The Prohibition Enquiry Committee recommends nation-wide prohibition in India by April 1958

December 24
India retains the Asian Quadrangular Football Championship for the fourth year in succession beating Pakistan in Dacca

Padmaja Naidu

August 8
Communal riots break out in Ahmedabad to protest against the announcement of a bilingual state of Bombay

August 11
Lok Sabha unanimously passes the States Re-organisation Bill

September 1
121 persons are killed and several injured when a 20-ft bridge over a swollen rivulet near Annampalli, 60 miles from Hyderabad, collapses, throwing into the stream two bogies of the Secunderabad-Dronachalam Passenger

September 1
Life Insurance Corporation of India inaugurated.

September 1
Rajya Sabha passes the Indian Post Office (Amendment) Bill, laying down postal charges in terms of the naya paisa

September 11
Prime Minister Jawaharlal Nehru announces the main conclusion of the Netaji Enquiry Committee that Netaji did die in an aircrash

October 14
Dr B R Ambedkar and about two lakh Scheduled Caste men and women convert to Buddhism in Nagpur

October 18
Padmaja Naidu is appointed Governor of West Bengal

October 21
Nizam of Hyderabad retires from public life

November 23
152 passengers are killed and several injured when the Madras-Tuticorin Express plunges into a swollen river near Ariyalur, 174 miles from Madras

November 25
Railway Minister Lal Bahadur Shastri resigns, owning moral responsibility for the Ariyalur accident

December 8
Lok Sabha passes the Standards of Weights & Measures Bill

"What we have to learn to do, we learn by doing."
— Aristotle, Nicomachean Ethics, Bk II

Can it be that the idealism of the first decade is flagging? That people are getting set in their ways, falling into set patterns of thinking? India has to answer these questions as people all over the country exchange the heady nationalism of the Freedom Struggle for the desire to better their own lives — individually or as a community. The regional voice starts surfacing, and has to be answered. But before that, so that the efforts of the last few years is not lost, consolidation work must continue. If social change is inevitable, in a democracy it must also be accompanied by attempt to bring the greatest good for the greatest number.

Conflict is an inescapable component of growth, and India struggles externally as well as internally to make the various transitions to full-fledged success. Goa is brought into the Indian fold with the military defeat of the Portuguese and the complete annihilation of colonialism in the subcontinent. Neighbours who covet land within India's borders are more contentious, less easy to vanquish.

The plans made have been ambitious, but if the test is in the implementation, the scope for failure becomes very real, and sometimes paralysing. The need for a national language of subcontinental origins is imperative. Yet it turns into a conflagration of enormous proportions, as Hindi is violently rejected in the South and East. The solution cannot be through orders, it must be through consensus. Democracy must triumph.

There is also the loss of heroes to be faced — frightening and debilitating though this seems. India is orphaned by the loss of those who strode across her breadth with vision and accomplishment. But hope cannot be lost. The engine is running, the gears are changing. The only way is ahead.

India
50
The making *of*
a NATION

1957

1966

STARS, SONGS, SOLIDARITY

1950s

The film industry helps heal the wounds of Partition and assists in national integration

"Today I bring for your scrutiny - and approval — a new toy my generation has learned to play with, the CINEMA! — you include the cinema among evils like gambling, sutta, horse-racing etc... Now if this statement had come from any other person, it was not necessary to be worried about them... You are a great soul, Bapu. In your heart there is no room for prejudice. Give this little toy of ours, the cinema, which is not so useless as it looks, a little of your attention and bless it with your smile."
— *Film-maker Khwaja Ahmed Abbas in a letter to Mahatma Gandhi in 1939.*

IF an assassin's bullet had not felled Gandhi on January 30, 1948, perhaps he might have lived to see how and why Khwaja Ahmed Abbas was right. The cinema, which he had derided, is to play a crucial role in holding a young and uncertain nation together.

Post-1947 and ravaged by Partition, India needs a medium which will sublimate the trauma of the recent past and help people rediscover the rhythm of normal life. This comes from the din and dust of studios where painted faces and costumed bodies emote to a director's diktats, cavort and contort

The Big Four: *Dilip, Dev and Raj with Jawaharlal Nehru*   Screen

to music and song, the slow whirr of the camera capturing reels and reels of make-believe magic on celluloid.

This cosmetic depiction of reality, the seemingly escapist nature of cinema which Mahatma Gandhi had feared, in fact unites India like never before.

October 30, 1952. Mehboob Khan, producer of films like *Andaz* (1949) and *Aan* (1951) receives a letter from Hollywood moghul, Cecil B de Mille. "Dear Mr Khan," it reads, "Thank you for showing me your recent picture *Aan*. I found it an important piece of work, not only because I enjoyed it, but also because it shows the tremendous potential of Indian motion pictures for securing world markets. I believe it is quite possible to make pictures in your great country which will be understood

and enjoyed by all nations without sacrificing the culture and customs of India. India has always held great fascination for us, and we all look forward to the day when you will be regular contributors to our screen fare with many fine stories bringing us the romance and magic of India." In the same year, an international film festival is held in India for the first time. Indian cinema has entered its Golden Age.

The film industry, with its liberal ethos, becomes the distillery where the creative juices of people from various parts of the country and belonging to all religions and backgrounds is poured in, stirred, stewed. The mix that emerges is potent, the effect heady. From the highest political office downwards to the common man, popular cinema strikes a chord in every heart. Sometimes subtle, sometimes gaudy, often surreal, these films capture the imagination of a people looking for escape, relief, self-belief. From this strange and exciting pastiche of romance,

Hit pair: *Nargis and Raj Kapoor*

song, dialogues, dance, fights and fisticuffs, emerges an extraordinary bonding of the people.

Heading this epic post-Partition revival of the film industry is a host of brilliant men and women, actors, directors, singers, music directors, technicians who inspire and feed on each other's talent to create an era of unparalleled excellence. There is a passion and commitment in the making of films which is symptomatic of the idealism that pervades the country in the first decade after Independence. There are film makers like Mehboob Khan, V Shantaram, A R Kardar, B R Chopra, Bimal Roy, Guru Dutt, S S Vasan, Chetan Anand who choose themes of social and national relevance without sacrificing the needs of commercial cinema.

Their films not only make pleasant jingles at the box office, but also convey a message. Mehboob's *Andaz* and *Aan* are starkly contrasting films and, apart from rewriting the box-office records, earn him comparison with the Hollywood master, Cecil B de Mille. Shantaram's approach to socially relevant themes is radically diferent — replete with songs, dance and an enchanting surrealism — but no less successful. Bimal Roy and Guru Dutt,

Tragic love: *Vyjantimala and Dilip Kumar in Devdas*

less ostentatious, are no less sensitive, especially to an individual's struggle against himself and society. B R Chopra, more macro in his vision, sees the problems of communities and countries in a rapidly changing world.

But mere strong themes are not enough. Music and songs are the staple diet of Indian life, and hence imperative in films. With the increasing impact of radio, they become even more important, putting a premium on the quality of music directors and singers. The 1950, this is boom time. Naushad's genius brings it with it all the nuances of classical music plus the earthiness of Uttar Pradesh. S D Burman has the folksy touch of the hills of the North East. Shankar is a Maharashtrian while Jaikishan is a Gujarati, but together they blend admirably to make magical notes and tunes. O P Nayyar, with one ear to the ground and the other towards the West, provides a fusion of sounds that has the country toe-tapping and humming.

The singers, obscured from public adulation, are nevertheless often the life and soul of films. With *Mahal* and *'Aayega aayega, aanewala'*, Lata Mangeshkar grows out of the influence of Noorjehan and comes into her own. With *Shree 420* and *Awara*, she establishes herself as the new Nightingale of India, the Queen of Melody. With Lata Mangeshkar also rises Mohammed Rafi, whose rich seven-octave voice and intrinsic humility marks him out as the favourite of heroes and music directors alike. Between them, Lata and Rafi not only win the affection and admiration of an entire nation, but become the singers with the largest audience in the world, an industry in themselves. There are also Mukesh, Manna Dey, Talat Mehmood, Geeta Dutt and Lata's younger sister Asha Bhosle, who make the playback scene unforgettably tuneful.

Nothing in films, of course, has more appeal than those who stand before the camera and emote, and in the 1950s, the Indian film industry is blessed with some superb talent. Prithviraj Kapoor and Ashok Kumar are household names for their perceptive portrayals of difficult characters. Balraj Sahni, a card-holding member of the Communist Party of India, is carving out a niche for himself in off-beat roles. Guru Dutt, when he is not making films, is an actor of calibre and depth.

Amongst the heroines, Nargis has established herself as the numero uno after *Andaz*, but with *Mahal*, the moon-like beauty of Madhubala has the nation obsessed with her. When

The making of
a NATION

Jitendra Arya

The new nightingale: *Songstress Lata Mangeshkar*

Baiju Bawra become a hit, Meena Kumari compels attention. This trio is soon challenged by Nutan, Nalini Jaywant, Geeta Bali, but the competition only serves to enrich the film industry.

Yet nothing in this era matches the impact or importance of Dilip Kumar, Raj Kapoor and Dev Anand, whose charisma sweeps the nation like never before. In the past there have been big stars. Kundan Lal Saigal, who died tragically in 1947, was a minstrel whose hypnotic voice had the entire country singing with him till a penchant for alcohol cut him short in his prime. Prithviraj Kapoor, the handsome Pathan from Peshawar, was another mass favourite, and Ashok Kumar, the eldest of a bunch of supremely talented singer-actor-brothers from Bengal, has shown matchless talent in some of the films he has acted in. But the trio of Dilip, Dev and Raj becomes unique, and in many ways the symbol of the creative greatness of the film industry in the 1950s.

Born within a couple of years of each they come from vastly differing backgrounds. Dilip and Raj both come from Peshawar. Raj is from a family devoted to theatre and films— his father Prithviraj has already laid the foundation for a dynasty that will dominate the industry for decades. His younger sons Shammi and Shashi will also taste considerable success, the latter becoming and international star with films like *Householder* and *Shakespearewallah*. Dilip is a fruitseller's son who spurns the family trade for artistic satisfaction. Dev Anand, an arts graduate from Lahore in search of similar fame, completes the troika.

All three make their entry in films in the mid and late 1940s, make their mark by the turn of the decade, and by the mid-1950s have established themselves as the industry's most successful stars. Their names spell success at the box-office. like. The Big Three they are called as they deliver hit after hit. Over this period, they also develop distinct acting styles which offer a fascinating study in contrast.

Raj Kapoor's poor hobo with the big heart is derived from an acceptance of socialism that has more to do with Charlie Chaplin's prowess as a fim-maker than any great understanding of Karl Marx's *Das Kapital*. The happy-go-lucky tramp, however, is a heart-stealer, and Raj Kapoor, now producer and director of his own films, perfects this act into becoming India's best known been product overseas.

Dev Anand is the streetsmart, suave, slick hick whose playing field is the big metropolis. He reflects the powerful influence of the West on India and finds ready acceptance in a young nation. His mannerisms are inimitable, but Dev'ss hairstyle and sartorial style become a rage.

Dilip Kumar, a student of Stanislavsky's method acting doctrine, is the intense young man grappling with destiny, despairing of love, coming to terms with his own existence. He has a brooding presence, his dialogue delivery is cultured and mastered to a fine nuance, the inflections reflecting the mood of the character he is playing.

Raj Kapoor is known as the tramp. When he launches into a highly successful career as producer and director, he becomes the Showman. Dev Anand, having apparently drunk from the Fountain of Youth, will become an Evergreen hero, apart of course from a highly successful film-maker. And for the kind of roles he first plays, Dilip Kumar becomes the Tragedy King before he becomes the Thespian, an actor's actor.

But in the 1950s, the Big Three are not merely film stars, they are national influences and much sought after for political and social causes. In many ways this is apt for through their roles and their personalities, they also reflect the spirit and personality of the prime minister and the essence of India's objectives in the first decade. In Raj Kapoor's tramp, Nehru finds an echo of his Fabian leanings, in Dev Anand, the need for modernisation and in Dilip Kumar, a symbol, not only of India's secularism, but also the pangs of his own acute artistic urges. It is hardly a surprise that Nehru is a personal friend of the Big Three, and that Dilip, Dev and Raj are ready to espouse the cause of the Congress.

1957, Mother India, Mehboob Khan's magnum opus extolling the virutes of Indian womanhood and India's essential rural spirit, family values and community ethos, which has broken all box-office records back home, is nominated for an Oscar as the best foreign film. The same year, Satyajit Ray's *Aparajito* wins the Golden Lion award at the Venice Film Festival. The Golden Age of Indian cinema is at its zenith. ∎

New heights: *Sunil Dutt, Nargis and Rajendra Kumar in Mother Inadia*

THE RENAISSANCE MAN
The genius of Satyajit Ray
By Iqbal Masud

SATYAJIT Ray, the greatest Indian film-maker of the 20th century has so many facets to his persona and role, that it is impossible to do justice to them in a brief essay. Perhaps the best point of departure would be to take up the usual description of Ray as the last Bengali renaissance man, but to explore it from a different angle. The subject of the Bengal renaissance and what Chidananda Dasgupta *(The Cinema of Satyajit Ray)* called the Tagorean synthesis is a vast one. Briefly, the heroes of the renaissance were Raja Rammohun Roy (1772-1833), Michael Madhusudan Dutt (1824-73), Pandit Ishwarchandra Vidyasagar, and of course the 'formidable' Tagore clan. Marxist critics have dismissed the word "renaissance" in Indian conditions because there were vital differences as compared to the European renaissance — it did not shift India from feudalism to capitalism.

Still, it threw up a new middle class. Ray has traced the process in *Jalsaghar, Kanchenjungha* and other films which delineate the shift from the traditional middle class to the new one. What the Tagorean synthesis is has been brilliantly explained in a recent essay by Amartya Sen, 'Tagore and His India'. Sen quotes the famous *Geetanjali* lyric. "Where the mind is without fear/ and the head is held, high;/ Where knowledge is free;/ Where the world has not been/ broken up into fragments by/ narrow domestic walls;/ Where the clear stream of reason/ has not lost its way into the/ dreary desert sand of dead habit;.../ Into that heaven of freedom, my/ Father, let my country awake". The point of this magnificent passage is, as Satyajit Ray said of Tagore's paintings' the evocation of "joyous freedom".

The analysis of Tagore by Sen conveys an important aspect of Ray's cinema: a deep aversion to any commitment to the past that could not be modified by contemporary reason; hostility to communal sectarianism (Sen quotes Isaiah Berlin on Tagore: "Tagore stood fast on the narrow causeway, and did not betray his vision of the difficult truths"), rejection of authority. Be it of the Brahmin or the Englishman; hostility to the growth of cultural separatism as for instance, the risen of Hindu nationalism today (see one of Ray's last films *Ganasatru* and of course the great *Ghare Baire)*. The Tagorean synthesis was an instinctive alliance of British, Muslim and Hindu cultures.

Ray's first film, *Pather Panchali* (1955), did not contain all the elements discussed above. What was remarkable about it was its spontaneous attempt to explore rural India. A remarkable feature of Ray's cinema present in *Pather Panchali* has often been missed by the critics. This is Ray's peculiar vision — "seeing timings for the first time". He reminds you of Ghalib's great line: *"Abr Kya Cheez Hai, Hawa Kya Hai"* (What are clouds? What is air?). Along with this goes Ray's obsessive exploration of age and death, which goes up to his last films.

One might pause here to set Satyajit Ray in the context of Indian cinema. The age of Ray ('50s onwards) was also the golden age of Hindi commercial cinema. Ray from the beginning very consciously and very deliberately sought to fabricate cinema as "cinema". That is, a distinct art form drawing upon a million other art forms but distinct from all of them. A second feature was that such cinema was regional. Ray explored Bengal and so to say, made Bengal the "world". Hindi commercial cinema, from the beginning, was equally deliberately and consciously not art but mass media. If you look at commercial cinema from this angle, what are considered its defects — use of song and dance, "irrelevant" comedy, exaggerated rhetoric, are not 'defects' but as features essential to its existence — its *raison d'etre*.

There were some great exceptions like Guru Dutt. But he remains an exception. Guru Dutt brought personal misery and a heightened egoism to his cinema in a lyrical form. Ray stepped away from all this. Take for instance his Apu growing up — *Aparajito* (1956) and *Apur Sansar* (1959). The 'rural' comes to town. The tortures and glories of the geographical transition and of adolescence and youth are captured in a fashion never so far equalled in Indian cinema. On a personal note, as I watched the last two films, I said: "This is me". I felt that kind of emotion only with one other film-maker — Guru Dutt.

One point about Apu should be noted. As Chidananda Dasgupta has noted, Apu was, in a very deep sense, a Brahmin. He represented a generation of Indians which was instinctively attached to moral values. In fact, for all their occasional slipping back, they lived on a high moral plane. Their tragedy

Cinema as art: *Satyajit Ray*   Jitendra Arya

arose from this fact. The importance of this point will be clarified later when I come to Ray's films of the '70s and '80s.

Ray was an objective observer. He never lost himself in the film like many top directors of Hindi commercial cinema. His objectivity enabled him to explore the shift from the traditional middle class to the thrusting, new, vulgar money-making class in *Jalsaghar* (1958). This process was further followed up in a brilliant comedy satire *Kanchenjungha* (1962). There is a clash of cultures in the film — a culture of the traditional sophisticated upper class and of the lower middle class.

The tensions and tribulations of urban middle class life are examined with superlative results in the adaptation of the Tagore novella in *Charulata* (1964). The brilliance of *Charulata* is manifold and it is not possible to examine it even superficially here. But I will make one point. At one level the narrative structure of *Charulata* is not very different from that of the commercial film. There is also plentiful use of close-ups and zooms.

What raises *Charulata* above the commercial cinema is the fact that narration is lit up by insight, wit and humour. *Charulata* is no ordinary triangle. Here again there is a clash of cultures — 19th century academic liberalism versus the urgent sensuality of the moment. With great respect to Tagore, it must be said that Ray's cinema has gone deep into the Tagore tale. Tagore nuanced, Ray plunged into the possible psychological tragedy.

Picking one's way through a large number of excellent films, I would like to comment on the period of Ray's films which are called metropolitan films namely *Jana Aranya* (1975), *Ganasatru* (1989), *Shaka Proshaka* (1990) and *Agantuk* (1991). These are films with varied brilliance and it might be thought crude to dump them in this fashion. However, in their totality, they represent an exploration of modern life, meaning '80s and post-80s life.

This holds true even if historically some of the films like *Ganasatru* belong to an earlier period of time. Broadly speaking, this is the world of New Brahmins — people who have some memory or consciousness of morality but are compelled by forces of our time to survive and not merely to survive but to survive in an affluent fashion. This is a subject of great complexity which Ray has 'investigated' magnificently. However, a lot still remained to be said. Despite his age, Ray had still not finished his masterpieces.

Indian cinema scene began to look blank after Satyajit Ray's death. However, the challenge of the times is being taken up in a very different fashion by people like Adoor Gopalkrishnan and Amol Palekar. In their films, history is being explored in an original fashion unmasking hidden contradictions, ironies and even a kind of acid humour.

It is a mistake to think that Ray's humanism is old-fashioned or 19th century. He had become aware of the erosions of morality and even of ordinary decency of life caused by historical forces in the last part of this century. What may be called the burden of historical, moral pessimism has to be carried and moderated by his successors.

LAST BASTION FALLS

December 17, 1961

The Army liberates Goa from Portugal. And India's break from imperialist rule is complete

"YOU'VE got to shoot a bull, otherwise it will finish you." Ancient wisdom from Kenneth Kaunda of Northern Rhodesia or just timely advice? He speaks at the Seminar on Portuguese Goa in Delhi from October 24 to 28, 1961. For Africa and Asia, the continued Portuguese occupation of Goa is a slap in the face for freedom, an untenable sustenance for outdated forces of colonialism. Jawaharlal Nehru, India's prime minister, will declare at the seminar that India's attitude to Goa is guided not just by its theoretical attachments to non-violence, but by practical considerations.

But the story of Goa begins sometime before the events of late 1961. The western state on the Indian subcontinent was colonised by the Portuguese after Vasco Da Gama's historic visit in 1498. The British, much as they ruled India, had a treaty with Portugal that went back to the 14th century, making them "historic allies". The British Empire allowed Portugal to hold Goa, Daman and Diu, and the French to hold Chandernagore and Pondicherry. But unlike the French, who left graciously when India gained Independence, Portugal hung on. Goa was not a colony. It was part of metropolitan Portugal and therefore Lisbon's problem.

Not all Goans, however, saw it quite that way. From 1654, Goans had fought for freedom, and the first attempt was made by a Roman Catholic priest called Castro. Over a hundred years later, in 1787, the Portuguese crushed the Pinto rebellion, where a group of priests tried to overthrow the colonial rulers. In 1852, Dipaji Rane led an uprising, which lasted three and a half years and ended only when the Portuguese loosened some of their restrictive measures.

In 1895 and 1912 again, Dada Rane rose against the Portuguese. Repressive measures were used to quell these violent protests. But by the early 20th century, as the Indian freedom movement was sweeping across the country, Goa's freedom fighters were affected by these winds too.

In 1928, the Goan National Congress, under Dr Tristao Braganza Cunha, adopted non-violence as the guiding principle.

The move was now to educate the people, to instil the desire for civil rights and liberties. Goans responded in substantial measure, taking part in meetings and rallies, breaking the laws that denied them these freedoms. They suffered for their cause. In 1946 alone, some 1,500 Goans were arrested and variously beaten up or kept in police custody.

1947. Freedom comes to India. The Portuguese have no intention of leaving they say, yet they confer with the Nizam of Hyderabad over becoming part of his state when he makes his bid for independence. Goans are made vague promises, filling some of them with hope of a solution. But when Dr Gaitonde is arrested and deported to Portugal in February 1954, the cry from prominent Goans, addressed to others is to "free themselves and unite with India".

July 21, 1954. Members of the Azad Gomantak Dal liberate the small Portuguese stronghold of Dadra and Nagar Haveli, north along the western coast from Goa. Satyagrahis within and outside Goa rejoice: their turn can only come next. August 1955 and hundreds of Satyagrahis, Goan and Indian, are fired upon by Portuguese troops, arrested, beaten up. The Indians are left off lightly, but the Goans are sentenced to up to even 28 years imprisonment. Between now and 1961, hundreds of Goans will be similarly treated, many deported to convict settlements in Africa and Portugal. The pressure on India to act is tremendous.

The Goan drama is also being played out on the international stage. Nehru's principles of non-violence and peaceful co-existence, of negotiation before action, are now associated with his name all over the world. The United Nations is all for negotiation and talks between Portugal and India. Both countries are now accusing each other's troops of border-crossing, and of covert military provocation. Patience is not just running thin, it is practically in tatters, as Asian and African countries align themselves with India, the West with Portugal. The European country's contention that Catholics in Goa would suffer from union with India is countered by the fact of many more Christians enjoy full religious freedom in India.

The making of
a NATION

Farewell colonialism: *A rousing welcome for the Indian Army*

Handing over: *Portuguese and Indian officers*

Ministry of Defence

An economic blockade of Goa is not successful. The result is widespread smuggling and Goan nationalists, hampered by the lack of direct traffic, feel left out and weak. Worse, Portugal turns to Pakistan for help. The Azad Gomantak Dal attacks Pakistan for violating the principles of the Bandung Conference. Nehru's policy of waiting and watching is a failure, from all appearances. The Portuguese show no sign of relenting, the international community is very slow in applying pressure. The American ambassador in India, John Kenneth Galbraith, advises caution. Nehru replies, "Step by step, we were drawn into this whirlpool, much against our will." Evidently, the wind has changed direction — from peaceful negotiation to military action.

But in Goa itself, law and order is breaking down. Goans are fleeing into India. Portuguese troops infiltrate Indian territory and pick up insurgents against their regime. The time to act seems to have come, Defence Minister Krishna Menon tells Nehru.

December 17, 1961. Indian troops move into Goa, under the charge of Lieutenant-General J N Chaudhuri, GOC-in-C, Southern Command. Air Force planes drop pamphlets telling the people that their hour of freedom is at hand. Indian warships move into the sea around Goa. In 24 hours, Goa is taken. Casualties are few. The only untoward incident is when Portuguese guns fire on Indian ratings after flying the white flag of surrender.

The takeover is practically painless and peaceful. The Governor-general of Goa surrenders, in defiance of orders from Lisbon. Contrary to Portugal's assertions, Goans do not fight to the last breath to defend their colonial masters.

December 19, 11 pm. Troops at Marmagoa lay down their arms when the Indian Navy sails into the harbour. The last Portuguese resistance is over. Daman and Diu have already surrendered earlier in the day.

The international community is appalled. India has gone back on her own principles. In Goa itself, there is widespread jubilation. The Indian flag is flown from rooftops.

The Portuguese National Assembly announces in February 1962 that it does not accept the Indian invasion and takeover of Goa. Tomas Prisonro Furtado, a member of the Portuguese National Assembly, and a lawyer in Margao, says that since Goa has joined the motherland, it is the duty of every Goan to work for the progress of the country. He and the other Goan members of the assembly send in their resignations to Dr Salazar, Prime Minister of Portugal.

The bull has been shot.   ∎

Union Territories

1 Delhi Size: 15,000 Population: 94,21,000	5 Daman and Diu Size: 0.1,000 sq km Population: 102,000
2 Andaman & Nicobar Islands Size: 8,000 Population: 281,000	6 Pondicherry Size: 0.5,000 sq km Population: 808,000
3 Lakshadeep Size: 0.03,000 sq km Population: 52,000	7 Chandigarh Size: 0.1,000 Population: 642,000
4 Dadra and Nagar Haveli Size: 0.5,000 sq km Population: 138,000	

COLONIALISM IN GOA
The effects of Portuguese rule on the population
By Dr. Teotonio R de Souza

CONTRAFACTUAL methodology could provide us with different images of Goa that could be, and one such virtual reality could be similar to several other districts in the Konkan neighbourhood of Goa, without any special attraction that distinguishes the 25th state of the Indian nation. What made Goa different is certainly the long-term, almost 450 years of treatment to which it was subjected by the Portuguese colonial regime.

Whatever the nationalist reactions of some Goans or their latter-day political sympathisers with an anti-colonial bend of mind, it should not be forgotten that individual or class interests have often defied wider interests and sought collaboration that could be termed as political betrayal. If Timmayya or Timaji had not offered his advice and collaboration to the Portuguese empire builder, Afonso de Albuquerque, Goa would perhaps have had a different past than it has had.

Also, between the first and the second (definitive) conquest of Goa, the Portuguese could not have survived without active assistance of the Goans from the either side of the Mandovi river. During and soon after the conquest, Goan nayaks were competing with each other to decapitate their former Muslim chiefs and hand over their heads to Albuquerque's officials in exchange for monetary rewards or other forms of patronage. If the Goan Saraswat Brahmins had not continued to run the fiscal machinery of Goa as tax-collectors for the Portuguese administration and as food-suppliers, the Portuguese rule over Goa could have been short-circuited.

Many Goan men and women of humble castes seemed to have found a once-in-a-life-time opportunity to opt for social mobility by throwing their lot with the new masters. Portuguese mesticos were many born from this native option, and there resulted also a new native caste of Charde, with many of the Maratha collaborators in the early war of conquest and control acquiring the Kshatriya status following their conversion to Christianity. It has a parallel in Sri Lanka, where lower castes entered the Salagama caste of the cinnamon gatherers that cooperated with the Portuguese.

In return for the newly acquired social rise, the Charde of Goa were the steadfast supporters of the Portuguese regime, unlike their rival Brahmins who manifested their discontent against the colonial rulers on different occasions. Bishop Matheus de Castro Mahale, most of the Pinto Conspiracy partners, and a great number of 19th century Goan liberal politicians countering the white Portuguese interests were Brahmins.

Another interesting case of Goans who acted as close military allies of the Portuguese during the 17th century,

The making
a NATION

Portuguese influence: *Vasco de Gama's statue at Viceroy's Arch*

defending the frontiers of the Bardez, and also by sending a detachment of soldiers of Ceylon to fight the Portuguese adversaries there, is of the Ranes. In the late 19th century, when the Goa railway project got underway and the timber of Satari forests became a valuable item, several foreign firms from British India sought parcels of Satari lands as concessions, allegedly for plantations, but in reality to exploit the forests for their valuable timber. The origin of Rane revolts ought to be sought there, and not in any nationalist sentiments aimed at liberating the Goans from the Portuguese rule. If they were converted into mythical freedom-fighters in the Goan folk songs, it was the invention of the Salcete Brahmins who composed the folk songs to irritate the Portuguese officialdom that meddled in the local elections, checking the political ambitions of the Brahmin candidates.

Left to themselves, the Goans may have continued till date their game of petty collaboration and resistance, given their inability to organise any effective joint resistance that could put an end to the colonial rule. Contrary to what was believed, the collaborators were not always the Goan Christians. The Goan Saraswat Brahmins, who did try quite effectively to preserve the Hindu cultural traditions of Goa, did find an effective political challenge in the Goan Catholic community. It is the political ambition of the Saraswats to dominate the Goan scene by trying to communalise the politics that lies at the origin of the exaggerations about Goan Christians being pro-Portuguese.

The same ambition was also manifest in the political battle over the official language of the state. The Saraswat Brahmins tried to force Marathi as the official language, and had it not been for the militance of the Salcete Christians, the Goans would have neither won the Opinion Poll of 1967 that saved the territory against a merger into the neighbouring Maharashtra, nor the Official Language case in 1986, which resulted in winning the statehood for Goa. This leads us to conclude that the conversion methods of the Jesuits in Salcete (unlike those of the Franciscan friars in Bardez, and mixed methods in Tiswadi) have left a lasting impact upon the ethos of their converts in the Salcete taluka of Goa. The political militancy of the sashtikars has been visible in the post-liberation politics of Goa.

One great benefit of the Portuguese rule in Goa was an early exposure to Western ideas and education. Goan emigration to British India and African colonies, and later to several countries of the West, was largely facilitated by this factor. In the world of growing globalisation and cultural interaction, the Goans have many plus points. What the Goans lacked was a sufficient resource-base to assert effectively their sentiments of political independence within Goa. This was possible in British India, and Goan liberation had to wait till independent India could intervene to put an end to the Portuguese colonial presence in Goa.

There was enough consensus among the Goans about the need of liberation, and the large communities of Goans in India played an important political role in pressuring the Indian authorities to act. Many Konkani proverbs convey the native cultural identity and unwillingness to surrender to colonial rule forever. One such significant folk saying advises a Goan to distrust a Portuguese in the same way as he distrusts even a baby cobra (sarop munncho nhoi daktto, ani paklo mhunncho nhoi amcho). The Goa-born cardinal Valerian Gracias of Bombay was one of the leading voices. Within Goa the expression was muted due to oppressive measures adopted by the Portuguese dictatorial regime. It was not different in Portugal itself till 1974.

HOPE OF THE VALLEY

1963

*Kashmir's tortuous history is dominated by mismanagement and intrigue.
And the towering figure of Sheikh Abdullah*

DECEMBER 26, 1963, after midnight in a cold, hard winter. The Mo-e-Muqaddas, the hair of Prophet Mohammed, is discovered to be stolen from the Hazratbal shrine.

December 27, 1963. News of the loss of this Holy Relic becomes public. Kashmir burns with anger as crowds gather and demand action from the government.

But Kashmir has no proper government. The current prime minister Khwaja Shamsuddin is a puppet placed there because it was necessary to remove his predecessor, Bakshi Ghulam Mohammed. Too many charges of corruption and too much unrest have sent Mohammed off to be part of the Kamraj plan, conceived for leaders like him who need to be out of power and back to the grass-roots.

The real problem, however, lies quite somewhere else. It is behind bars, with the man whom all Kashmir has respected and loved for many, many years. Soon, the anger over the theft of the Mo-e-Muqaddas is accompanied by demands that Sheikh Mohammed Abdullah be released from jail. For almost 10 years now, the flame of the Chinar, leader of the National Conference, has been incarcerated. In the tortuous history of Kashmir's accession to India, the career of Abdullah has been equally chequered. From one of India's strongest symbols of secularism and democracy, the Sheikh has fallen from grace. For many of those 10 years, his enemies — in Kashmir itself and in Delhi — have tried to implicate him as a traitor with Pakistani sympathies.

The Kashmir Conspiracy Case, as this infamous affair is called, is itself shrouded in mystery and ambiguity. It is born out of the Sheikh's own vacillations over whether to accede fully to India or to pursue a path of independence for Kashmir. The idea of accusing him of favouring Pakistan is almost ludicrous to his followers — he has rejected the idea again and again, shown contempt for Mohammed Ali Jinnah and his friendship with Indian Prime Minister Jawaharlal Nehru is practically legendary. Yet, in spite of that friendship, Abdullah is in jail.

Abdullah's period of darkness, unfortunately, is also one for the Valley. A veil of despair creeps over Kashmir, as people are disappointed by the government of Bakshi Ghulam Mohammed, once Abdullah's trusted lieutenant, of the apparently changing positions of India, of their beloved leader in jail. In India, Hindu fundamentalists damn Kashmir's hesitation to become a complete part of India. In Pakistan, no effort is spared to bring Kashmiri sentiment around to its side. The one man who can help is locked up and away from his people.

January 4, 1964. The Holy Relic is recovered, whether by divine intervention or that of the Intelligence Bureau is never made clear. However, what is clear is that at least one crisis has been averted, although there are rumours that the returned relic is a fake. There are demands for a special Deedar or public viewing of the Mo-e-Muqaddas. There are also demands for the release of Sheikh Abdullah.

January 6, 1964. Jawaharlal Nehru suffers a stroke at the Bhubaneshwar session of the Congress. India is shaken at the thought of losing its first prime minister. Nehru's ill-health

Kashmir connection: *Sheikh Abdullah greets Jawaharlal Nehru*

gives ample opportunity for Pakistan to wreak havoc in Kashmir, which still has no effective leadership. In India, from minister without portfolio Lal Bahadur Shastri onwards, the need for Sheikh Abdullah's release is emphasised.

January 10, 1964. Experts proclaim that the Relic is genuine, there is jubilation in the air as cries of *"Mubarak Ho!"* are heard all around. For now, the trouble-makers are silenced. Yet, there are repercussions. Kashmir is agitating like never before, almost every village affected. Far away, Calcutta sees terrible rioting over the loss of the Relic. And Abdullah is still in jail.

Nehru, sick though he may be, knows he has listened to

his advisers for too long, instead of trusting his instincts. He calls his Cabinet colleagues and informs them that if the people can revolt so thoroughly, obviously their Kashmir policy for the he decides to visit Pakistan first, and is due to be Nehru's guest on May 29. Pakistan, overjoyed as it is at this coup, is disappointed in Abdullah, who does not toe the expected pro-

past 15 years has been ill-judged. Of those who insist on harping on the Kashmir Conspiracy Case, Nehru makes short shrift: "If a damned thing can't be proved in four years, in six years, there's obviously nothing to be proved."

April 5, 1964. Kashmir's new prime minister, G M Sadiq, announces that the Kashmir Conspiracy Case against Sheikh Abdullah has been withdrawn.

April 8, 1964. Sheikh Abdullah is released. There are scenes of tumultuous joy in Kashmir, where he is given a hero's welcome. The Sheikh would now like to follow the idea of a confederation between India, Kashmir and Pakistan. To this end

Pakistan line. But the ultimate disappointment is Abdullah's. Nehru dies on May 27, and he has missed the chance to meet his old friend. On another level, he has lost the chance to solve the Kashmir tangle, to sort out the skeins and bring Kashmir into secularism and democracy with honour and dignity.

Post-script

After Nehru's death, Abdullah takes up Pakistan's demand for a plebiscite in Kashmir. His detractors in India raise the red flag once again. A meeting with Chou-en-Lai is seen as deliberate provocation and Abdullah is arrested again on May 8,

1965 by a government headed by Lal Bahadur Shastri. He will stay there, mainly in Kodaikanal in Southern India, till January 2, 1968, when he is released by Nehru's daughter, the Indian Prime Minister Indira Gandhi.

Unfortunately, in too many ways, it is too late for Kashmir. Abdullah himself, although an India lover to the end, is disillusioned by the country. His goal remains what he sees best for Kashmir, but his long years away from his state have taken the people of Kashmir in many doomed directions, solutions to some of which are still being sought. Indira Gandhi is less of an ideological visionary than her father, but she is a stronger political manipulator. However, the machinations of the Congress in Kashmir do not help, and her relationship with her father's old friend rides through a see-saw of emotions and events.

Abdullah himself remains something of a contradiction. There are allegations that his National Conference is not averse to encouraging anti-India activities.Still he starts a dialogue with Indira Gandhi, to reach closer to India rather than Pakistan and advises his people not to look at Pakistan for a solution. Especially not Pakistan after 1971, when the formation of Bangladesh vindicates his stand on the two-nation theory. His problems with India continue as both sides have lost the ability to trust each other. Yet, when he dies, on September 8, 1982, his body is wrapped in the Indian flag. Mourners chant his old slogan from the '40s: *"Sher-e-Kashmir ka kya irshad? Hindu, Muslim, Sikh ittehad"*.

This call for inter-religious unity is significant at this late stage, when the whole of India is ready to make a mockery of secularism. It shows how wrong so many early decisions about Kashmir were, how short-sighted so many policies, how dangerous too much talk without positive action. It also shows why Kashmir still burns today. ∎

Poor replacement: *Bakshi Ghulam Mohammed*   Jitendra Arya

The Hazratbal shrine   Meraj-ud-din/India Today

The History of Hazratbal

The legend goes that it is in 1635 that the Mo-e-Muqaddas or the hair of Prophet Mohammed arrives in India. Shah Jahan is on the throne in Delhi. The Holy Relic is brought to Bijapur by Hazrat Syed Abdullah, till recently Mutwali at the main shrine in Medina, now banished by the Sultan after a fight with his cousin. Bijapur bequeaths a jagir on Abdullah. When he dies, it passes to his son, Syed Hamir.

However, in 1686, Aurangzeb attacks Bijapur, and Hamid has to flee, impoverished, to Jahanabad. There Hamid meets a Kashmiri trader, Noor-ud-Din, who helps him considerably. Noor-ud-Din asks Hamid for the Holy Relic, but is refused. That night, though, Hamid has a dream where the Prophet asks him to hand over the hair to Noor-ud-Din. After he does so, Noor-ud-Din has a dream where he is asked to take the Relic to Kashmir and install it by a lake.

Noor-ud-Din sets off, showing the Relic to the faithful along the way, which Aurangzeb gets to hear about. After Noor-ud-Din falls ill in Lahore, Aurangzeb orders that the Relic be brought to him. Noor-ud-Din's servant Medanish takes the hair to the Mughal emperor, warring in the Deccan at the time, who first convinces himself that the hair is genuine. Aurangzeb rules that such a sacred object should not be in private possession and sends it to the Dargah Saheb in Ajmer. Noor-ud-Din is imprisoned. However, Aurangzeb then has a dream where he is told that the Relic must be taken to Kashmir by Noor-ud-Din immediately. Aurangzeb sends word to Medanish, but it is too late for his master — the shock of losing the Relic has killed him. Medanish exhumes his master's body and leaves for Kashmir.

The Relic arrives in Shopian in 1700. It is scheduled to be kept at the Khanqa Naqashband shrine in Srinagar, but the place proves too small for the huge crowds that gather. The governor orders that it be kept at the Bagh-e-Sadiq Khan, built by Shah Jahan on the shores of the Dal lake. The *Mo-e-Muqaddas* has found its resting place. Over time, the shrine acquires the name Hazratbal and a village and several legends grow around it.

This is only one.

THE FLAME OF THE CHINAR
Sheikh Abdullah was synonymous with Kashmir throughout his life

By Farooq Abdullah

FOR the State of Jammu and Kashmir, the decision to align and identify its lot with India in October, 1947, was a deliberate one and made against heavy odds. It has not been a mere addition of a few thousand square miles to an already gigantic mass of land, its true import for both was much more vital and wider on ideological and historical frontiers. It brought about an irrefutable extension and reaffirmation of the truly secular borders of the Republic of India. As fate had determined, it came about after our country was gasping for life following a major surgery carried out on a communal diagnosis.

When stalwarts like Mahatma Gandhi, Jawaharlal Nehru and Maulana Abul Kalam Azad had, with reluctance, submitted to Partition, Sheikh Mohammad Abdullah stood up to prove that the 'Two Nation Theory' was a blunder. When the Indian leadership was faced with reverses threatening its very secular conviction, the late Sheikh provided them a raison d'etre for the survival of their secular faith. Mohammad Ali Jinnah, with his Two Nation Theory, presented himself as a man possessed, who would not concede any quarter on this territory. Jinnah's ideological armada overwhelmed Khan Abdul Gaffar Khan's impregnable bastion, the North West Frontier Province.

In this dark helplessness, a tall leader from the Pirpanjal Himalayas, Sheikh Mohammad Abdullah stood as the torch-bearer of sanity. The advancing hordes unleashed by the two Nation Theory faced an insurmountable challenge from him. This 'miracle' of the Sheikh was as dramatic as it was heartening for believers in a composite culture and communal harmony. It occurred when, apparently, the hopelessness was complete. For Gandhi, it was a resurrection of his otherwise dying secular principles. He said with great relief, "Only in Kashmir do I see a ray of hope."

Sheikh Abdullah's bold initiative was novel and compelling. It was an ideological odyssey. Besides bringing about mass destruction of life, property and institutions, Partition also threw age-old value systems into total disarray. If the culture of communal harmony had to be salvaged, it needed unceasing augmentation to its depleted resources of conviction and ideology. To make his point, the Sheikh launched the revolutionary package of land reforms and abolition of absentee land-lordism. These epoch-making land reforms carried to a logical conclusion the Sheikh's unrelenting desire for change for the better. Significantly, these reforms were brought about when they seemed impossible and detractors said that the Sheikh could not fight against the money power of the big landlords.

For the first time in independent India, Sheikh Abdullah brought down an autocratic ruler. He also started an ambitious mass literacy project and personally began to guide it as Education Minister (education was the only portfolio which the Prime Minister of Jammu and Kashmir chose to keep with him). There were other important steps which gave succour and sustenance to his long-suffering people. It had a fine-tuned message as well — raising the aspirations of those very people who had rejected the Two Nation Theory. The people were convinced they had charted the right course for their future. He did not relent in his march — no looking back for the Sheikh. He did not allow to concretise what an Urdu poet had visualised:

شہر جاناں کا یہی کچھ ہے دستور
مڑ کے دیکھا اور پتھر ہے گئے

This indeed is known of the Beloved's
unforgiving city
He will be stone, the departing lover
who at its gates, looks back

This was the finest hour for the Kashmir-India handshake. Protagonists of the Two Nation Theory, across the border, had reached the telling conclusion that the Sheikh had, after all, made them lose the battle for Kashmiri' hearts. This feeling emboldened Nehru to challenge Pakistan to resolve the Kashmir issue, if they dared, through a reference to its people. The response from Pakistan was such that comes from one sensing defeat. Instead of accepting Nehru's challenge, they went on picking holes in the United Nations resolutions to avoid a showdown with the people of Kashmir. Sheikh Abdullah's towering stewardship, his bold initiative, subtly and unobtrusively, influenced the making of the Indian Constitution through import of his ideals and actions. He, along with three of his colleagues, was a member of the Constituent Assembly and thus among the distinguished galaxy of its founding fathers. By committing the Muslim majority State of Jammu and Kashmir to India, he reversed the entire cycle of unhealthy winds that lashed the subcontinent. It changed the soul and spirit of the Indian Constitution like a whiff of fresh mountain air. The fathers of this momentous document assimilated the meaning of Sheikh's faith and thus Article 370 was included in this document. This article is a testimony and recognition of the Sheikh's vision of Jammu and Kashmir to remain as a distinct entity within the sustaining arms of a sovereign Indian Republic.

Sheikh Abdullah's convening of the State Constituent Assembly was primarily meant to transfer the victory sign to the soul of his beleaguered people. He was conscious of the pipers playing their pernicious tunes from across the border and wanted to exorcise this ghost. The convening of State Constituent assembly in 1950 made the ramparts of his vision invincible. Unfortunately, he was not allowed to guide

The making *of*
a NATION

the course of this Assembly for long, yet in barely a year's time, he had set its course. The Assembly ratified the accession. He also made it the platform to make his statement of a fully autonomous State of Jammu and Kashmir, with a separate constitution and a separate flag of identity to fly alongside the National tricolour; and of course, a separate State emblem. His vision was so powerful and his sincerity so transparent that in spite of his arrest and detention in 1953, it did leave its imprint on the document when finalised in 1957.

The siege of August 1953 as the Sheikh describes it in his biography *Aatish-e-Chinar* took place when his partner in Delhi unceremoniously dumped him. This was the handiwork of desperate elements who nibbled at his greatness but could not match it. Vested interests who had been dislodged by his radical measures, reactionaries who could not come to terms with authentic secularism. Personal ambition had consumed their integrity and they forged an underhand alliance to get rid of him. These elements in the state had the patronage of a few in Delhi who could neither comprehend nor reconcile with the progressive ways of the Sheikh. His self-respect and refusal to bend at the knee, was the last straw. The unconstitutional dismissal and arrest of a stalwart became a precedent for many constitutional excesses which are still not over. His first five years of incarceration without producing him before a Court of Law was as unethical as it had been illegal.

He was released for a 100-odd days in 1958. But this release was made just to tighten the noose of a conspiracy case around his neck. Evidence was fabricated, stock witnesses produced and all that is forbidden in law books was attempted to frame him. The Sheikh was conscious of this trap and yet his larger concern remained that his people did not abandon the path of sanity and secularism he had set them on. On January 30, 1958 he was out of jail for a few days. He then issued the following statement coinciding with the 10th death anniversary of Mahatma Gandhi:

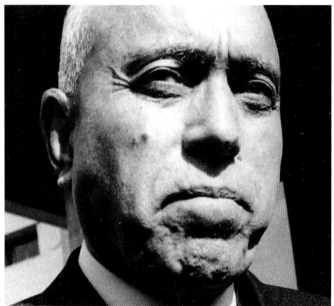
Lion in winter: *Sheikh Abdullah*   Mid-Day

"Mahatma Gandhi was among the greatest personalities of his time. He struggled throughout his life for the emancipation of mankind, for truth and for non-violence. He sacrificed his life for his ideals. I, on the 10th anniversary of his martyrdom, appeal to millions of his followers that they should deal with Kashmir with truth and non-violence."

After his arrest on April 29, 1958, Sheikh was made the principal accused in a conspiracy case. The so-called Kashmir Conspiracy Case was forged with a twin purpose, that of keeping the Sheikh away from his people and to hoodwink world opinion which had not taken kindly to his detention without a fair trial. When Kashmir was simmering with anger and longing for their Sher-e-Kashmir, the Daily Telegraph of London wrote in its banner news 'The Sheikh on trial, but India in the dock'.

Nehru had by now become disillusioned with his proteges in Kashmir. They had literally held both the people of the state and the Indian nation to ransom for personal pelf. In long detention, the Sheikh's shadow started growing longer. His silence became very loud and resounding. The 1962 Sino-Indian conflict shook both Nehru and the nation. It dealt a cruel blow to the Government of India's myopic vision. In 1963 Kashmir exploded with the theft of the Prophet's Holy Relic from Hazratbal. The agitation in Kashmir awakened Nehru and his establishment in Delhi. The message was clear. The Sheikh had to be released. His release came about with the withdrawal of the so-called Kashmir Conspiracy Case against him. Nehru learnt his lesson the hard way. He accepted the writing on the wall that Sheikh Abdullah's monumental sacrifice, suffering and credibility in the subcontinent could alone play the vital role at that crucial juncture of history. Nehru requested the Sheikh to use his fame and charisma to unravel the difficult knot of Indo-Pak relations. The Sheikh, his usual statesman-like self, agreed to lend a helping hand in the interest of his people and India and Pakistan. The Sheikh went to Pakistan to break the ice. He alone had the stature and broad shoulders to act as a bridge between the two feuding neighbours.

He also had the blessings of men like C Rajagopalacharya, Vinoba Bhave, Jayaprakash Narayan and others. He was received in Rawalpindi with great warmth. People came out to receive him in thousands and President Ayub Khan welcomed him with adoration. Ayub Khan in a joint statement with the Sheikh, announced a visit to India and desire to talk frankly to Nehru. A dawn seemed in the offing. This was the night of May 26, 1964. Never, before or after, was such optimistic euphoria witnessed. But, alas! This was too good to be true. The next day, May 27, Nehru suddenly passed away. That was a cruel stroke of destiny at a crucial time. A tearful Sheikh rushed back to Delhi to attend the funeral. A sobbing Sheikh near the mortal remains of Nehru, is perhaps the most poignant picture of that tragic day.

While the Sheikh's foray to Pakistan was a climax, its anti-thesis proved more enduring. After Nehru's death, Sheikh's voice was lost in a din. This was a prelude to many a tragic event. In a year's time a wave of terror and hate was unleashed in 1965 by the neighbour. The Indo-Pak war devastated many hopes. We have yet to recover from the aftermath of that and earlier disasters.

HINDI-CHINI BYE BYE

1962

When friend turns foe, India is left gasping for answers. And arms.

"As a soldier, I cannot even envisage India taking on China in an open conflict on its own. It must be left to the politicians and the diplomats to ensure our security."
— General K S Thimayya, Chief of Army Staff, 1962

"China is a great and powerful country with enormous resources. But India is no weak country to be frightened by threats and military might. We shall build up our strength, both military and economic, to win this battle of Indian freedom. We shall always be willing to negotiate a peace but that can only be on condition that aggression is vacated. We can never submit or surrender or to aggression. That has not been our way, and that will not be our way in the future."
— Prime Minister Jawaharlal Nehru, October 21, 1962

"You have displayed an impressive degree of forbearance and patience in dealing with the Chinese. You have put into practice what all great religious teachers have urged and so few of their followers have been able to do. Alas, this teaching seems to be effective only when it is shared by both sides in a dispute."
— American President John F Kennedy to Nehru, October 27, 1962

Only a few years ago, the air of Delhi was thick with cries of *"Hindi-Chini Bhai Bhai"* as Prime Minister Jawaharlal Nehru and Chinese Premier Chou-En-Lai brought Asia's two largest countries together in non-alignment.

Yet, by 1959, that short-lived friendship is over. Changing world alliances take China away from India and towards questioning the McMahon line, India's border with China in the Aksai Chin area of the Himalayas. The border is a legacy of the British Raj; the need for argument has to do

The making of a NATION

Across enemy lines: *A soldier watches the Chinese rebuild a border post*   TOI

with China's quest to establish itself as a world power, reach an understanding with Soviet Russia and with the intransigence of Tibet. Non-alignment cannot stand in the way of vaulting ambition.

In 1959, aggressions on the border in Ladakh and North East Frontier Agency begin. There are reports of Chinese troops building up. There are also, strangely, intelligence reports that this military build-up is not threatening. Meanwhile, Nehru avoids confrontation and tries negotiation. China blows lukewarm and cold. But never stops her military operations, and always stops short of resorting to force. Even if India is no mouse, China affects a very convincing cat. The game is afoot. And only China knows the rules. Simply, Indian territory in the Aksai Chin must be handed over to China without argument. Nehru cannot possibly agree.

September 8, 1962. A frantic message from the Post Commander at Dhola in the NEFA reports that 600 Chinese soldiers have crossed the Thagla Ridge at 8 am and come down to the Dhola post. A log bridge on the supply route has been cut

Jubiliant jawans: *Out of Chinese captivity*   Ministry of Defence

Sorry state: *Nehru inspects an Indian Army bunker*

Ministry of Defence

and water supply threatened.

The games are over. China has made the first move. And Dhola is unable to defend itself.

The blame is shared all around — the Army Command has made half-hearted and haphazard preparations for war, the Intelligence Bureau has lulled everyone into believing that China would not attack because it had not done so before. Flawed as that logic is, it seems to appeal. Meanwhile, Defence Minister V K Krishna Menon keeps his military chiefs in the dark — he knows best and they must accept that.

This concerted hamhandedness explodes in the face of Indian troops, sent higgledy-piggledy to the freezing cold of the Himalayan winter, with no winter clothes, no equipment and no weaponry. That any fighting is done at all is a tribute to the resilience and tremendous spirit of the Indian Armed Forces. That any victories emerge is nothing short of a miracle.

Chinese soldiers are better prepared for war in the mountains; they have, after all, been in a state of preparedness for close to four years. They have been acclimatised to the cold and have the latest weapons. In a way, there is no contest.

Yet, the Indian army soldiers on. The defence minister and the chiefs of staff issue contradictory statements and instructions. Troops are sent back and forth across unfamiliar and difficult terrain. The obvious is overlooked for the obscure. In Thagla, in Towang, the Se La Pass, Tseng Jong, the story of blunder is repeated, and hapless troops try to follow orders. And the country is being kept in ignorance about what is happening.

October 20, 1962, 5 am. The Chinese fire two Verey lights. After this signal, a cannonade of over 150 guns and heavy mortars. Indian positions at Tsangdhar come in for heavy bombardment. The battle of Namka Chu has begun. Entire platoons are destroyed to protect India's honour and stop the Chinese advance, spread too thin with no supplies. At the end of the battle, only six per cent of the 7 Brigade is alive.

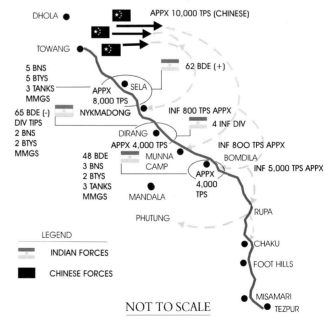

POSITIONS OF CHINESE AND INDIAN FORCES
17 NOVEMBER 1962

NOT TO SCALE

Sandeep Patil

Tense times. *Nehru with Defence Minister V K Krishna Menon*   Jitendra Arya

China announces to the world that, "At 7 am (Peking time) in the morning of October 20, the aggressive Indian forces, under cover of heavy artillery fire launched massive attacks against the Chinese Frontier Guards all along the Kachileng River and in the Khanzemane area." Nothing could be further from the truth.

October 21, 1962. 'India is at War' announces the *Hindustan Times. The Statesman* of the same day quotes Menon saying that India, "had not conditioned her reserves for war purposes... I want you to understand there are some difficulties in this matter".

October 23, 1962. The country is aghast to learn that it is at war with China. Congress Members of Parliament meet in Delhi to complain that they had been misled by Menon. *The Statesman* of October 25 states: "Parliament has been told time and again that conditions were not altogether favourable in Ladakh to check the Chinese advance [but] an air of confidence had been created in the country about the position in NEFA."

Soon it is clear that all confidence is misplaced. Demands for Menon's dismissal surface. Responsible for the growing debacles or not, he is held to be so. The Chief Ministers of states

Star support: *Film actress Nargis with the troops in Ladakh*

Ministry of Defence

make their position clear and even President Sarvepalli Radhakrishnan prevails upon Nehru.

October 31, 1962. It is announced that Menon is being relieved of the Defence portfolio, which Nehru will now hold himself.

But the political manoeuvrings of Delhi cannot yet offset the disaster of the Indian defence strategy. At Se La and Bomdila, troops are massacred as headquarters are moved away from well-stocked fortresses. The concept of fortress defence is negated, and the consequences are fatal. Nehru tells Menon on October 28, "I do not know how I shall explain to Parliament why we have been found lacking in equipment. It is not much good shifting about blame. The fact remains that we have been found lacking and there is an impression that we have approached these things in an amateurish way."

Now, even Nehru cannot stem the tide of the Chinese advance. He tries to boost the morale of the troops, he refuses to officially declare war against China or break off diplomatic relations or go to the United Nations for help. Gradually, the international community is concerned and help is proffered, from Krushchev in Russia, from Harold Macmillan in Britain, from the United States, as India begins to ask.

November 7, 1962. Y B Chavan, Chief Minister of Maharashtra, is persuaded to take over as Defence Minister. Nehru keeps his negotiations alive, China keeps its attacks up. British philosopher and mathematician Bertrand Russell, an admirer of China and Nehru both, acts as an emissary on India's behalf, but China will not relent. The strategists of the Indian Army still flounder under their own inadequacies, propped only by the bravery of fighting battalions. The threat to Assam is very real by November 20 and the prime minister's assurances in Parliament do little to assuage fears.

But by November 20, the tide is beginning to turn. The end of the Cuban crisis means that the USA can offer substantial help. The offer from Russia is also encouraging. China realises that it does not need an Indian side bolstered by outside help. That night, Chou-En-Lai calls the Indian *charge d'affaires* to his residence and declares China's intentions.

November 21, 1962. China announces a cease-fire. The war is over.

December 1, 1962. Chinese Frontier Guards retreat to 20 km from the line of actual control which existed between India and China on November 7, 1959. China holds some 2,500 sq miles of Indian territory. India has been taught a big lesson.

The education is not just in the necessity for military preparedness, although that is important. To that end, Chief of Army Staff L N Thapar resigns and is replaced by Lieutenant-General J N Chaudhuri, GOC-in-C, Southern Command. The controversial Lieutenant-General B M Kaul, who masterminded the Indian strategy is replaced by Major-General Sam Maneckshaw. The perils of politicising army operations, of running a war from a defence ministry rather than through military thought have been painfully brought home. These mistakes will, thankfully, not be repeated again. India has also to learn to separate diplomatic soft-sell from the hardware of battle stations.

The defeat by China has a painful effect on India. But perhaps even more on a most-loved leader. ■

		Indian Casualties		
Area	Killed	Wounded	Missing	Total
NEFA	1,150	500	1,600	3,250
Ladakh	230	50	60	340

Source: The Indian Army by Lt Gen S L Menezes (Retd)

A LEGEND PASSES

May 27, 1964

Jawaharlal Nehru dies. The world loses a statesman.
India feels orphaned

Jawaharlal Nehru: *Wearing the lines of history*

Jitendra Arya

"This prime minister happens to be very much alive at the present moment."

— *Jawaharlal Nehru on a question of his succession, at a press conference in Delhi, on October 9, 1963*

"I want these (my ashes) to be carried high up into the air in an aeroplane and scattered from that height over the fields where the peasants of India toil, so that they might mingle with the dust and soil of India and become an indistinguishable part of India."

— *From Nehru's will, written in June 1954*

MAY 27, 1964, 6 am. Prime Minister Jawaharlal Nehru suffers a rupture of the abdominal aorta. Sleep is induced through painkillers. Nehru slips into a coma. *May 27, 1964, 2 pm.* The Prime Minister is dead.

"We have become orphans," cries a woman at Lonavla station to her nine-year-old son. He does not understand. But across India, millions of men and women do. They have, indeed, been left behind by a man, who for 17 years, epitomised India. Not since the death of Mahatma Gandhi have Indians felt so bereft and alone.

Huge multitudes crowd into Delhi to get a last glimpse of a man they had loved so well. The grief is spontaneous, immense and unstoppable. Chacha Nehru to India's children, a protector to India's minorities, father-figure, disciplinarian and inspiration to all Indians, it has been Nehru's spirit which has moved India since 1947. It is a deep sense of bereavement that moves it now. The waves of people are so great that the administration brings troops into Delhi to control them. But people have come here out of love, not hate, out of pain, not anger.

"The light has gone from our lives," Nehru had said on Gandhi's death. Now, something else has gone as well. An inner spirit, a vision, a sense of belief in India and an almost childlike idealism.

Nehru is dead. India is orphaned.

But he leaves behind a legacy. One that will occupy India for many more years. And even if the hero-worship turns to disdain, if the sentiment turns to scorn, much of India today would have been impossible without Nehru's drive and imagination. India's industrial base, planning ability, strong sense of secularism, pride in the international arena all derive from Nehru. If he was flawed it was from being not challenged enough. And being let down by inadequate followers.

But all that is in the future. For India in the present, there is a loss to be assimilated and understood. Thousands throng his cremation, many more are moved by the publication of his will. He dedicates himself to his country, even in death with only one small request: "The Ganga, especially, is the river of India, beloved of her people, round which are intertwined her racial memories, her hopes and fears, her songs of triumph, her victories and her defeats. She has been a symbol of India's age-long culture and civilisation, ever-changing, ever-flowing, and yet ever the same Ganga... I am proud of that great inheritance that has been, and is, ours, and I am conscious that I too, like all of us, am a link in that unbroken chain which goes back to the dawn of history in the immemorial past of India. That chain I

Miles to go: *Nehru on his last journey*

Men of their times: *Nehru with Rajendra Prasad and Sardar Patel*   _{PIB}

would not break, for I treasure it and seek inspiration from it. And as witness of this desire of mine and as my last homage to India's cultural inheritance, I am making this request that a handful of my ashes be thrown into the Ganga at Allahabad to be carried to the great ocean that washes India's shore."

Nehru's love for India, of course, is never in question. It is there in his books, in his writings, in his speeches. It is there in every brick he built, every institution he laid down, every thought he tried to instil. But death is cruelly final and memory is short. Nehru's desire for no religious rituals after his death is disregarded by his daughter, Indira Gandhi. Similarly, over the years, much that is touted in the name of Nehru will be in name only.

Like so many Indians, it was the Jallianwala Bagh massacre of 1919 that moved a young Nehru to rid his country of a foreign ruler. He was 30. From then on, this somewhat effete young man, educated at Harrow and Cambridge, never looked back. He brought back from England the socialism of the Fabians and soon represented the young radicals of the Congress Party. In him, Gandhi found an ideal lieutenant: "He combines with the heart of a child a towering intellect, wide learning and an ability which can stand comparison with any in the world... Jawahar is a real *jawahar*." Jewel to Gandhi, perhaps, but not to everyone, especially not within the Congress. The rise of the jewel is resented by others who might have shone brighter if it were not for him.

But pettiness must be swept aside, understood, dealt with or accepted. The judgments of history will see to that. What transpires is that by the time Independence dawns on India, it is Jawaharlal Nehru for Prime Minister. Gandhi's matchless words become prophecies here as Nehru towers over India and the world.

Yet, in his last years Nehru can see the disparities in the country he has wrought. Within the Congress Party, there are divisive tendencies. The rise of regional satraps eats of out his influence and power. The formation of the Kamraj Plan, to take the Congress back to the grass-roots is disquieting in itself.

Almost 20 years in power has led the Congress away from the people and towards corruption and the loaves and fishes of office. The country's industrial growth has not been as it should, nor its agricultural output. The population is growing alarmingly. And then comes an unwarranted aggression from a former ally.

As Nehru becomes an old man, age extracts its price. In 1962, when he is 72, he contracts a viral infection that keeps him bed-ridden for a month. At the end of that year, the war with China and the debacle of India's defeat breaks some of his seemingly dauntless spirit.

January 6, 1964, Bhubaneshwar. Nehru suffers a stroke, on his left side. He will not rest for long enough. But he does seem to know that the end is coming. Those famous words from Robert Frost never leave his bedside, as if he craves the lovely, deep and dark woods, with miles to go before he sleeps. The last months of his life see him spending more time with India's second President, historian and philosopher Sarvepalli Radhakrishnan, coming to terms with life.

And death.

"Looking back, I agree with those who say Nehru made a mistake in not dividing the Congress into its socialist and non-socialist components by retaining the Congress as his political vehicle. After the struggle for Independence had been won, Nehru was hampered by the power of the right-wing, which increasingly came to dominate the Congress Party. This domination was only held in check by his own leadership and command over the population of India. The price, however, of having to reconcile the powerful economic forces which the Congress comprised with his hopes for democratic socialism, was the emasculation of the latter programme. India has a slow growth rate and remains stricken with poverty and disease. Nehru's own efforts to alter this would have succeeded more had his party been forthrightly socialist with an opposition in Parliament representing the very forces that now dominate the Congress."

— *Bertrand Russell, British philosopher, in an obituary in The Times, London* ∎

Mass appeal

A MAN OF VISION
Nehru's secularism and ideals stand the test of time
By Mushirul Hasan

I have no personal memories of Jawaharlal Nehru, free India's first Prime Minister. He was dead when I joined the University. Yet many of us felt that the country had lost a charismatic figure, a man who nursed a vision for free India, and plotted its trajectory with foresight and imagination. We learnt a great deal more about Nehru and the nationalist movement after reading his *Autobiography* and *The Discovery of India*.

Even as undergraduates in a university which took pride in its association with the Prime Minister, we sensed that these books were not just autobiographical narratives, but major statements on political, social and intellectual affairs. The *Autobiography*, published in 1936, appeared to be a political manifesto, a document with hazy ideas but reflecting a strong commitment to a modern, united and secular India. *The Discovery of India*, we discovered later, was in the nature of a

journey into India's past, a journey that led its author to discover the roots of composite and syncretic ideas and movements, an exercise that strengthened his conviction in the historical/intellectual underpinnings of secular nationalism. I believe it is hard to find a more lucid exposition of India's composite past.

So many of my colleagues in the academia, however, think differently about the man and his writings; in fact, the tribe of Nehru-baiters has swelled considerably over the years as more and more educated Indians become sensitive to the slow and tardy economic progress over the last 50 years, the collapse of our most cherished institutions, including the party system, the erosion of democratic values and the diminishing importance of values and principles in public life. Most share these concerns and agree with the critique of the Nehruvian legacy in certain circles.

But, surely, before we write him off we need to know more about the man and his legacy, place him and his policies in perspective, and examine the breakup of the Nehruvian consensus from the 1960s through to the 1990s, looking in particular at the reasons for the growth of communal activity and the retreat of both Muslims and Hindus into communal political camps. We need to consider, moreover, the political options or choices that were available in 1947-8. If we do so, we may well discover that Nehru, more than anybody else, was nicely groomed by his father and the Mahatma to cope with the changes ushered in by Independence and the upheaval caused by Partition. He was, above all, intellectually and ideologically better equipped to lead a truncated nation through an extremely difficult phase of nation-building.

It is, of course, a tall order to assess the contribution of any political leader or statesman at any given moment of history. For example, we have yet to hear the final verdict (if there can ever be one) of the British historians on Lloyd George and Winston Churchill, the two war heroes. The evaluation of Robespierre, the French revolutionary, goes on relentlessly in France. The same is true of Nasser in Egypt, Tito in Yugoslavia and Soekarno in Indonesia who were, along with Nehru, the main architects of the Non-Aligned Movement.

Evaluating Nehru, on the other hand, is a particularly awesome task, more so because he occupied centre-stage for so many decades and performed a variety of roles. Starting as an activist in the Congress movements in the early 1920s, he rose to become, in somewhat exceptional circumstances, the Mahatma's political heir. He emerged, thanks to his exposure to the Bloomsbury group in London, the exponent of socialism within the Congress and the rallying point for scores of radical groups. In the mid-1930s and 40s, he steered the Congress ship through the rough currents of Indian politics and ensured that the nationalist movement, still guided by Gandhi, did not lose sight of its democratic and secular goals. He was on the move throughout his public life, eager to learn, exhort, mobilise, and leave his imprint on his party and government. That is why he endeared himself to the masses, the minorities and other socially under-privileged groups. In the words of his distinguished biographer, Sarvepalli Gopal: "To a whole generation of Indians he was not so much a leader as a companion who expressed and made clearer a particular view of the present and vision of the future. The combination of intellectual and moral authority was unique in his time."

Consider Nehru's role in the years immediately after Independence. India had tasted the fruit of freedom on August 15, 1947. There was much to celebrate. Fair enough. But the country was brutally partitioned, fragmented socially and politically. Nehru's dreamworld collapsed. His defence of and justification for a secular ideology seemed unreal and hollow. Yet his personal ingenuity and strong secular commitment, coupled with the weighty secular traditions of the nationalist movement, enabled him to pull through difficult and turbulent times. He, as also his comrades in the Constituent Assembly who shared his passion for a secular state and society, kept the secular flag flying in India even though it was being lowered in other newly-liberated countries of Asia and Africa.

Nehru's secular and enlightened concerns had a great deal to do with his upbringing in Allahabad, a city with a glorious record of inter-community harmony and cultural and social mingling, his interactions with liberal and Left-wing groups in England, and the profound influence of his father Motilal Nehru who, along with the lawyer and liberal politician Tej Bahadur Sapru, fashioned a secular and composite ethos in Allahabad. Yet family life and western

education alone do not explain Nehru's secular trajectory. After all, not everybody who lived in Allahabad was inspired by the cosmopolitan outlook of the Urdu-speaking elites. Take the case of Madan Mohan Malaviya, a distinguished citizen of the same city, who was the chief protagonist of 'Hindu' causes and a major critic of Motilal Nehru's liberal and eclectic world-view. M A Jinnah shared Nehru's social and educational background, but changed his trajectory to lead the campaign for a separate Muslim homeland. He should not have done so against his earlier political convictions, even if he was wronged by Gandhi and Nehru, or because a section in the Congress pursued anti-Muslim policies. Here lies the difference between Nehru and Jinnah. Whereas Jinnah trimmed and tailored his ideological garb to suit political exigencies, Nehru remained firm in his secular beliefs. He did not waver as Jinnah did. This was largely because his profound secular commitments were consistent with his world view which was in large measure influenced by socialistic ideas.

It is doubtless true that Nehru and Jinnah were not cut out to work harmoniously, but their contemporaries hoped that they would do so on account of their broadly liberal and secular orientation. The predictable 'parting of ways' took place in 1937-38, when Jinnah launched his tirade against the performance of the Congress ministries in various provinces of British India. The criticism was harsh, as indeed based on flimsy information, but the message was loud and clear. Nehru's secular rhetoric, so implied Jinnah in his letters and speeches, was not good enough. The Congress alone could not decide India's future political agenda in its negotiations with Pax Brittanica. Muslims must have a say and he, as their sole spokesman, had an equally important role in deciding whether India remain united or divided.

Nehru, too, can be faulted then and later for some of his utterances, his recklessness, his political miscalculations, his arrogance, and his inability to deal with his adversaries on equal terms. At the same time, his secular convictions stand in bold relief. When the chips were down, he refused to be swayed by the Muslim League rhetoric or the Hindu propagandist viewpoint. He could not single-handedly stem the communal tide in the 1940s or thereafter. Nor could he prevail upon the Congress to reject the insidious Partition Plan. He could at best marshal his political will and resources to provide the healing touch after the bloodbath in 1947, instil confidence in the Muslim communities that remained in India, and create the institutional structures that would help contain the anti-secular tendencies. This he did in ample measure. In so doing, he pursued not a typically Nehruvian goal, but a goal set by the Mahatma, by the secular wing of the Congress, and by the Left formations. A secular state as a political solution for modern India was based on the contention that it afforded the optimum freedom for the citizens to develop into fully integrated beings. This was a modern goal, rational and scientific, and in addition a specifically Indian goal. These values should have been apparent to all, and it was because of this that they were for Nehru and his colleagues the final legitimation for the secular state.

Nehru's adversaries in the Congress party's higher echelons did not approve of his sledgehammer efforts to change the fabric of Hindu society, his lenient policy towards Pakistan, and his undue tenderness for the Muslims. But Nehru repudiated such criticism, as he had time and again: "Whatever the provocation from Pakistan and whatever the indignities and horrors inflicted on non-Muslims there, we have got to deal with this minority in a civilised manner. We must give them security and the rights of citizens in a democratic State. If we fail to do so, we shall have a festering sore which will eventually poison the whole body politic and probably destroy it."

"For all of us in India", he told the chief ministers in May 1950, "the issue of communal unity and a secular state must be made perfectly clear. We have played about with this idea sufficiently long and moved away from it far enough. We must go back and go back not secretly or apologetically, but openly and aggressively." The past was a constant reference point. The Prime Minister invoked the Congress record to legitimise its secular discourse after Partition. In this context he pointedly referred to the Mahatma's message of communal peace and his exemplary courage in extinguishing the flames of religious hatred. In so doing, Nehru tried to settle the issue of whether the government and the party were going to adhere to old Congress principles in regard to communalism or whether the country as a whole was going to drift away from them.

This had been the impulse behind Nehru's brainchild, the Muslim Mass Contact Campaign, launched in March 1937. The idea was to approach the Muslims not as a collective fraternity but as a segment of an impoverished population. The principal motivation was to convince them that they did not constitute a 'nation', and that their fortunes were not tied to their Muslim brethren per se but to fellow-artisans, peasants and workers in other communities. Nehru conducted dialogue with Jinnah on these lines, questioned the rationale of 'Muslim nationalism' in a society traditionally anchored in cultural and religious pluralism, and criticised the creation of 'Muslim Identity' in the garb of Islam. He tried in vain to delink issues of proportion and percentages of seats from the more basic contradictions between nationalism and colonialism. He expected Jinnah to draw his constituency into this just and legitimate struggle as co-citizens and not as a preferential religio-political collective.

The basic premise of Nehru's defence of a secular state and society was valid. There was nothing wrong in arguing that religious solidarity should not be the basis for political activism, or that religious symbols of disunity be shunned in public life. He had stated as early as 1927 that "there can be and should be religious or cultural solidarity. But when we enter the political plane, the solidarity is national, not communal; when we enter the economic plane the solidarity is economic." The alternative strategy, worked out by B G Tilak in Maharashtra or the swadeshi leaders in Bengal, had serious political implications in so far as it created fissures in the liberation struggle, offended Muslims in those regions, and enfeebled the intellectual underpinnings of secular goals set by the Congress.

Nehru was not the sole champion of secular nationalism; yet he, more than anyone else, enriched its content. He provided depth to debates on secularism within the Congress, as also in Left circles, by introducing complex but relevant historical and contemporary themes drawn from India and other societies. He did not do so on the basis of abstract principles of Western democracy — a charge leveled against him by his detractors — but because of his own acute understanding of the wider social and political processes in history. There is no reason to believe that his perceptions were flawed, or to doubt his motives or intentions.

As we celebrate 50 years of our freedom from colonial rule, we may do well to pay heed to the following lines in Nehru's *Discovery of India:*

"Many of us are utterly weary of present conditions in India and are passionately eager to find some way out. Some are even prepared to clutch at any straw that floats their way in the vague hope that it may afford some momentary relief, some breathing space to a system that has long felt strangled and suffocated. This is very natural. Yet there is danger in these rather hysterical and adventurist approaches to vital problems affecting the well-being of hundreds of millions and the future peace of the world. We live continually on the verge of disaster in India, and indeed the disaster sometimes overwhelms us... A divided India, each party trying to help itself and not caring for, or co-operating with the rest, will lead to an aggravation of the disease and a sinking into a welter of hopeless, helpless misery. It is terribly late already and we have to make up for lost time... There are still many people who can think only in terms of political percentages, of weightages, of balancing, of checks, of the preservation of privileged groups, of making new groups privileged, of preventing others from advancing because they themselves are not anxious to or are incapable of doing so, of vested interests, of avoiding major social and economic changes, of holding on to the present picture of India with only superficial alterations. That way lies supreme folly."

Child's play: *With grandson Rajiv*   Nehru Library

FALL, RISE, THEN ECLIPSE

1964

India lose the hockey Olympic gold in 1960, regain it in 1964, but the slide has begun.
Never to stop

"The Indians play and their stick is in turn their fork, their spoon and their knife. It also serves them as a waiting tray.... Up whistles the ball, and they catch it on the outside of their stick and there it lies, as if it were tucked away in a lady's workbasket and they run away with it at express train speed... The Indian ball seems ignorant of the laws of gravity. One of those tanned diabolical jugglers stares at the ball intently; it gets upright and remains suspended in the air... This is no longer the game of hockey. It's a juggling turn. It is splendid."

— *gleaned from Dutch sports writing in the early 1960s*

I T is not only creative journalists who are inspired into purple prose on watching the Indians play. Over the last three decades, the wizardry of the Indian hockey players has captivated the world and won them millions of followers. Speed on the field, dexterity with the stick and imaginative passing have earned the Indians six successive Olympic gold medals, apart, of course, from international renown. It is a golden run, unparalleled in the history of the game or the Olympics. Then, one fine day, it ends, the myth of invincibility is shattered..

1960, October, Rome Olympics. It is the final of the hockey tournament, and the two arch rivals from the Indian subcontinent are pitted against each other. Pakistan, the fledgeling nation, are to challenge India for the top honours. It is a tense match which both sides are loathe to lose. Given the peculiar historical background to any India-Pakistan contest, the paranoia is understandable. But fear cramps the Indians more, and the unthinkable happens. Pakistan strike once, and India's monopoly over the Olympic hockey gold is over, making it a galling moment for skipper Leslie Claudius who is playing his fourth Olympics, and sending the entire nation into a pall of gloom. The loss here is more than just a medal; it is a severe blow to national pride and heritage.

To the perceptive and the less prejudiced, this setback was perhaps on the cards. Pakistan has grown by leaps and bounds in stature, while India has begun to stagnate, their suzerainty, ironically, becoming a constraint to growth. In the 1956 Olympics at Melbourne, India had struggled to get past Germany 1-0 in the semi-final, and in the final, only a penalty corner conversion by Randhir Singh Gentle staved off a fierce challenge from Pakistan. Four years later, the Pakistanis are not to be denied. The mantle of champion

The making of
a NATION

Revenge is sweet: *The Indian hockey team, with captain Charanjit Singh on the podium, after winning the gold medal at the 1964 Olympics*

Associated Press

hockey nation had passed on to another.

India's rise to hockey greatness makes for one of the more colourful stories of sport. Hockey had been introduced to India by the British Army. Before the colonial master could be banished from Indian soil, the colonised had however eclipsed them at the game. Supple, speedy and slippery, Indian players revealed a natural flair for the sport which soon made it the most popular game in the country. Hockey spread fast, first from Calcutta in the East, then Bombay in the West, encouraged by the armed forces naturally, but soon by many institutions. Dominated initially by Anglo-Indians, the 'natives' make it a virtually *desi* 11 by the time of the 1928 Olympics at Amsterdam where India win their first gold medal.

By 1932 at the Los Angeles Games, India also has its first Indian captain, Lal Shah Bokhari. But that becomes an academic point of discussion after the team flays one opposition after another, and by astounding margins. The United States, for instance, is beaten 24-1 which is not only an Olympic record, but a resounding message to the world of India's expertise in this fast-paced, glorious game.

The pick of this team is a short-statured genius called Dhyan Chand. He has extraordinary dribbling skills which make him the most rivetting player in the world and the despair of opponents. Foreign critics were to call him a sorcerer, a magician and a demon and each of these was apt description of a man who used the hockey stick like a wand.

By the 1936 Berlin Olympics, Dhyan Chand was the most well-known player in the world and also the captain of the Indian team. Around Dhyan grew a cluster of outstanding players like his brother Roop Singh, K D Singh Babu, Kishan

Before the fade-out: *Ajitpal Singh with the 1975 World Cup*

Lal, M N Masood, A I S Dara to name only a few. The Indians were to exhibit brilliant skills in retaining the hockey gold, beating Germany by a whopping 8-1 margin in the final. While the rest of the world looked at American sprinter Jesse Owen's four track gold medals as a rebuff to Adolf Hitler's quest for Aryan supremacy, India's blistering hockey victory was no less significant.

For the next two decades, there was to bo no opposition to India's hockey juggernaut. When the Olympic Games were resumed in London in 1948 after the War, India were to reestablish their lien on the hockey gold medal, beating England 4-0 in the final. At Helsinki four years later came the fifth gold after a 6-1 whipping for the Netherlands. But by now, Pakistan were slowly beginning to make their impact. The rivalry between the two teams draws its fire from the fact of Partition. Yet, the style of the players from both sides was the same, having been honed in the same finishing school as it were. By the 1958 Asian Games in Tokyo, the Pakistanis had caught up, winning the gold on a better goal average. By 1960, they have stunningly gone ahead....

1964 Olympics, Tokyo. It's India versus Pakistan again in the hockey final. The passage till here has been smooth for both sides, but crunch time has now arrived. It's a grudge match, and both teams know this. The Indians, trained by a strict disciplinarian, Habul Mukherjee, have shown not only dashing form, but also tremendous staying powers. Skipper Charanjit Singh has also been an inspiration. The team is hungry for success. The match is marked by long periods of mid-field play as both sides forget their natural flair and settle for attrition. But finally India strike, then hold on to the lead. As in the previous

The wizard: *Dhyan Chand in middle age*

Associated Press

WHAT AILS INDIAN HOCKEY
Getting India back on the field
By M M Somaiya

D HYAN Chand, K D Singh (Babu), Kishan Lal and Roop Singh may have turned in their graves many times over. Balbir Singh, Leslie Claudius, Udham Singh and Perumal may be equally shaken, probably tearing off their last strands of hair in disbelief. These and a host of others who played during the glory days of the pre-1960s may be well asking: how has this game of hockey been transformed beyond recognition? What has happened of the grand empire that they had built?

Sagging morale and unfulfilled promise pushes one to invariably wonder whether, have playing levels fallen here or has the rest of the world grown and caught up. Against such a backdrop it seems criminal that the great victories of the past were not recorded for posterity. It may have provided us a lead to answer this very important question.

As I see it, there has been a bit of both. Indian players of the golden era were definitely a more dedicated lot. Hockey was their only gateway to recognition and glory. Stories abound of how Dhyan Chand practised in the twilight to sharpen his reflexes and timing, of how Balbir (Sr) perfected his strike from the top of the circle by tireless individual training, of how K D Singh Babu weaved his way between stones placed close to each other to perfect his dribbling. The focus on particular individual techniques was possible since national duty beckoned only once in four years and for the remainder it was back to sharpening skills away from pressures of international engagements.

The '70s, '80s and '90s saw a pronounced change. The Asian Games was introduced in the '50s, the World Cup came into existence from the '70s. The Champions Trophy became a permanent fixture in the '80s after having been tested in the late '70s. The birth of so many prestigious tournaments saw the Indian Hockey Federation adopt a new training method for national players. Long, gruelling coaching camps were the order of the day, in which leading national players spent almost the entire year. Team training is no doubt vital for coordination but on the flip side, individuals did not bother to master the basics of fine-tuning their strongest suits. Hitting, trapping, flicking, the dribble and the reverse hit were most often neglected. Major parts of team training during these years unfortunately revolved around developing strength and stamina and as a result even team cohesion could not reach desired levels. Extraordinarily skilled players became a rarity. Ajitpal Singh, Ashok Kumar and Mohammed Shahid were a few gems of a fast fading species. In retrospect the team training methods and regimen introduced in the '80s and a large part of the '90s seemed counter-productive. Fortunately wisdom has now dawned and in recent years shorter camps are the order of the day.

While India was slipping a bit what was the rest of the world doing? In the '60s and '70s itself the seeds of tactical

The making *of* a NATION

two Olympic finals between the two sides, the match is decided by a solitary goal. For India, this time, it is sweet revenge for the Rome debacle. The return of the gold sends the country into a tizzy. The greater joy in winning the medal lies in beating Pakistan. Huge crowds throng the Delhi airport to welcome back the heroes from Tokyo. India's hockey glory appears to have been salvaged. Sadly, this victory is just a mirage

Postscript

In fact, India win only one Olympic hockey gold medal after 1964, a pyrrhic victory at Moscow in 1980 when most of the top nations, including Pakistan, West Germany and Australia have boycotted the event. Indeed, after the 1964 win, Indian hockey slides downhill, first steadily, and after the introduction of astro-turf in the mid-1970s, fairly rapidly.

Pernicious officialdom, poor infrastructure and even poorer adaptability by the players sees India tumble ignominiously from hockey's prime standings. From a bronze at the Mexico and Munich Olympics in 1968 and 1972 respectively, it is shockingly down to seventh place at Montreal in 1976.

In the World Cup tournaments, there is a rise from the silver at Amsterdam in 1973 to the gold in 1975 at Kuala Lumpur, then a free fall which sees India finish 12th and last in the 1986 tournament at Willesden. By this time, hockey has lost its power, prestige and position as a national sport, or even a spectator sport. There are only epithets and epitaphs of India's pristine glory. Alas, that is too far in the past to be gratifying. ■

Rare talent: *They don't come like Ajitpal Singh in India anymore*   All Sport

hockey? The sentiments and charm reserved for hockey in days gone by still linger. But very shortly we will be swamped by an entire new generation. A generation not as fortunate to be fed first-hand information of the glory days of hockey to be inspired enough to play. With hockey relegated to just an iota of coverage in the media, especially on television, it may not catch the fancy of the new lot. The hockey fraternity has a real job on its hands. It would help if the matter is handled from the roots so that its popularity is not shortlived.

The training for the Indian team is now no doubt more focused. The number of astro-turfs have also increased and there are a fair number of tournaments at the junior level to spot talent early. Attempts are afoot to rope in sponsors by showing greater credibility in organisation. But there remain few avenues that could provide resources in terms of quality players.

Hockey in India must be taken to schools, colleges and clubs. Till a decade ago the Combined University team was a stepping stone to the national squad, but not anymore. In the golden era, players won their plaudits while representing their clubs. Teams like the Bhopal Wanderers, Lusitanians of Bombay, Manavadar XI and HAL, Bangalore kept players in great form and the turnstiles ticking. In the current context it would be prudent to introduce a professional National Hockey League with the intention of encouraging club level participation again. The tournament could attract foreign participation as well. Focus must also shift to recognising and developing talent in areas away from metros which do not get adequate exposure.

Hockey has been traditionally popular in a few pockets. Sansarpur, a village in Punjab which has produced a host of Olympians, is slowly developing a training schedule for youngsters there. The Adivasis from the Bihar-Orissa belt are another hockey-inclined set. Bhopal and Jhansi, one-time nurseries of Indian Hockey, are sadly dying and need to be revived. The Coorg district in Karnataka has had a clutch of internationals. Necessary infra-structure with astro-turf and coaching manpower needs to be made available. The net for trapping hockey talent must be cast in these and other selected places. The base for hockey must be broadened to ensure that the under-14, under-16 and under-18 teams have a steady flow of players. These would be finally feeder teams for the National squad.

The ultimate goal must be to fix standards in personal mastery. Even in a highly cohesion-oriented game like hockey, the impact of a team would depend greatly on the skills of each individual. And a lift in the standard of play would bring back the crowd in droves. For a game like hockey where spectator interest is dwindling even at the international level this would be a fillip. The weaving dodges of Pakistan's Shahbaz Ahmed, magnet-like control of Xavier Escude of Spain, the hare-like speed of Holland's Van Den Honert and our own Dhanraj Pillay's swishing reverse sweep are all examples that even today hockey can be tantalisingly exciting. The most important, factor – that could be a tonic for Indian teams and players – is increasing self esteem and pride,. It is said that most games are won and lost in the mind. Sadly for India this has been the major stumbling block in recent times.

hockey had been sown. Recording matches on tape, analysing and improving was top on their agenda. Soccer formations, mostly ultra-defensive, were introduced to blunt the free-flowing play of the Indians and Pakistanis. From the 4-2-4 formation in the '60s to the 4-4-2 formation in the '70s to the current 3-3-3-1, the world, and in particular European countries, innovated. While these strategies blunted the edge of the five-man Indian frontline, it provided flexibility for a roving centre-forward to break away on counter attacks whenever necessary. This, along with close marking and intelligent overlapping, posed a constant worry for the Indians. Moreso since at home they had been exposed to the rigid 5-3-2 formation.

Besides the tactical play which the Indians found hard to even comprehend initially, they suddenly had to cope with players with some exciting stick skills. Gone were the days when one body feint by the Indians could sway six to seven defenders. Defences manned by seven to eight players hardly give any elbow room. In attack too the Europeans and Australians developed a flair for what they still call the Indian dribble. Ties Kruize, Ric Charlesworth, Peter Hasselhurst and Stefan Blocher were ball players par excellence. Penalty corner conversion became a strong and lethal weapon. Paul Litjens, Craig Davies, Floris Bovelander and Carsten Fischer sunk many an Indian dream with their bludgeoning drives. It was evident that the competition had moved ahead.

In the wake of major criticism, allegations and counter-allegations, is there light at the end of the tunnel for Indian

WAR, PEACE AND A PRICE TO PAY

1965

*Kashmir leads to another military conflict between India and Pakistan,
and an international effort to find solutions*

The joy of victory: *Indian soldiers atop a captured Pakistan tank*

Ministry of Defence

IS there any irony in the fact that in October of 1964, Lal Bahadur Shastri, Prime Minister of India, had met President Ayub Khan of Pakistan in Karachi? After a 90-minute cordial talk, a communique issued stated that the two leaders had agreed to Indo-Pak "relations needed to be improved and conducted to their mutual advantage as good neighbours".

In international relations, however, all statements are open to interpretation. For Pakistan, an invasion of India through the remote and extreme western corner of its subcontinental landmass in early 1965 may have been advantageous. For India,

Pakistan's aggression ultimately led to the Indian military's being able to regain the honour, prestige and morale lost in the 1962 war with China.

April 28, 1965. Prime Minister Lal Bahadur Shastri speaks in the Lok Sabha: "If Pakistan continues to discard reason and persists in its aggressive activities, our Army will defend the country and it will decide its own strategy and employment of its manpower and equipment in the manner which it deems best."

So the soft, 'little man of India' sends a clear message to

Pakistan that neither he nor his country are entities to be trifled with. Pakistan's aggressions in Kutch start with infiltrations into Indian territory in January and blow up into skirmishes with the Border Security Forces in March. Pakistan takes Karanjot and then opens the door for talks — assuming, of course, that Karanjot is now Pakistani territory. India refuses to accept these terms. By now the Indian Army has replaced the border police and repulses attacks, from Pakistani tanks and 100-pounder guns. The army has also moved into the borders of Punjab to repel any moves into that state. However the Indians remain defensive, refusing to be drawn out by Pakistan's provocations. Good sense, as it later turned out. Softness, like most things else, is also relative.

The Kutch episode ends after a series of talks and a couple of broken ceasefires, brokered by British Prime Minister Harold Wilson. Shastri and Ayub meet in London on June 17, during the Commonwealth Prime Ministers' Conference to work out the ceasefire proposals. But as Neville Chamberlain discovered in 1939, all peace bought cheaply is peace bought weakly.

July 1, 1965, the ceasefire comes into force.

Force, being another word open to interpretation, will come into strong focus in a couple of months.

August 13, 1965. Prime Minister Shastri speaks to the nation. If Pakistan "had any idea of annexing part of Indian territory by force, she should think afresh. I want to state categorically that force will be met with force and aggression against us will never be allowed to succeed."

These are not words spoken in isolation, because Pakistan's postures are getting increasingly belligerent. Something, clearly, is afoot as through August thousands of Pakistani guerillas disguised as Kashmiris enter the paradise state. Pakistan's attempts to garner local support are scotched by the Kashmiris themselves — who pass on the information to the Indian forces. The Indian Army takes the Haji Pir Pass on August 28 to secure the Srinagar Valley. Covert operations by Pakistan have failed.

When the big attack comes, however, it is not expected in either its form or intensity. Nor is Shastri's swift and exceedingly effective retaliation.

September 1, 1965. Pakistan launches a full-scale attack on India in the Chhamb area of Jammu. Chhamb is tank territory and close to Pakistan's Sialkot and Kharian cantonments. Shastri gives the Indian Armed Forces full freedom in dealing with the aggressor who has moved in with 75 Patton tanks. Kutch, it now becomes clear, was a testing ground for Pakistan's new American equipment, a forerunner for the big fight to come. Shastri plans a three-pronged attack, with support to the ground forces from the Indian Air Force.

To draw Pakistani troops away from Kashmir, India decides to target Lahore. This will cut off Sialkot from Lahore and hit at Pakistan's war machine. The Indian Air Force crosses the ceasefire line in Kashmir to make sorties into Pakistani territories, targetting military bases. Pakistan hits back furiously, but its fervour is let down by poor tactical moves and results in a loss of several new tanks. Fighting is fierce on both sides, but soon Pakistan flags as it loses manpower and ammunition.

January 7, 1966: *Just before Khan and Shastri sign the treaty*   Times of India

January 10, 1966: *Shastri and Khan share a joke*

January 11, 1966: *Kosygin and Khan carry Shastri's body*   Times of India

Pakistan starts appealing to the international community for help. The US refuses to intervene directly. Shastri takes Pakistan's peace moves with several, deserved, pinches of salt. He says on September 16: "... if past experience is any guide, these remarks would be part of a propaganda to beguile the world. Previously also, President Ayub Khan had talked of peace and followed it up by unprovoked aggression against India in Kutch and subsequently in Kashmir." Doves may be gentle birds of peace, but evidently they have sharp beaks.

But Pakistan cannot afford to continue this conflict it has started. Its good friend China tries to help by badgering India on the North-Eastern borders in Sikkim, to take the pressure off Pakistan. But Shastri is not easily frightened. "The might of China will not deter us from defending our territorial integrity," he tells Parliament on September 17. But Pakistan is foiled by its western ally's disapproval of China's effort to help. Ayub Khan cannot afford to offend Washington.

It falls on U-Thant, Secretary-General of the Security Council, to work out a ceasefire. The miltitary position is at a stalemate, with the Indian Army sitting just outside Lahore, and over 500 km of Pakistani territory under its control. *September 20, 1965.* The Security Council of the United Nations adopts a resolution jointly sponsored by the USA and USSR. Firing must cease on September 22 at 2430 hours. India accepts immediately. Pakistan dithers, but finally accepts it at midnight.

The 22-day war ends. The UN has left the two countries with no option — economic sanctions and worse are implied in the strong resolution. Nor can both countries afford a long-drawn-out war. But the ceasefire cannot cease hostilities. The brew is put on simmer by the United Nations. For Shastri, though, the 22-day war has been a triumph. He has shown his strength and come out stronger. For Ayub Khan there is humiliation that must be avenged.

It is left to the Soviet premier, Alexei Kosygin, to bring the two together. He invites the President of Pakistan and Prime Minister of India to Tashkent to meet across the negotiating table. Kosygin drives a hard bargain as the two countries agree on terms for withdrawal of troops. Both countries agree on a modus operandi. Then Kosygin comes up against the brick wall of Kashmir. Pakistan wants to use every opportunity to get Kashmir. India will not negotiate on other pretences. Finally, the Soviet leader gets the two to agree to disagree. The Tashkent Pact states: "... the interests of the peoples of India and Pakistan were not served by the continuance of tension between the two countries. It was against this background that Jammu and Kashmir was discussed, and each of the sides set forth its respective position."

January 10, 1966. The Tashkent Pact is signed. Shastri is due to return a hero to India. The mild-mannered prime minister, operating under the shadow of the colossus of Jawaharlal Nehru, has done his country and his predecessor proud.

January 11, 1966. Lal Bahadur Shastri dies of a heart attack in Tashkent. India is denied her hero. But Shastri's glory is not negotiable. ∎

Core of steel: *Lal Bahadur Shastri* Times of India

A FINE EXAMPLE
Memories of Lal Bahadur Shastri
By Anil Shastri

I was just eight years old when my father Lal Bahadur Shastri resigned as Union Railway Minister since he felt morally responsible for a railway accident that took place in South India in 1956. After relinquishing his office when he came back home he asked me if I felt bad at not being the son of a minister any longer.

Though 41 years have passed since then I very well remember having told him that I was in fact happy that he was no longer a minister because he would be able to spend more time with us in the family. He smiled and passed by.

But to my great disappointment this never happened in reality because my father's routine after resignation became busier and he had less time for the family than when he was a minister.

The second general elections were approaching fast and there were more people coming to see him and his tours around the country became more frequent and longer. He would leave early morning when I was fast asleep and when he returned late at night he would again find me sleeping. Hence, I would not see father for five to six days at a stretch and sometimes even more than a week. My siblings and I all had the same complaint — that he had all the time for everyone in the country but us.

In spite of the fact that he held high offices in Government, my father remained simple and modest all along. After becoming Prime Minister, he was addressing a press conference. An American correspondent remarked that though Mr Shastri wore simple clothes such as dhoti and kurta his sons preferred to wear trousers and shirts. My father replied that he was the son of a poor schoolteacher whereas his children were the sons of India's Prime Minister.

When he was the Union Home Minister, my brothers and I used to go to school in a tonga whereas our friends in the same school had cars for their use. Their fathers were Government officials and some of them in fact were working under my father in the Home Ministry. We used to feel bad that though we were the Home Minister's sons we had no car. One day all three of us decided to take up the matter with father. One late evening when father returned home he was surprised to find us awake. We asked him as to why we, as the Home Minister's sons, could not have a car for going to school. He, as usual, smiled and said he had no car of his own and all he could do was to provide a government car for us. We were happy. But he cautioned that this facility would be available to us only as long as he was a minister. Once he was out of office we would again be going to school in a tonga. We realised immediately that it would be difficult switching over to a tonga after having travelled in a car. We, therefore, ultimately preferred to continue with the tonga.

We realise today that our decision was not wrong. Even today I do not find it difficult to accommodate and adjust myself to an unfavourable situation for which I owe a lot to my father. The values of life that I have learned from him are much more than perhaps what I would learn from a hundred thousand books.

My father's integrity was beyond doubt. It was because of this quality that he earned respect and confidence amongst people. Once Jawaharlal Nehru said, "No man can wish for a better comrade and colleague than Lal Bahadur. He is a man of the highest integrity, loyalty, devoted to ideals and a man of conscience and hard work."

We made one more request for a car when he became Prime Minister. One evening he said he had decided to buy a car and we were thrilled that finally we would own one. He requested his private secretary to find out his bank balance and the price of a new car. His bank balance was about Rs 4,000 and a car cost at that time about Rs 12,000. We were shocked that as India's Prime Minister he had only Rs 4,000. However, father did not disappoint us. He applied for a loan from the government as Prime Minister and bought the car for us. After a year he died and the loan remained unpaid. Although the Government offered to waive it, my mother decided not to accept the offer and repaid the loan from her monthly pension amount. Associated with this car are values and memories which our family will always cherish. My father did not leave behind any house, money or property in any other form.

It was the Pakistan war in 1965 which was most vital during his short tenure as Prime Minister. It was about 8 pm when my father, surprisingly, was having an early dinner. His private secretary contacted him over the telephone to tell him that General J N Choudhary and Air Marshal Arjun Singh had come to see him. He left his meal and went to the drawing room to meet the Service Chiefs. In about five minutes he came back to finish his meal. As usual he had a smile on his face. When we asked what had happened, my father only said we should be prepared for war. We were stunned and also bewildered to find him as calm and composed as ever. He further elaborated and told us that the Service Chiefs had informed him that the Pakistan Army, with about 100 Patton tanks, had crossed the international border in the Chamb Sector. He had, therefore, given them instructions to retaliate with full force and even if it meant marching towards Lahore.

During the war, due to shortage of food, he had appealed to the country to miss a meal once a week. Before his appeal he had told my mother not to cook food on Monday evenings. Nobody in the family would eat on Monday evenings. My father never asked us to do anything which he did not practise himself. For example, if he advised us to do our own work he did his work too. He would wash his clothes and polish his shoes regularly. On seeing him, my brothers and I also did our own polishing.

I remember once I had slapped my younger brother Sunil who was hurt in the eye and started crying. My mother complained to father. Since I had gone to bed, nothing happened. But next morning he called me and said he would not speak to me for one week and asked me to leave his room. After that, for seven days he actually never spoke to me. I would purposely go near him or even pass by him expecting a word from him but he had meant what he said. This was no small punishment for me. Its impact was great. This was enough for me. I went to my room and sobbed and sobbed for hours. After that I decided that I would never raise my hands on my younger brothers and actually I never did. I am sure that had my father given me a beating it may not have produced the same result.

A few days before he left for Tashkent I requested a photograph with him. Surprisingly, I had no separate photograph snapped with him till then. He called my mother and three of us had ourselves snapped. He even gave his autograph with his good wishes on the print which I have treasured. Very few people knew that I was to accompany my father to Tashkent since my mother for some reason was not going with him.

I do not know what happened and my programme was suddenly cancelled just one day before his departure. I felt extremely bad as I had told all my friends that I was going to the Soviet Union. Father called me and told me not to be disappointed and promised to take me along on his forthcoming visit to the United States. Though that was some consolation, I was depressed and unhappy. I even did not see him off at Delhi airport and in fact I was only one not to do so because the entire family went to wish him success at Tashkent.

It was January 3, 1966, when my father was about to leave at 7 in the morning. I was awake, tossing in bed. He passed by, kissing me with a smile. That was the last I saw of my father.

EAST MEETS WEST

1960s

A chance encounter between Ravi Shankar and George Harrison makes scintillating music for the world

RAVI Shankar has never heard of the Beatles when he meets George Harrison at a party in mid-66. The way Shankar remembers it, Harrison says he wants to learn from him and the sitar maestro answers that the Beatle would have to give it time.

Starting here is a relationship that will take the music world by storm — both in India and the West. The meeting of Indian classical music and western pop music happens at a time when a new, youthful spirit is overtaking the world. The generation born after World War II is looking to break away from the regimentation of their parents' lives and anything that will do the trick — from psychotropic substances to sitar playing — will do. Shankar does not walk lightly into this new age, and although he is criticised for trivialising the pure and hallowed traditions of Indian classical music, he takes his art very seriously.

Like sarod-player Ustad Ali Akbar Khan, son of his guru

Ustad Allauddin Khan, Shankar also sets up a music school in the US, Kinnara in 1968. He is thrilled at the way American students take to Indian music, the dedication and devotion that they show to the long and laborious journey to perfection. Shankar uses this school to correct many of the wrong impressions about Indian music and Indian religion that the flower children have spread. It is with great joy and elation that he performs at the Hollywood Bowl Indian Music Conference to an audience of 17,500 and a stage decorated with flowers and alpana. His fellow musicians are no less illustrious. Ustad Bismillah Khan on the shehnai, Ali Akbar Khan, with his son Ashish and accompanied by Mahapurush Misra, K V Narayanaswamy accompanied by V V Subramanyam on the violin and Palghat Raghu on the mridangam. Shankar himself is accompanied by Ustad Alla Rakha on the tabla, a long and fruitful musical relationship between the two now well on its way.

Fusion maestros: *Alla Rakha with George Harrison and Yehudi Menuhin with Ravi Shankar*

Pulling the right strings: *Ravi Shankar's music still mesmerises audiences the world over*

However, it is not just through the Beatles — arguably the world's most popular music band — that Shankar puts Indian classical music on the international stage. Sometime before he and George Harrison attempt fusion in the Age of Aquarius, Shankar has already met, in 1952, Israel's Yehudi Menuhin, the greatest violin player of his time.

"We immediately became the best of friends. I always admired him as a musician, and he, from the beginning, was so interested in Indian music," Shankar will say later. This life-long bond saw fruition in concerts like the 1966 West Meets East collaboration organised by the United Nations, where music lovers thrill to the two masters playing Swara-Kakali together, a Shankar composition based on the Raga Tilang. If the Beatles connection brought Shankar fame of the Andy Warholian 15-minute variety, right up there in psychedelic media-painted colours, his work with Menuhin would give two cultural imperatives the chance to push each other's boundaries further, and come closer together. In 1972, Shankar would play with the London Symphony Orchestra, under the baton of Andre Previn. By this time, his flirtation with western

pop is wearing thin, although he plays at the seminal Woodstock concert with Alla Rakha in 1969 and at the Dark Horse concert with Bob Dylan, Ringo Starr, Ali Akbar Khan and Harrison in New York's Madison Square Gardens in 1971. Pop audiences, he finds, lack the necessary commitment — a problem he and other musicians will also face in India when classical music becomes fashionable. Instead Shankar tries to inculcate in his Indian audiences the discipline of the western classical music lover. East meets West, again.

If Shankar's name becomes synonymous with Indian sitar in the west, he grows no less famous in India. Critics attack him, but people throng to listen and watch. For a man who learnt to play the sitar at the relatively mature age of 18, this is no mean achievement. Shankar was born in Benaras on April 7, 1920. His career started as a dancer in his famous brother Uday Shankar's troupe. That is when he first felt the pulse of the people as a performer. He then joined All India Radio in 1949. Shankar worked with AIR for almost seven years. In 1956, he took his sitar abroad for the first time, and in 1958, he and Alla Rakha had their first major world tours, starting with Japan. It was also in

Jitendra Arya

1956 that his music for Satyajit Ray's *Pather Panchali* earned accolades.

It would be a discredit to India's other great classical music exponents to call Shankar the greatest. However, he is definitely one of the greatest, as all his colleagues are eager to testify. He has played with generations of Indian musicians, and has inspired all of them. Not afraid to break through artificially created barriers, Shankar opened the doors and windows of North Indian classical music, much as Rukmini Devi Arundale reinvented Bharat Natyam earlier this century. He explained the music he played to his audiences in English, simplifying its intricacies. This too earned criticism — why would he not speak in Hindi? Shankar will not be curbed by this "language nonsense" however: "I can speak in Hindi or Bengali — but somehow music is easier to explain in English. So I get confused."

His sitar, however, speaks a universal language and there is no confusion there. Says Ustad Amjad Ali Khan, the great sarod player, "It was destiny that the country produced an artiste of Panditji's calibre." ∎

CLASSICAL EXCELLENCE

Ustad Bismillah Khan singlehandedly lifted the shehnai, a wind instrument, to the international platform. The man who plays on the steps of temples in Varanasi is today synonymous with this musical instrument.

Son of Hafiz Ali Khan, **Amjad Ali Khan** is known for his individual sarod sound and tantrakari innovations. Belonging to Gwalior gharana, his fast jhalas, elaborate alaps and extensive laykari make him a terrific performer. Brought Ekhare tans into sarod, earlier played only on sitar.

 The flute and **Hari Prasad Chaurasia** are inseparable. Has cut discs and travelled extensively both in and outside the country for performance. Along with Pandit Shiv Kumar Sharma (santoor), has directd music for films like *Silsila* and *Chandni*.

Son of Ustad Alla Rakha, **Zakir Hussain** developed the sounds of tabla with flamboyance and elan. His sense of beat, tremendous ability to innovate according to situations and a classic rapport with the audience makes this a handsome tabla player a performer par excellence. He has excelled both in jugalbandi and solo performances. Has acted in Merchant-Ivory's *Heat and Dust* and Sai Paranjape's *Saaz* opposite Shabana Azmi. Now settled in America.

 Dr L Subramaniam The young violin player from Chennai, now settled abroad, is known for his 'east-west' fusion. Has performed with the legendary Yehudi Menuhin. Has performed in numerous concerts in the international circuit.

The making *of* a NATION

A Bharatnatyam danseuse and the founder of Darpana Academy of Performing Arts at Ahmedabad, **Mrinalini Sarabhai** has choreographed several works without diluting the traditional base and "extended the language of dance with innovations and thematic content, reflecting contemporary issues." With an active dance career spanning four decades she and her daughter Mallika Sarabhai have worked together in various dance projects.

 Kelu Charan Mohapatra has a big hand in popularising the temple dance of Odissi in the country and abroad. His notable disciples include the late Sanjukta Panigrahi, Sonal Mansingh and Ilean Citaristi.

Kathak exponent of Lucknow gharana, **Birju Maharaj** has mesmerised his audience wherever he has performed.

 Born in 1916 in Madurai, **M S Subbulakshmi** is a Carnatic vocalist of supreme order. Known for her devotional songs in Hindi. particularly Meerabai's bhajans. Has acted in films. Also plays on the veena.

Pandit Bhimsen Joshi's Bhimsen's bhajans are rated among the best while his Khayal renderings are legendary. His gayaki is a sangam of Kirana, Agra and Gwalior traditions.

TONGUE LASHING

1960s

The issue of Hindi as a national language divides the country with acrimony and violence. Regional pride and concepts of statehood take precedence over all else

"If under sentimental urges we should give up English, we would cut ourselves off from the living stream of ever-growing knowledge. English is the only means of preventing our isolation from the world."
— *Dr Sarvepalli Radhakrishnan, Second President of India*

"I feel we have no respect for mother tongues as we should. We cannot develop all potentials of our language until education given to the child from the beginning to the highest level is in his mother tongue."
— *Morarji Desai, Fourth Prime Minister of India*

"English cannot be in India, anything but a second language. A language spoken and understood by persons less than five per cent could not have the status of the first."
— *Jawaharlal Nehru, First Prime Minister of India*

ONE of the most divisive battles fought in modern India is over language. A country with 14 scheduled spoken languages in the Constitution and innumerable dialects has a piquant situation at hand — very few of these languages are understood across the length and breadth of the land. In this respect Dr Radhakrishnan is undoubtedly right. English not only prevents our isolation from the world, but also from each other. But English is a foreign language, imposed upon us by an alien ruler, taught to us to assist in his administrative needs. Jawaharlal Nehru is also right. And then, there is the contention of Morarji Desai. Every Indian language, written and spoken, is rich in its own culture and traditions. It provides every Indian with a base and a ground for laying down roots. The mother tongue cannot be ignored.

Three valid points of view. No solution. Impasse.

There is one suggestion however. A suggestion that has been waiting in the wings almost since Independence became a goal. A suggestion that was put off when India became free because of the dangers it held within it. A suggestion whose alarm has been set for January 26, 1965. It is on this date that Hindi will become India's national language. Its official language. For lurking behind Nehru's indictment of English is his vindication of Hindi. Spoken by the largest percentage of Indians, it seems the most appropriate common medium. The trouble is that it is not spoken at all by an even larger percentage

Tamil supremacy: *Demonstrators in Madras opposing the imposition of Hindi*

The Hindu

of Indians. The bigger trouble is that many of these Indians see the imposition of Hindi as a new form of colonialism, from the heartland of India — Bihar, Uttar Pradesh, Rajasthan, Madhya Pradesh. What right has this backward area — economically and culturally both — to dictate terms to the rest of the country?

January 17, 1965. C Rajagopalachari, Independent India's first Governor-General convenes the Anti-Hindi Conference at Tiruchi in Tamil Nadu. The conference is attended by representatives from non-Hindi speaking areas like West Bengal and Maharashtra. The decision is to launch an agitation over the imposition of Hindi.

January 25, 1965. Effigies of the demon Hindi are burnt all over Tamil Nadu. The Dravida Munetra Kazhagam party in Tamil Nadu has decided that Republic Day would be a day of mourning to protest the arrival of Hindi as

NEVER HINDI
Why the South won't relent

IN 1934, when the Congress Party is looking for a language that can serve as a national binding force, it picks Hindustani. A compromise choice between Hindi and Urdu. But later, the differences between Hindustani, Hindi and Urdu will seem trivial compared to their collective differences with India's other languages.

In 1937, provincial elections are held throughout India. C Rajagopalachari of the Congress, just elected Prime Minister of Madras, announces that Hindi will be compulsory as a second language in all schools.

September 5, 1937, Tirunelveli. Dismayed academics start a society to protect Tamil from Hindi. Soon after, the Tamilian Association joins in. The movement has turned political. It now waits for its most important player.

Erode Venkatappa Ramasami Naicker, 59, is known as an atheist and iconoclast. He will now be known as the

India's official language.

January 26, 1965. The Tamil Nadu Anti-Hindi Council has its peaceful campaign planned — black flags, processions, burning copies of the Constitution. But as Congress workers and protesters clash, peace vanishes. Two persons in Madras burn themselves to death. In a police firing incident in Chidambaram, a student is shot dead.

January 27, 1965. Over 300 student leaders are rounded up and arrested.

January 28, 1965. Prime Minister Lal Bahadur Shastri appeals to the people of Tamil Nadu to stop protesting. Even if Hindi is the official language, English is to continue as an associate language until non-Hindi speaking states have switched over.

To no avail.

February 10, 1965. Students go on a rampage across the man who will lead the revolt against Hindi, who will forever be associated with Dravidian pride against Aryan invaders, and with the caste turnaround of most of South India, ending Brahmin domination. Little wonder that he will be called Periyar by his followers — Tamil for great, venerable sage.

June 1, 1938, the first anti-Hindi procession marches through the Madras heat to Rajagopalachari's house. It is followed by protests throughout the state. The government backs down, minimising the focus on Hindi — no examinations, to be taught for only two-and-a-half hours a week. The protests continue, as more and more associations join in. Periyar and over 300 people are arrested. In jail with Periyar is Canjeevaram Natarajan Annadurai, just out of college.

With no sign of the agitation ending, the Hindi notification is withdrawn in 1940. Rajagopalachari's ministry has already resigned by then. The Justice Party, which he had trounced in the 1937 election becomes the Dravida Kazhagam in 1944, headed by Periyar. Five years later, it will split and the Dravida Munetra Kazhagam will be launched by Annadurai, never to look back. But whatever the name of the party, the stance remains — no Hindi.

The making *of* a NATION

Dravidian Pride: *Periyar*

The Hindu

state. Buses are burnt, trains are stoned. At least 35 people are killed and as many injured in police firings. Two policemen are burnt to death.

The violence continues over the next five days. Immolations, police firings, and the cry of 'Long live Tamil'. The unofficial count puts the final death toll at 150, of the wounded at 500.

Union Food and Petroleum Ministers, C Subramaniam and O V Alagesan, both from Madras state, resign from the Cabinet.

February 12, 1965. Acharya Vinoba Bhave goes on an indefinite strike to protest against the violence. He breaks it five days later when the Centre accepts his conditions — no violence over the language issue, Hindi not to be imposed upon non-Hindi speaking people, no English on Hindi-speaking people.

February 22, 1965. The protest is called off.

February 25, 1965. After negotiations with student leaders, the Official Language Act of 1963 will be amended so that English remains and the all-India pan-Hindi decision is delayed further. A three-language formula for all states is considered — the mother tongue, Hindi and English.

But though the protest may have been called off, it is far from over. Two years later, the DMK will come to power in Tamil Nadu and the state will never accept Hindi as any sort of language — first, second, third, official, national. Language not only touches the chords of the growing regionalism which is engulfing India, but also at pride and identity. In Punjab, far away as it is from Tamil Nadu, and so much closer to Hindi, the Sikhs will demand their own state so that Gurmukhi can get its rightful due as a language. In November 1966, Prime Minister Indira Gandhi will agree to split Punjab and carve out Haryana — for Jats, Hindi-speaking Punjabi Hindus. To try and mollify the angry South,

Down with Hindi: *...up with English!*   The Times of India

Haryana introduces Telugu as a third language, and Bihar, Tamil. There are few solutions more foolish than those that are politically motivated.

The problem spills over even in the rest of the subcontinent, as East Pakistan rejects West Pakistan's imposition of Urdu over Bengali. Language, suddenly, is the tie that binds us all together.

The simmering discontent will lie low for 10 years. In 1977, the Janata Government comes to power and the importance of Hindi resurfaces. The focus shifts from Hindi versus regional languages to Hindi versus English. Says the controversial Raj Narain, Union Minister for Health and Welfare, "The 14 languages in the Constitution are all sister languages. Hindi is the eldest sister of all. Since the others are younger sisters, the eldest, that is Hindi, naturally wishes the best for all the others." The three-language

Crossing boundaries: *Bombay protests too*   The Times of India

formula is now sought to be implemented with zeal in schools across the country. Except Tamil Nadu, which has only two languages and not one of them is Hindi. When Doordarshan, India's state-run television broadcaster, starts its National Network, for national transmission, with the news in Hindi and English, Tamil Nadu does not even telecast the Hindi news. Tamil Nadu must speak in either Tamil or English.

Part of the objection in most non-Hindi speaking states is not so much of recognition of their own tongues — as with Gurmukhi — but with the inferiority of Hindi. The Dravidian languages, Bengali and Marathi are all rich in literary tradition and show great linguistic growth. Hindi has not made the same strides. Why should it get precedence?

Not one of these questions is satisfactorily answered. It could be that there is no answer. Or, that there are too many, as with Radhakrishnan, Desai and Nehru. ■

POLITICAL STARS
The South's brightest heroes

M G Ramachandran

ARGUABLY Tamil cinema's most popular star, M G Ramachandran was also one of the few living people to have a temple dedicated to him. For the people of Tamil Nadu, MGR was not just a film star, he was also chief minister and akin to a god. His 136 films saw him as the conquering hero, vanquishing all manner of villains.

When MGR switched over from the khadi of the Congress for the fiery speeches of C N Annadurai, he also became a champion and supporter of the Dravida Munetra Kazhagam. His political associations began in the 1950s, and by 1972 he was confident enough to break away from the DMK and form the AIADMK. Chief Minister of Tamil Nadu from 1976, MGR unfortunately did not live up to expectations as in

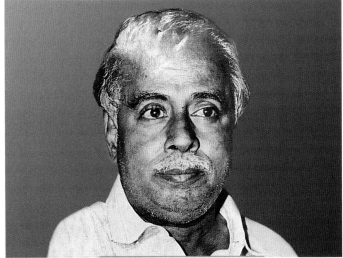
Fiery leadership: *C N Annadurai*   The Hindu

his reign autocracy masqueraded as democracy. Yet, when he died on December 24 1987, aged 70, all Tamil Nadu cried. And in his honour, made his widow Janaki chief minister. She was soon ousted by MGR's other heir, the Puratchi Thailavi,J Jayalalitha.

N T Rama Rao

People's hero: *N T Rama Rao*   Mid-Day

N T Rama Rao was to Andhra Pradesh much what MGR was to Tamil Nadu. The star of a series of mythological films starting from the 1940s, NTR soon became identified with the roles he played — Krishna, Ram and Venkateshwara. When he launched the Telugu Desam Party in 1982 in reaction to the increasingly corrupt Congress ministries which ruled Andhra, his success was assured. But NTR soon fell prey to the inadequacies of his own ill-thought-out social reforms and lost power. He, however, returned in triumph and after his death in 1995 his heirs fought over succession. His new wife Lakshmi Parvathi ultimately lost to his son-in-law Chandrababu Naidu who now leads the Telegu Desam Party and the state.

Star to icon: *M G Ramachandran*

The making *of* a NATION

HAPPENINGS

1957-1966

January 5
Central Sales-Tax Act, 1956
comes into force

January 22
Trade agreement between India
and Pakistan signed in New
Delhi.

February 12
The British aircraft carrier, Hercules,
is bought for the Indian Navy

March 8
B G Kher dies in Poona

April 10
About 200 pilgrims are
drowned when two boats
capsize in the river Godavari
near Bhadrachalam

May 13
Dr Rajendra Prasad and
Dr S Radhakrishnan sworn
in as President and Vice-
President respectively

May 15
Lieutenant-General
K S Thimayya takes over
as Chief of Army Staff

June 2
Twenty-two people die
in a suburban electric
train collision at
Wadala, Bombay

January 1
A collision between the Pathankot-bound
Delhi Janta Express and the Ambala-Delhi
passenger train at Mohri kills 30, injures 90

January 8
British Prime Minister Harold Macmillan
arrives in New Delhi

Janaury 26
Eminent social reformer and educationist
D K Karve is awarded the Bharat Ratna

February 22
Maulana Abul Kalam Azad, Union
Minister for Education, dies in
New Delhi. A stalwart of the Freedom
Struggle, he parted ways with Jinnah
remaining a pillar of the Congress

March 11
Aga Khan, Prince Karim, is
installed as Head of the Indian
Ismaili community in Bombay

June 14
Dr C V Raman
receives the Lenin Peace
Prize at Kremlin

June 28
Mridulaben Sarabhai is
expelled from the
Indian National
Congress

Maulana Abul Kalam
Azad

February 1
Indira Gandhi succeeds U N Dhebar
as Congress President

February 10
Martin Luther King, leader of the blacks
in the US, arrives in New Delhi

April 29
A Dakota aircraft crashes
near Hailakandi shortly after
taking off from Agartala, killing
all 24 persons on board

May 20
Ramanathan Krishnan
wins the men's singles title
in the London Lawn
Tennis Championship
Tournament

January 1
Pilots of Air India International strike work

February 11
Nikolai Khrushchev, prime minister of
the USSR, arrives in New Delhi

April 20
Air India International
inaugurates its Boeing 707
service to London

May 1
The new states of
Maharashtra and Gujarat
come into being

January 21
Queen Elizabeth and the Duke of
Edinburgh arrive in New Delhi

January 26
Dr B C Roy and Purushottam Das Tando
are awarded the Bharat Ratna

February 22
Former British Prime Minister,
C R Attlee, delivers the first of the two
Azad Memorial Lectures in New Del.

February 24
The Government of Madras decides
that Madras State be referred to as
Tamil Nadu

March 7
Govind Ballabh Pant, Union
Minister for Home Affairs, dies in
New Delhi.

April 26
Maharaja Hari Singh, former
ruler of Jammu and Kashmir,
dies in Bombay

May 14
Ramanathan Krishnan u
the men's singles title at t
International Tennis
Tournament in Wiesbade

May 27
Noted geneticist Professor
J B S Haldane's request
Indian citizenship accepte

1957   1958   1959   1960   1961

August 25
India wins the World
Polo title

September 5
The Rajya Sabha passes the
Wealth Tax Bill

October 3
All-India Scheduled Castes
Federation is formally dissolved and
the Republican Party of India is
formed

October 29
G B Pant is awarded the
Bharat Ratna

November 9
Dr Rajendra Prasad inaugurates the
15th World Vegetarian Congress
at Bombay

November 23
The Calcutta Mail derails near Igatpuri,
at least 50 die

November 25
The fifth report of the Law Commission
suggests that the vast majority of British
statutes still in force in India
should be repealed

December 15
A group of 60 Harijans enter the
Vishwanath Temple at Varanasi

December 20
British philosopher and mathematician
Bertrand Russell is awarded the Kalinga
Prize for 1957

July 8
V Shantaram's Do
Ankhen Barah Haath
wins an award from the
International Catholic
Film Bureau.

July 22
India's first milk
sterilisation plant opens
at the Aarey Milk
Colony, Bombay

July 25
The Indian Institute of
Technology is
inaugurated in Bombay

December 11
Wilson Jones wins the World Amateur
Billiards title for India in Calcutta

Wilson Jones

September 15
Television is introduced in
India with the setting up of a
pilot TV centre

December 3
The government declares that all
foreigners living in India should take
residential permits

December 5
Well-known cricketer S Duleepsinhji, dies
in Bombay. Nephew of the legendary
Ranjitsinhji, Duleep had played
international cricket for England. The
Duleep Trophy, a major domestic
tournament, is named after him

December 9
Dwight D Eisenhower, President of the
United States, arrives in New Delhi

December 24
India beat Australia in the second Test at
Kanpur, Jasu Patel claiming 9 wickets

July 16
Milkha Singh wins the
440 yards race in the
British National Athletic
Championships

September 8
Feroze Gandhi, Lok Sabha
member and husband of
Indira Gandhi, dies in New
Delhi of a heart attack

October 30
M A Chidambaram is elected
President of the
Board of Cricket in India.

November 29
Crown Prince Akihito and
Princess Michiko of Japan arrive
in New Delhi on an eight-day
state visit

December 11
Nandu Natekar wins the singles title in the
25th National Ball Badminton
Championships in Trivandrum

December 18
The National Museum is inaugurated in
New Delhi

October 29
New All-India Muslim League is
formed

October 29
Nineteen persons are killed and 57
injured when the engine and three
bogies of the Tundla-Farrukhabad
passenger train are derailed between
Mainpuri and Bhogaon stations

November 1
The first Indian-made transport plane
Avro-748 makes its maiden flight
at Kanpur

November 11
Lt Col G Bhattacharya of the Indian
army is convicted and sentenced to eight
years' rigorous imprisonment in Dacca

November 29
Soviet Cosmonaut Yuri Gagarin
arrives in New Delhi

Bertrand Russell

Mansur Ali Khan
Pataudi

January 11
Lala Shri Ram, prominent industrialist,
dies in New Delhi

January 16
Fifty persons are killed and 25 injured when
two massive air-locks burst inside a 72-ft
deep pier for a railway bridge being built on
the Mahanadi at Naraj, 38 miles from
Bhubaneshwar, Orissa

January 31
Government decides to designate the peacock
as the National bird of India

February 9
Naresh Kumar and Ramanathan
Krishnan win the doubles title in the
Asian Lawn Tennis Championships in
Calcutta. Krishnan went on to win the
singles title the next day

February 28
First President of India, Dr Rajendra
Prasad dies in Patna

March 12
Jacqueline Kennedy, wife of the
US President John F Kennedy,
arrives in New Delhi on
a nine-day visit

April 18
India loses the fifth and final
cricket Test match at Kingston
for a series scoreline of 0-5.
Mansur Ali Khan Pataudi
becomes the youngest captain in
the history of cricket when he
takes over in the Third Test from
Nari Contractor who suffered a
serious head injury from a
Charlie Griffith bouncer

May 11
Dr Sarvepalli
Radhakrishnan is elected
President of India

May 7
India defeats Japan to
win the Eastern Zone
Davis Cup
Championship in Tokyo

May 22
Rohini, a glider made at
the Aircraft
Manufacturing Depot of
the Indian Air Force is
successfully flown in
Kanpur

June 3
All 29 persons aboard
an Indian Airlines
Dakota are killed when
it crashes in flames near
the Sarna railway
station, five miles from
Pathankot

February 17
An IAF Ilyushin-14 aircraft crashes,
killing 13

March 8
Twenty-two people are killed and
34 seriously injured when the
Calcutta-bound Express from
Madras runs into a goods train at
Banpur station on the
South-Eastern Railway,
about70 miles from Cuttack

April 17
Jagjit Singh is the first Asian to
be selected for 1963 Kalinga
Prize, for popularising science

June 1
Naya paisa
becomes paisa

January 3
R. Krishnan retains his title at the Asian
Lawn Tennis Championship

Janaury 24
Rani Guidaliu, who as a young girl, was
worshipped as a goddess by the Nagas, dies

February 6
Pratap Singh Kairon, former
Chief Minister of Punjab, is shot
dead near Delhi

April 13
An IAF Dakota carrying four
officers and five other defence
personnel crashes in the
Mokokchung area of Nagaland,
killing all on board

Mihir Sen

April 15
Renowned painter Nand
Lal Bose dies

April 18
An all-women expedition
led by Pushpa Athavale of
Bombay scales Mt Koktang
(20,166 ft high) in
Western Sikkim

1963   1964   1965   1966

July 23
The French Senate
adopts a Bill
thorising ratification
f the treaty by which
nce ceded her Indian
possessions to India

October 7
The Congress-PSP
coalition in Kerala ends

October 18
Cowasji Jehangir, noted
industrialist, dies in
Bombay

Dr Sarvepalli Radhakrishnan

August 8
India endorses the partial
Nuclear Test Ban Treaty

August 27
The first consignment of
250 tons of bananas from
Maharashtra and Gujarat
are despatched to Kuwait
from Bombay

September 2
A severe earthquake claims a
heavy toll of life in the Badgam
Tehsil of Kashmir Valley

September 11
All 13 passengers and a crew
of five die when an IAC
Viscount crashes near Dholpur,
33 miles from Agra

October 6
Veteran Sikh leader Baba Kharak
Singh dies in New Delhi

October 31
K C Mahindra, well-known
industrialist, dies in Bombay

Rohini

August 5
Jayaprakash Narayan is
awarded the Ramon
Magsaysay Award for public
service

August 15
A daily television service
begins in New Delhi

August 21
Ten people are killed in an
explosion at the explosive
factory at Kirkee near Poona

Rita Faria

August 24
Mihir Sen successfully
swims the tricky Straits
of Gibralter, from Spain
to Morocco

September 4
An IAC Caravelle crashes on its
training flight on a 700-ft hill
33 miles from Bombay, killing
all four on board

September 12
Mihir Sen becomes the first
person to swim the Dardanelles
when he successfully crosses from
the Marmora to the Aegean Sea

September 21
Mihir Sen crosses the Bosphorus

September 26
C P Ramaswami Aiyar, eminent
educationist, dies in London

October 13
The Hyderabad Kazipet Express
collides with the Kazipet
Express train at Ghatkesar,
killing 100 people

October 30
Mihir Sen swims the
Panama Canal

November 17
Rita Faria, an Indian medical student,
becomes Miss World in London

December 21
India wrests the Asian Games Hockey title
from Pakistan in Bangkok

Less than three decades after the lofty idealism of India's beginnings, complacency sets in with dire consequences. Mighty resolutions will inevitably be followed by smaller realities. But there are inherent dangers in shifting complete focus to individual or sectarian problems and so ignoring the bigger picture. Eternal vigilance is, indeed, the price of liberty.

That liberty is lost by a rejection of the Constitution when a government driven by power-lust and terrified of dissent tramples the essence of democracy — freedom. New though it may be, the Constitution is India's most hallowed document, most revered institution. It is the chart that navigates a nation and its basic tenets must be sacrosanct. The Emergency stifles fundamental  rights and brings home, in stark and brutal urgency, the importance of free thought, expression, disagreement. Indeed, the uncontestable need for unfettered democracy.

The lesson is harsh. But it is one that India will not easily forget. In a triumph of the democratic process, welcome elections break the handcuffs of autocracy. The sanctity of the Constitution is restored. The Emergency may be over, but its follies must always be alive in public memory.

There is, though, a significant off-shoot of the Emergency. Politics now takes centre-stage over ideology as states and leaders realign themselves. New thoughts and new alliances emerge. Experimentation abounds in India's states as local considerations become the driving political force, laying the ground for change at the centre of power. Democracy, dominant.

REVOLUTION!

1960s

The Naxalite Movement uses force to bring land to India's peasants, inspires a generation of students and then fritters away its own advantage through excessive violence

"It is a peal of spring thunder."

— *Chinese Premier Mao Tse Tung on the Naxalbari uprising of 1967*

RADIO Peking is, in fact, a major supporter of Bengal's version of the peasants' revolt of the late 1960s. However, this revolt is distinguished from others in the incipient violence that it advocates and inspires — ultimately across much of the nation and over the decades. Charu Mazumdar, founder of the Naxalite Movement and the Communist Party of India (Marxist-Leninist) believes in annihilation as the route to eliminating class differences. Armed peasants and small militant squads to take the land back from the exploitative bourgeosie. And the Naxalite movement does start as an armed rebellion by peasants. A peal of spring thunder, even, perhaps.

Show of hands: *Naxalite activists being arrested in Calcutta*

The Statesman

Naxalbari is a small, unprepossessing village in the Siliguri division of Darjeeling district in Northern West Bengal. Much like so many other Indian villages, where the wealth and the land is concentrated in the hands of a few rich landowners and farmers. Little has changed in 20 years of Independence, and the cliched image of the poor peasant shows here in stark reality. But in fact, Naxalbari was the centre of a peasant movement in 1959. Destiny was not kind then. Would it be different now?

March 1967. Jotedar Iswar Tirki of the Bangla Congress tries to plunder the paddy stock of a local share-cropper, Bugul Kishan. The United Front Government, a coalition of Left parties has just come to power in West Bengal. The time for revolution has to be now. Farm workers and share-croppers in Naxalbari stand with Bugul. Armed with bows and arrows, they attack the local jotedars and forcibly take their paddy stocks. The revolution has begun. Over the next two months, the jotedars' land deeds and documents will be burnt, animals and implements seized and land redistributed among the landless poor.

But the United Front, even if it is well aware of the problems of Bengal's peasants and is committed to helping, cannot condone lawlessness. Then, there are the jotedars. Powerful, rich and ruthless. The police are sent in.

May 23, 1967. Police inspector Soman Wangdi, is killed.

May 24, 1967. The counter-attack is harsh. Agitators use women and cows as a cordon, but the police are unsympathetic. In the ensuing firing, six women, two children and two men are killed.

The Naxalbari incident is, still, small and the amount of land seized even smaller. But it stands as an example of class struggle, the beginning of a war that escalates because of the neglect that this part of Indian society has faced for so long. Extremists in the Left pick this up as an ideal way to put their ideas into action. The Naxalbari uprising has been masterminded by Charu Mazumdar, implemented by Kanu Sanyal, both members of the Communist Party of India (Marxist), the main constituent of the United Front Government. They will now take their struggle across as much of Bengal as they can, taste success in Andhra Pradesh and Bihar and then, concentrate all their efforts on Calcutta.

The Government finds itself caught in a bind. The Left considers peasants one of its main supporters. But peasants suddenly want all their grievances attended to immediately and are unforgiving of an administration that is working through talks and negotiations. Have not they already suffered enough under 20 years of Congress misrule? Have not the jotedars acquired this land illegally in any case, in collusion with corrupt politicians and through money power? Armed rebellion, Mazumdar tells his men, is the only way. The Government struggles to explain that this haste is unfair, that all it wants is a little time. Biswanath Mukherjee, one of the ministers sent to the area with a six-member Cabinet Mission points out that the Government has "adopted a sober and progressive" attitude.

But sober is not what the Naxalites want. And progressive is open to interpretation. Youth power is at its zenith worldwide in the 1960s and the plight of India's downtrodden peasantry is more than urban idealism can bear. Although the Naxalbari uprising is crushed by August 1967 and Mazumdar and Sanyal expelled from the party soon after, the cry for revolution shifts to Calcutta's streets. College Street, repository of some of the country's most respected educational institutions resounds with the explosions of bombs. The bows and arrows of the peasants are quickly replaced by rifles, machine guns, hand grenades. Mao's peals of spring thunder translate into the blast of power from the barrel of a gun.

Mazumdar, Sanyal and the other leaders of the Naxalite Movement go underground, while Calcutta burns above. The class struggle, says Mazumdar, must involve the industrial proletariat.

Naxalbari sees an echo in Srikakulam; After all, Andhra Pradesh — Telengana in particular — has long been a hotbed of peasant resistance. Mazumdar is joined by Nagi Reddy in 1968 and together they form a coordination committee of Communist Revolutionaries. But differing on the fundamental issue of the foundation of a new party, they part ways. The Communist Party of India (Marxist-Leninist) is formed on April 22, 1969. Kanu Sanyal makes a formal announcement on May 1, 1969 at Calcutta's maidan. Sanyal is secretary, Mazumdar is chairman.

In 1970, The Peking Review hails Mazumdar as the "beacon light of the movement" in an article about the peasant movement in Srikakulum. But the light is fading. Not only are not enough peasants interested in armed rebellion, but gradually, nor are the CPI(ML)'s members enamoured of Mazumdar's theories of annihilation. Important lieutenants like Ashim Chatterjee and Santosh Rana express their differences by 1971.

Outside the Naxalite Movements, winds of change are blowing through Bengal and India. The United Front Government is summarily dismissed. The new Congress regime comes down relentless on Naxalites, with harsh shoot-to-kill orders. And then India helps Bangladesh win freedom. India's youth, the bulwark of the Naxalite struggles, are infused with a new patriotism.

July 18, 1972. Charu Mazumdar is arrested in Calcutta. Soon, his other comrades will follow him to jail. A sick man, Mazumdar will die soon after. The Naxalite Movement peters out in Bengal, only to become resurgent in Andhra Pradesh years later.

But unfortunately for rural India, although the points raised were all valid and vital, very little was done to answer them. The lost dream of Naxalbari might still live wherever there is unwarranted exploitation. ■

Peoples' Revolution: *Peasants inspired by China's Mao Tse Tung*

'C' IS FOR CHARU
On the inspiring force behind the Naxalite Movement
By Vara Vara Rao

Spearheading change: *Charu Mazumdar and Kanu Sanyal*   The Statesman

CHARU Mazumdar and Naxalbari. Or, it should be Naxalbari and Charu Mazumdar...? I wrote a song in jail in 1974, as an undertrial prisoner in the Secunderabad Conspiracy Case, for my second daughter who was to go to school that year, to start her with the alphabet.

"A" for Arms, "B" for Bengal and "C" for Charu Mazumdar — one has to learn the alphabets with these words.

Is it not more correct and coherent to learn class struggle, communism, cultural revolution and Charu Mazumdar in that order or priority, starting with big "C". When it comes to people and their emotional identity, these rationalities don't work. In 1971 or thereabouts, I interviewed Kaloji, the people's poet for Srijana, a Telugu literary monthly, about his views on future course of Indian politics. He is a Gandhian. He said there are only two options left — Darovodayam or Charu Mazumdarayam.

What was the message of Naxalbari? To put it simply, the message of his "light documents against revisionism" is to ask the landless poor and agricultural labourers to:

1) seize lands from the illegal occupation of landlords — the jotedars;

2) resist the goons or police who will naturally come in support of the landlords; and,

3) seize power in the villages with a progamme or, all power to the village peasant committees.

This micro study and programme was tried in Therai, before Naxalbari in 1967 and its micro-implementation in Naxalbari, Kherebari and Parasbiga on May 23, 24 and 25 1067 is the key to the open-war path to the New Democratic Revolution based on agrarian armed struggle. As Sri Potlapalli Rama Rao, Telugu short story writer, put it in the Telengana Armed Struggle days, the countryside in this country did not remain the same after Naxalbari, though many Naxalbaris were oppressed crushed and faced setbacks in Srikakulum (Andhra Pradesh), Mughabari, Lakshmipur, Kheri (Uttar Pradesh), Jalandhar (Punjab), Wyanad (Kerala) and elsewhere by 1970-71.

The struggle lies in Charu Mazumdar's understanding and analysis of China's great proletariat cultural revolution, as the third world revolution after the Bolshevik Revolution of 1917, as well as China's People's Revolution of 1949. And then applying these to Indian conditions, which he characterised as semi-feudal, semi-colonial and comprador bourgeoisie, with even the social evil of untouchability intact after 20 years of so-called Independence.

Naxalbari paved the way for the formation of the Communist Party of India (Marxist-Leninist). Today, we find that for the last 30 years, one or more Marxist-Leninist parties continuing armed struggles, boycotting elections and adhering to the path laid down by Naxalbari under the leadership of Charu Mazumdar.

The pitched battles fought in Jalandhar and Calcutta Universities, Presidency College in Calcutta, the students' movements in Punjab and the sacrifices in Andhra can only be compared to the Spanish Civil War, where the cream of society sacrificed their lives for democracy and freedom.

Generally, the urbanised middle class comes to conclusion that intellectuals are not attracted to Naxalbari politics today as in 1970s, and the middle class is distancing itself from revolutionary politics. It is true that the leadership for the Marxist-Leninist movement in the 1970s came from the petty-bourgeoisie intellectuals, and that the revolution had a romantic appeal for those who were at the periphery or outside the movement. They assumed that they were in the orbit of that egalitarian ideal dream or New World.

As a Chinese saying goes, the "Dragon of Revolution entered into the Fort of the Prince and its fumes are felt with its sound and heat."

We are in its midst — whether it is Telengana, Bihar or Dandakaranya — of a revolution. And the wavelength? It is not those same petty-bourgeoisie intellectuals but grassroots-level people who are in process coming into leadership — whose language, etiquette, articulation (or no etiquette? and no articulation?) are something which we are not used to. It is very difficult for us to shed our middle class egos and accept the leadership of Puli Anjaiah, Adoni Lakshmi, Orugallu Sudersan or Chintala Venkataswamy as we could easily accept the leadership of K G Satyamurthy, also a great poet, Vinod Misra and, of course, Souren Bose.

Charu Mazumdar asked students, youth and intellectuals to go to villages and organise the landless poor against the class enemy. That's exactly what the Radical Students, Radical Youth League and Jana Natya Mandali cultural activists started doing from 1978 onwards in Telengana and parts of Andhra.

The dream of Charu Mazumdar started at a micro-level in Naxalbari in a single spark that spread like wildfire in parts of the country. That's why Charu Mazumdar is remembered today as the torch-bearer of Naxalbari for the Indian Revolution.

WOE TO HER FOES

1969

Indira Gandhi breaks the Syndicate, splits the Congress and establishes her supremacy

"We will have a pretty face for a time and she will be burdened by the weight of her father's and Mr Shastri's misdeeds. To that we can safely add the weight of her own misdeeds."
— *Dr Ram Manohar Lohia, 1966*

BUT it is always a mistake to underestimate the faces that you meet, however pretty they may be, which Dr Ram Manohar Lohia might not have realised when he made this remark about Indira Gandhi, India's third prime minister in 1966. For, in the years between 1966 and 1969, Indira Gandhi is to lay the foundation that will make her one of modern India's most significant prime ministers — continuing long after Dr Lohia is consigned to the graveyard of forgotten men. The burden of her misdeeds — that is for history to judge, and it undoubtedly will. But Dr Lohia, who died in 1967, could not have known how prescient he was being.

However, all that is much, much later. To many, in the country and in the Congress Party, Mrs Gandhi is little more than a pretty face, beloved daughter of the country's charismatic first prime minister, Jawaharlal Nehru. If he had wanted her to succeed him as prime minister, he certainly never said so. After his death in 1964, the powerful Syndicate, that runs the affairs of the Congress party, determines that Lal Bahadur Shastri be prime minister. When Shastri dies unexpectedly in Tashkent in 1966, it picks the information and broadcasting minister in Shastri's Cabinet as prime minister. Indira Gandhi is to be pretty malleable in their hands, a puppet prime minister pulled by powerful strings.

The Syndicate is a group of state leaders, formed in Tirupati in 1963, headed by Kumaraswamy Kamaraj Nadar,

president of the Congress, former chief minister of Madras, N Sanjiva Reddy, chief minister of Andhra Pradesh, S Nijalingappa, chief minister of Mysore, Atulya Ghosh, Bengal Congress chief, S K Patil, Bombay city Congress chief and union minister. They represent the newly emerging power centres in the South, West and East of the country.

Waiting in the wings, deprived for the second time of the prime ministerial chair since Nehru's death, is Morarji Desai, also a Syndicate member. Mrs Gandhi is up against the Syndicate's stranglehold over the Congress party. Or is she? She spends her 14 months in power before the general elections, watching and learning. And getting the measure of the Syndicate.

February 25, 1967. The Congress wins the fourth general elections, but with none of the glory of the past. The Syndicate has suffered heavy losses. Kamaraj has lost in two constituencies, S K Patil in Bombay, Ghosh in Bengal. Mrs Gandhi has campaigned the country tirelessly, invoking the Nehru mystique, presenting herself as a champion of the people. She has won. It is the candidates hand-picked by the Syndicate who have lost.

March 12, 1967. The post of Congress Parliamentary Party leader is hers. So is the Prime Ministership. Mrs Gandhi's Cabinet effectively demonstrates her new clout in the party. Syndicate membership is limited, notably Desai as deputy prime minister and finance, although what he wants is home. Her own main supporters are in the form of Fakhruddin Ali Ahmed (industrial development and company affairs) and Jagjivan Ram (food and agriculture).

The first show of strength comes over the candidacy of the new President. Sarvepalli Radhakrishnan has already had two

The making of a NATION

The smiles before the storm: *Indira Gandhi with Congress President K Kamaraj in happier days*

terms and the well-known scholar is also going blind. The Syndicate wants him to continue, the opposition parties put forward former chief justice, K Subba Rao. Indira Gandhi wants Vice-President Zakir Husain. He is sworn in on May 13, with her other candidate, V V Giri, as Vice-President.

Not quite just a pretty face now.

Kamaraj's term as Congress President expires and the question of his successor arises. He is not willing to stand for another term — although that is what Morarji Desai wants. The Syndicate favours Patil, but Mrs Gandhi does not. The new, vociferous section of the Congress, known as the Young Turks, led by Chandra Shekhar, has its own ideas. Finally, the leader of the Congress Parliamentary Party and the outgoing Congress President agree on a compromise candidate — S Nijalingappa.

If Indira Gandhi appears to give in when it comes to the Congress President, the President of India is another matter. Dr Zakir Husain dies of a heart attack on May 3, 1969. Vice-President V V Giri is sworn in as acting President.

Earlier in the year, Mrs Gandhi has set the wheels in motion to abolish the privy purses — the allowances paid to India's princes after the post-Independence integration of states into the Indian Union. These had varied from $ 350,000 for the Maharaja of Mysore to $ 25 to the Talukdar of Katodia, annual and tax-free.

July 9, 1969. Indira Gandhi sends a note to the Congress Working Party on the nationalisation of major banks. This proposal has been floating about for some time, but is not liked by Finance Minister Morarji Desai. Then, Mrs Gandhi, much like her father before her, does not like much about Desai anyway. The CWC meeting in Bangalore approves the note on July 11.

July 12. the CWC nominates N Sanjiva Reddy as the Congress candidate for President of India.

July 12. Vice-President Giri announces his candidature.

The Syndicate and Mrs Gandhi meet again.

July 16. Mrs Gandhi relieves Desai of the Finance portfolio — though he is welcome to stay on as deputy prime minister. Taken unawares, Desai, known for his strong principles among other things, has no option but to resign. No sooner does he, than the Acting President promulgates an ordinance to nationalise 14 major banks. The Young Turks are applauding. So are the left parties. So are the people. On the heels of the abolition of privy purses — taking money away from the feudal and exploitative rich — this is one more step that proves that Indira Gandhi cares for the people. Had she not said, two years before, during an election speech in Rae Bareilli, "...my burden is manifold, because scores of my family members are poverty-stricken and I have to look after them."?

Nationalisation is supposed to mean more loans for poor people, a more equitable spread of the country's resources among the country's people, an encouragement of entrepreneurship.

The Syndicate, of course, is not happy. They will soon have even less cause for clapping.

Sanjiva Reddy as President is not acceptable to the prime minister, to the Young Turks within the Congress, to the opposition. Mrs Gandhi refuses to issue a whip for voting in line with the CWC choice and the official Congress candidate. Instead, she is in favour of a "conscience" vote. "The Congress cannot merely be a machinery for winning the election of candidates

chosen by a small group and by making alliances divorced from policies," she says, "It has to be a live political organisation of the masses, pulsating with activity at every level." Freedom of voting, argues the Syndicate, will make a mockery of the Congress candidate. Can it be that Indira Gandhi is not aware of this?

August 20, 1969. V V Giri is elected as President of India, on what is known as second preference voting. The stakes are now no more a question of who is more powerful — Indira Gandhi or the Syndicate. It has become a question of the future of the Indian National Congress.

There is a move afoot in the Congress to discipline those who resorted to conscience voting in the presidential elections. Mediators and the unabashed conscience voters warn of serious consequences. Peace-makers flit between the two camps as both make confrontational noises. The growing feeling within the Syndicate and right-wing elements is to expel the leader of the CPP. So the August 25 Congress Working Committee passes a unity resolution. Perhaps the unity lies in the fact that everyone recognises that matters have reached a head.

Certainly nothing gets better as Nijalingappa resists Mrs Gandhi's moves to convene an All India Congress Committee meeting and all talks between them come to nothing.

November 1, 1969. and Nijalingappa drops C Subrahmaniam and Fakhruddin Ali Ahmed from the CWC. Both are Indira Gandhi's men.

November 1, 1969. Indira Gandhi calls for an AICC meeting in Delhi.

November 9, 1969. The CWC expels Indira Gandhi from the party. The Congress Parliamentary Party expresses its faith in the leadership of Mrs Gandhi — 330 of the 427 Congress MPs present. At the special AICC session, she gets support from 448 of the total 711 delegates.

The Indian National Congress is now formally known as the Congress (Old) and Congress (Ruling). The party that gave India independence now graduates to petty politics. Mrs Gandhi explains on November 8: "It is a conflict between two outlooks and attitudes in regard to the objectives of the Congress and the methods in which the Congress should function. It is a conflict between those who are for socialism, for change and for the fullest internal democracy and debate in the organisation... and those who are for the status quo, for conformism and for less than full discussion inside Congress."

The implications are clear. Congress (R) is forward-looking, pro-people. The Congress (O)? Reactionary and conservative at best.

But even if Mrs Gandhi is supported not only by her split Congress, but also by the opposition parties in Parliament, she needs more than that to knock the final nails into the Syndicate's coffin. Meanwhile, the Supreme Court has struck down her nationalisation bill as well as the abolition of privy purses as unconstitutional. The need for more action is upon her.

December 27, 1970. The President dissolves Parliament and calls for fresh elections in March '71, a year earlier than scheduled. The Syndicate splinters all over the country, as partymen rush back into Mrs Gandhi's arms. The Congress (R) wins 352 of 518 seats. The Syndicate 16. Pretty or not, Joan of Arc had nothing on her, you might say. ■

Pretty as a picture: *Gayatri Devi, one of the world's most beautiful women, made a successful transition from princess to politician*

Jitendra Arya

ROYAL CHARADES
From patrician to plebian,
India's royalty learns to cope

Till the outcome of the Revolt of 1857, it might be said that most of the resistance to the British in India came from India's princely states. From Tipu Sultan to, finally, the Rani of Jhansi, many of India's rulers laid down their lives to save their lands from foreign domination. But it might also be said that the British may not have built their stronghold in India so successfully without the cooperation of India's princely rulers. Playing one against the other till they dominated them all, India's princes, who ruled two-fifths of India's landmass, found that they controlled nothing. The British resident handled the affairs of state, while monarchs fell to quibbling over the number of guns in their salute or organising marriages between their dogs or taking the Viceroy on duck shoots. So it was, when Independence came for India, except for a few progressive states like Cochin and Travancore and a few progressive rulers like the Nawab of Bhopal and Jam of Nawanagar, India's princely states found themselves without nanny and rein-bearer. The integration of these states into India was successfully carried out by Sardar Vallabhbhai Patel, and there were those rulers who showed their political prowess and understanding. Some, like the Maharajah of Baroda, showed their ability to cut their losses and run — he was the first to sign the Instrument of Accession and then his family later shone as a bright Indian jewel on the international celebrity circuit. Others involved themselves in the handover of power to their subjects and the new political awakening in the country.

By 1969, when Prime Minister Indira Gandhi abolished the privy purses promised in perpetuity to the princes after Independence, most of these hereditary rulers had had their day or were carving new positions for themselves. The Scindias of Gwalior, for instance, were becoming a political family — harking back to their Peshwa origins? — and today, Rajmata Vijayaraje and her daughter Vasundhara align with the Bharatiya Janata Party while Madhavrao Scindia is part of the Congress. Karan Singh, yuvraj of Jammu and Kashmir, was made Sadar-e-Riyasat of his father's erstwhile kingdom soon after accession and had to deal with the troubles which have engulfed it since. Maharani Gayatri Devi of Jaipur was jailed by Mrs Gandhi during the Emergency for opposing her policies.

Others would shine in different fields. The Nawabs of Pataudi, *pere* and *fils*, would become famous cricketers and the awe they inspired would come from their heritage as much as their undoubted prowess. If there is any irony in Tiger Pataudi — who also descends from the Nawab of Bhopal — advertising suit material brand-named Gwalior, rest assured it is overwhelmed by the romance of royalty. Cricket and royalty in India, however, have a long history, evident in two national tournaments named after former royals, outstanding cricketers themselves — the Ranji trophy after Ranjitsinhji of Nawanagar and the Duleep trophy after his nephew Duleepsinhji.

But heredity is not always apparent. The Nizam of Hyderabad fought hard to keep his state independent, yet his descendant has been satisfied sheep-farming in Australia. *Sic transit gloria.*

AN INDIAN SUMMER

1971

This is a story of two acts, two series, two amazing victories. It is a story of a team raised in controversy but destined for glory. It is a story of how Indian cricket comes of age

Home are the heroes: *Mammoth crowds greet the motorcade carrying the victorious Indian players after their return from England*

Courtesy Ajit Wadekar

Prologue

ON a cold wintry December day in 1970, Vijay Merchant pulls off the biggest *putsch* in Indian cricket history. Employing his casting vote as chairman of the selection committee, he casts aside Mansur Ali Khan, the erstwhile Nawab of Pataudi, as captain of the Indian cricket team. In his place comes Ajit Wadekar. Pataudi has been captain since 1962. He is highly regarded for his dashing batting, brilliant fielding and dynamic captaincy. But there have also been some complaints of high-handedness, there have been some poor results and Pataudi's own form has been suspect. Merchant has found ground to take a radical decision.

By this time strong gusts of change are also blowing across the country and Pataudi Jr finds himself on the wrong side of the drift as it were. Prime Minister Indira Gandhi has split the Congress, nationalised banks and stopped the privy purses for princes and nawabs. Stripped off his exalted status, Pataudi Jr is no more a holy cow. By replacing him with commoner Wadekar, Merchant, in a sense, is accentuating the definition of India's new social structure in which the patrician has become obsolete, dispensable, and the plebian has come to rule.

Merchant's decision, however, shocks the country. Pataudi Jr, in spite of his royal aloofness, has been a much-loved figure. There are some accusations that the ouster of Pataudi has a history behind it, or more pertinently, vengeance. In 1946, when Merchant was easily India's best batsman, he was overlooked for the captaincy to the tour of England, that honour being bestowed on Iftikhar Ali Khan, the Nawab of Pataudi Sr. An act of revenge therefore, claim Pataudi Jr's supporters. But this dissenting voice is brushed aside as Merchant brings in sweeping changes into the Indian team in early 1971.

His clarion call is 'Catch 'em young', but the 1971 team to the West Indies is really a mix of experience and and youth with no apparent claim for greatness. There is no Pataudi, the miffed former noob opting out of the tour for "personal reasons". But Wadekar has M L Jaisimha, Dilip Sardesai, Erapalli Prasanna and Salim Durrani for advice. Supporting these seniors are the classy spinners S Venkatraghavan and Bishen Singh Bedi, and a host of youngsters, most with less than two years experience. The most promising amongst the newcomers is a dimunitive opener from Bombay, Sunil Gavaskar, who has forced his way into the team with a string of high scores in domestic cricket. Though he is the youngest player in the team the senior players would do well to follow his example," Merchant tells the squad at the send-off dinner, marking Gavaskar out as the player to watch.

But such optimism is lost on critics who see this as a makeshift team put together as a desperate gamble, and unlikely to make an impact against the West Indies, especially on their own wickets. The previous tour's scoreline, 0-5, is intimidating. Will history repeat itself?

Tale of two skippers: *Ajit Wadekar and Tiger Pataudi*   Bristol Photo/Mid-Day

Act I

"...It was Gavaskar
The real master
Just like a wall
We couldn't out Gavaskar at all
You know the West Indies couldn't out Gavaskar at all."

— *From a calypso composed by Lord Relator in honour of the 1971 Indian cricket team to the West Indies*

February 19, Kingston, First Test. The first day's play has been washed out. On the second, it seems the match will be a wash-out. Before tea, India are reduced to 75 for 5 and the ghost of 1962 seems to have been resurrected before young Eknath Solkar joins the seasoned Dilip Sardesai, and some sense is restored to the proceedings.

February 20. By tea on the third day, the match has swung dramatically. The partnership between Sardesai and Solkar fetches 137 runs for the sixth wicket. For the ninth, Sardesai finds a stubborn ally in Prasanna. These two put on 122 runs. By the time India are bowled out, Sardesai has made 212 runs in just over eight hours, the first double century by an Indian against the West Indies, and the total is a healthy 387.

February 21. The West Indies are bowled out for 217. From 183 for 3, the collapse is sensational and triggered by the off-spinning duo of Venkatraghavan and Prasanna giving India a lead of 170 runs. When, a little later, Ajit Wadekar walks in to enforce the follow-on, there is utter shock in the West Indies dressing room. Captain Gary Sobers, inarguably the greatest cricketer in the world, is ignorant that in a game reduced to four days, the follow-on margin is also reduced from 200 to 150 runs. In his education, there is also humiliation. The match is drawn, but India have won an important psychological battle.

March 6, Port of Spain, Second Test. The West Indies bat first and are bowled out in under a day for 214. Advantage India.

March 7. The first wicket partnership between Ashok Mankad and debutant Gavaskar puts India on the road to a high score. They put on 68 runs, Gavaskar goes on to make a reassuring 65, but the substance to the innings is again provided by the heroes of the first Test, Sardesai and Solkar. They add 114 for the fifth wicket, and India coast past the West Indies score, with Sardesai scoring his second century in succession. India total 352, a lead of 138 runs.

March 9. When play resumes after the rest day, the cricket is taut and players from both sides are tense. By midday, however, it seems that the West Indies have repulsed the Indian threat. The deficit has been wiped out for the loss of only one wicket, and Fredericks and Charlie Davis are looking good.

March 10. India get a fortuitous breakthrough even before play starts. At nets, Davis is hit on the right eyebrow and taken to hospital to repair the gash which has allowed much blood to pass. Soon after play commences Fredericks is run out at his overnight score, and the West Indies are on edge again. After some chilling overs in which Clive Lloyd tries desperately to break free of the stranglehold, Wadekar plays a masterstroke. He brings on veteran Salim Durrani to bowl at the restless Lloyd and positions himself at short mid-wicket. Promptly, the impetuous Lloyd lashes a delivery into Wadekar's hands. The next ball from Durrani is a vicious breakback that beats Sober's defensive jab, goes between bat and pad and dislodges the leg stump bail. If ever two balls could win a Test match, it were these. The spine of the West Indies batting has been cracked. They fold up for 261 runs, leaving India 124 runs to win. The West Indies fight back like wounded tigers, but India are not to be denied. Before the day is through, the verdict is out. India have beaten the West Indies for the first time ever.

Gavaskar's debut marks the arrival of a master batsman. By the time the series is through he will have amassed 774 runs with four hundreds, including a century and a double century in the last Test which stymies the West Indies' bid to level the series. It is a performance which makes not only the subject of calypsos in cricket-obsessed Trinidad but a household name all over the world.

The making *of*
a NATION

The Rock: *Sardesai's solid batting provides India the fillip to bid for victory*   Mid-Day

TOP INDIAN PLAYERS 1947-71

Vijay Merchant: Orthodox opener who did not play too many Tests but earned universal renown for his matchless technique and appetite for big scores. After retirement he served as commentator, selector, administrator and social worker.

Tests 10, Runs 859, Ave 47.72

Mushtaq Ali: Aggressive opening batsman who believed attack was the best form of defence. Forged a good partnership with Merchant in pre-Independence days, their contrasting styles frustrating opponents.

Tests 11, Runs 612, Ave 32.21

Rusi Modi: Right-hand batsman of polish and precise timing. Hit the high spot with 560 runs in the 1948 series against the West Indies, a record which stood for more than two decades.

Tests 10, Runs 736, Ave 46.00

Vijay Hazare: Graceful middle-order batsman who vied with Merchant for the status of best batsman in the country. Often he was that man, as when he made two hundreds in the same Test against Don Bradman's side in 1948.

Tests 30, Runs 2192, Ave 47.65, Wkts 45, Ave 32.91

Lala Amarnath: Dashing all-rounder with maverick ways. As a swing and seam bowler, he was sans pareil in his heyday, and when he made a hundred on Test debut, the toast of an entire nation.

Tests 24, Runs 878, Ave 24.38, Wkts 45, Ave 32.91

Vinoo Mankad: A superb all-rounder whose wily left-arm spin was just a notch higher than his reliable batting, Mankad was arguably India's most valuable cricketer through the late '40s and '50s.

Tests 44, Runs 2109, Ave 31.47, Wickets 162, Average 32.32

Vijay Manjrekar: The youngest of the trio of masterly Vijays that succoured Indian cricket post Independence, Manjrekar supplemented superb technique with punchy strokes all round the wicket, the pick of these being a rasping square cut.

Tests 55, Runs 3208, Ave 39.12

Polly Umrigar: Evolved from utility cricketer to hard-hitting batsman to pillar of the side through the late 50s and early 60s.

Tests 59, Runs 3631, Ave 42.22, Wkts 35, Ave 42.08

Subhash Gupte: A leg-spinner par excellence, Gupte became independent India's most well-known matchwinner in the '50s. He had a baffling googly and deadly flipper to boot.

Tests 36, Wkts 149, Ave 29.55

Chandu Borde: A leg-spinner, Borde became one of the pillars of the Indian batting in the 60s. He had a tight defence, fine shots and a sound temperament.

Tests 55, Runs 3061, Ave 35.59, Wkts 52, Ave 46.48

Dilip Sardesai: Stocky batsman with wonderful footwork and superb balance. He had all the shots and the urge to play these.

Tests 30, Runs 2001, Ave 39.23

Salim Durrani: The erratic genius of Indian cricket, his career figures do his all-round talent little justice. When in the mood, though, he could be peerless, bagging wickets on plumb tracks or hitting sixes at will.

Tests 29, Runs 1202, Ave 25.04, Wkts 75, Ave 35.42

Ramakant Desai: Nicknamed 'Tiny', Desai made up in pace and fire what he lost in inches. He had an easy, flowing run-up, a good action and strong shoulders which propelled the ball at high speed towards unsuspecting batsmen.

Tests 28, Wkts 74, Ave 37.31

M A K Pataudi: An imperious batsman and outstanding cover fieldsman, Pataudi Jr was easily the most charismatic cricketer to have played for India. The loss of one eye in a car accident did not kill his zest for the game; indeed it made critics wonder how great he might have been with both eyes intact.

Tests 46, Runs 2793, Ave 34.91

Ajit Wadekar: A stylish left-hand batsman who loved to cut and hook, Wadekar made a belated entry into international cricket but made himself a permanent member of the side soon after.

Tests 37, Runs 2113, Ave 31.07

The Oval Salute: *Skipper Wadekar and Chandrashekhar respond to the cheers of Indian supporters a*

Act II
"It's all over, the match is yours. They'll want you up on the balcony."

— *Former England batsman Ken Barrington to Ajit Wadekar after the 1971 Oval Test*

August 24, The Oval. Skipper Ajit Wadekar has the amazing ability to doze off after he has been dismissed and this time it is no different though India are chasing another sensational victory. Is he cocky or simply confident? Perhaps he is plain tired, for this has been a nerve-racking, fatiguing Test match in a long and hard season. While the gripping run hunt is on, Wadekar snores.

But that is getting ahead in the story, which begins with the Indian team's arrival into England in the second half of a wet and cold summer. Wadekar's team has come here with some changes from the side which beat the West Indies a few months earlier, the selectors replacing Jaisimha, Durrani, rookie wicket-keeper Jeejebhoy with Abbas Ali Baig, mystery wrist spinner Bhagwat Chandrashekhar and another young wicket-keeper Syed Kirmani. Also available for the Test matches is dashing wicket-keeper batsman, Farokh Engineer.

India's victory over the West Indies has stimulated enough excitement for the English critics and cricketers to treat Wadekar's side with some respect, and lots more contempt. England is not the sunny Caribbean isles nor is there an aging West Indies team to battle. On green wickets and difficult conditions, the Indians are yet to be tested. And surely this side is no match for Ray Illingworth's lions who have only the previous season mauled the Australians.

The first Test is a humdinger. After four exciting days, however, the fifth day is unfortunately rained off with India needing 38 runs and England two wickets to win. There are arguments for and against the two teams, a plethora of ifs and buts. But one thing is certain — India are no pushovers.

In the second Test, the fifth day's play is rained off again, but this time to India's clear and great benefit. Set to score 427 runs to win, India lose Gavaskar, Mankad and Wadekar reaching

ing England ·   Courtesy Ajit Wadekar

a precarious 65 for three before the rain gods smile on them. On to The Oval with honours even.

August 19. Third Test, first day. England win the toss and make merry. Before the end of an entertaining day's play, the score reads 355 runs to England's credit.

August 20. No play as rains hold sway. The forecast from the met office is bleak, and even bleaker from the newspapers. Victory should be easy for England.

August 21. Premature, presumptuous and contemptuous as this forecast seems, India's batting appears to justify the assessment when play resumes. At 125 for 5, the die seems to have been cast. Then comes the recovery through the lower order, stretching the total to 284. And yet, England's lead is a substantial 71 runs.

August 23. After the rest day, the storm. England, looking to capitalise on this lead, are stunned into submission by Chandrashekar's leg-spin of unpredictable bounce and delivered at near medium-pace. The close-in catching is outstanding, with Wadekar, Solkar, Abid Ali and Venkatraghavan hovering around the bat like vultures. England collapse unexpectedly and ignominiously to 101 all out. Chandrashekhar, brooking no defiance, claims 6 for 38, and India now need 172 for a win. The early loss of Gavaskar for a duck, is a big setback, but from there, the innings recovers gradually through the two senior pros, Wadekar and Sardesai.

August 24. Wadekar, in a needless mix-up, is run out immediately on resumption and India are again on tenterhooks. The skipper returns to the pavilion, strips off his pads and gloves, and finds a nook in the dressing room to doze off. Meanwhile, the action in the middle approaches a tantalising climax. Ten runs later, Sardesai is caught behind and at 134 for five, the match is pregnant with possibilities. England's hopes, however, are dashed by the flamboyant Engineer, who brings India close to the target with a flurry of fours. With two runs to get, little Vishwanath hoping to hit the victory stroke, is caught behind. But the largehearted Abid Ali, kissing his talisman and invoking the name of god, cuts Luckhurst for a boundary to prompt an invasion of the pitch and for Barrington to rouse Wadekar from his slumber with the news that in one glorious summer, the history of Indian cricket had been rewritten. ∎

THE GAVASKAR ERA
The Little Master's great effect on Indian cricket
By K N Prabhu

AMONG the many drawbacks of Indian cricket in the early years was the lack of opening batsmen of any substance and bowlers who were quick enough to secure a break-through and deter the opposition from indulging in intimidatory short-pitched bowling which passed unnoticed by the umpires. These deficiencies, however, were corrected to a large extent in what is recognised as the 'Gavaskar Era'.

After Vijay Merchant and Mushtaq Ali, the opening positions were subject to experiment. Vinoo Mankad's brilliance and Pankaj Roy's painstaking performances never did instil the necessary confidence, Contractor lasted for too brief a while and in later years Engineer, Abid and others failed to establish themselves with any degree of authority.

Hence Gavaskar's arrival on the scene in 1971 with a string of prolific scores was of tremendous significance. India came to be accepted in the inner councils of the game as a force to contend with. Interestingly, it coincided with another landmark in our history. When Indira Gandhi was returned to power in the 1971 general elections, after worsting the Old Guard who formed the Syndicate, by a happy coincidence Gavaskar had set the seal on India's triumph at Trinidad. In later years it used to be said that while Mrs G was supreme at the Centre, Gavaskar's writ ran unchallenged in our cricket councils.

The history of Indian Cricket can be divided into four distinct phases: the Age of Elegance of the 1930s, when it was a passing pageant of artistes like Merchant and Mushtaq, Mankad and Amarnath; then the Years of Endurance, when the pseudo-professionals made it a thing of scorn; followed by the Years of Recovery under Pataudi and Wadekar and, finally, the Gavaskar Era.

Gavaskar arrived at a time when Indian cricket was at the crossroads; the Old Guard, Jaisimha, Sardesai and Wadekar had retired and soon it was time for the great exponents of spin to follow. It is to Gavaskar's credit that he nursed and encouraged the new young recruits. When Vishwanath was on the wane, his place was filled by Vengsarkar, when Bedi and Prasanna were done with Yadav and Doshi took over. Then Ravi Shastri was picked from "out of the blue" and promoted to the top ranks till he was ever willing to fill any slot in the bowling and batting. And for one a couple of seasons, Sivramkrishnan raised hopes of being another Subhash Gupte in the making.

There was no dearth of talent, for Azharuddin raised visions of being a superb craftsman in the style of Vishwanath and also a master builder like Gavaskar. And with Kapil around, there were any number of young sturdy men to follow in his footsteps. In truth Gavaskar had been a trail-blazer, ready to hand over a flaming torch to a future generation.

The making *of* a NATION

Gavaskar's sequence of tall scores is now a statistician's dream; his technique as the "broadest bat in the game" has been studied, dissected and analysed by shrewd observers. He has been compared to Bradman in his aptitude to play a long innings and acquire runs. There is one other aspect which has not received the attention it deserves. It is no secret that bodyline bowling was devised to curb Bradman. Having seen it in operation, I would submit that Gavaskar's mastery over the conventional type of fast bowling, prompted Clive Lloyd to direct his fast bowlers to resort to short-pitched bowling in the infamous Kingston Test of the 1975-76 series. This in itself is an indirect tribute to Gavaskar's powers of batsmanship.

Around this time there was also a radical change in the character of the Indian attack. Through the '60s it had banked heavily on spin. In 1962 Prasanna had teased and puzzled the batsmen; then in the late '60s Chandra and Bedi joined forces with Venkat, while Prasanna turned to more serious occupations before returning to the Indian team. The start of the Gavaskar era was also to mark the decline in the dominance of India's great spin bowlers. Bedi and Prasanna were over the hill and Chandra seemed to have lost all heart in bowling on flat wickets. Only Venkat soldiered on faithfully though his appearances depended on the whims of the selectors. At this stage Gavaskar found in Kapil Dev an all-rounder of inestimable value.

It is said that Bradman buoyed up Australia's spirit during the great depression of the '30s. I would believe that Gavaskar's batting in the Australian summer of 1978-79 and later in Pakistan was cheering news during the dark days of the Emergency. For a brief while Gavaskar toyed with the idea of joining the Packer Circus but his loyalties in the end were always with India.

It was also the age which saw the growth of player power. On the West Indies tour of 1975-76 Gavaskar had spoken up for the players. Their allowances were pitiful and there were few incentives to the deserving. The Indian Board made huge profits and there was no reason why this should not be equitably distributed among the players. Gavaskar used the media to highlight all these grievances.

The mid-70s marked the high noon of the Gavaskar era. He himself touched the high meridian of his powers as a batsman, with every calendar year marking an aggregate of a thousand runs in Test matches. As a captain, too, he looked well nigh invincible. His batting was neatly balanced, with Vishwanath chipping in with superbly crafted centuries, Vengsarkar batting with a vigour and vitality quite often absent formerly in the middle order. And above all the presence of Doshi and Yadav was some assurance that Kapil would not have to go it, all on his own.

In later years there was a lack of empathy between him and Kapil. The differences between them were exploited and blown out of all proportion by the tabloids. But Gavaskar conducted himself with great dignity.

Gavaskar was also accused of playing for himself and of chasing records, but a glance at the scorebooks will prove that many of India's exciting victories were forged after he had given the innings a head start, whether it was 102 in April '66 at Trinidad, where India chased a target of over 400, 166 on a fiery wicket against Imran and company in January '79 or even in the contentious Melbourne Test a year later when he made 70.

Sunny days: *Gavaskar's brilliant batting raises India's stock even as it gathers runs and records*
Graham Morris/Mid-Day

"There never was great man made ignoble talk of." The Shakespearian tag has much truth in it. Bradman was said to be fallible on drying pitches. And Gavaskar, it was pointed out, was never truly tested by spin. The answer was always there and it was emphasised in his last Test innings on a turning pitch at Bangalore against Pakistan. Gavaskar made 96 (the next best was Azharuddin's 26) against Iqbal Qasim and Tauseef Ahmed. He almost carried the day till he was out to a doubtful decision. But it was not the end. There was one more blank to be filled. He did it with superb timing which had marked his batsmanship with a century at Lord's – after which he officially announced the end of the Gavaskar Era.

MASTER CLASS

Sunil Gavaskar
Tests 125, Runs 10122, Highest 236★, Ave 51.12, Hundreds 34, Fifties 45, Catches 108.
One-day cricket: Matches 108, Runs 3092, Ave 35.13, Highest 103, Hundreds 1, Fifties 27

Bishen Singh Bedi
Tests 67, Wickets 266, Ave 28.71, Best 7 for 98.

Bhagwat Chandrashekhar
Tests 58, Wickets 242, Ave 29.74, Best 8 for 79.

Erapalli Prasanna
Tests 49, Wkts 189, Ave 30.38, Best 8 for 76.
Srinivas Venkatraghavan
Tests 57, Wkts 156, Ave 36.11, Best 8 for 72.

★ Not out

WAR, PEACE. AND A NEW NATION

1971

The genocide unleashed by Pakistan on its Eastern sector draws India into a complicated conflict.
But India wins the war. And Bangladesh is formed

Surrender!: *General Niazi (right) lays down arms to Jagjit Singh Aurora (left)*

Ministry of Defence

DECEMBER 3, 1971. 17.40 pm. The Pakistan Air Force attacks Indian military airports on the western sector — Srinagar, Pathankot, Amritsar and Avantipur. In air sorties through the night, Ambala, Agra, Jodhpur and Uttarlai are also attacked.

Prime Minister Indira Gandhi is in Calcutta, addressing a public rally.

Chief of Army Staff, General S H F J Maneckshaw calls Chief of Staff, eastern sector, Major-General Jack Jacob in Calcutta. He is to inform the prime minister immediately. Commander of the operation, Lieutenant-General Jagjit Singh Aurora meets the prime minister while Jacob organises her departure. Indira Gandhi flies back to Delhi in an Air Force jet. The Cabinet is ready for her and an emergency meeting is held.

December 4, 1971. Just after midnight. Indira Gandhi speaks to the nation.

"Since last March we have borne the heaviest of burdens and withstood the greatest of pressures in a tremendous effort to urge the world to bring about a peaceful solution and prevent the annihilation of an entire people whose only crime was to vote democratically. But the world ignored the basic causes and concerned itself only with certain repercussions...

"Today a war in Bangladesh has become a war on India. This imposes in me, my Government and the people of India a great responsibility. We have no other option but to put our country on a war footing... We are prepared for any eventuality."

India is at war.

December 4, 1971. The Indian Air Force hits back hard at Pakistani air bases. In the West, Chanderi, Shorkot, Sargodha, Murid, Mianwali, Masroor, Risalwala and Changamanga. In the East, the Dacca and Narayanganj airfields and the Chittagong oil refinery.

The making of a NATION

The fury of the Indian response is neither anticipated nor expected. Fighting a civil war for almost a year, General Yahya Khan takes a calculated risk when he attacks India, trying to deflect attention from the genocide which the Pakistan Army was carrying out in its Eastern wing, now self-styled as Bangladesh. For all that time, millions of refugees have been swarming into India, causing a gigantic human rights problem and increasing local discontent. For all that time, India has been pressing for a political solution, appealing to the international community to stop Pakistan's excesses on the Bengali self-determination movement in the East.

This war is fought on two sectors, but it is, understandably, on the East that the major action takes place. The Mukti Bahini (Freedom Army), a committed and dedicated group of guerrilla fighters has been attacking the Occupation Pakistan Army in Bangladesh. Made up of erstwhile officers of the Pakistan Army, these warriors make up in courage and skill what they lack in weaponry. Fighting on familiar terrain, they manage to capture Pakistan Army bases and liberate part of the country they are fighting for. The Indian Army has been asked to help them, but covertly, without open confrontation. In West Pakistan, negotiations have almost broken down and Sheikh Mujibur Rehman, head of the Awami League and now head of the struggle for Bangladesh, is in prison.

The Indian Air Force keeps up its bombardments and gains control of airspace in the East. On December 4 itself,

Major triumph: *Field Marshal Sam Maneckshaw*

19 Pakistani planes are destroyed. In the Bay of Bengal, the Indian Navy sets up a blockade. Cox's Bazar and Chittagong Harbour are attacked from the aircraft carrier, Vikrant. Pakistani gunboats are destroyed, hangars and fuel dumps set on fire.

If operations on the West are largely defensive, on the East, the Indian Army, aided by the Mukti Bahini is offensive. By December 6, Jessore has been taken and the thrust is very clearly towards the capital, Dacca. That is also where the Pakistan Army is converging, partly on the run from the Mukti Bahini.

December 6, 1971. The Indian Government officially recognises the People's Republic of Bangladesh. Pakistan breaks off diplomatic relations with India.

Also breathing fire and brimstone is the United States of America. Pakistan is its ally. The United States cuts off all military and economic aid to India, while continuing to support Pakistan. It asks, in the Security Council of the United Nations for an immediate cease-fire in the Indian subcontinent. The Soviet Union vetoes the move. Foreign Minister Andrei Kosygin calls Pakistan the aggressor.

December 9, 1971. The US sends its Seventh Fleet into the Bay of Bengal. The ostensible reason is to rescue American nationals stranded in Dacca. The implicit reason is clear to everyone, however.

December 9, midnight. In an emergency meeting between the prime minister and the chiefs of army staff, it is decided to ignore the American presence. The Army will march on to Dacca. However, a message is sent to the Soviet Union and a Soviet fleet in Vladivostok sails towards the Bay of Bengal.

Dacca is not too far away.

From now on, the pressure on the Pakistan Army in the East to surrender is enormous. Hampered by the swiftness of Indian retaliatory action and by the absolute lack of intelligence gathering from a hostile Bengali population, the Pakistan Army

APPENDIX 2

INSTRUMENT OF SURRENDER SIGNED AT DACCA AT /63 HOURS (IST)

ON 16 DEC 1971

The PAKISTAN Eastern Command agree to surrender all PAKISTAN Armed Forces in BANGLA DESH to Lieutenant-General JAGJIT SINGH AURORA, General Officer Commanding in Chief of the Indian and BANGLA DESH forces in the Eastern Theatre. This surrender includes all PAKISTAN land, air and naval forces as also all para-military forces and civil armed forces. The forces will lay down their arms and surrender at the places where they are currently located to the nearest regular troops under the command of Lieutenant-General JAGJIT SINGH AURORA.

The PAKISTAN Eastern Command shall come under the orders of Lieutenant-General JAGJIT SINGH AURORA as soon as this instrument has been signed. Disobedience of orders will be regarded as a breach of the surrender terms and will be dealt with in accordance with the accepted laws and usages of war. The decision of Lieutenant-General JAGJIT SINGH AURORA will be final, should any doubt arise as to the meaning or interpretation of the surrender terms.

Lieutenant-General JAGJIT SINGH AURORA gives a solemn assurance that personnel who surrender shall be treated with dignity and respect that soldiers are entitled to in accordance with the provisions of the GENEVA Convention and guarantees the safety and well-being of all PAKISTAN military and para-military forces who surrender. Protection will be provided to foreign nationals, ethnic minorities and personnel of WEST PAKISTAN origin by the forces under the command of Lieutenant-General JAGJIT SINGH AURORA.

(JAGJIT SINGH AURORA)
Lieutenant-General
General Officer Commanding in Chief
Indian and BANGLA DESH Forces in the
Eastern Theatre
16 December 1971.

(AMIR ABDULLAH KHAN NIAZI)
Lieutenant-General
Martial Law Administrator Zone B and
Commander Eastern Command (PAKISTAN)
16 December 1971.

Terms and conditions: *The surrender document*

Running scared: *Refugees from war-torn Bangladesh*

is caught in a bind. Young West Pakistan officers who had boasted that they were being sent to improve the gene pool of the Bengalis now faced a distinctly uncomfortable option: surrender as prisoners of war to India, as per the Geneva convention, or face the wrath of angry Bangladeshi mobs lusting for their blood.

Yahya Khan's last-ditch desperate move of forming a civilian government with Nurul Amin from East Pakistan as Prime Minister and Zulfikar Ali Bhutto as deputy, has no effect.

December 11, 1971. Major General Farman Ali appeals to the UN for help in repatriating Pakistani troops from Bangladesh. Pakistan shoots it down as an unauthorised appeal. The United States continues to pressure for cease-fire, stopped by the Soviet Union. There are fears that this will become a proxy war between two world powers. Meanwhile over 2,000 Pakistani troops surrender.

December 12. Six Pakistani vessels carrying fleeing troops are sunk by Navy aircraft off Chittagong harbour. Indian paratroopers are dropped to the north of Dacca, along the Brahmaputra. A message from Maneckshaw asks that all towns be taken. Indian troops led by Lieutenant-General Jagjit Singh Aurora are advancing from Comilla, Akhaura and Mymensingh.

December 13. Lieutenant-General A A K Niazi, Commander of the East Pakistan operations, sends a message to GHQ in West Pakistan: "Dacca under heavy pressure. Rebels

have already surrounded the city. Indians also advancing. Situation serious. Promised assistance must take practical shape by 14 December. Will be effective in Siliguri, not NEFA and by engaging enemy air bases."

General Maneckshaw steps up demands for surrender. Niazi's call for an immediate cease-fire comes, interestingly, routed through Washington.

December 15. Maneckshaw replies: "I have received your communication regarding a cease-fire in Bangladesh at 2.30 pm today through the American Embassy in New Delhi... Since you have indicated your desire to stop fighting, I expect you to issue orders to the forces under your control in Bangladesh to cease fighting immediately and surrender... Should, however, you not comply with what I have stated, you will leave me with no other alternative but to resume my offensive with the utmost vigour at 9 am (IST) on the morning of December 16."

December 16, 9 am. No reply. Then a call asking for an extension of the deadline till 2.30 pm.

December 16, 4.31 pm. The lawns of the Race-Course Maidan in Dacca. Lieutenant-General A A K Niazi surrenders unconditionally to Lieutenant-General J S Aurora. In one voice, former East Pakistanis shout, *"Joi Bangla".* Bangladesh has been liberated.

Maneckshaw calls Mrs Gandhi: "Madame, we have defeated them."

Indian generals are now keen to take Pakistan on the West, where troops are waiting just outside Lahore. But the Indian Prime Minister calls for an immediate cease-fire.

December 17. India orders a unilateral cease-fire effective from 8 pm. Yahya Khan agrees.

The 14-day war is over.

But the hostilities are not. Pakistan is in turmoil, humiliated and stung, Bangladesh is jubilant, crowing with victory. India is stuck in between, with a growing problem of refugees, close to 15 million. Yahya Khan is forced to step down and Bhutto becomes Prime Minister. For all his earlier jingoistic speeches, he is eager to make peace with India. The two prime ministers agree to meet in Simla in June.

July 3, 1972, Simla. The Simla agreement is signed by two prime ministers. According to its terms, the two governments are "resolved that the two countries put an end to the conflict and confrontation that have hitherto marred their relationship and work for the promotion of a friendly and harmonious relationship and the establishment of durable peace in the subcontinent".

Brave words. The agreement goes on to state that the two countries will try and solve problems bilaterally and not through war, that they will respect each other, avoid propaganda against each other, start trade and cultural communication, withdraw forces to their own sides of the international border, accept that the line of actual control in Jammu and Kashmir is as it stood on December 17, 1971.

The pact is hailed by all except war-mongers. If few are naive enough to believe that all agreements will be adhered to, there is a definite feeling that beginnings had to be made.

Success or failure, since the Simla Agreement, India and Pakistan do not enter into direct military conflict. The rest is another story. ∎

IN OUR DEFENCE
Why India needs a strong military
By Jasjit Singh

TILL 15 August 1947, the defence of India included two tasks: that of defending Indian territory, and the defence of the Imperial Raj and its interests. Independence coalesced the two into one, that of defending India and its interests. The problem since then has been that we lost much of our territory. And the less we focused on our territories occupied by others, the greater has been the tendency to think of defence as defending "every inch" of the territory! The result, of course, has been a politico-military doctrine that requires a huge land army, mostly infantry oriented. Therefore, the question in the 50th year of Independence that must be addressed is how to approach the issue of defence in the coming decades. But before we get to answering that question, we need to be clear on some, what may be termed the key lessons of half a century of defending India.

The central lesson is that, while our defence forces are one of the most professional and dedicated volunteer military in the world, we have not been particularly successful in defending our territory. Pakistan occupies nearly one-third of the state of Jammu and Kashmir since 1948, and China occupies 48,000 sq km of our territory since the 1950s besides the 10,000 sq km illegally ceded by Pakistan in 1962 (and the 90,000 sq km constituting the important state of Arunachal Pradesh claimed by China). In both cases we have not taken any steps, or even clearly signalled that the territories occupied through military aggression will be recovered.

In the case of J & K, restricting war to the boundaries of the state in 1947-48 not only weakened our case on the state being an integral part of India, but it became a major factor in Pakistan's calculations to initiate the 1965 War. A major assumption, reinforced by its operations in the Rann of Kutch in April that year was that India would again restrict defence to the territory of the state of J & K where terrain factors are a handicap for India. That this was also the prevailing assessment among US strategic analysts could only add to the belief. The war was won finally because our forces were authorised to fight across the international border and launch a counterattack towards Lahore.

Parliament had passed a strong resolution in 1962, which continues to be valid even today, that the territories occupied by China must be recovered. But why did we lose that territory to China?

The main reason is that this was a unique situation for which we were grossly under-prepared. There had been no roads through the high Himalayas leading up to the borders. The construction of roads was started only in 1957 by which time China had already built a road through the Aksai Chin plateau. The rebellion in Tibet in 1959 precipitated the situation and the nature of dialogue to resolve the border issue changed fundamentally. There were many failures that finally led to the disastrous war — the only war that independent India lost. Many individuals failed, and the focus of analysis and history has been on those failures.

But it was really a systemic failure. The system and organisation for higher direction of defence and its management had even stopped functioning by the time we got to November 1962. Krishna Menon, who was responsible for really advancing India's indigenous base of self-reliance in defence, unfortunately virtually ignored the system set up after Independence. The Defence Minister's Committee had stopped functioning a couple of years before that, and so had

India at war: *Soldiers with a field gun*

Ministry of Defence

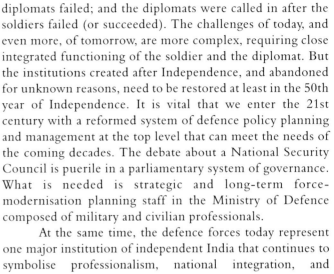

The Eastern Front: *Initial deployment and moves to concentration areas*

the Defence Committee of the Cabinet. Military operations in Goa in 1961 do not appear to have been decided or directed by any such committee — and nor was their planning for defence in 1962.

The result was a series of flawed decisions with deep influence on strategy and the strategic situation. For example, this was the only war where the combat component of the Indian Air Force (deployed for the task since 1959) was not employed although, even in US assessments, it would have made a "material difference" to the ground battle. A so-called forward defence posture was adopted when there was limited capability to sustain it militarily. Almost every military commander was changed at all levels during or just prior to the war. Many more examples can be cited.

But what is worrisome is that by focusing on individual failures, the lesson of systemic failure does not seem to have been imbibed. The disjunction between the higher military leadership and the "government", inherited perhaps from the historical caste disjunction between the Kshatriya and remaining society, has, if anything, increased since then. Notwithstanding our democratic credentials of half a century, we are a unique, and only democracy in the world that keeps the military professional outside the governmental framework and defence decision-making processes. No greater example of this disjunction could be cited compared to the reports that our production and possession of chemical weapons (and the decision to eliminate them in the 50th year of our Independence) was kept a secret from the military leadership! Or the fact that the eighth five-year Defence Plan could not be finalised even after the plan period was over!

The challenges of defence have become more complex. Traditionally, soldiers were asked to step in once the diplomats failed; and the diplomats were called in after the soldiers failed (or succeeded). The challenges of today, and even more, of tomorrow, are more complex, requiring close integrated functioning of the soldier and the diplomat. But the institutions created after Independence, and abandoned for unknown reasons, need to be restored at least in the 50th year of Independence. It is vital that we enter the 21st century with a reformed system of defence policy planning and management at the top level that can meet the needs of the coming decades. The debate about a National Security Council is puerile in a parliamentary system of governance. What is needed is strategic and long-term force-modernisation planning staff in the Ministry of Defence composed of military and civilian professionals.

At the same time, the defence forces today represent one major institution of independent India that continues to symbolise professionalism, national integration, and dedication to duty. In more than one respect, the defence forces are India itself. The Indian Army will be 250 years old in this year of India's golden jubilee of Independence. One comes across seventh generation officers in the same regiment. The defence forces have consistently displayed selfless dedication to national defence. We are now in the 26th year (32nd if 1971 is rightly treated as a unique event) without a war — the longest period in history without the military in India engaged in a war.

All previous wars, big and small, had been imposed on India. The fact that we are living for more than a quarter century without another being imposed, is a direct tribute to the defence forces and the preparedness that has deterred potential aggressors. This success, in fact, is already raising its own questions. A whole generation is now used to the absence of war. The success of defence contains the seeds of future un-preparedness, as much as it did in earlier days. National allocation for defence has had no force modernisation for more than a decade now. Conventional capability has been eroding. Nuclear challenges require a strategy of recessed deterrence and diplomacy that vigorously pursues the goal of a nuclear weapon-free world. The critical issue here is the development and deployment of intermediate range (up to 5,000 km-range) missile systems.

Self-reliance in defence equipment, where tremendous progress has been made in a country that had been de-industrialised during the previous two centuries, will need to be given a fresh impetus based on interdependence and joint ventures/collaboration in design, development, production, and sales. Decades of prevented wars have tended to use the army for an internal security role, patently a wrong instrument for the task. This will have its short and long-term negative effects. Many factors point to the need for restructuring defence forces and capabilities to meet future needs. But above all, 50 years after Independence, the defence forces now must compete for quality manpower with other sectors if the leadership needs of tomorrow are to be adequately met.

The making *of* a NATION

PAST DIVISIONS
The absurdity of the two-nation theory and the socio-political context in which it places India's Muslims
By Ali Sardar Jafri

THE two-nation theory is as absurd and confusing as the one-nation theory. There's no single definition of a nation which could be applicable to all kinds of nations existing on Earth. There are one language-nations, two-language nations and multi-lingual nations like India. If you ask who the father of the two-nation theory is, almost every nationalist Indian will say Mohammed Ali Jinnah with disgust and disapproval, and every Pakistani will say Mohammed Ali Jinnah with pride. According to me, he's not, but ultimately he accepted it and used it for the formation of Pakistan. And I also believe that Pakistan was a political bargaining counter for him. He did not get it by his own efforts. History and our own national movement collaborated with him.

India in the 19th century was emerging from feudalism and all kinds of feudal institutions, good or bad, survive till today. In the feudal period, we lived in communities. There was no concept of the modern nation that arose after the industrialisation of Europe, out of which our concept has been born. The Urdu word *'qaum'* is used for community — *baniyon ki qaum, dhobiyon ki qaum*. People like Sir Syed Ahmed Khan used it for communities when he said 'Muslim *qaum*' and 'Hindu *qaum*', because the formation of the nation had not been completed at the end of the 19th century.

These communities lived in harmony till the advent of the British. There were occasional clashes but not the situation which we are facing today of hostile communities ready to destroy bridges of understanding. So actually the differences between communities were exploited by the British, and this two-nation theory was started by Lord Curzon with the partition of Bengal in 1905. As far as I know, there was no demand for the partition of Bengal. It was opposed by Hindus, it was opposed by nationalist and secular leaders in the forefront of the movement, and ultimately they succeeded in reuniting Bengal in 1911. But the seed of trouble was sown.

The movement was so powerful, in which *Vande Mataram* was used as a slogan in Bengal, that one could not imagine that any patriot or national leader will demand partition of the country in one form or the other. Surprisingly, however by 1924 such an eminent leader as Lala Lajpat Rai, in a series of articles in the *Tribune* supported the partition of Bengal and Punjab.

"Punjab should be partitioned into two provinces, Western Punjab with a large Muslim majority to be a Muslim governed province and the same principle can apply to Bengal. Under my scheme the Muslims will have four provinces, the NWFP, West Punjab, Sind, Eastern Bengal." He clarified:

"But it should be distinctly understood that this is not a united India. It means a clear partition of India into a Muslim India and a non-Muslim India."

Will it be wrong to call Lala Lajpat Rai, a Congress President, the father of the two-nation theory and Mohammed Ali Jinnah his follower?

The Lahore Resolution of Muslim League of March 23, 1940 reads:

"Resolved that it is the considered view of this session of the All-India Muslim League that no constitutional plan would be workable in this country or acceptable to Muslims unless it is designed on the following basic principles, namely, that geographically contiguous units are demarcated into regions which should be so constituted, with such territorial readjustments as may be necessary, that the areas in which the Muslims are numerically in a majority, as in the North-Western and Eastern Zones of India should be grouped to constitute independent states in which the constituent units shall be autonomous and sovereign."

After the Lahore Resolution was passed, by 1942-43 the Communists had given it the ideological base and support of the party. This sent people like Mia Iftekharuddin, a prominent Punjab leader, to the Muslim League. Within the national movement itself, Rajagopalachari and Bhulabhai Desai had a sympathetic view of Jinnah's demand and finally Lord Mountbatten succeeded in persuading Pandit Jawaharlal Nehru and Sardar Vallabhbhai Patel to accept partition, which was later called the Mountbatten Plan. And ultimately, Mountbatten persuaded Gandhiji to support it.

Gandhiji said in a prayer meeting that people should accept Partition because, "It was the willing act of the Congress and the Muslim League." He absolved every one: "I cannot blame the Viceroy. He stood for a united India till the last. I cannot blame Jinnah. Perhaps we did not do enough to allay his fears. I cannot blame my own people. Obviously they had no choice."

The Muslim League celebrated the occasion by distributing sweets. Qaid-e-Azam Mohammed Ali Jinnah was a different man. Addressing the Constituent Assembly of Pakistan in Karachi on August 11, 1947 he said: "You are free, you are free to go to your temples, you are free to go to your mosques or to any other place of worship in the State of Pakistan... You may belong to any religion, caste or creed... that has nothing to do with the State... We are starting in the days when there is no discrimination no distinction between one community and another... We are starting with the fundamental principle that we are citizens and equal citizens of one State."

But so much communal venom had been generated during the struggles and the conflicts of over hundred years that the dream of a modern State was drowned in blood. The question of the identity of Pakistan on the basis of two-nation theory remained unsolved. Who are we? Where have we come from? And where are we going? How are we related with the Indo-Mughal composite culture of undivided India? These and related questions started bothering the writers and intellectuals of the new state of Pakistan.

Twenty-four years after the famous speech of the

Qaid-e-Azam, in the Constituent Assembly the distinguished progressive poet of Pakistan who is equally loved and respected in India, Faiz Ahmad Faiz, tried to define the national and cultural identity of Pakistan. He wrote in the April-June 1975 issue of the Urdu magazine, *Ghalib*, published from Karachi, of which he happened to be the chief editor.

"Before the partition of the subcontinent, the Muslims had a kind of political and social identity. A basic change occurred after the formation of Pakistan. Accordingly we should have formulated the (new) concept of our culture, which we did not do.

"As a result of the division of the subcontinent, a new country came into being called Pakistan and a new nation called the Pakistani nation. Pakistan is composed of different regions with their distinct cultures and ways of life (or life style)... We should not forget that these different regions have certain common features/factors which provide the basis of our culture. The most important among them is the unity of religion (*Ishtirak-e-Deen* —Islam)."

Trying to clarify the contours of the new national and cultural identity Faiz wrote:

"No doubt, our cultural heritage includes Delhi and Agra, Mir and Ghalib. Similarly Samarkand and Bukhara, Hafiz, Saadi and Rumi are parts of our cultural heritage. However, a little discrimination (*tafreeq*) is necessary between the cultural treasures and manifestations which are found in our land and those which belong to other lands.

"Of course, our relationship (*rishetey*) with Taj Mahal, Red Fort, Samarkand and Bukhara are very close or deep; yet they are not our property. Our property is Mohenjodaro, our property is Takshila, our property is Lahore, Multan, Khyber."

In the final analysis, it means that for the glory of the new Pakistani culture and nation it is necessary to keep a distance from Agra and Delhi, from Taj Mahal and the Red Fort, from Ghalib and Mir who are symbols of the beautiful composite culture of India. It is a *karishma* of the two-nation theory that an enlightened poet like Faiz has indulged in this kind of argument.

Similarly, another distinguished poet of Pakistan, Jamiluddin Aali, preached till 1997 that there should be a cultural wall of China between Hindustan and Pakistan. The irony is that Aali is from the family of the Nawabs of Loharu. He migrated from Delhi to Karachi and writes the beautiful and chaste Urdu of Delhi. He has made a name by popularising sensitive dohas of Hindi style in Urdu. The wall of China did not pass through his heart.

It is clear, therefore our national leaders and communities did not understand what was going on from a historical perspective. The British were consistent. The mistakes committed by the national movement also contributed to the partition of the country. There are controversial accounts of Nehru refusing to form a government in 1938 according to pre-election agreements with the League. I personally feel that had the Cabinet Mission Plan succeeded the history of United India would have been written differently.

H Surhawardy, who was a disciple of C R Das, after the Muslim League victory in Bengal, offered to form a joint government with the Congress, which was refused. Finally, the bitter experiences of the Interim Government (with Liaquat Ali Khan as finance minister) destroyed all the chances of keeping the country united. If we look at these factors, we find that Partition is not the victory of any political party but the failure of our national movement, just as the creation of Bangladesh can be said to be the failure of the two-nation theory.

But now we should try and look ahead, and not back. We should try to forget the trauma of that period and look at the future of the subcontinent which includes India, Pakistan, Bangladesh and Sri Lanka. India being the big brother and the inheritor of the traditions of Buddha and Gandhi should take the lead in building a modern subcontinent on the basis of mutual understanding because our interests, economic and political, are common and we need to take an enlightened view of the situation. Our celebration of the golden jubilee of Independence should be a harbinger of a better future because South Asia means the subcontinent and it has got all the potentialities of becoming a great world power, not only economically, but even spiritually.

THE EVENING OF TASHKENT

Let us make merry in a feast of love,
For the stink of blood has disappeared.
The clouds of gun-power have rained and vanished,
The war's last lightning has flashed and gone.
It is now evening in Tashkent, so fragrant with roses.

Awaken the ambergris nights of the beloved's tresses,
Light the camphor candles of those silvery arms,
Fill to overflow the goblets of long kisses.

Raise this red goblet — to the beauties of Tashkent,
And this green goblet — to the fair-ones of Lahore,
To the sirens of Delhi raise the white goblet
In which is poured the colour of love's sun.

Many hued smiles glitter on the horizon —
A sweet breeze stirs from the gentle talk —
From every lip falls a nourishing dew,
Which shall cleanse and bring forth our hope's dawn,

No grief shall now dishevel any tresses —
No youth shall have to cross the valley of fear —
Brave men shall not disembark on the death's shores —
Never shall blood and dust smear a bride's hair—
"Good News" shall never come again to a mother —
No one shall ever "Congratulate" orphans.

Though a horde of flowers shall spring from this land,
No one will know whose eyes have become narcissus,
Whose forehead this rose, whose lips this poppy,
Whose outstretched arms these dancing branches!

Only this will be said: This land is of the braves,
Of the nameless monarchs of the beauty's kingdom,
Of the lovers who dreamt of roses and died for dew.

May this dew rain endlessly on this land.
May this land never thirst for blood again.

New Delhi, January 10, 1966

The making of a NATION

THE AWAKENERS
1973

Vinoba Bhave, Sunderlal Bahuguna and Baba Amte strive to keep the conscience of the nation alive — with mixed success

"What do the forests bear? Water, soil and pure air."
— *Chipko slogan, 1970s*

APRIL 1973. Villagers in the Garhwal region of Uttar Pradesh demonstrate against the felling of ash trees in the Mandal forest.

March 1974. A group of 27 women stop contractors from felling trees.

Over the next five years, this spontaneous satyagraha by the people will be known as the Chipko movement and will spread across the Garhwal Himalayas to other forested regions of India. Inspired by the teaching of Mahatma Gandhi, encouraged by his disciples Mira Behn and Sarala Behn, the Chipko movement will gradually be associated with another Gandhian, Sunderlal Bahuguna. Like the Mahatma, Bahuguna would shame the authorities into action by fasting. He would act as a conscience for the nation, give active voice to the people's protest.

The Chipko movement is unique in its simplicity. Women of the area simply hug the trees so that contractors cannot fell them without killing them. *"Aaj Himalaya Jagega, Krur Kulhara Bhagega"* is the slogan of the 1970s, as the movement reaches its finest moment.

December, 1977, the Adwani forests are scheduled for felling. Women of the area, including the wife of the village chief who is also a contractor, tie threads round the trees, swearing protection. The contractors are driven away, only to return with armed police, in February, 1978. Again, they are foiled by women hugging trees. In December 1978, Bahuguna will go on an indefinite fast to stop trees being cut in Badiyagarh. He is arrested and confined.

When he meets Prime Minister Indira Gandhi in 1980, Bahuguna convinces her that commercial green felling in the UP Himalayas needs to be banned. The Prime Minister recommends a 15-year ban. The movement now spreads to other parts of the country, through Bahuguna's almost 5,000 km

Spring cleaning: *Bahuguna saving the Ganga for our souls*   Bhawan Singh/ India Today

march from Kashmir to Kohima, from 1981 to 1983.

The foot march is a venerable Indian method of arousing national interest. No one used it better than Gandhiji during the salt march to Dandi in 1930. In Independent India, it was one of his most dedicated non-political disciples who inherited his mantle and worked with the heart of India. It was this man who also inspired generations of activists — like Bahuguna — who would try and act as the conscience of the nation. Vinoba Bhave walked around India for 14 years with his Bhoodan movement. The principle was simple. "I have come to loot you with love. If you have four sons, consider me as the fifth, and accordingly give me my share," says Bhave to his audiences. And so they give him land, which is given to landless labourers and impoverished tenants. Bhoodan — the gift of land.

April 18, 1951, Telengana. Bhoodan is born. Bhave is holding a Harijan baby in his arms, during a visit to a Harijan

Looting with love: *Vinoba Bhave appeals to a nation's generosity*

Friends of trees: *Chipko Andolan's women activists*   Bhawan Singh/India

colony. Curious, he asks the Harijans how much land they would need to solve their problems of poverty, illiteracy, unemployment themselves? About 80 acres is the answer. Would some local landlord give it to them? In the shocked silence, V R Reddy, landowner stands up. "I will give 100 acres," he says.

The Bhoodan movement eventually translates into the Gramdan movement, where entire villages are donated and run as cooperatives. Its success flags eventually, but it proves that India has a conscience, that India can hear a voice, if someone cares to make themselves heard. Certainly, another follower of Gandhiji and Bhave hears it. At the age of 35, in the late 1940s, the Deputy Chairman of the Warora Municipal Corporation sees a young man lying in a gutter, his face and limbs festering with sores, crawling with maggots. Murlidhar Devidas Amte gets nightmares at the thought of his family suffering from leprosy. After months of inner turmoil, Anandawan is born in 1949, a rehabilitation home for lepers, in the Chandrapur district of Maharashtra. And with Anandawan, Murlidhar Devidas becomes Baba Amte.

Bhave, who died in 1982, will spend the last few years of his life trying to get cow slaughter banned. A Gandhian to the last, he never lived far away from the villages of India, simply and honestly. Both Bahuguna and Amte get international recognition and fame. Bahuguna wins the Right Livelihood Award of Norway — known as the alternative Nobel — in 1982; Amte the Magsaysay in 1985. But rather than let this turn their heads, they turn their attention to the ecological destruction of India by wanton commercialisation and unintelligent development in the 1980s and 1990s. Bahuguna trains his guns on the Tehri Dam in the Garhwal region. Amte leaves his beloved Anandawan in 1990 to camp on the banks of the Narmada to try and stop the gigantic Sardar Sarovar Dam.

India has changed since both men started on their life of sacrifice and commitment — more cynical, less spontaneous, more selfish and more greedy. But hopefully not changed so much that it cannot hear its own conscience.   ∎

The making *of* a NATION

Narmada Bachao: *Baba Amte being stopped at the Gujarat border on his way to the site of the Sardar Sarovar dam*   Namas Bhojani/ India Today

UPHILL JOURNEY
1975 —

The search for a solution to the problems in the North-East leads instead to more secession stories

JANUARY 13, 1975. A police jeep drives up to the office of the Inspector-General of Police, Mizoram. Some men in police uniforms jump out and walk into the police headquarters. They enter the room where the IGP, G S Arya, is in conference with his staff, Deputy Inspector-General of Police, L B Sewa and Superintendent of Police, K Panchapakesan. They shoot all three dead, point-blank range and walk out the way they came. No one hears them, sees them or even pretends to do either.

Arya's crime was simple. He was trying to boost the morale of the Mizoram Police, trying to recruit and trust local people, trying to use the people of Mizoram to counter the insurgency that has been crippling the state since 1947. Clearly, he was a threat to the Mizo insurgents of the Mizo National Front and Mizo National Army. Mobilising the police force would prove an effective counter to insurgency. Arya had to go.

Arya is significant in that he was the first police officer in Mizoram, to realise that insurgency cannot be contained by ignoring and sidelining the local population. However, the Indian Government's stand on the North-East has long been marked by ignorance and indifference. The British policy of non-interference — not to "meddle in the feuds and fights of savages, but to encourage trade with them as long as they are peaceful towards us," said Lord Dalhousie as Viceroy in 1879 — was carried on by Independent India.

But this is an area that is vital for India's defence, if not for the rights of the people who live here. China looms large all round the North-East and demands that due attention be paid to securing India's borders. Largely tribal in character — 116, speaking 420 of India's total 1,652 languages and dialects — the North-East, isolated by geography and alienated by ignorance and administrative indifference, suddenly found itself, on Independence, in a new country, with new rules and laws. After years of following various tribal laws, this was both difficult and to some extent unreasonable.

The North-East was also severely affected by Partition. Now completely landlocked, its supply routes which used to pass through East Bengal were now cut off. This left its already hard-to-reach regions almost completely inaccessible. Food, essentials, employment were hard to come by. Under such circumstances, frustration and added support to secessionist movements were perhaps inevitable.

The fact that subsequent governments at the Centre largely ignored the North-East or left these states to their own

Constant presence: *The Army is never far away in the North-East*

North by North-East: *The Seven Sisters*

resources, did little to inspire confidence. Most solutions attempted were ill-considered sops, and the magnanimous gesture of offering statehood to these regions hardly answered their problems. Although elections were held periodically, the people discovered that politicians, whether local or national, can be equally corrupt and callous. India's first Prime Minister, Jawaharlal Nehru, refused to have any truck with secessionists, trying instead to convince mainstream leaders that the area would not be submerged by India. Indira Gandhi played both secessionists and elected political leaders against each other, a tactic that backfired as much as it worked.

The Janata Government in between her two regimes helped considerably in making matters worse. Prime Minister Morarji Desai, on a visit to Mizoram in October 1978, spent his time sermonising rather than listening to problems. In remote and hilly areas, good roads are essential. However Desai remonstrated with the chief secretary for wasting government money on roads. In his inimitable style, Desai offended government workers and the tribal population both. Insurgency, rather than being quelled by his visit, was only encouraged.

Mizoram, however, with the work of Congress leader Lalthanwala, with the MNF's Laldenga, former chief minister Brigadier T Sailo of the People's Congress and a series of talks

between Indira Gandhi and later Rajiv Gandhi, managed to find some answers in democracy. Insurgency has been contained to some extent, since the people feel they have a government which looks after their own interests.

April 9, 1975. The Indian Army moves into Gangtok, the capital of Sikkim, surrounds the palace of the ruling Chogyal and places him under house arrest.

April 10, 1975. Kazi Lhendhup Dorji, Chief Minister of Sikkim and the Sikkim Assembly abolish the institution of the Chogyal and declare that Sikkim, so far a protectorate, is a constitutional entity of India. In a referendum held on April 14, the merger is approved by overwhelming vote.

April 26, 1975. Sikkim is India's 22nd state through the Thirty-sixth Amendment to the Constitution, ratified by Parliament on May 16, dated retrospectively. It is also India's least troublesome North-Eastern state, although it will have problems balancing a monarchic past with a democratic future.

Nagaland is not so lucky. With the winds of freedom and democracy and self-realisation blowing through the world in the 1940s, the fiercely independent Nagas started their own search for their identity and rights. Under the leadership of Z A Phizo, the Nagas had started looking for independence before August 1947, and were wary of Indian claims that they would get full constitutional rights. With Phizo truculent and adamant, the movement turned violent. Phizo was arrested in 1948, thus beginning the Naga secessionist movement. A long series of discussions and accords now began, often leading nowhere. Phizo fled India through East Pakistan and arrived in England, where he lived in exile till his death in 1990. But he continued to control events in Nagaland from his distant perch.

November 11, 1975. The Shillong Accord is signed with the Nagas. Insurgents agree to give themselves up, work overground. But hope is short-lived. A group of Naga leaders living in China at the time refuse to acknowledge the accord. Phizo himself repudiates it, so do his two lieutenants, who then also turn against Phizo. As the movement itself gets increasingly factionalised, violence only increases as does crime. Insurgency killings go up from 35 in 1990 to over 200 five years later. The political process is equally ineffective and constant complaints by the people of the corruption of Congress Chief Minister S C Jamir are ignored.

Surrounded by insurgency movements and intensely proud of their tribal identity, the Meiteis of Manipur under N Biseshwar, also search for self-determination resulting in an ethnic cleansing of Manipur's large population of Kukis. In Tripura, the situation is complicated by the influx of refugees from East Pakistan and later Bangladesh. There is constant fear of tribal identity being lost.

At no time are Pakistan and China far away from these movements. The more corrupt the local government, the greater the frustration of the people, the greater the chance of a hostile country using the situation to its advantage. Every insensitive comment, every callous act, every example of corruption only drives the North-East further to the edge. It may only be India's good fortune that it has not fallen off, 50 years since the trouble began. ∎

Covert war: *Bodo rebels arming themselves*

INSULAR APPROACH
Fear of outsiders turns Assam against itself

FEBRUARY 18, 1983, 8 am. A massive mob surrounds the village of Nellie, 45 km from Guwahati in Assam. Guns, spears, swords and daos catch the early morning light. There is no beauty in the sight, however, as enraged Lalung tribals wreak death and destruction on this settlement of 15,000 Muslim refugees from East Pakistan. The brutal attack goes on for 24 hours, and the bodies that are cut, slashed and fall into heaps are largely of women and children. As the stench of death rises nauseatingly on Saturday morning, conservative estimates put the toll at 600; the truth might be closer to over 1,700.

Nellie stands as an incident of national shame. Where were the paramilitary forces, otherwise so visible in Assam? Where was compassion, human consideration? But Nellie was also an accident waiting to happen. Assam has been sitting on a keg of explosives, since elections were called by Prime Minister Indira Gandhi. The All-Assam Students Union boycott the elections. Their leaders Prafulla Mahanta and Bhrigu Phuken, known to be moderate, are under arrest, leaving the field open to extremists. Assam burns as all over the state riotous mobs confront the police. In the days before the Nellie massacre, after polls open on February 14, there are rumours that Assamese villages have been burnt and 1,000 people killed. The investigating police find that the Assamese struck back by targetting Bodo villages and killing 30 Bodos. The final death toll is 100.

February 16, five Lalung children are found dead near Nellie. The Lalungs are against the polls, the Nellie immigrants, siding with the Congress (I), definitely for them. The Lalungs also feel that the immigrants have taken away their land. The stage is set for Nellie.

The Congress (I) wins the election with a comfortable majority and Hiteshwar Saikia is the new chief minister. But the election is also seen as a farce, in which no main Assamese parties have participated. Nor have the people of Assam — only 17.6 per cent of total votes are cast. Democracy cannot work if the people do not cooperate — or worse, if their voice is not heard.

Does the Assam problem begin with Partition when Bengali Hindus poured in from East Pakistan? With the Bangladesh War of 1971 when the state was deluged by an influx of Bengali Muslims from Bangladesh? Or did it get infinitely worse in 1979, when, under the direction of the Janata Chief Minister Golap Borbora, Deputy Inspector General of Police Hiranya Bhattacharya discovered 47,658 'foreigners' — Bangladeshis — on the electoral lists of Mangaldoi? From here, the anti-immigrant protests start burning through Assam, culminating in the polls of 1983.

These ill-judged elections create giant clefts of hatred between the Assamese, the tribals (looking for their own identity through a demand for Bodoland and formation of the Bodo Autonomous Council) and the Bengalis. Saikia tries to negotiate with the AASU and has some degree of success, as the people themselves seem horrified by the bloodshed. The AASU agrees to stop demanding the expulsion of immigrants, pre-1971.

But the United Liberation Front of Assam is not so amenable. Formed by Paresh Barua, ULFA uses terrorism to give more body to AASU demands. Robberies, kidnappings and extortion are preferred ULFA methods, and through the late 1980s, early 1990s, tea garden staff and businessmen are their targets. Pakistan, Bangladesh and the tribal insurgents in neighbouring states all help ULFA.

Assam, however, continues to try and make democracy work. In December 1985, the Asom Gana Parishad with Mahanta as chief minister comes to power, with a government mainly comprising former AASU leaders. However, before the government's five-year term is up, it is brought down by charges of corruption, ironically, from the AASU.

FIGHTING INSURGENCY
Low on policy, high on politics
By K F Rustamji

WHEN we look back at the 50 years of insurgency that we have had, we find that it has helped us to strengthen the nation in the military sense but it has retarded development and prevented us from dealing with poverty and illiteracy in the right way.

From the first day of Independence we have faced hostility over Kashmir as a continuation of the Muslim League policies of undivided India. After the attempt to annex the state failed in the first Kashmir war (1948), we had frequent attempts to incite comunal trouble, and then in 1965 well-trained commandoes, about 3,000 in number, were pushed into the state to raise a revolt, capture Srinagar, and declare that the state had acceded to Pakistan. The plan failed mainly because the Kashmiri people resisted it to a man, and the Indian Army was quick to rush to the defence of Kashmir.

Then the focus shifted to the North East when the Nagas, under Z A Phizo launched a movement for independence with a series of well-planned ambushes in which they captured weapons. The demand for separation began spontaneously as an off-shoot of the conditions created by World War II. Pakistan soon stepped in to train hostiles and make the insurgency difficult for India. It took years of continuous army pressure to subdue the movement. In the end, a group led by Jayaprakash Narayan, Rev Michael Scott and Chaliha (Chief Minister of Assam), worked out the basis of a settlement. Breaches of it have been frequent, and from time to time there is a resurgence in the shape of a crime wave. The basic fact that applies here, and probably to all insurgency areas, is that whenever there is serious unemployment and food shortage, young men are drawn towards it. Soon after, Mizoram exploded like a bomb and it was a real test of the army's endurance and skill to restore order.

From time to time there were numerous variations of the theme in Assam and Tripura and insurgency has now become one of the methods of political progress. Then the scene shifted to Punjab when the Khalistan movement provided another opportunity to Pakistan to support the movement which threatened our stability. Pakistan poured into Punjab the weapons supplied to them for fighting the Russians in Afghanistan.

Simultaneously camps for training hostiles were established in occupied Kashmir and other parts of Pakistan and hundreds of men were returned into Jammu & Kashmir to create an 'Azadi' movement. In Punjab and Kashmir, the police and paramilitary (Border Security Force and Central Reserve Police) fought alongside the army to defeat insurgency.

For some years to come the large number of weapons that are present in Pakistan and in India are likely to create problems. In Pakistan, Karachi became a battleground, and now in various parts of Punjab, a Shia-Sunni conflict has arisen owing to the availability of weapons. In India, apart from insurgency, the weapons are being used for crime on a large scale.

Both in Punjab and in Jammu and Kashmir we were more or less unprepared for the onslaught unleashed against us. Slowly and with considerable sacrifice, our security forces with the support of the local people, have blunted the thrust of insurgency. But all that has happened has had a deep impact on India and may make any type of reconciliation difficult to achieve.

Allegations of excesses have often been made. Many of them were false or deliberately exaggerated to secure the support of outside agencies stoking insurgency.

Some charges, however, were proved to be true and firm action was taken against the miscreants. The National Human Rights Commission has also stepped in to ensure that no excesses are committed. At the same time, the weaknesses of our criminal justice system have not received the attention that they deserve, and this had made the task of dealing with the problem more difficult.

The wars between India and Pakistan were clearly an extension of, or even directly caused by, insurgency. The attempts to capture Jammu and Kashmir by inducting Kabalis and Pakistan troops led to two wars in 1947 and 1965. That left a deep gash in the Indian mind and when the opportunity came in 1971, India seized it to support the struggle of the Bengalis and in the process partitioned Pakistan.

Have the two sides learnt a lesson? Both sides have paid a heavy price. The Zias and the Bhuttos may have been defeated, but there is a segment both in Pakistan and India that wants the enmity to continue. Nawaz Sharif holds out a slim hope, and in Inder Gujral we have a man who is prepared to sponsor peace. Will the leaders of the two nations be able to support peace? The conditions that Pakistan wants to lay down for a settlement of what is termed the Kashmir problem is not clear. If it means annexation of Jammu and Kashmir, it is out of the question. If it wants a plebiscite with only India and Pakistan as the options, it would be meaningless because some may want independence. If it means only a plebiscite on the Indian side and not on the Pakistan side, it would be quite inconclusive. It seems to us in India that the Kashmir problem is only a bogie used by Pakistan to keep alive an enmity which is traditional in politics, and useful to get support from abroad.

On the other hand, if there is a genuine desire to be friends there could be a confederation of some type, even a unification which would give all of us the status that we deserve in the world.

An important development has taken place in Pakistan, India and Bangladesh. It is significant that it has taken place in all these countries at the same time. The leaders have lost the trust of the people, and instead the people have begun to assert themselves and create new leaders. It is now the people who are leading in all three countries. That is the true success of democracy. The election results in all three countries have proved it. If we do not accept the voice of the people as the voice of God, let us at least show some faith in our culture, the bonds of history and geography, and the urgent, compelling need to pull our people out of poverty and illiteracy.

FUNDAMENTAL BLUNDER

June 26, 1975

After the Allahabad High Court revokes her election to Parliament, Indira Gandhi clamps a state of Emergency on an unsuspecting nation

THE President has proclaimed an emergency. There is nothing to panic about.

June 26, 1975 and democracy takes a leave of absence from India. Indira Gandhi saw the need for panic in the build-up to the proclamation to Emergency. Once proclaimed, she had, truly, little to panic about. Yet.

J R D Tata, arguably India's most respected industrialist, says, "Things had gone too far. You can't imagine what we had been through here — strikes, boycotts, demonstrations. Why, there were days I couldn't walk out of my office on to the street. The parliamentary system is not suited to our needs."

But truly, this story begins somewhere before President Fakhruddin Ali Ahmed invoked the powers conferred on him by clause 1, Article 352. At its very origins may lie the discontent sensed by a country which felt itself suppressed by a government machinery that fed it with platitudes and not essentials. The euphoria of the victory over Pakistan in the 1971 Bangladesh war is over.

Prime Minister Indira Gandhi's Garibi Hatao (Remove poverty) programme seems now more like a 'remove the poor' operation. There are promises, but never any results as politicians grow more corrupt. Strikes and protests spread across the nation. Workers are arrested, leaders jailed.

But nothing happens. Till an almost forgotten Gandhian emerges out of Bihar. Jayaprakash Narayan. He starts a countrywide campaign against corruption. His cry is 'sarvodaya', the welfare of the community made popular by Vinoba Bhave, whose disciple Narayan had been. The village as the unit that will take the country forward. To a country to whom all other paths had led nowhere, it might as well be this.

Contrast Narayan with the politicians in power. He is not self-seeking, self-serving, power-hungry. He had refused ministership in the '50s. He promises a revolution that is social, economic, political, educational and ethical. He tells a group of students in Bihar that his call for "total revolution" was "more peaceful than the freedom movement led by Mahatma Gandhi". He also says to government servants, "Your loyalty is to the National Flag and the Constitution, not to the Prime Minister or the Government of the day."

Words spoken fearlessly, brave and true. But this is February 12, 1975. India has still not come to terms with the leeway given to the people by democracy. Politicians are still feudal lords. And the Nehru dynasty is in control.

If JP's stirring, revolutionary speeches are not enough to create trouble for the Congress government led by Indira Gandhi, the Allahabad High Court rules on June 12, 1975 that Mrs Gandhi's election to the Lok Sabha from the Rae Bareilli constituency in March 1971 is void because of corrupt electoral practices. Her opponent was Raj Narain, a man who would play Fool to the Janata Party's King Lear in the days to come.

Amazed as the Congress party and Gandhi are by this, they move the Supreme Court. A conditional stay is granted on the Allahabad judgment — she can remain as Prime Minister but cannot vote in Parliament. Clearly, an untenable situation.

JP and his motley group of opposition parties — Organisational Congress, Jan Sangh, BLD, Socialist Party, Akali Dal — announce that they will launch a nationwide satyagraha. The call is for Gandhi's resignation, with a satyagraha to court arrest outside her house on Sunday, June 29.

But before Section 144 of the Criminal Procedure Code can be violated, democracy itself is under threat. "A climate of violence and hatred has been created," says the prime minister in a broadcast on June 27, 1975, "...The Opposition parties had chalked out a programme of countrywide gheraos, agitation, disruption and incitement to industrial workers, police and defence forces in an attempt to paralyse totally the Central Government."

The verdict is in. India is not fit for democracy. Fundamental rights are curtailed. Political leaders — including JP — who oppose the government are jailed. The press is heavily censored.

But the emergency is not seen quite the same way by all Indians. Some, like Tata, find it necessary in a climate that is unconducive to industrial progress. Others — the intelligentsia not least among them — say that yes, perhaps Indians need the boot if they are to be made to work. The British had it right all along. Ironically and tragically, the Emergency finds itself with a lot in common with the worst excesses of the Raj.

No freedom of expression and thought, no right to protest, no right to private property. These cannot exist without adequate responsibility, the country is told, and the determination of 'adequate' will come from the state. One newspaper protests by printing a blank front page. Others give in: the country has never performed better, progress is actually being made, the 20-point programme is terribly effective.

George Orwell's thought police could not have done it better.

Then, there is the son. Sanjay Gandhi, the good-looking rebel, is at his mother's side. His dream is for a people's car, for a country that is effective in its population control, cities that are clear of slums.

His dreams. Nightmares for those who live them out.

Thousands of men are rounded up in towns and villages by Sanjay Gandhi's workers. They are forced to undergo sterilisation operations. There is no question of consent here. If the people do not volunteer, force them. The goal is the ultimate good of the country. The ends justify all means. Stories that trickle out include old men and young boys, victims both of this untrammeled "enthusiasm". Posterity will find other words.

Even in a state of suppression, noises of dissatisfaction can be heard. *'Nasbandi ke teen dalal. Indira, Sanjay, Bansilal'*, is one slogan that meets sterilisation vans. Indira Gandhi's ears are well covered by Sanjay's pet monkeys — all is well. Perhaps it would be with almost 35,000 in jail under the Maintenance of Internal Security Act. Such draconian measures of imprisonment without trial will raise their totalitarian heads

(opposite): Dark days: *Indira Gandhi rejects fundamental rights*   India Today

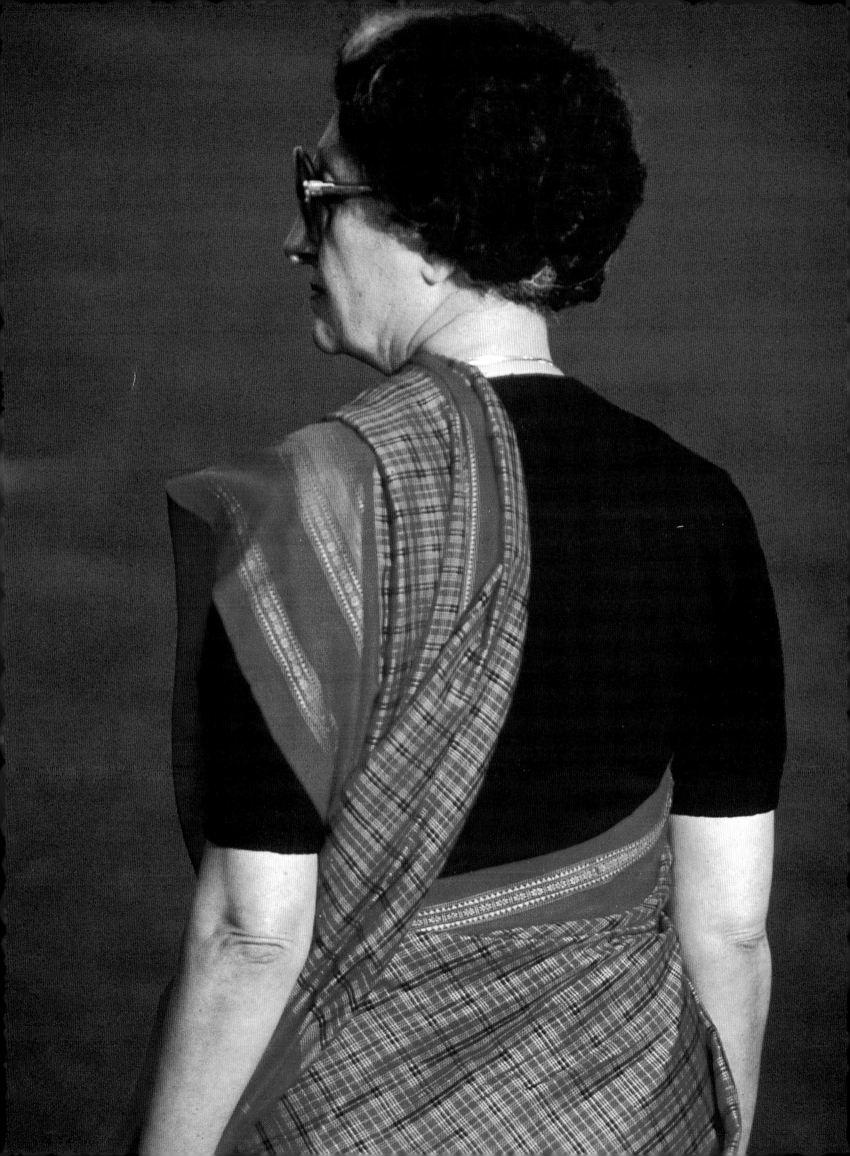

Power and folly: *Indira Gandhi and her son Sanjay*   Pramod Pushkarna/India Today

20-Point Programme

1. Steps to bring down prices of essential commodities. Streamlined production, procurement and distribution of essential commodities.

2. Implementation of agricultural ceilings and speedier distribution of surplus land and compilation of land records.

3. Stepping up of provision of house sites for the landless and weaker sections.

4. Bonded labour, wherever it exists will be declared illegal.

5. Plan for liquidation of rural indebtedness. Legalisation of moratorium on recovery of debt from landless labourers, small farmers and artisans.

6. Review of laws on minimum agricultural wages.

7. Five million more hectares to be brought under irrigation. National programme for use of underground water.

8. An accelerated power programme. Super thermal stations under Central control.

9. New development plan for handloom section.

10. Improvement in quality and supply of people's cloth.

11. Socialisation of urban and urbanisable land. Ceiling on ownership and possession of vacant land.

12. Special squads for valuation for conspicious constructions and prevention of tax evasion. Summary trials and deterrent punishment of economic offenders.

13. Special legalisation for confiscation of smugglers' properties.

14. Liberalisation of investment procedures. Action against misuse of import licences.

15. New schemes for workers' association with industry.

16. National permit scheme for road transport.

17. Income-tax relief to middle class. Exemption limit raised from 6,000 to 8,000.

18. Essential commodities at controlled prices to students in hostels.

19. Books and stationery at controlled prices.

20. New apprenticeship scheme to enlarge employment and training, specially for weaker sections.

again, but perhaps none will cause as horrific a shiver as MISA. An additional 72,000 people are in jail under the Defence of India Regulations. Not just enemy politicians — radical professors, left-wing students, trade union leaders all meet in jail.

But all is certainly not well. Sanjay and friends have targeted the area around Delhi's Jama Masjid. Does it matter to them that these Muslims have lived here for centuries? That Jawaharlal Nehru and Maulana Abul Kalam Azad had convinced them that they did not have to go to Pakistan, that Delhi was their home? Now, they beg the daughter and grandson of India'a first prime minister to spare their homes from property developers looking for quick prosperity.

April 18, 1976. The inhabitants of Turkman Gate put up a resistance to the demolition squads. The police fire. Twelve people die, many more are injured. The appeals of Sheikh Abdullah, even the President of India, Fakhruddin Ali Ahmed have come to this.

The reign of Sanjay is complete. He and his men and women — V C Shukla, Jagmohan, Bansilal, Jagdish Tytler, Ambika Soni — have free rein to wreak terror. And they do. His mother, when she hears criticism, is stung: "Those who attack Sanjay attack me". And so the world turns.

And, so do worms. International approbation begins to take its toll. In Bangladesh next door, Sheikh Mujib-ur-Rehman is assassinated. In the Congress party, Jagjivan Ram defects to form the Congress For Democracy. Other leaders in jail, with JP, now suffering from a kidney ailment that will soon debilitate him, contemplate their moves.

On *January 18, 1977,* Indira Gandhi makes an unscheduled broadcast that the Lok Sabha will be dissolved and elections will be held in March that year, "to restore the political processes on which we were compelled to put some curbs".

On *January 20,* the Janata Party is launched, as leaders of the opposition are released from jail — Morarji Desai, Charan Singh, L K Advani. The Congress finds a strong opposition for the first time. And it also hears the voice of the people. March 21, 1977 sees the Congress utterly trounced at the polls. Indira and Sanjay both lose their seats — she to Raj Narain, her old contestant.

The Shah Commission will say of the Emergency in its report, six years later:

"There is no evidence of any breakdown of law and order in any part of the country — nor of any apprehension in that behalf... But Madam Gandhi in her anxiety to continue in power, brought about instead a situation which directly contributed to her continuance in power and also generated forces which sacrificed the interests of many to serve the ambitions of a few. Thousands were detained and a series of totally illegal and unwarranted actions followed involving untold human misery and suffering."

Indira Gandhi herself would say, objecting to the attitude of the west towards her actions: "... the worst part of being under a foreign rule was the constant humiliation. Going to jail or being beaten up was a very small part of our suffering. The really galling part was that you were constantly being humiliated in your own country."

Surprisingly, many of her countrymen felt similarly during her Emergency.   ■

UNPALATABLE ORDER
How the constitution was undermined
Soli J Sorabjee

ON June 25, 1975 a Proclamation of Emergency was issued under Article 352(1) of the Constitution on the grounds that the security of India was threatened by internal disturbance. It was notified in the Gazette on June 26, 1975. As a consequence, the basic freedoms guaranteed by Article 19 of the Constitution, including freedom of expression and freedom of the press, got suspended by virtue of Article 358 of the Constitution.

For the first time in free India pre-censorship was imposed by promulgating a Censorship Order dated June 26, 1975. On June 27, 1975, a Presidential Order was issued under Article 359 suspending the right to move any court for the enforcement of the fundamental rights conferred by Articles 14, 21 and 22 of the Constitution.

Veritably, democracy in India suffered a temporary demise. Numerous persons, including senior and respected leaders of the Opposition were arrested, without any reasons being given, under the hateful Maintenance of International Security Act, notoriously known as MISA. As a result of the Censorship Order, no news, comment, rumour or other report relating to any action taken under certain provisions of the Defence of India Rules, or any action taken under MISA, could be published unless it was previously submitted to the Censor for his scrutiny and his prior permission was obtained.

Taking advantage of the Emergency, numerous repressive measures were adopted in the form of executive non-statutory guidelines and instructions were issued by the Censor to the press. One of the instructions of the Censor was "nothing is to be published that is likely to convey the impression of a protest or disapproval of a governmental measure". Consequently, anything that smacked of criticism of governmental measures or actions was almost invariably banned, even if the criticism was sober and moderate. The Censor's scissors were applied capriciously and, in a few cases, the decisions "bordered on the farcical" — quotations from Gandhi, Tagore and Nehru were banned. A statement by the chairman of the Monopolies and Restrictive Trade Practices Commission criticising the working of public sector undertakings was blacked out. Other ludicrous instances are the bans imposed on news about a member of a former royal family, Begum Vilayat Mahal, squatting at New Delhi railway station, a report about junior lawyers marching to the Delhi High Court and the news about a meeting of the Wild Life Board, which considered the grant of a hunting licence to a certain maharajah's brother.

Some of the Censor's directives were sinister, like the ones prohibiting any reference to the transfer of state high court judges, banning publication of judgments of high courts which ruled against the Censor, "killing" news of the opposition of certain state governments to proposed constitutional amendments, banning reports of alleged payoffs made during the purchase of Boeing aircraft and suppressing criticism of family planning programmes. The object was not merely withholding of information but manipulation of news and views to legitimise the Emergency and make it acceptable. One tragic consequence was that inhuman practices like forcible sterilisation of young men came to light much later after the events, by which time family planning had become an anathema to the rural masses. An urgent and important programme suffered a serious setback thanks to suppression of freedom of expression by the Censor.

By the Constitution (Thirty-Eighth Amendment) Act 1975 and the Constitution (Forty-Second Amendment) Act 1976, the powers of the judiciary were severely curtailed. Judicial review was sought to be excluded in various matters such as declaration of Emergency and imposition of President's Rule in the states.

The role of the national press in this was disgraceful. In the memorable words of L K Advani, when the press was asked to bend it chose to crawl. Leading newspapers and their editors fully realised both the absurdity and the illegality of the Censor's action but were unwilling to challenge it in a court of law. They had their own reasons. *The Hindustan Times,* one of the leading English language dailies, headed by Mr K K Birla, a prominent Indian industrialist and a staunch supporter of the Congress Party, became an unabashed supporter of the government. *The Times of India*, one-third of whose directors were government nominees, soon surrendered its independence and toed the official line. Political cartoons disappeared overnight and no one dared put out any cartoon of Mrs Gandhi which was in any way unflattering. One of India's most brilliant and popular cartoonists spent a good bit of his time worrying about the loss of his personal liberty on account of his previous sarcastic political cartoons and his portrayal of Mrs Indira Gandhi with a large nose a la Cyrano de Bergerac. *The Hindu* believed discretion to be the better part of valour and acted accordingly. The honourable exceptions were the *Statesman* and the *Indian Express*, who had to pay a heavy price for their independence and courage.

Fortunately there were a few in the press world who were willing to stick their necks out. Amongst others, they were Minoo Masani, who published a monthly journal, *Freedom First,* Astad Gorwala, the intrepid publisher of the weekly, *Opinion,* and Rajmohan Gandhi, publisher of the weekly, *Himmat.* These courageous souls challenged the arbitrary orders of the Censor in the high courts. *Sadhana* and *Janata,* Marathi and English papers, had also to wage legal battles to avert forfeiture of their presses and the orders for deposit of securities.

The role of the state high courts in protecting press freedom was commendable. The High Court of Bombay, in its landmark judgment in Binod Rao v Masani delivered on 10 February 1976, declared: "It is not the function of the Censor acting under the Censorship Order to make all newspapers and periodicals trim their sails to one wind or to tow along in a single file or to speak in chorus with one voice. It is not for him to exercise his statutory powers to force public opinion into a single mould or to turn the press into an instrument for brainwashing the public. Under the censorship order the censor is appointed the nursemaid of democracy and not its grave-digger... Merely because dissent, disapproval or criticism is expresed in strong language is no ground for banning its publication..." The State High Court of Gujarat in its judgment in C Vaidya v D'Penha castigated the censorship directives for imposing upon the people "a mask of suffocation and strangulation".

These judgments were delivered at a time when "inconvenient" judges were transferred from one state to another in India. Notwithstanding this, the high courts rose to the occasion. Indeed, it was their finest hour.

This was in sharp contrast to the role of the Supreme Court which in its judgment in ADM Jabalpur ruled, overruling eight high courts, that during an emergency an order of detention proven to have been passed mala fide could not be challenged in a court. In order to neutralise the effect of disastrous decisions, during the time of the Janata government at the Centre, Article 359 of the Constitution was amended by the Constitution (Forty-Fourth Amendment) Act 1978. Thereby Article 21, which guarantees the right to life and personal liberty, was made non-suspendable even in an Emergency.

The lessons of the infamous Emergency of 1975 are clear. Freedoms are not meant for the craven and the cringing. The role of the press in guarding its freedom and in protecting human rights of the disadvantaged and the oppressed will not depend only upon statutory and constitutional provisions. It will lie in its commitment to act as a vigilant sentinel, ever ready and unafraid to speak out against terror and oppression, embodying the spirit of Benjamin Franklin who told his compatriots: "They who would give up essential liberty to purchase a little temporary safety deserve neither liberty nor safety."

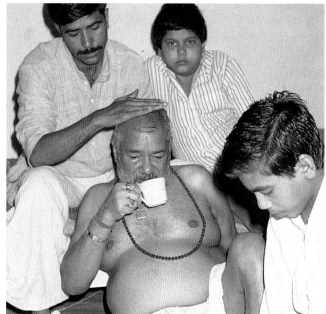
Indira's nemesis: *Raj Narain*

India Today

Rogues' Gallery

BANSI LAL

One of Sanjay Gandhi's main Gang of Four during the Emergency, Bansi Lal was Defence Minister in Indira Gandhi's Cabinet. However, he was most closely involved in the compulsory sterilisation programme, which he implemented stringently and brutally in his home state of Haryana. The extent of Bansi Lal's reign of terror and its effect on the populace was clear when he lost the 1977 elections by a margin of 1,71,000 votes.

V C SHUKLA

Flamboyant and suave, Vidya Charan Shukla was Information and Broadcasting Minister during the Emergency. This role he took very seriously so that censorship meant castration and criticism, treason. He was part of the Gang of Four (with Sanjay Gandhi, Bansi Lal and Om Mehta) and quite the ladies man in his heyday, Shukla later quit the Congress for the Janata Party to try and regain the political respectability lost during the Emergency. He then re-joined the Congress.

CANDY

The mysterious glamour girl of the Emergency. Candy, (also called Vijayakumari, Vidyabala and Vidhubala from time to time) was foisted by V C Shukla, information and broadcasting minister during the Emergency, on the Pune Film Institute. Candy, whose acting talent was debatable, did however manage to get her way at the institute through her ministerial connections. "Vidya" recalling erotic times spent with him.

AMBIKA SONI

November 1975, on the day she turned 34, Ambika Soni was elected president of the Indian Youth Congress. She was its first woman president. During the Emergency, the India Youth Congress had been chosen to play a major role in implementing the government's policies. For power seekers, her proximity to Sanjay Gandhi made her a friend to be both treasured and feared

RUKSHANA SULTANA

Glamorous and quite the socialite, Rukshana Sultana was famous during the Emergency for her string of sterilisation camps and rabble-rousing activities in Delhi's Muslim quarter. In less than a year, Sultana is supposed to have got 13,000 men sterilised. After the victory of the Janata Party in 1977, Sultana faded to obscurity, only to re-appear as actress Amrita Singh's mother.

JAGDISH TYTLER

Youth Congress and friend of Sanjay Gandhi, the bearded Jagdish is best remembered for his participation in Indira Gandhi's younger son's Clean-up Delhi for the developers campaign. His role in the diabolical demolitions of Muslim homes at the capital's Turkmangate area led, eventually, to his political isolation. A few years later, his political career was resurrected, but Tytler never had the same clout again.

(India Today)

FLAMING SUCCESS

August 15, 1975

The success of Sholay gives India its first curry western. And audiences a taste for violence and excess

Comrades in arms: *Dharmendra and Amitabh Bachchan as criminals fighting for justice*

UGUST 15, 1975. *Sholay* is released in cinema halls all over India. It is advertised as a film with "the greatest story ever told", "the greatest star-cast ever assembled". Lack of modesty perhaps, but the flames lit by *Sholay* will brighten up Indian cinema for some time to come.

Not for film critics, however.

Says an August, 1975 review in *The Illustrated Weekly of India:* "The stereophonic and other technical innovations redeem *Sholay* from the shallows. Ramesh Sippy has introduced a feeling of verve and some of the action is gripping. But no sooner you are out of the theatre, it is gone; you realise that a story built on negative emotions like hatred and violence can have no lasting impression on the mind."

The review goes on to say: "Where the film fails is in its music — there is not one song that can be singled out as a noteworthy composition. Either R D Burman has run out of ideas or he has lost the urge to create."

Damning words. But not isolated in thought or expression. *December 1975.* Another reviewer, this time in *India Today:* "But, a film cannot live by technique alone and it is here that *Sholay* looks like a dead ember."

Yet, by December 1975, it has already been established that *Sholay* is a film burning bright and long, like no other in the great Indian theatre of reel life. It certainly does have an impressive star cast. Sanjeev Kumar, Dharmendra, Amitabh Bachchan, Hema Malini, Jaya Bhaduri, and a powerful newcomer, Amjad Khan, playing the villain. It has a hard story of revenge and violence. It is

shot like a Western, all horses and holsters and stark countryside. It has catchy dialogue and catchy tunes. It has the admired technique — stereophonic sound, a 70 mm screen, slick camerawork. Damned by faint praise, *Sholay* shrugs off the insults and touches a very powerful — and lucrative — chord in Indian hearts.

The critics are quick to catch on. From being a dead ember, *Sholay* is seen as a film that is representative of its times. These are hard and cynical days for India, the 1970s. Life is tough, and after the 1971 war with Pakistan over Bangladesh, there has been little to inspire the more positive human emotions. The imposition of the Emergency by Indira Gandhi in 1975 has meant that whatever little juice was left in life has been squeezed out. Indeed, the rumours whisper, even Sholay almost had its flames doused. The producer, G P Sippy and his director son Ramesh, goes the gossip, had to pay Rs 20 lakh to get the film passed by the Censor Board, with its violence and all intact.

The violence in *Sholay* is not to be taken lightly. In no story shown on screen in India before has physical brutality been depicted with such severity and style, and to so many whistles and clapping. The plot, curry Western or not, is simple. A police officer catches a dangerous and notorious dacoit, who escapes from custody. The dacoit then kills the police officer's entire family, and after the officer retires and comes home, captures him and cuts off his arms. The dacoit lives practically on the officer's doorstep, wreaking his terror across the district. Seeking revenge, the officer contacts two former jailbirds of his acquaintance — petty thieves with tremendous courage and hearts of gold — and

The end for Gabbar: *Amjad Khan's sinister style takes India by storm*

employs them to get the dacoit.

Before the story itself opens out, then, *Sholay* has already established its blood and revenge theme. The violence is both suggested and graphic, making it a first for Hindi cinema. In many ways, this film will be a precursor for the later gore-and-guts C-graders that will take over cinema halls. Yet, the violence of *Sholay*, in a time when films were more romantic, more family and social dramas, is strangely refreshing. And, at the same time, more appealing and reflective of society. An avid *Sholay* fan assesses his reaction a few years later: "What we see in *Sholay* is a society that is corrupt. Criminals have the power. Innocent people are made to suffer. This is exactly what we find in the society in which we live. The way things are portrayed in Sholay, there is no hope of change through peaceful means. If society continues the way it is now, more and more people will be subject to hardships and unfair treatment. Therefore things have to change. If the only way available is violent means, people will be forced to use it to create a better society."

Yet *Sholay* appeals on various levels — not just that of discontentment with society, a common attraction with popular Indian cinema. *Sholay* is also immensely popular for its dialogue, its derivative story by hit writers Salim-Javed, its songs and the acting of its multi-starrer cast. Sanjeev Kumar as the police officer, Thakur Saheb in the film, is all controlled power and rage-under-the-surface. His is undoubtedly the pivotal character in the film, and the kingpin on which the plot revolves. His acting skill is never in doubt, Kumar fits into his role, down to the empty, flapping sleeves, of a man handicapped by both his physical impotence and his all-consuming anger. The two thieves, Veeru and Jai, played by Dharmendra and Amitabh Bachchan, are counters to Thakur Saheb's personalised revenge. Professionals, very close friends and ultimately, do-gooders in spite of their criminal past, Veeru and Jai play the role of popular heroes. Yet, here too, *Sholay* achieves a shift. The film-maker's focus is, not unnaturally, on Dharmendra, who plays a slightly oafish Veeru and is the bigger star at the time. But the thunder is already being stolen by the lanky Jai — Amitabh Bachchan has already tasted success with Zanjeer in 1973. *Sholay* is going to catapult him to levels never seen before in Indian cinematic history. Given Dharmendra's higher billing, the film concentrates its romantic interest on the scenes between him and the village *tangewali*, played by an ebullient Hema Malini. But it is the long, lingering looks exchanged between Jai and the Thakur's widowed daughter-in-law — his only surviving family member — played by Jaya Bhaduri that catch public attention.

The character, however, who is the real find, is Amjad Khan as the dacoit, Gabbar Singh. His exaggerated style of dialogue delivery, manic laughter, perverse humour make him into a household hero. When children cry at night, mothers tell them to go to sleep quickly or Gabbar Singh will get them, Khan announces menacingly at the start of the film. Yet, all over India, it is children who will imitate Gabbar Singh, and find him fascinating so that within a few years, this venal, even bestial character, will be used to sell biscuits — to children of course.

Many later screen villains will try and copy Khan's success with Gabbar Singh — the actor himself included — but this charisma can never be repeated.

An apt, if hyperbolic, reflection of society, or just a happy

Powerhouse performance: 'Thakur' Sanjeev Kumar   Sippy Films

ART OF THE MATTER
The growth of parallel cinema in India
By Shyam Benegal

POPULAR cinema in India did not change with the coming of Independence. With a form inherited from the popular urban theatre of the late 19th century and a tradition, however tenuous, going back to the folk performing arts, popular cinema shapes its content to suit its form. The form itself is notable for some compulsory features — song and dance interludes, a central romance and familial melodrama. This format gives films of the popular cinema a familiar, perennial and unchanging look.

However, to conclude that there is very little to choose between one film and another in the popular film genre would not be quite correct. There were and continue to emerge some outstanding film-makers in this genre.

In pre-Independence India, there were film-makers like Sohrab Modi, Mehboob, V Shantaram, Fatehlal and Damle, who made memorable films. The first three among these continued their illustrious careers well after Independence. Many of their films had a strong nationalistic sentiment disguised in stories set in mythology, history and contemporary fables, particularly during the colonial period when censorship was very strict and any hint of anti-colonial sentiment was ruthlessly put down.

In the immediate post-Independent India, several film-makers emerged who dealt with social issues echoing the hopes and expectations of a newly independent nation within the popular cinema format. Among the most outstanding of these were Raj Kapoor, Bimal Roy and Guru Dutt. What caused a new cinema to happen was the fact that the format of popular cinema seemed incapable of rendering a realistic portrayal of life, nor did it seem capable of individual artistic expression. Some tentative moves in this direction took place even before India became free. These included Khwaja Ahmed Abbas's *Dharti Ke Ld* (banned by the colonial government) and Chetan Anand's *Neecha Nagar*.

The first International Film Festival held in India in 1952 was a catalyst in this process. The post-war movements in the cinema of Italy, France, the USSR and Japan served as the inspiration, particularly the neo-realist films from Italy which brought cinema closer to the dream of everyday life.

By the mid-50s, Satyajit Ray had made his first film, *Pather Panchali*, to be soon followed by Ritwik Ghatak's *Ajantrik*. Bimal Roy had made *Do Bigha Zamin* a couple of years earlier. Mrinal Sen made his first film too during this time. Much of this was confined to Bengal. This was a seminal phase of what a couple of decades later would be seen as the parallel cinema movement. It was in 1952 again that the government of India set up the S K Patil Committee to look into the problems of the film industry and articulate a film policy. The creation of institutions such as the Film and Television Institute of India, the Film Finance Corporation (later the National Film

blending of the right ingredients in the right place at the right time, *Sholay* runs, for instance, for 267 weeks at Minerva Cinema in Mumbai between 1975 and 1980. During and after its theatre-run, it is seen and re-seen on the video circuit. Long-playing records and cassettes are made of its dialogue, memorised by children and adults alike. Mimicry artists make a fortune out of playing roles from the film — from the huge Gabbar Singh to the tiny cameo played by Jagdeep as a timber merchant to Dharmendra's drunken suicide-proposal scene to Hema Malini. R D Burman's throaty *'Mehbooba, Mehbooba'* is heard in discotheques even 20 years later.

Multi-starrers, with violence as the main theme, have now arrived in India for keeps. But nothing, perhaps, can create the right chills as Gabbar Singh's characteristic call. *Arey ho Saambha?*, he still shouts, down the generations.   ■

10 Top Hits of Indian Cinema Since 1947

1	Mother India (1957)
2	Mughal-E-Azaam (1960)
3	Sholay (1975)
4	Jai Santoshi Maa (1975)
5	Ram Teri Ganga Maili (1985)
6	Maine Pyaar Kiya (1989)
7	Aankhein (1993)
8	Hum Aap Ke Hai Koun..! (1994)
9	Dilwale Dulhaniya Le Jayenge (1995)
10	Raja Hindustani (1996)

Source: *Trade Guide*

Development Corporation) and the Children's Film Society were designed to encourage the making of films that would be responsive to the aspirations of a newly independent country.

By the 1960s, some film-makers in Kerala had made films that fit the definition of new cinema. Several of them based their work on acknowledged literary works. These films were notable for their realistic portrayals of life dispensing with the conventions of popular cinema. When the first graduates of the FTII came on the scene, the new cinema took on the aspects of a movement. Film-makers like Adoor Gopalakrishnan spread the movement in Kerala. Girish Karnad and B V Karanth – neither of whom were from the FTII – made their first films in Kannada. By the beginning of the 1970s, film-makers in Mumbai like M S Sathyu, Basu Chatterjee, Mani Kaul, Kumar Shahani and Shyam Benegal heralded its presence in the Hindi cinema while Satyadev Dubey and Govind Nihalani jointly made films that were the first of its kind in Marathi.

It was in the '70s that the new cinema had come to stay. With the new cinema came a new breed of actors, particularly in Hindi. Most of them had learnt their craft either from the National School of Drama, the FTII, institutions set up by the government after Independence, or from the stage. Many of them did not possess the kind of conventional looks favoured by the film industry. Their credentials depended on their high acting ability.

Among the first generation of these actors are the very well-known Shabana Azmi, Smita Patil, Anant Nag, Naseeruddin Shah, Amrish Puri, Om Puri, Kulbhushan Kharbanda, later to be followed by Anupam Kher, Anita Kanwar, Ila Arun, Neena Gupta, Soni Razdan, Satish Shah, K K Raina and even later by Seema Biswas, Rajit Kapur, Pallavi Joshi, Rajeshwari Sachdev and many others. Each generation brought a new set of actors on the scene. Today, actors like these have become indispensable to the film and television industry as a whole, not necessarily to play romantic leads but in roles that get well-defined by the very fact of their playing them.

Shabana Azmi is the name that first comes to mind as one of the finest dramatic actresses to emerge from the parallel cinema. The three-time National Award winner for her performances, Shabana comes from an illustrious family. Her father Kaifi Azmi is one of the best Urdu poets of his generation. But not possessed of the conventional looks sought by the film industry, she represented the situation of Indian women on the screen that was to have great influence in the manner in which women's roles would be conceived and played in the cinema over the next two decades after her initial appearance in *Ankur.*

Smita Patil, her spectacular but brief film career cut short by death, was the other icon of parallel cinema. Unlike Shabana, she was not a trained actress. An abundance of natural talent and her ability to give highly focused performances won Smita several national laurels and a very large following.

Starting his working life as a bank clerk, Anant Nag made his debut in the cinema with *Ankur.* His film career really took off in Kannada films where he went on to become a matinee idol. However, even more than films, politics has been his passion. He is now a minister in the Karnataka cabinet.

Naseeruddin Shah is arguably one of the best actors working in cinema today. He was the mainstay of many a film of the parallel

Actors' actors: *Naseeruddin Shah and Shabana Azmi*   India Today

cinema since the '70s. He is an actor both by profession and vocation. Acting is an all-consuming passion with him. His commitment to the cinema is matched by his commitment to the theatre.

Another actor who shares many of the traits with Naseer is Om Puri. A fellow alumnus at the National School of Drama and FTII, Om Puri too appears to have been born to be an actor. With his pronounced unconventional looks and bearing, it was doubtful that he would have been able to make any kind of headway in popular cinema if it wasn't for the memorable performances he gave in films of the new cinema genre.

Amrish Puri, an indispensable actor of popular cinema for the last two decades, started his professional acting career after a stint in insurance. It was during that time that he became well-known in theatrical circles in Mumbai for his finely-etched performances in Satyadev Dubey's productions of Mohan Rakesh's and Girish Karnad's plays. He followed this with exceptional performances in films of the new cinema like *Nishant, Manthan* and *Bhumika.* This led him to the mainstream popular cinema where his career took a dramatic upturn when he became the archetypal villain you most loved to hate. He has been a continuing asset to popular cinema for over 20 years with a career that has only been overshadowed by Amitabh Bachchan.

The movement itself, if it could be called that, started to decline with the coming and proliferation of nationwide television. The single biggest reason, of course, was the moving away from cinema to television of its most loyal audience – the urban class. Then the quality of many of these films deteriorated because of their shoestring budgets The support of the state by way of the National Film Development Corporation helping to produce such films was a double-edged sword. It offered an opportunity to make films that, left to the market forces, could not have been made. But this support weakened the motivation of the film-makers to reach an audience. This often led to films that were obscure, uncommunicable, poorly or ineptly executed.

A third factor, equally important, has been the escalating production costs of films. Considering the overall market for such films, the cost increase makes them less viable than before.

With real estate prices having skyrocketed in urban India, cinema houses have become less profitable to run. Unless multiplexes with multiple screens with seating capacities varying between 200 and 300 seats are built, cinema as an industry is in jeopardy. The fate of the new cinema, curiously enough, is tied to that of the popular cinema. Once multiplex cinemas become the rule, there is no doubt that the film industry as a whole will look up.

HAPPENINGS

1967-1976

Dr J V Narlikar

January 1
A mob sets fire to the Eden Garden cricket stadium in Calcutta, charging that the authorities oversold seats, the West Indies win the series 2-0

January 23
Ariyakudi Ramanuja Iyengar, doyen of Carnatic music, dies

February 8
Prime Minister Indira Gandhi is hurt on her nose and mouth in a stone-throwing incident during an election meeting in Bhubaneshwar. She is operated on two days later

February 24
The Nizam of Hyderabad dies and Barkat Ali Khan, 34, is recognised as his successor

May 4
Dr J V Narlikar, eminent scientist, is awarded Cambridge University's Adams Prize for his research work on Gravitation and Cosmology

May 9
Dr Zakir Hussain is elected President of India

February 13
A B Vajpayee is elected President of the All-India Jan Sangh

February 20
Asia's first heart transplant operation is performed by Indian surgeons at KEM Hospital, Bombay

March 12
The Indian cricket team wins their first overseas 'rubber' against New Zealand 3-1

March 19
The Deccan Express rams into the stationary Birur-Hubli Passenger at Yalviga, 47 km from Hubli; 56 people are killed, 41 injured

April 20
Ramu, the wolf boy, admitted into Balrampur hospital, Lucknow, since January 1954, dies

April 23
Celebrated musician, Ustad Bade Ghulam Ali Khan, dies

May 27
The second Jawaharlal Nehru Award for International Understanding for 1966 is awarded to Reverend Martin Luther King posthumously

June 28
Air-India gets a $ 60 million US loan to buy two Boeing 747 aircraft, popularly known as the Jumbo Jet

February 3
Tamil Nadu Chief Minister, C N Annadurai, dies

March 20
Lieutenant-General S H F J Manekshaw is to be the next Chief of Army Staff

May 3
Dr Zakir Husain, President of India, dies of a heart attack in Delhi. Vice-President V V Giri is sworn in as Acting President

June 4
Sucha Singh and two other accused in the Pratap Singh Kairon murder case are sentenced to death

June 8
Lieutenant-General J S Aurora takes over as General Officer Commanding-in-Chief of the Eastern Command

June 13
Prahlad Keshav Atre, Marathi writer, dramatist and editor of Maratha, dies

January 23
Reservations for Scheduled Castes and Scheduled Tribes in Parliament and State legislatures are extended for 10 years

February 19
The Union Government appoints a committee, headed by Justice K N Wanchoo, to suggest measures to counter evasion of direct taxes

March 23
Two successive earthquakes around the town of Broach in Gujarat leave 35 dead and over 200 injured

April 17
Violinist Yehudi Menuhin is chosen to receive the 1968 Jawaharlal Nehru Award for International Understanding

April 20
For the first time in Independent India's history, President V V Giri appears in a court of law as a respondent witness in a petition challenging his election as the Head of State, which the Supreme Court upholds on May 11

May 7
A procession of 10,000 people is attacked in Bhiwandi, 30 km from Bombay, causing week-long communal riots, about 200 people are killed, The riots spread to Jalgaon, Mahad and Thana

May 29
Dr Telo Mascarenhas, 71-year-old Goa freedom fighter, is released from a Lisbon jail where he had spent 10 years

January 25
Himachal Pradesh becomes India's 18th state

May 4
Noted sarod exponent Amja Ali Khan wins the first prize at the second International Music Forum for Asia held in Paris

June 6
The second report of the Law Commission suggests a drastic overhaul of the Indian Penal Code to provide, among other things, rigorous punishment for gheraos and attempted self-immolation for political purposes and a time-limit for the prosecution of minor offences

---

1967   1968   1969   1970   1971

October 9
About 7 lakh people are rendered homeless and 60,000 houses damaged in a cyclone that hits Cuttack and Balasore

October 12
Dr Ram Manohar Lohia, Samyukta Socialist Party leader, dies in New Delhi

November 9
Krishna Hutheesing, sister of Jawaharlal Nehru, dies

November 14
C K Nayadu dies. India's first cricket captain, renowned for his legendary batting and brilliant fielding

November 14
Bishamber Singh wins the silver medal at the World Freestyle Wrestling Championship in Delhi

December 11
Several cities in Western India including Bombay, Poona, Panaji, Surat, Hyderabad and other places are hit by an earthquake. The worst devastation is at the epicentre at Koyna Nagar. Over 210 people are officially stated to have been killed, over 1,900 injured

October 2
President Dr Zakir Husain inaugurates the Gandhi Birth Centenary celebrations

October 16
Dr Hargobind Khorana, an eminent scientist of Indian origin now settled abroad, shares the Noble Prize for Physiology and Medicine

December 29
Jaideep Mukherjee wins the men's single title in the Asian Lawn Tennis championship

July 25
A fire at the thatched stables at the Palace Grounds in Bangalore kills 39 race horses, including some top class animals

September 18
The worst communal riots since Partition are sparked off when a Jagannath temple is attacked by a Muslim religious procession, in Ahmedabad. Riots continue for eight days, 150 die and 1,000 are injured

October 1
Frontier Gandhi, Khan Abdul Gaffar Khan arrives in India after 23 years to take part in the Gandhi Centenary Celebrations

October 26
The Apollo-11 astronauts are welcomed in Bombay

November 7
A cyclone kills 110 people in the coastal districts of Andhra Pradesh

July 21
13 passenger buses and five taxis carrying pilgrims to Badrinath, six goods truck and a military vehicle are washed away by the flooded Alaknanda at Belakurhi in Uttar Pradesh

August 5
Tiger shooting is banned for five years in 10 states and two Union Territories

October 23
Prime Minister Indira Gandhi addresses the Silver Jubilee session of the United Nations

November 15
Indian driver Nazir Hussain wins the second Asian Highway Motor Rally

December 22
The 11-member Samyukta Vidhayak Dal ministry, headed by Karpoori Thakur, becomes the eighth to assume office in Bihar since the 1967 general elections

August 2
Parliament approves the Medical Termination of Pregnancies Bill seeking liberalisation of the abortion law

December 9
All 20 passengers and crew on board an Indian Airlines flight from Trivandrum to Madras via Madurai are killed when the Hs-780 Avro crashes near Chinnamanoor about 140 km from Madurai

December 18
Indira Gandhi is awarded the Bharat Ratna

Dr Zakir Hussain

Balraj Sahni

January 4
The Institute of Criminology and Forensic Science, the first of its kind in Asia, is inaugurated in New Delhi

January 9
India becomes self-sufficient in rice with an all-time record production of 412.45 million tonnes in 1970-71

January 9
India becomes the top film producer in the world with a record 4,334 feature films made in 1971

January 23
Film producer B N Sircar is awarded the 1971 Dadasaheb Phalke Award

January 24
The Government of India announces an increase in car prices. The ex-factory price of Ambassador goes up by Rs 127, the Fiat by Rs 259 and the Standard Herald by Rs 459

January 26
A national memorial to the 'Amar Jawan' is installed at India Gate, New Delhi

March 31
Actress Meena Kumari dies in Bombay. Known as the tragedy queen of the silver screen, her roles in Baiju Bawra, Saheb Bibi Aur Ghulam and Pakeezah are memorable

April 14
85 Chambal ravine dacoits lay down their arms before the Sarvodaya leader, Jayaprakash Narayan, in Jaura, Madhya Pradesh

April 24
Noted artist, Jamini Roy, dies

June 3
The first modern warship built in India, IS Nilgiri, is commissioned

Dr Karan Singh

January 1
Vidya Wati, mother of Shahid Bhagat Singh is awarded the honorific 'Punjab Mata' and a monthly pension of Rs 1,000

March 16
Dr Karan Singh, Minister of Tourism and Civil Aviation, resigns from the Cabinet, accepting moral responsibility for the crash of an Indian Airlines Avro trainer aircraft in Sikanderabad, killing all three pilots in the plane. It is not accepted

April 13
Balraj Sahni, well-known film character actor, dies

April 28
Ramdhari Singh 'Dinkar' wins the 1972 Bharatiya Jnanpith Literary Award for 1972 for his poetical work Urvashi

June 5
M S Golwalkar, Rashtriya Swayamsevak Sangh chief, dies in Nagpur

February 4
Dr Satyendra Nath Bose, physicist and noted professor, famous for his 'Bose Statistics' dies

February 19
Oil struck at a depth of 962 metres in the first well drilled by ONGC's 'Sagar Samrat' at Bombay High

February 21
In a head-on collision between the Dehra Dun Varanasi Janta express and a stationary goods train near Moradabad, 42 people are killed and 54 injured

April 29
Thirty-three people are killed and 23 injured when a Kerala State Road Transport Corporation bus rolls into a 1,500 ft ravine near Munnar in Kerala

April 29
India completes the repatriation of about 93,000 Pakistani Prisoners of War and civilian internees who surrendered to the Joint Indo-Bangladesh Command in Bangladesh on December 16, 1971

May 12
Sheikh Mujibur Rahman, Prime Minister of Bangladesh, arrives in New Delhi on a five-day official visit

May 21
A Calcutta-bound bus skids into the Ganga near the Pahelzaghat railway station in Bihar, killing 80

Dr Salim Ali

January 2
Railway Minister L N Mishra is injured in a bomb explosion at Samastipur at the inauguration ceremony of the Samstipur-Muzaffarpur rail link. He succumbs to his injuries the next day

January 29
India loses the fifth and final cricket Test and the rubber 2-3 to West Indies at Bombay

March 15
India wins the Third World Cup hockey tournament at Kuala Lumpur, defeating Pakistan 2-1

March 17
Dr Sarvepalli Radhakrishnan, former President of India, dies in Madras

April 24
2,500th anniversary of Lord Mahavira's Nirvana observed

May 2
Padmaja Naidu, former Governor of West Bengal, dies in New Delhi

January 6
About Rs 1,500 crore is admitted to the government upto December 31, 1975, in the Voluntary Disclosure Scheme

January 17
Prakash Padukone creates a new Indian record when he wins the men's singles crown for the fifth year in succession in the National Badminton Championship

February 1
Dr Salim Ali, Indian ornithologist gets the J Paul Getty Wild Life Conservation Prize

February 2
The 11th Shahi Imam of Jama Masjid, Syed Hamid Bukhari, dies in New Delhi

February 7
Ritwik Ghatak, well-known film director, dies in Calcutta

February 16
After completing the formality of winning the men's singles crown within two minutes, top-seeded Niraj Bajaj of Maharashtra goes on to bag the men's doubles crown at the 37th National Table-Tennis Championship in Jaipur

March 22
Prices of passenger cars are reduced substantially with immediate effect; Premier Padmini becomes cheaper by Rs 4,037, Ambassador by Rs 4,160, the Standard Gazel by Rs 1,059. New all-inclusive prices: Premier Rs 32,905, Ambassador Rs32,170, Gazel Rs 254,041

April 16
The National Population Policy raises the minimum marriage age for boys and girls to 21 and 18 respectively

May 18
India and Pakistan decide to resume diplomatic relations and restore all severed links within a week from July 17

1973   1974   1975   1976

August 15
The six-digit Pin Code (Postal Index number) system of addressing letters for speedy sorting, transporting and delivery comes into effect

October 2
The Bombay TV Centre is commissioned

October 11
The 40 km long Leh-Nobra road in Ladakh, the highest roadstrip in the world, is opened to traffic

October 19
Former shipping magnate, Dharma Teja is sentenced to rigorous imprisonment for terms extending to three years and fined Rs 14.3 lakh on eight charges of criminal breach of trust, forgery and falsification of accounts of the Jayanti Shipping Company

November 18
The Indian Board for Wild Life adopts the tiger as the National Animal in place of the lion which had enjoyed this honour since 1967

na Kumari

July 29
Vijay Amritraj wins the men's singles title in the First Volvo International Tennis Tournament at Bretton Woods, New Hampshire

September 13
President V V Giri decides to forgo with immediate effect 10 per cent of his net emoluments in view of the country's economic situation

November 1
Mysore is renamed Karnataka and the Union Territory of Laccadive, Minicoy and Mindivi Islands is called Lakshadweep

Begum Akhtar

August 20
Fakhruddin Ali Ahmed is elected India's fifth President

August 25
The Supreme Court rules that the President and Governors of states shall exercise their normal constitutional powers only upon and in accordance with the advice of their ministers

August 31
M S Subbulakshmi, noted singer, receives the 1974 Ramon Magsaysay Award for public service

October 6
V K Krishna Menon, former Defence Minister, dies in New Delhi

October 29
The All-India Lawn Tennis Association decides not to play South Africa in the Davis Cup final at Poona because of the latter's apartheid policy

October 30
Begum Akhtar, noted ghazal and thumri singer, dies in Ahmedabad

October 31
A fire in a second-class bogey of the Sealdah bound Upper India Express kills 52 passengers and injures 36, near Allahabad

September 26
Rohini-300, a single stage sounding rocket, developed at Vikram Sarabhai Space Centre, Trivandrum, is successfully flight-tested from Thumba

October 2
K Kamaraj, former Chief Minister of Tamil Nadu and former President of Indian National Congress, dies in Madras

October 31
Sachin Dev Burman, music composer and director, dies in Bombay. His lilting music drew heavily from folk tunes His songs were associated with Guru Dutt and Dev Anand

November 23
Vijay Amritraj wins the Indian Grand Prix Tennis Championship at Calcutta, defeating Manuel Orantes of Spain

Mukeshchandra Zoravarchand Mathur

July 22
With the maiden run of the Amritsar-Lahore Express, rail links between India and Pakistan resume after a lapse of 11 years

August 22
An overcrowded public bus plunges 13 metres into an embankment at Lilji Dam near Rewa in Madhya Pradesh, killing 97 passengers

August 27
Playback singer, Mukeshchandra Zoravarchand Mathur, popularly known as Mukesh, dies in Detroit. He was known as the voice of Raj Kapoor

November 29
Prabhat Ranjan Sarkar, alias Anand Murti, chief of the outlawed Ananda Marg and four of his followers are sentenced to life imprisonment

December 12
Ramesh Krishnan, 15, scores a facile 6-2, 6-4 win over his father Ramanathan Krishnan in the men's singles final of the All-India Hard Court Tennis Championship

December 18
Nirupama Mankad wins the women's singles title in the National Lawn Tennis championship at Hyderabad defeating Susan Das 6-4, 6-3

December 30
International Subscriber Dialing between New Delhi and London is inaugurated by Communications Minister S D Sharma

"The good of the people is the chief law."
— Cicero, De Legibus, 3, 3, 8

A frail old woman, revered on the streets of a dying city is given the world's highest secular award for her services to humanity. Another old woman raises her voice against the inequities of the legal system. A grossly underestimated cricket team brings home the sport's most valuable trophy. It would seem like a decade of high achievement and honour. But hark!

Unmitigated hope bears the seeds of unmitigated disaster. A military assault on the most holy shrine of the Sikh religion leads to the bloody assassination of one of India's most enduring Prime Ministers. The death of Indira Gandhi leads to a new calibration of Indian politics. Even if she is replaced by her son, there is the undeniable conviction that an era has ended, and a new one is still waiting to be born.

In the interim, India grapples  with the problems of division and dissension Of new voices seeking attention in the amphitheatre. Of new communities, breaking out from traditional moulds. The nation's forgotten, downtrodden, dispossesed are looking for recognition and their might will reverberate into the future. In Bhopal, the country sees the horrific face of the world's worst industrial disaster, and in that will lie the realisation that economic growth must be contained within human compunctions.

For the moment, too many of the sounds heard will be of dissatisfaction, compounded and confounded by the current apathy. Tumult and turmoil, however, are still signs of growth, of a nation grappling with its problems. Some of these will be self-created, others will be historic, most will be a combination of these and other indefinable factors. But they all speak of a desire to be better, to do better. Much as the past is comfortable, the future beckons with all its signs of uncertainty and probable reward.

1977 4 *1986*

PROMISES AND LIES

1977 - 1980

Jayaprakash Narayan's promise of a people's government falls to the Janata Government's internal politicking

ALL India Radio interrupts its regular programming at 1.10 pm, March 23, 1979: Jayaprakash Narayan is dead. News agencies pick up the news and the nation is alerted. Well-wishers and reporters try to get into Jaslok Hospital where Narayan was being treated. President Neelam Sanjiva Reddy is on his way to Bombay.

1.15 pm, K S Hegde, Speaker of the Lok Sabha, informs the House, having just heard of JP's death from Prime Minister Morarji Desai. Two minutes silence is observed. The House is adjourned.

Half an hour later, Janata Party President Chandra Shekhar announces from a loudspeaker outside Jaslok that JP is, in fact, alive. His debilitating kidney ailment does mean, though, that he is in a critical condition.

So, another day, another monumental blunder for the Janata Party Government in power.

Conceived in jail and born in freedom on January 20, 1977, the Janata Party holds the hopes of a nation shattered by the emergency in its hands. But old, venerable and various as these hands are, guided as they are by a gentle Gandhian with a

dream of social change that will bring peace and prosperity to all India, they soon appear to be woefully inadequate.

This inadequacy is all the more apparent because of the obvious lack of unity. The Jan Sangh, the Organisational Congress, the Bharatiya Lok Dal, the Socialist Party and Congress dissidents form the Janata Party — the party of the people. Narayan picks Morarji Desai for prime minister. This is the octogenarian politician's third and last chance to be *primes inter pares.* But waiting in the wings is Charan Singh, the Jat leader of rich farmers. There is also Jagjivan Ram, leader of the lower castes, who will not mind a shot at the top job.

But first, the country is put back to normal. Prisoners are released. Constitutional rights restored. Press censorship removed. A commission headed by Jayantilal Shah, former chief justice of the Supreme Court, is appointed to enquire into the excesses of the emergency.

The Janata Party is in power, all's well with the world.

This is a government that is committed to social welfare. But it is also a government which cannot agree with itself. First, more money is allocated to agriculture in the Sixth Plan. But farmers

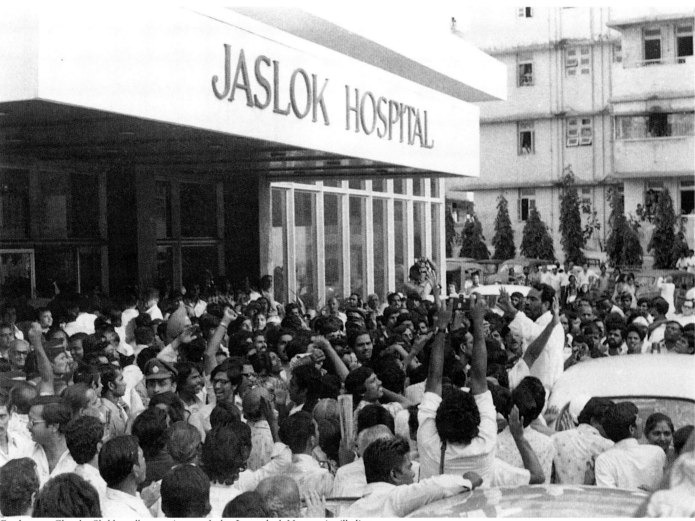

Fatal error: Chandra Shekhar tells mourning crowds that Jayaprakash Narayan is still alive

Gautam Patole

Courting martyrdom: *Indira Gandhi awaits arrest*   Raghu Rai/India Today

allegations that the prime minister's son is corrupt, it is of pictures of Jagjivan Ram's son in *flagrante delicto*, it is of health minister Raj Narain declaring that modern medicine is useless. It is of Indira Gandhi winning an election to the Lok Sabha from Chikmaglur in Karnataka in November 1978 by a landslide margin. It is of the government arresting her and her son Sanjay and putting them in jail for a week and overturning her election. It is of turning Indira Gandhi into a martyr by a tragic lack of government action and programmes.

The Congress splits in 1977 and the Congress of Indira is the larger and more powerful. As the Janata Party flounders and bumbles along, people turn again to their old patron and their old party. But Indira does not really have to show her hand.

July 12, 1979 and Charan Singh, with the help of H N Bahuguna, a fellow Cabinet member and former foe, decide to oust Desai from the prime ministership. Increased Hindu-Muslim riots in the North, with certain involvement of Hindu fundamentalist parties, mean that a common front must be forged to "fight the fascist forces, represented by those who believe in the Hitlerian theory of ethnic purism, religious supremacy and bigotry".

Unable to sustain the attacks from within, Desai resigns on July 27. Charan Singh forms a government, with help from another old enemy turned ally, Indira Gandhi.

Or so he thinks. On August 20, Indira Gandhi regrets that she cannot support his government. On August 22, the President dissolves Parliament and Singh is to continue as caretaker prime minister till then. Elections are announced for January 2, 1980. It surprises no one that the Congress (Indira) wins.

Of Jayaprakash Narayan, little is said anymore. By killing him six months before his death on October 8, 1979, the parties and men that came together to serve the people have exposed their petty inadequacies. Says journalist Arun Shourie, after the false death announcement, "The only truthful action of the Janata Government so far has been to prematurely announce his death. They killed his promises and now they are bent on killing him as well."

There can be no worse — or better — epitaph for a government that meant so much when it started, only to work so hard to debase itself so totally. ∎

are no better off. Then, foreign companies are thrown out. Coca-Cola, the American soft drink giant leaves. The government decides to make its own soft drink. A government-owned bakery, Modern, starts manufacturing Double 7 — or significantly, 77-which very few people see, less drink. But then, perhaps governments ought to be more concerned with development than aerated waters.

This is also a government that is made up of men that the people can trust. Of JP's dream of "good men". This is not a government of corrupt Congress-type politicians, who care little for what happens to the people as long they can feather their own nests. This is a government of the upright and true, of people who care for the common man over the rich and influential.

Said journalist and political commentator Inder Malhotra of the Janata Party government in April 77: "Those who took so much time to finalise the composition of the Cabinet or allocation of portfolios, showing themselves terribly touchy over minor matters of personal pride and prejudice, may well turn out to be even more quarrelsome when differences over high policy, affecting various classes having conflicting interests are concerned. The problem used to be acute even when the Congress was in power. It cannot but be worse at a time when the four constituents of the Janata Party have different social moorings and political predilections."

What is worse for the Janata Party, though, is not just the question of administrative or developmental issues. It is of

Political pastiche: *(left to right) A B Vajpayee, Morarji Desai, Charan Singh and Mohan Dharia*
– India Today

COALITIONS MUST WORK
The importance of government by consensus
By V P Singh

IF you look at the graph of the experience of coalition governments you will see an improvement in 1997. The National Front did not split as the Janata did in 1977. And the United Front Government is a further improvement.

In 1990 the National Front did not split. It was only the Janata Dal faction within it that split. Chandra Shekhar went away with a small faction of the Janata Dal. The major chunk of the Janata Dal remained.

After 1977, the Janata Party just vanished. But later the Janata Dal and the National Front did not, the Front is intact.

The great change in the 1989 coalition was that the opposition came of age through it. Now it has come to stay, and I have been a party to it. The 1977 government failed to become a real political entity, 1989 could give it that. That was a major contribution to the maturing of Indian democracy. That was because the 1989 coalition laid the foundation for drawing regional parties into the national scene.

The present government is a further improvement on the 1989-1990 government. Here a change has come. H D Deve Gowda went as prime minister, I K Gujral took office. But there has been no split in the UF because of this. If there was a difference, it was over election of the party president. But on account of the coalition itself there was no split. Even the Janata Dal has not split.

They have managed a transfer of power which the earlier two coalitions could not. So the experience of coalitions is maturing.

The political reality of coalition governments is now gravitating towards economic and social reality. And this can be a very positive development so far as the unity of the country is concerned. The illusion that if a single party is ruling, that will strengthen the unity of the country is misplaced. That can mean only single party hegemony.

What happened during that hegemony in the past? Various regional parties emerged. They could find a voice in the government. So they flourished and successfully challenged the Congress. They were being labelled fissiparous, seccessionist. Sly remarks were made about them. And they felt alienated. Delhi was distant, their state was to them far more important.

Now, under some conditions of course, they have become the managers of national affairs. They are in Delhi, they are Delhi. This has had a tremendous effect on them. That we are ruling India, that we are India. Not just some people in a corner.

Their role as complainers, that Delhi is not this and not that, has gone away. Their situation was negative. You cannot get elected merely by asking voters not to support Janata or to oppose the BJP. You will lose out if you don't rule. People want to elect a party that rules, so why not send someone who will rule in Delhi?

And, speaking of compromises, any government has to make compromises. The state is the final manager of conflicting interests. These average out, that is a part of the function of the state.

In coalitions that sort of thing comes into focus. Every section voices its views in public and private fora. If this is kept in abeyance, that can lead to a break-up. So, there is a need for every view to be expressed. But to run a successful coalition government there must be a vast area of commonality. Secondly, there must be conversation at both formal and informal levels. The informal channels must be kept open because so much gets decided before formal meetings.

Thirdly, there must be a realistic understanding of each other's strength at the ground level for ticket distribution. Luckily, what made the United Front and the National Front governments run without breaking up, was that the area of influence of each has been individual and different from one another, there is no overlap. For example, the DMK, TDP, the Left, in Assam. This is making it all work. If there was an overlap, that would make it more difficult. The United Front should not give up its regional parties. In fact the regional parties are the United Front.

The voter may get confused when he sees an obvious contradiction when his party aligns itself with another for the sake of convenience over ideology. But, for instance, in 1989, when National Front got outside support from the BJP, what was the choice? Can you have a country without any government at all? Not having a government is not an option. Now the BJP is looking for a coalition with the BSP. If the Congress makes a bid for power, how can it do so except in coalition? These are just realities. The BJP is also in coalition today in Maharashtra. The two are often in conflict. It is also in coalition in Haryana and with Badal. And also UP.

The voter is not in a predicament. He must vote for a party he thinks is the right one. If a coalition develops later, then that is the compulsion of the situation. There is not a preferential voting system when you have a first choice, second choice, third choice and so on. Such a system has other problems. Though in India it may be possible to have a system that demands anyone should get at least 50 per cent of the vote to get elected. And if that fails, to go for a second round. This could work, the pressure will be against fissiparous tendencies and consensus will be emphasised. It can be a counter to the fear that seats will go to any particular caste. It will force candidates and parties to look for policies of synthesis. I have been talking about this, but, in India there are no takers for it.

As for the ethics of divergent parties coming together under one umbrella, when it comes down to the brass tacks, parties represent various interests. Not narrow interests, but I mean in the larger sense. These interests can come across as ideologies, so that ideological differences are really a clash over the interests they represent. When you look at the adjustments being made by parties, look at the interests that they are adjusting.

Take the Gita, for example. It is a great religious work,

Great experiment: *Jayaprakash Narayan with leaders of the first coalition government*

but it is not a political force today. It was in the days of the Mahabharata. There was a political offshoot to the religious content of the Gita. The ideology was a cover for waging a war. So that there was then an important political input, not just religious or spiritual.

Or look at *Das Kapital*. It is linked up with political interests. When it comes to the political potential, then it must link up with some interests. So when we look at the ethics or ideology, we must look for political interests.

In coalitions it may be inevitable that parties with small electoral gains find themselves in the driver's seat. That number of, say, 30 or 40 is only the formal part of it. The political reality is that decisions are taken in consensus with those who support you. There is no hegemony. If anyone is hurt by a decision, they will make a lot of noise. No one can get away with doing just anything. No party can go about breaking institutions. There are checks and balances. These things take time to work, it is not as quick as in one-party rule. But it has its positive side. Unless, of course, the deadlocks become so strong that nothing works.

In India the political structure rests very much on the social structure, if it does not do so absolutely. When the equilibrium of social forces shift, then the political fortunes of the parties also shift. The Congress used to have the support of the Scheduled Castes, the Muslims in the North, of the backward classes in the South. Now the vote of many of these social sections has been moving, and the stability of the Congress support has been vanishing. That support came to them earlier because of the stability of the social conditions. Now some of the upper caste vote that went to Congress is going to the BJP. Janata Dal or Samajwadi supporters vote Congress when they have no choice. The Scheduled Caste

vote in U.P is now going to BSP.

But the Congress can get back support of the minorities. The Muslim anger with the Congress came at the time of the Babri Masjid demolition and was associated with Narasimha Rao. If the electoral equation of the Congress with the United Front changes, then the whole equation can change. There are sections angry with the Congress who vote BJP.

But the total support for BJP is not very great. They lost in Ayodhya.

In 1989 and even now, the threat to coalition governments comes from outside, from national parties. It was the BJP then, this time it was the Congress. They get away with it, the regional parties are blamed. It is not a question of *'Chal nahin paate'*. It is *'Chalne nahin detey hain'* The threat to coalitions comes from national parties, the regional parties get blamed for it.

But we are going through the stages of learning how to run a coalition. There was no experience of this at the national level. In West Bengal, in Kerala, yes. Now all parties are maturing into learning how to run a coalition. But by itself there is nothing wrong with outside support. The beauty of democracy, as I like to recall that saying, is not that it produced great men, it lies in that small men can come together and do great things. Now the crisis was managed by all parties coming together, it was their own collective effort.

There should be a debate on the presidential form of government. As more and more coalitions and regional parties come up, the presidential system can give political expression to the unity of the country. But there are forms andforms of presidential government. If the president is too strong, institutions can be jeopardised. There is need for a debate on this.

FAITH, HOPE, CHARITY

1979

Mother Teresa wins the Nobel Peace Prize and the love of an entire nation

IT is 1979. Calcutta has 300,000 pavement dwellers, 300 slum clusters and one saviour. Since 1947, Mother Teresa has been doing God's work amidst the "poorest of the poor". All these years later, the world has chosen to honour her with the highest secular award known to man "for outstanding service to humanity and saintly devotion".

But what does the Nobel Peace Prize mean to one who has dedicated herself to life as a bride of Christ? To living with the most desperate, the most despairing, the most desolate people of her teeming city? A year after winning the prize, Mother Teresa would say that the publicity she received after winning has interfered with her work of service to the poor. So she would not "participate in any more receptions". But she does say at the time, "It is a victory of the poor". And the bulk of the money is to go to leprosy patients.

It is not always easy to understand Mother Teresa. She speaks of service, of love, of God, of Jesus - ephemeral concepts to most. But she is always strong and certain and easily placeable within the Christian ethos. "Actually we are touching Christ's body in the poor. In the poor it is the hungry Christ that we are feeding, it is the naked Christ that we are clothing, it is to the homeless Christ that we are giving shelter," she said to British journalist Malcolm Muggeridge in 1969. The rest of the message is in the Bible itself: "And when the time comes to die and go home to God again," she explains some years later, "we will hear Him say, 'Come and possess the Kingdom prepared for you, because I was hungry and you gave me to eat, I was naked and you clothed me, I was sick and you visited me. Whatever you did to the least of my brethren, you did to me'."

Mother Teresa, then, works for her own salvation. But in doing so, she brings succour and salvation to untold numbers of others. It is essential to understand this much about her.

Agnes Gonxha Bojaxhiu first heard the call in Skopje in Yugoslavia when she was 12. Born to Albanian parents on August 27, 1910, Agnes was a shy girl with a club foot. Although she did not go to a Catholic school, priests encouraged the children to find their vocation according to God's call. "It was at that time that I knew I was called to the poor," she says, working with a young people's group in her parish called the Sodality. It was not till she was 18 that she decided to become a nun.

Agnes joined the Irish order of the Sisters of Loreto, well-known for their work in India, which she had always wanted to visit. After a year at Rathurnam in Ireland, Agnes took a P&O liner in 1929 bound for Calcutta. In 1931, she took her vows and the young novice was now Sister Teresa, after St Teresa of Lisieux, the Little Flower of Jesus. Loreto is largely a teaching order and the Bengal Mission runs several schools. Teresa was sent St Mary's in Calcutta's Entally district, not as posh as Loreto's other schools. She taught Geography and catechism, learnt Bengali and Hindi, and became principal in 1944. Always physically frail, she contracted tuberculosis and was sent to the hill station of Darjeeling to recuperate and make her retreat.

It was on the train, on September 10, 1946, that she heard the second call. God wanted her to save the poorest of the poor, to give up everything. The first sacrifice was to be the order of the Loreto nuns. The process to leave the order began within the bureaucratic processes of the church, from applying to the archbishop of Calcutta on to the final permission from the Pope, then Pius XII. Teresa was allowed to be a non-claustral nun in 1948, not without opposition from within her own old order.

But even before she heard her second call, Sister Teresa had started serving the poor. The Bengal famine of 1943 had left over five million dead, and between classes, Sister Teresa could be found in the Motijheel slums. The high boundary walls of Loreto, she was to say, "seemed to me at that moment like a prison wall".

The archbishop of Calcutta was not well-disposed to Teresa's bid for independence. "I know this woman as a novice. She could not light a candle in the chapel properly and you expect her to start a congregation," Ferdinand Perriers was fond of asking. Indeed, her colleagues for 19 years at Entally remembered Teresa most for her physical weakness and ordinariness. But physically weak, and even ordinary perhaps, Teresa was not to be shaken from her chosen way of life. Her ordinariness seemed subsumed into a new saintliness, so evident to all those who come across her, then and now. In 1948, even as she lived in a small room in the Little Sisters of the Poor, even as she worked alone in the Motijheel slums, people had started to call her 'mother'. In March 1949, she got her first missionary of charity, Subhasini Das, one of her senior students, who took the name Sister Agnes, for Mother's christened name (Sister Agnes died in 1997, of cancer). There would be no looking back. October 1950, the Feast of the Most Holy Rosary. Permission to start a new congregation is granted by Rome and consecrated by the Pope. The Missionaries of Charity order is born, to give "wholehearted free service to the poorest of the poor".

But missionary has rarely been a pleasant word in the Indian context. Even liberal thinkers balk somewhat at the thought of people being saved from dire poverty or a lonely death only to be introduced into the Christian faith. Others justify the conversion by the fact that at least, Mother Teresa is doing something. Still others — especially those who have felt her touch, been healed in spirit by her presence — simply dub her a "living God". As the Missionaries of Charity has grown from the slums of Calcutta to a worldwide organisation, criticism has been raised about money accepted from all sources, about refusal to condemn politically suspect patrons, or even those whose moral and humane standards are corrupted.

Amidst all this acclamation, where does Mother's association with the dreaded Duvaliers of Haiti fit in, with Robert Maxwell, with Charles Keating of the infamous US savings and loan swindle? Perhaps, it does not. Perhaps, the Missionaries of Charity take what they can to do the work they do, without questioning where it comes from. Perhaps they even believe that forgiveness can come from bad money being put to good use.

Jawaharlal Nehru once declared, "Believe me, Mother, we need you as much as the poor do." Maybe, maybe. ■

(facing page): Mother Teresa: *Serving the poor*   Shailesh Rawal/India Today

MR BOX OFFICE

1982

Amitabh Bachchan's stellar quality breaks all records and brings a nation to its knees

Great fighter: *Amitabh Bachchan emerges from Breach Candy Hospital to the relief of his fans*

Bhawan Singh/India Today

"Amitabh Bachchan is number one to 10, all other stars come after that."

— *Film-maker Manmohan Desai on the sets of Coolie*

"This man is not just a star. Amitabh Bachchan is an industry."

— *French producer Alain Chamas*

JULY 24, 1982, Bangalore. "Action!" commands Manmohan Desai on the sets of his new venture *Coolie* and young Puneet Issar bounces into the range of the camera unleashing a kick to Amitabh Bachchan's stomach. As the camera whirrs, the hero reels, spins around, then falls heavily on the steel table, the edge hitting his mid-riff with a big thud. The take has gone perfectly. Desai is so pleased with his star's performance that he breaks into applause. Then his expression changes. Bachchan, who had recovered from the fall on the table with an agonised look that seemed like an extension of the scene, stands up, takes a couple of tottering steps rubbing his stomach, then collapses on the floor.

July 25, St Philomina's Hospital. Bachchan's personal physician Dr K M Shah, flown in from Bombay, is extremely displeased at seeing his patient. The injury looks serious. The previous day's ministrations of sedatives and painkillers have failed to quell the pain. The X-rays taken earlier in the day reveal no damage, but Dr Shah is not sure that this is conclusive proof

that Bachchan is out of danger.

July 26. Bachchan is fully conscious, which also means that he is in complete agony. It's been almost 48 hours since the injury. Dr Shah is in a dilemma. Should Bachchan be shifted to Bombay?

July 27. The gravity of the injury hits the film industry, indeed the entire nation. Bachchan's childhood friend Rajiv Gandhi asks for periodic health reports. Taking a cue from the prime minister's son, local and state politicians start doing the rounds of St Philomina's. Meanwhile Dr Shah calls in Dr H S Bhatt, a leading urologist to examine Bachchan. Dr Bhatt wastes no time in pronouncing his decision. Operate immediately.

July 28, News of Bachchan's injury now hogs the national headlines. St Philomina's is mobbed by friends, fans and vicarious thrill-seekers. The operation takes over three hours and is performed by three specialists. Bachchan's innards reveal a hole where the small intestine meets the big. As the day progresses, his condition worsens. The word inside the hospital is that Bachchan is critical. The buzz outside is that Bachchan is dying.

July 31. The action shifts from Bangalore to the intensive care unit of Bombay's Breach Candy Hospital. Over the last 24 hours there has been some improvement in Bachchan's condition. But there is an accompanying fear. He has developed mild jaundice.

August 2. Another operation becomes imperative. This

one lasts eight hours. The battle for survival become more grim. Doctors are unwilling to provide false hope. There is only one hope. Prayer.

By now the entire country has realised the seriousness of Bachchan's injury and the response from his fans and well-wishers is overwhelming, unparalleled. Hundreds of women join Jaya Bachchan in her invocations at Sidhdhi Vinayak temple in Bombay everyday. There is, it seems, a prayer on every lip as millions all over the country go to temple, mosque, church, gurudwara seeking divine benediction to save this one life. Clearly, the appeal of Amitabh Bachchan transcends caste, creed and custom. Now it engulfs an entire nation.

August 8. Prime minister Indira Gandhi visits Bachchan immediately on her return from the United States. While Bachchan's political clout gets a fillip, his health remains a matter of deep concern. Nevertheless, he has recovered enough to be fed some liquids. The milling crowds outside Breach Candy Hospital greet this bit of information with explicit joy. Elsewhere, director Ramesh Sippy, responding to a query about Bachchan says. "You don't know what a fighter Amitabh is. He just never gives up."

Flashback

If Amitabh Bachchan was not a fighter he would never have survived the Indian film industry. Acting is neither in his genes nor is it his expertise. His father is the renowned Hindi poet Harvanshrai, from Uttar Pradesh. His mother Teji is a Sikh from Karachi. They are influential people, counting the Prime Minister among their personal friends. But neither is interested in films. When Bachchan chucks up a promising career as a corporate executive to try his luck in films, nobody is more surprised than his parents.

Having failed to get a foothold in Bollywood via a national talent contest, Bachchan is condemned to doing the rounds of cynical producers and directors who find his bamboo-thin physique, his extraordinarily long limbs and an intense face with sunken eyes ill-suited for the audiences.

The struggle is hard and long. The few interesting films that come his way, get interminably delayed or scrapped for want of finance. Khwaja Ahmed Abbas gives him a break in *Saat Hindustani*, a film based on the liberation of Goa. The film takes longer to release than it did to make, and when it is finally shown, there are no viewers. Sunil Dutt's *Reshma aur Shera*, a moving if slow-paced film is another casualty at the box office having spent too much time in the cans to make an impact on the screen. Bachchan's impressive cameo performance as a mute coward is lost as the film bombs.

Succour to a sagging career comes from the gifted director Hrishikesh Mukherjee who sees in Bachchan's brooding presence and deep-set voice an ideal foil to Rajesh Khanna's happy-go-lucky terminally ill cancer patient in *Anand*. As Khanna's doctor-friend, Bachchan is restrained and sober, suitably underplaying the character to allow the bubbly Anand to win the sympathy of the audience.

Mukherjee's next film, *Namak Haram*, pits Amitabh and Rajesh Khanna together again as friends from contrasting backgrounds. This time Bachchan has equal billing and a meatier role than in *Anand*. As the self-indulgent, pleasure-seeking son of an industrialist who chooses to atone for his father's sins, he shows an amazing range of emotions before the camera. *Namak Haram* gets critical and box office acclaim.

A stroke of luck helps him make the big leap from supporting actor to main hero. Producer Prakash Mehra, spurned by veteran actor Raaj Kumar, offers the lead role in *Zanjeer* to Amitabh Bachchan. He has to play a revenge-seeking neurotic cop haunted by the memories of his parents' murder. It is a complex, demanding role in which Amitabh revels. Backed by a crisp script from the talented duo of Salim and Javed, he invests in the character a rage and an energy that captivates audiences all over India. The Angry Young Man of the Indian screen is born.

In the next few years, Amitabh distills into the Angry Young Man image an all-encompassing, enduring persona that gradually becomes an unorthodox anti-establishment crusader who relies on native wisdom and inherent courage to win the battles of life. Bachchan's keen sense of perception, his utter friendliness with the camera, his intrinsic intensity, his splendidly controlled voice, clubbed together with some strong author-backed roles, make a promising star into a superstar.

Zanjeer is followed by *Deewar* then Sholay and later *Amar Akbar Anthony*, each a golden jubilee hit. Through the late 1970s, he is established as the magic mantra for the box-office, the most recognisable face in the country, the industry's highest paid star, reportedly commanding Rs.35 lakhs per film plus a cut from gross earnings from known producers. From newcomers, Rs one lakh a day would be just fine. The money, seemingly obscene, is nevertheless justified.

Bachchan's appeal is universal, bordering on a national obsession — young women love him, young men ape him, old

The making *of* a NATION

Hero No 1: *Bachchan resumes the fight in Coolie, and for life*   Mukesh Parpiani

People's choice: *Bachchan as a politician*
Namas Bhojani

people adore him. He is loyal friend, lover, brother, son. There have been superstars before him — Ashok Kumar, Dilip Kumar, Rajendra Kumar, Rajesh Khanna. But never one like Amitabh Bachchan.

Cut to Present

September 24, 1982. It's approaching noon. Outside Breachy Candy Hospital thousands of people wait expectantly. Suddenly, a roar breaks the silence. A tall man, in a simple churidar and a kurta draped with a shawl, emerges into view. Amitabh Bachchan looks gaunt and spent. But he manages a weak smile as he walks gingerly towards his car supported by son Abhishek, brother Ajitabh, and film-maker Manmohan Desai. It's been two months since his injury. The world appears distant, different. Then, as he nears the gate of the hospital. Bachchan regains some control. He raises his hand and gives a clenched fist salute to signify victory. The crowd goes delirious with joy. Many break down and weep. The prayers have been answered. Amitabh Bachchan is alive. The nation breathes a sigh of relief.

Post-Script

Recovering swiftly from his injury thereafter, Amitabh completes *Coolie*, then turns to the more serious task of helping his friend Rajiv Gandhi win the elections following Indira Gandhi's assassination. Bachchan contests on a Congress ticket from Allahabad and beats veteran H N Bahuguna hands down. The tryst with politics, however, is short-lived. Unable to survive the Machiavellian machinations within his own party, and especially after the Bofors scandal breaks, Bachchan quits politics and returns to films. In spite of a continuous bout with the nervous disorder myacsthena gravis, Bachchan pursues acting with zest. By now he has become bigger than any role, and hence completely stereotyped. While his performances do not flag, inevitably, his films do. He takes a hiatus from films, then returns with much fanfare in the 1990s only for the industry to discover the unthinkable — Bachchan's films have started to flop. But even as he becomes unaffordable in terms of cost and unpredictable in terms of box office success, Amitabh Bachchan never ceases to make news. In success or failure, he is a phenomenon, adored or envied but impossible to ignore. ∎

BOLLYWOOD BEWILDERED
Mainstream Indian Cinema
tries to regain its voice
By B K Karanjia

THE best thing to have happened to the Indian film industry in the post-Independence period was the establishment by the Government in 1951 of the Film Enquiry Committee to put the industry's house in order. The Enquiry Committee's Chairman was S K Patil, and among its members were film stalwarts like B N Sircar and V Shantaram. The Committee's deliberations resulted in the founding of the Film and Television Institute at Pune, the institution of the National Awards to recognise and reward merit in film-making and the establishment of the Film Finance Corporation, which in the late '60s initiated the New Cinema movement.

The Committee's major recommendation was a statutory body (on the lines of the French Centre Nationale de la Cinematographie and the Australian Film Commission) to regulate, not control — the distinction is vital — the film industry's affairs. But the government, while welcoming this idea and realising the necessity of such a body, did nothing to pursue it, and the more vocal sections in the industry, some with underworld connections, resisted the idea. The moment of truth passed the industry by.

A house divided against itself, Indian cinema has the dimensions of an industry without its disciplines. As it grew in the '60s and '70s, its problems multiplied, with certain inbuilt and bewildering paradoxes: the more the problems, the greater the number of films being made; the worse the ravages of the star-system, the higher the price paid to stars; the stricter the censorship, the more prurient the appeal of these films; the scarcer the finance, the more lavish the expenditure...

The Indian film industry today provides the strange spectacle of being subject to control without regulation when the crying need is for regulation with the minimum of control. We cannot, in this day and age, return to the studio system, but we have to devise some sort of system to at least return to the values that prevailed in our cinema in the pre-World War II years.

The industry, weakened from within, has been attacked from without. Some time ago a young man caught in a crime confessed to the police that he was "inspired" by Amitabh Bachchan playing the errant son in the film *Shakti*. The police noted down his confession and the press duly reproduced it. Of course, no police officer came forward to declare that he was similarly inspired to act above and beyond the call of duty by the example of Amitabh Bachchan's police inspector father, played by Dilip Kumar, in the same film.

This is the bizarre new element introduced into the Indian film scenario. Up till now politicians blamed the

Bare necessity?: *A scene from Raj Kapoor's Ram Teri Ganga Maili*

art of story-telling in which, as Jack Valenti prophesies, lies the secret of the creative future of motion pictures.

It is no use blaming the audience, still less use pretending to be mystified by the utter unpredictability of its likes and dislikes. We have the largest, most patient, most grateful audience in the world. Touch their lives and their hearts at some point, so that what they see becomes for them an enriching experience, and they will respond, as they have always done since Dada Saheb Phalke unspooled Raja Harischandra. In generous measure. This is what the social responsibility of cinema is all about. Today there is a noticeable disquiet in our cinema audience: in this very disquiet there is hope for tomorrow's cinema.

In spirit and blood this is the same audience that thrilled in our film industry's salad days to films of the calibre of *Duniya Na Mane, Amrit Manthan, Achyut Kanya, Aurat* and *Devdas*. Already in the films released in the '70s and '80s traces can be seen of the same social consciousness repossessing our film makers. Not only in small films with a rather specialised appeal like *Bheegi Palkein*, but also in big commercial projects like *Prem Rog, Nikaah, Swami Dada* and *Vidhaata*.

What is needed today, and what indeed is happening in our cinema, is a going back to the past for creative sustenance, a recapture that might well become a renewal.

sex and violence in cinema for crime in society. Now criminals themselves have joined the politicians in claiming films to be their source of inspiration. Can you imagine an unlikelier or unholier alliance?

But logic and reason do not enter the scenario at all. Cinema, given a bad name and hanged, is now in the process of being drawn and quartered. This adds to the pervading gloom with studios, cinemas and laboratories closing down one after the other, distributors dragging their feet when coming forward with the promised advances, and films flopping for no apparent reason.

But there is hope in that with box-office earnings going down, tax revenues will also go down and the state governments in the first instance and the Centre later are bound to sit up and take notice. Film taxation's unwritten law is that the lesser the number of golden eggs to be collected, the greater the concern for the goose's health. And the goose too is being internally rejuvenated with the film trade's apex body, the Film Federation of India, coming down to the grass-roots of statistics and research in place of speculation.

There is hope also in the new awareness dawning on film makers that the formula is no longer valid. There is growing appreciation of "the eternal verities" of the ancient

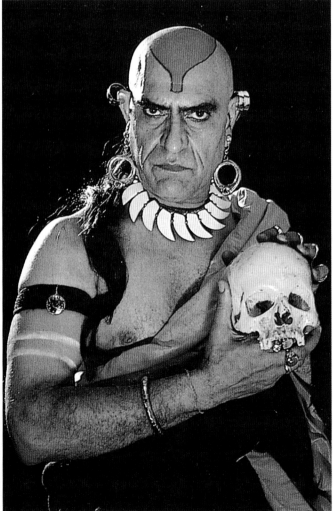

Spell-binding: *Amrish Puri plays the essential villain*

GAMES PEOPLE PLAY

1982

The IXth Asian Games prove that India can organise a world class event and bring Rajiv Gandhi to the forefront. But can India produce world class athletes?

"These Games will serve as a renewal of contacts."
— Jawaharlal Nehru at the inauguration of the 1951 Asian Games in Delhi

"We welcome you all to these celebrations in this ancient land of ours... to this awakened land of ours."
— Amitabh Bachchan reading out the hymn at the inauguration of the 1982 Asian Games in New Delhi

BUT in early 1982, the awakened land is in some turmoil which could ruin Jawaharlal Nehru's vision of the Asian Games being a vehicle for the constant renewal of contacts between nations from this part of the hemisphere. The IXth Asian Games due in November, are imperilled by logistical and political problems. Will the infrastructure be completed in time for an event of this magnitude? Will the Punjab issue be resolved, or at least contained, to enable the safe conduct of the Games?

By the 1960s, it must be remembered, all major international sports events had become politicised, and if they were not entirely manifestations of a political system, as in East European countries, they were surely representative of the might of the ruling party. Even so, holding the Asian Games in 1982 is an awesome task for India, and succeeds only because all bureaucratic stops are unplugged by a coterie of committed sports lovers and ambitious young politicians with the son of the prime minister in the driver's seat, heading the challenge.

The previous Janata government had in fact won for India the rights to host the 1982 Games. But riven by internecine battles, the government had put the Games on the backburner. When the Janata Party is ousted in the 1980 elections, it seems as if it is already too late to save the Games. Till Rajiv Gandhi arrives to salvage not only the Games, but use this as a vehicle for enhancing national esteem. Weaned on the wonders of screwdriver technology, like his brother before him, and driven by the desire to take India into the First World in one gigantic leap, Rajiv Gandhi's political clout and indefatigable enthusiasm makes the Asian Games not only possible, but into a showcase event for the rest of the world. New Delhi gets a facelift and essential infrastructure. New stadia, new freeways and new hotels sprout up at various places and in double quick time. Bureaucratic delays and bungles are minimised as the son of the prime minister ensures that licences and clearances are provided quickly. There is mounting criticism in the world that India is not up to the task, that it is already too late. If the Asian Games have to be held at all, work has to be completed on a war footing. The man put in charge of field operations as the secretary general of the Asian Games Special Organising Committee is Sankaran Nair, a no-nonsense, self-motivated former head of the Research and Analysis Wing. Nair, reporting directly to Rajiv Gandhi and with a team of industrious men working under him, is given under two years to ensure that the job is completed.

"We had to go through a hell of a lot of problems," Nair was to say later, "It normally takes six years to organise the Games, but we had less than two years at our disposal. But it was a matter of the nation's prestige and there was no question of looking back. We had to form various monitoring committees to check at each stage and take quick decisions. Steel, cement etc were procured from all available sources and the government supported the Special Organising Committee in every way. In fact the chairman of the SOC, Buta Singh (who was also the sports minister) had been given such wide-ranging powers that he was actually speaking on behalf of the Cabinet and could issue directions to all the government departments to cooperate with the SOC."

Such sweeping authority facilitates the urgent creation of the infrastructure in the capital. But for the Asian Games message to percolate right through to the smallest village and the lowest population denomination, dissemination of information becomes equally critical. Television is getting to be the new fix for Indians, and colour TV has already made its advent in some prosperous homes. There can be no better way to transmit the achievement of the government than through exciting, colourful visuals of sport.

In a radical decision aimed at helping sport as well as winning popular support, the import duty on colour TV sets brought into India is slashed drastically as the Games approach. Suddenly, there is an avalanche of colour TV sets coming into India. That accomplished, there arises the need for faultless

Great start: *The '82 Asiad's colourful opening spectacle*

broadcast to ensure that the TV viewers don't feel cheated. The big push theory comes into play for Doordarshan too.

In a record time of six months, 20 transmitters are installed all over the country, including the remote North-east states. A tie-up is signed with INTELSAT for beaming capsules of the Games. Four colour outdoor broadcast vans, 15 electronic cameras and sundry other hardware necessary for a top class telecast are purchased without delay. Foreign technicians are flown in to train the Indian personnel. The cost for such training alone is Rs 80 lakh, that for the buying of hardware undisclosed. The overall cost of hosting the Games is reckoned to be more than Rs 150 crore, but no official figures are forthcoming.

By the end of 1982 what is clearly emerging, however, is that the Asian Games can be held. The infrastructure, barring some spit and polish jobs, is nearly complete, the participating nations have confirmed their entries, the Indian athletes too have trained hard. What remains a thorn in the flesh is the threat from the Akalis in Punjab that they would disrupt the Games to highlight their problem.

The last couple of weeks before the Asian Games are scheduled to begin are tense. Some protests by Akalis turn ugly. The government clamps down seriously on troublemakers. Suspicious-looking people crossing into Delhi from the Punjab border are stopped, questioned, and then turned back or allowed in depending on their ability to convince the investigators. In New Delhi itself, there is a crackdown on potential miscreants by the Lieutenant-General Jagmohan, whose ruthless methods during the Emergency are still recalled with awe and fear. Indeed, by the time the Asian Games are due, New Delhi resembles a city

Silver streak: *Golden Girl PT Usha wins two silver medals* India Today

under siege from security forces, but understandably so.

November 19,1982. The Jawaharlal Nehru Stadium in New Delhi is filled to capacity by the time Amitabh Bachchan's baritone voice resonates around the ground expounding India's essential virtues. More than 75,000 people have occupied its newly constructed terraces as the weak winter afternoon sun prepares to make a premature exit from the rapidly darkening sky. These include, apart from the genuine sports lovers and those who love to be seen on any occasion, the who's who of India, including Prime Minister Indira Gandhi.

Touted as the biggest event of the decade, the spectacular opening ceremony shows why this may not be an exaggeration. As the sun dissolves into the horizon, the evening unfolds into a never-seen-before pageant of sights, sounds and colours. More than 5,000 athletes are joined by 7,000 folk dancers and 32 elephants and the President's guard on bay steeds in an extravagant symphony of dance and parade. Simultaneously, 2,000 pigeons are released, and all this to the tune of Pandit Ravi Shankar's original, lilting composition. Then the traditional flame is lit amidst a deafening roar of applause. The IXth Asian Games have finally begun.

December 3, 1992. The Jawaharlal Nehru Stadium is filled to capacity again. This time there is no opening hymn by Amitabh Bachchan, no music by Ravi Shankar, no orderly march past. The closing ceremony of any such event is an occasion to relax and rejoice and the mood of the athletes and other participants reflects this through the unsynchronised dance steps, the spontaneous celebrations.

Yes, these Games had athletes too, and as always there has

India Today

Twice world amateur billiards champion (1981, 1983) , **Michael Ferreira** has also won the world open championship once. An outstanding cueist, Ferreira is an outspoken votary for deprived sportspersons in India. Turned pro after Geet Sethi

Milkha Singh dreamt of doing what no Indian had ever done before — winning an Olympic gold medal. He came very close to pulling this off, breaking an Olympic record in the 1960 Rome Games in the 400 m heats. His time of 45.9 sec was bettered by three others with South Africa's Malcolm Spence beating him to the bronze. A sepoy in the Indian Army, Milkha took to athletics as a diversion to avoid daily parades. In the 1958 Asian Games, he won the gold medals in the 200 and 400 m and the 400 m gold in the 1962 Asian Games.

The most complete Indian player after Ramanathan Krishnan, **Vijay Amritraj's** talent was hailed with respect and admiration by the tennis world, as was clear when Bud Collins labelled him the 'A' in the ABC of tennis, placing him above Bjorn Borg and Jimmy Connors. He reached the Wimbledon quarterfinal in 1973 and 1981.Led India to the Davis Cup final in 1987.

Of all his achievements, **Prakash Padukone's** triumph in the All England Badminton Championships in 1980 will be long remembered. A touch player par excellence, the genial genius from Karnataka made his mark when badminton, like tennis, had become a 'power' sport. Winner of the National title nine times from 1971 to 1979, Prakash's international triumphs include five international titles in 1981, including the World Cup in 1981.

For a country which gave chess to the world, India has, strangely, produced few excellent players. Till **Vishwanathan Anand** arrived to make amends. Nicknamed the 'Lightning Kid' for the speed of his moves, Anand was India's first Grandmaster in 1987. By 1995 he was challenging Garry Kasparov for the Professional Chess Association title. After a flashy start, Anand lost to Kasparov, but had established his credentials as one of the greatest chess players of his generation.

Geet Sethi, at 19, was the youngest national billiards champion. Between 1984 and 1987, he won both, the national billiards and snooker championships for four years in a row. He has also been twice world amateur billiards champion and twice in a row world professional champion. The first Indian player to turn pro.

P T Usha made an unmatched impact not only in athletics, but also society. Inspired by her, many young girls, and especially from the South, chose to make sport their vocation. A fine sprinter, Usha switched to the 400 m hurdles in mid-career and missed winning the bronze medal in the 1984 Los Angeles Olympics by a whisker. At the Asian level, however, she was formidable and in the 1986 Asian Games in Seoul, won four golds and one silver to earn the sobriquet of 'Golden Girl'.

Ramanathan Krishnan is arguably the finest Indian tennis player yet. In 1960 and 1961 he was a semi-finalist at Wimbledon. He led the country to the Davis Cup final in 1966 after a courageous performance against Brazil in the semi-final in Calcutta. Ramanathan made up for his rather unathletic frame with a silken touch to reach the number three spot in the world.

In 1958 **Wilson Jones** became India's first billiards world champion. He claimed another world title in 1964 in New Zealand. Jones won the national billiards title a dozen times, the snooker title on five occasions. His technique and table manners were reckoned to be impeccable. Jones quit after his second world title when several felt he had plenty of years left.

been agony, ecstacy, the glory of winning and the sadness of losing. China, as expected, have topped the medals tally, Japan have come second. India have disappointed yet again, never more so than in the 1-7 rout in the hockey final against Pakistan. But there have been some superb efforts too. Charles Borromeo and M D Valsamma have set the track ablaze and the women's hockey team has atoned somewhat for the men's debacle. P T Usha, the dazzling sprinter, with two silvers has shown the promise that could win a gold medal. But not impressive enough for a host country with the second largest population in the world.

More importantly, through the two weeks, there has been no hitch, no trouble barring a minor protest here and there, and an avoidable fracas during a football match between North Korea and Kuwait in which a referee is badly beaten up. For the most, though, there was top class sports displayed by outstanding athletes covered brilliantly by television. The consensus opinion was that it had been a miracle no less.

Postscript:

It's time to breathe and soak in the laurels. The Asian Games have ended. Rajiv Gandhi has a broad, contented smile on his face. He is being queried about the expenses incurred for the Games. "We should be able to meet the actual cost of hosting the event by auctioning the Asian Games village. It should fetch something like Rs 150 crore," he says.

Elsewhere, Milkha Singh, India's greatest runner ever, is being questioned about the future of Indian sports after the Asian Games. "The task of taking Indian sport to great heights will have to begin without wasting any time. We have spent so much time, money and energy on them (the infrastructure) that we must make sure we use them all the time."

Shortly after, the Asian Games village is auctioned, and as Rajiv Gandhi had expected, the Rs 150 crore is recovered. However, 15 years after the Asiad, most of the stadia, as Milkha Singh had feared, remains in disuse. In a sense, with the 1982 Asian Games, India had arrived. In another sense, it never took off. ■

FROM PILOT TO POLITICIAN
The grooming of Rajiv Gandhi
By Vir Sanghvi

"HE says that his wife will divorce him if he joins politics," Indira Gandhi told Khushwant Singh when asked if Rajiv Gandhi intended to fill the void left by his brother Sanjay. For over a year after Sanjay's light aircraft crashed into Delhi's Willingdon Crescent, Mrs Gandhi kept up the pretence of denying that she had any desire of inducting her shy, older son into politics.

There was no doubt, however, that Indira wanted Rajiv to enter the fray, no matter what she said in public. When a group of MPs called on her, she feigned annoyance when Shivraj Patil entreated her to draft Rajiv. "He is not in politics. He is not interested," she snapped. Shivraj Patil did not look unduly chastened: a few months later she made him a minister in the central cabinet as his reward.

But what of Rajiv himself? His friends say that he had no interest in politics; that he did not get on with his younger brother; and that, during the post -Emergency period Sonia and he shut themselves up in their bedroom preferring to have meals sent up than to join the family at the dining table.

He was the one Gandhi who seemed determined to escape his destiny — and the dynasty.

But once Sanjay died, Mrs Gandhi stepped up the pressure. She insisted that he abandon his job at Indian Airlines arguing that one dead pilot in the family was more than enough. Once he resigned, Rajiv found that there was very little else that he could do — as Mrs Gandhi had perhaps guessed he would discover.

Reluctantly, he slid into politics claiming that all he was trying to do was "help Mummy".

Even so, he resisted being projected in the Sanjay Gandhi mould. He did not want to be a youth leader or to propound a national agenda. His priorities were more managerial. Rooted firmly in the system created by his mother and grandfather, his concern was to make that system function more efficiently.

He asked Arun Singh, an old school friend to give up his job with Reckitt and Colman, makers of Cherry Blossom boot polish and began to rely more on Arun Nehru (formerly of Jensen and Nicholsen, makers of multi-coloured paints), a distant cousin whom Sanjay had inducted into politics.

The trio took over a government bungalow on Delhi's Motilal Nehru Marg and set -up an alternative thinktank. Mrs Gandhi was indulgent but unwilling to accept many of their recommendations.

Instead, she made them undertake specific projects. The most high profile of these was the Asian Games. The Janata Government had rashly agreed to host the games but had forgotten to build the required infrastructure. Rajiv's men took it upon themselves to turn the Games into a showpiece for their vision of India.

The making of a NATION

Taking charge: *Rajiv Gandhi gains prominence after the Games*   P Pushkarna/IT

Seven new deluxe hotels were sanctioned, Delhi was dotted with spanking new flyovers, new stadia were constructed and enough money was spent to build new capitals for both Punjab and Haryana. In the process, Rajiv built up his own team: Sankaran Nair (formerly of RAW), Buta Singh and Amitabh Bachchan, an old friend who came in to help with the details of the spectacle.

When the Games went off without a hitch, Mrs Gandhi was delighted. Her son had proved himself. India had shown the world that it could do it.

It was, by any standards, a major triumph. But it was a managerial triumph not a political one. Unfortunately nobody recognised the difference then — and the distinction would come back to haunt Rajiv Gandhi when he finally succeeded his mother.

WHAT SPORTS POLICY ?
Petty officialdom and politics prevent India from becoming a top sports nation
By Michael Ferreira

THE ritualistic beating of breasts that accompanies India's failure to make any impact on a major sporting event like the Olympics would be amusing if it were not so tragic. How is it, the lament goes, that in spite of a population of 950 million, we are unable to get a gold medal; we should take steps on the traditional "war footing", and so on and so forth. The knee-jerk outrage subsides in due course as we cynics expect, and nothing substantial is done for the next four years.

I believe that in assessing the Indian sports policy, we have to decide what sports we are talking about. In recent years, we have enjoyed consistent success at the highest level (read: international titles/records/championships) in three sports, cricket, billiards and chess. Ironically, these sports are self-sustaining in the sense that they are untouched by whatever passes for a sports policy and the success they have achieved has been largely due to the talent of the persons concerned and not to any systematic national policy.

The real core area for India is, or should be, those sports which promote national health with the minimum equipment, those in which we have physical advantages (or in which we do not suffer from any physical disadvantages) and those in which we have had a tradition or history of excellence. Any dissertation on the failure of a sports policy should therefore focus on athletics, gymnastics and hockey and to a lesser extent, badminton and tennis.

There is no question that India has plenty of Milkha Singhs, PT Ushas, Ajit Pal Singhs and Prakash Padukones. It is a tragedy that in 50 years our pernicious system has been able to unearth only a few of these diamonds. Why is it that other nations continue to produce world class athletes while we, with some honourable exceptions, languish far behind? Is it money? Surely not, for even Ethopia, one of the poorest nations by WHO standards has produced gold medallists, and in the marathon, the most gruelling event of all. Is it climate? Many African countries have as bad or worse climatic conditions than ours and are still in the hunt for medals. It is physical attributes? Our magnificent specimens from the Punjab region are as good or have the potential to match the best in the world. Is it a vast and unmanageable population? Oh yeah? What about China?

The bitter truth is that we are among the most dishonest, corrupt, scheming, envious and hypocritical nations in the world with no thought for anything that does not serve our narrow and self-seeking ends. This miasma permeates our national life and it is hardly cause for wonder that it has filtered down to the way sports is handled in the country. Selection can never be guaranteed to be on merit — regionalism, favouritism and — horror of horrors — bribes in cash or kind, all play their nefarious part. Trips abroad are manoeuvred under various guises by managers who damage more than manage, as coaches, who are more interested in shopping or sight-seeing, or as "observers" that delightfully vague phrase that encompasses a multitude of sins. At a recent seminar, Ashwini Nachappa astonished us with the story of how the officials to an event in South-East Asia outnumbered the athletes! Par for the course is when the number of officials equals that of the atheletes.

The number of horror stories that I personally have experienced would fill a book.

I have routinely waited for clearance to travel to world championships till a couple of hours before departure. Some unfortunates in other sports have suffered the humiliation of being refused permission to board the departing aircraft with their colleagues as the government did not have the courtesy or the good sense to inform them or their Associations in reasonable time of its inability to fund the trip. Yet it is standard for beaming ministerial faces, especially during high-profile cricket events, to leap out of TV screens and the national dailies as if somehow they had a fundamental role to play in the goings-on.

Irrationality and prejudice are and have always been, the bane of many Indian sports associations. Where in the world would a player with a brilliant Davis Cup debut not even be called to the squad the following year because the Captain found the youngster's habit of listening to music on a Walkman in his spare time difficult to accept? Which country treats juniors with great potential as non-persons when they reach the senior ranks? Which other country is stupid enough to prepare a team for the Asiad in Seoul (where the temperature was in the low 20s) in the unbeatable 40 degree plus temperature of Delhi and its environs? Which country lives in a time where turning professional invites censure from the Association, where "making money" from sport places a sportsperson outside the pale of respectability, even though the officials can merrily do exactly that?

In this environment, it is hardly surprising that we have failed dismally to make the kind of impression in international sport worthy of the abundant talent in our country. In fact, the surprise is that we have managed to produce the names already mentioned and a few others.

Is there any hope for India? Leander Paes's Bronze medal apart (a one-off achievement which others will find perhaps impossible to emulate). I do not think that we will win any individual medal at the Olympic level in the forseeable future. It will take ages to create an ideal environment for ensuring that talent, and we have plenty of that, is brought to full bloom. First, the establishment of a genuine sporting culture at the government level which is not limited to inane appearances at cricket matches which merely pander to super-fatted egos and ambitions. Second, the emergence of individuals dedicated to the cause of sport for its own sake is a distant dream. The only way for that to happen is for these individuals to be paid handsomely for their services, but with total accountability for their actions. Treat sport as an industry with commensurate rewards and the results will follow.

BANDIT QUEEN

February 13, 1983

Circumstance and caste drive an innocent girl to a life of crime. And Phoolan Devi becomes India's most celebrated dacoit

Farewell to arms: *Phoolan Devi's dramatic surrender at Bhind*

Pramod Pushkarna/India Today

The making of
a NATION

"If I had money, I would build a house with rooms as large as the hall of this prison. But I know all this is a dream. If any woman were to go through my experience, then she too would not be able to think of a normal life. What do I know, except cutting grass and using a rifle."

— *Phoolan Devi, on what she wants from life, after her surrender.*

FEBRUARY 13, 1983, 9 am. The village of Bhind in remote Madhya Pradesh is packed as thousands of villagers have walked there to witness history, to see the legendary female dacoit, Phoolan Devi, Dasyu Sundari, heroine of many, wonder of the Chambal valley.

Just after 9 am. Phoolan Devi walks on to the stage, facing the crowd. She wears her trademark red bandanna, a new khaki uniform, a red shawl. Her rifle is over her shoulder, her gunbelt round her chest. She picks up one of three waiting garlands and puts it on a portrait of Mahatma Gandhi, then one for the Hindu goddess Durga. The third is for Chief Minister Arjun Singh. Then, she bends down and touches his feet. Walks to the edge of the stage and lifts her rifle and gunbelt above her head. Puts them down. The bandit queen has surrendered. To Durga, to Gandhi, to the law. India's most famous and celebrated dacoit is

carried away to jail, caged. Freedom lost.

It is a moot point, though, whether Phoolan Devi ever had freedom. She was born, 26 years before this, to the low caste of Mallahs, in the Uttar Pradesh village of Gorhi ka Parwa. Caste is very important in this part of India, and Phoolan's caste touches the lowest spot of Sudras. The geography of this barren area cannot help either. Poverty, hunger, humiliation, hard work, corporal punishment are the early lessons of Phoolan's life, with parents burdened with four daughters and no sons. By the time she is 11, she is raped by a husband 20 years older than her. But Phoolan is a fcisty girl with spirit. At 10, she has fought with her cousin, Maiyadin, who cut down her family's neem tree and got a Panchayat decision in her favour over some borrowed grain. But the feud with her cousin is not so easily decided.

Child marriages are the custom in Uttar Pradesh, even if they are banned by law. But custom also dictates that married girls live with their husbands only after they reach puberty. Phoolan is not so lucky. If there is any good fortune, it is in that her father rescues her soon after her husband assaults her, because she has fallen ill. But this does not last long enough. Her place is with her husband, she must go back to him and his nightly rapes. It is now that a girl of 11 swears revenge. *Khoon ka badla khoon.*

Phoolan finds a protector in Vikram, a Mallah like herself. He kills Singh — known for his cruelty to gang members and victims both — and marries her. He takes her back to her first husband so she can exact her revenge on him. As Phoolan Devi lifts that neem stick against Putti Lal, her fate is sealed. Crime will now answer where the justice system has failed. The Bandit Queen is born. The next stop is Maiyadin, who escapes her wrath under cover of darkness. His fate falls on his brother-in-law Mansukh. Egged on by Vikram, Phoolan kills Mansukh with the .306 rifle she has been learning to use. "Police dogs, this is in store for you, Phoolan Devi," says the note Vikram leaves on Mansukh's body on her behalf. Power flows through the barrel of a gun.

In her village, and for other oppressed communities in the area, Phoolan Devi is, truly, acquiring the stature of a goddess. For years, tortured by the Thakurs and Brahmins, the high caste Hindus, and shunned and beaten by the police, these low caste villagers have little hope of fair treatment, let alone justice. Old feudal systems and loyalties and age-old lines of division make a mockery of democracy. Phoolan Devi, with each rapist she thrashes, each cruel Thakur she kills, is only standing up for the downtrodden and the weak. Fighting back the only way possible where the law is steeped in the same traditional ways of life.

Her legend grows as stories of her exploits spread through the area. Phoolan Devi is the saviour of the oppressed. Villagers can only cheer when she kills those that they hate. But Phoolan's trials are not yet over.

August 13, 1980. Vikram is killed in a combination of

Caged: *By law and society*

Pramod Pushkarna/India Today

A pattern is now established, where Phoolan is rescued and returned. Finally, her husband files kidnapping charges against her parents. Bloated with corruption the Uttar Pradesh police may be, but child marriage cannot be countenanced. Putti Lal, her husband, is shooed off. Till Phoolan reaches puberty. The law cannot argue with custom. Only this time, Putti Lal is not interested in rape — he has taken a second wife. They both want a whipping boy, or girl, in this case. When she runs away now, it is for the last time.

There is little peace at home, however. Her parents are bowed down by years of degradation and Phoolan is the most outspoken member of her family. An altercation with the village pradhan, and she is gang-raped in front of her parents.

She runs away to a married sister, only to hear that her parents have been arrested, and she has been branded a dacoit, now a fugitive from the law. The accusation has been made by Maiyadin, and she is arrested, thrashed and raped to an inch of her life by policemen, confessing to any crime to save her family from threats made through the assaults. Phoolan is 15, forced out of childhood by cruelty and circumstance combined. Luckily, the judge frees her.

The next year, she is abducted by dacoits who ransack her village. Their leader, Baboo Gujar Singh wants her for himself.

Born again: *Phoolan Devi as an MP in 1996*

Thakur revenge and intra-gang rivalry. Phoolan is alone once more. Her protector and lover for the past year, gone. Phoolan is captured and then raped repeatedly by men of the Thakur caste, seeking revenge for her exploits against them. She is helped to freedom by sympathetic villagers, and forms her own gang with Man Singh. Her only thought is revenge for Vikram's death...

February 14, 1981, Behmai village, just south of Delhi. In cold blood, 22 Thakur men are gunned down. People say it is Phoolan's revenge. She is silent on the issue.

As Phoolan spends a year on the run in the harsh and rocky Chambal ravines, the question of dacoity reaches a climax in the region. In June, 1982, Chief Minister V P Singh resigns after his brother is killed in an attack. As much as the impact of Phoolan's actions is social, it is also political. Dacoity must be contained, and the surrender of the Bandit Queen would be a fine gesture. And so the long negotiations for a surrender begin. At 24, she has 48 major criminal charges against her, including murder, kidnapping and looting.

Phoolan demands that she surrender in Madhya Pradesh, not Uttar Pradesh, that her family be rescued from there, among other things. "What does it matter where she surrenders?" asks Prime Minister Indira Gandhi and the stage is set for one day in Bhind.

After her surrender, Phoolan Devi will spend 11 years in jail, waiting for the Supreme Court to release her. A celebrated and controversial film will be made on her life, books will be written.When she is released in 1994, the tough girl with the red bandanna has become a matronly woman. But there is fire in her belly — she wins a seat to Parliament and hijacks a train to keep an appointment. The Bandit Queen lives. ∎

Pramod Pushkarna/India Today

STILL THE SECOND SEX
Women in India wait for a fair deal
By Urvashi Butalia

HALF a century into the life of independent India is time enough to ask if things have improved for women in India. Important though the question is, it is a difficult one to answer. On the face of it, things seem to have changed. Women are more visible in what is known as the public sphere. At a policy and planning level, they can no longer be ignored. Ever since the Sixth Five Year Plan (1980-85) when, for the first time, a chapter was devoted exclusively to them, women have come to occupy more and more space in policy documents (although, activists would argue that, despite this, the attention paid to them is woefully inadequate); no political party has a manifesto that ignores women — although once in power, all do their best to do so! And there is perhaps the most significant development of all: reservation of 33 per cent seats for women in panchayats. Significantly, this move has not called up the same sort of opposition that the move for reservation in Parliament has — perhaps because power at the national level has more to offer to those who already have it, and they are not willing to give up a third of it to women.

In the early stages of the contemporary women's movement, attention was focused mainly on questions of dowry and rape — seen then as among the worst manifestations of violence against women. Among the first campaign that women's groups took up was the struggle against rape. This was sparked off by the rape of a young woman in Maharashtra and the decision of the Supreme Court to acquit the two policemen who were accused of raping the minor girl (despite the fact that the high court had indicted them). Four eminent lawyers addressed an open letter to the Chief Justice of India protesting the patent injustice of this decision, and this sparked off a countrywide campaign against rape. Several other key cases became part of this campaign which resulted, after years of protest, in the government agreeing to change the law on rape. The amended law was enacted in 1983 after long discussions with women's groups.

Although the anti-dowry campaign began somewhat differently — for example in many places pressure was brought to bear on offenders so that they could be isolated in the community in which they lived — it followed a similar trajectory in the end. Women found themselves protesting, and the government responded by changing the law on dowry, attempting to, but not succeeding in, giving it more teeth.

Very soon it became clear that changing the law was merely touching the tip of the iceberg. The real problem lay elsewhere. Rape and dowry were only two rather extreme manifestations of the systemic and structural violence women faced everywhere in their lives and if this was to be

Rising Violence Against Women							
Crime	Year					Percentage Variation in 1994 over	
	1990	1991	1992	1993	1994	1990	1993
Rape	9,518	9,793	11,112	11,242	12,351	29.8	9.9
Kidnapping and Abduction	11,699	12,300	12,077	11,837	12,998	11.1	
Dowry Deaths	4,836	5,157	4,962	5,817	4,935	2.0	-15.2
Torture	13,450	15,949	19,750	22,064	25,946	92.9	17.6
Molestation	20,194	20,611	20,385	20,985	24,117	19.4	14.9
Sexual Harassment	8,620	10,283	10,751	12,009	10,496	21.8	-12.6
Importation of Girls	-	-	-	-	167		
Sati Prevention Act	-	-	-	-	2		
Immoral Traffic (Prevention) Act	-	-	-	-	7547		
Indecent Representation of Women	-	-	-	-	389		
Total	68,317	74,093	79,037	83,954	98,948	45.0	17.9

Note: Figures pertain to crimes reported. Source: *Crime in India*, 1994

addressed, the women's movement would have to work at several different levels at once. Despite changes in the law for example, if the implementing authorities were lacking in the will, and the machinery, to implement them, little would come of lobbying them. Today, nearly a decade and a half after the laws on rape and dowry have changed, not even one person has been convicted in a case of dowry death, or indeed, punished even when — as in the Suman Rani case — the fact of rape has been proved and accepted by the court. Thus, statistics of violence continue to rise, and the perpetrators of violence continue to get away, often without being charged at all.

Perhaps the most stark example of this is the incident of widow immolation that took place in Rajasthan in 1987. Roop Kanwar, a young widow, was burnt to death on her husband's pyre, in full view of thousands of people. Yet, when the case came to the court, the court took the view that coercion could not be proved because there were "no witnesses". One cannot but wonder whether a public flogging of a man would have called up the same kind of response.

Roop Kanwar's death also highlighted another important question for women: Deorala, where the incident took place, is a village that, on the face of it, has all the trappings of "development": a school, reasonable wealth, electricity, markets and so on. Despite this, if people could continue to condone and endorse widow immolation, how far could what we see as "development" be said to have worked?

More recently, in 1992, another case in Rajasthan led to considerable rethinking on questions of violence and justice. Bhanwari Devi, a sathin working in Women's Development Programme (run by the state and Central governments, along with the support of non-governmental organisations) was gang-raped by high caste men of her village for trying to stop child marriages. When she reported the rape, Bhanwari faced obstacles and opposition at every point in the government machinery, and despite women's groups insisting that she, and other workers like her, be given some protection if they were to continue doing work for the state, little of this was forthcoming. Meanwhile, Bhanwari's rapists have been let off, and have used their considerable economic and caste clout to have her and her family isolated in the village and the community. How, activists have asked, is it possible to fight for

justice in such an environment?

It is important to ask why this is so. As the millenium draws near and India strides into the 21st century, it seems to me that its many, inherent contradictions are becoming sharper and deeper. There are women in all sorts of important positions in India today. Yet, we only need to scratch the surface to find a more sinister, hidden reality. This is the misogyny and fear of women that lies beneath. Some years ago, Ranganath Misra, then serving as the Chief Justice of India, castigated women for behaving "unnaturally" by moving outside their "natural" sphere, the home. What kind of justice can women expect at the hands of such a man? The same man later headed the National Human Rights Commission — women who had recently succeeded in getting women's rights recognised as human rights found this laughable. What kind of expectation could they have from him? What else but hatred and fear of women would push political leaders to make use of the "woman card" while electioneering, and then do their best to scotch women's entry into Parliament?

But look at panchayats: despite scepticism and doubts that women would be in there only as proxies for their fathers, brothers and other male kin (and surprisingly, no one has raised this question for men, who are often there in the same capacity) women have proved suited to political power, and have handled it intelligently by turning their attention to real, survival issues.

In terms of health and nutrition, attitudinal biases ensure that girls and women are fed less, educated less, given less care, and hitherto taboo things such as child sexual abuse and incest with girl children are only just being articulated. None of this is new. What is different and important though is that as the dimensions of the violence grow, women are becoming more and more determined to counter it. In this they are not alone, for they have the support of concerned men, without which things would be much more difficult. For while some women may be complicit in their own oppression, it is also clear to that violence against women is not the concern of women alone; rather it is an issue that men and women need to take up and address for a violent society is something that all of us need to be concerned — and worried — about.

The Indian woman: *Still searching for justice*   Sunil Mahadik

WINNING THE WORLD

June 25, 1983

*Kapil Dev's ragtag-and-bobtail team shocks the West Indies in the Prudential Cup final.
And a nation celebrates*

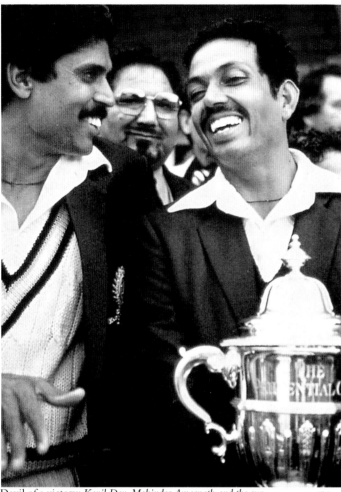

Devil of a victory: *Kapil Dev, Mohinder Amarnath and the cup*   All Sport

"Let's go out and fight."

*Kapil Dev to his teammates during the lunch interval after India had been
bowled out for 183 in the 1983 Prudential Cup final against the West Indies at Lord's*

The Indian cricket team's arrival in England in the summer of 1983 for the Prudential World Cup is nondescript. There is no battery of photographers at Heathrow to click Kapil Dev and his men, no savvy denizen of Fleet Street to weave a story of exotic Oriental willow wizardry or magical spin bowling. The romance of Ranji and Duleep has become as passé as the spendour of the Raj. In any case, in the late 20th century fix called limited overs cricket, only results matter, which is why India's arrival for the third World Cup hardly matters.

The media, however, is not being discourteous. The past offers no encouragement for the present. India's track record in this type of cricket is pathetic. In the inaugural World Cup in 1975, there was but one win to their credit, against lowly East Africa, which was no credit at all. And, in 1979, there was not even the one face-saving win, only more ignominy when Sri Lanka, then not even a full member of the International Cricket Conference, beat them too.

What then does 1983 have in store? Not much different say

the wise bookmakers at Ladbrokes by offering handsome odds of 60-1 on an India win. And if this seems condescending, there is worse. Most critics rubbish India's prospects in the tournament with David Frith, cricket historian and editor of theWisden Cricket Monthly, vowing to eat his words if India won the World Cup.

Look at this ragtag-and-bobtail side, they ask. No quality fast bowler barring one, no quality spinner at all, two outstanding cricketers sure, but aren't they now pitched against each other?

Indeed, the last is a niggling worry not just in England but even more in India. The two pillars of the side are Sunil Gavaskar and Kapil Dev, one a champion opener the other a brilliant all-rounder, both assured of their places in the Hall of Fame, but now both seemingly pushed into conflict. Or such is the fear, because captaincy has remained the most vexed issue in Indian cricket for 50 years – one that has spawned innumerable controversies, personality clashes and hence unstable teams.

In the latest round of musical chairs that the Indian selectors were wont to play, Kapil Dev, had replaced Sunil Gavaskar at the helm. The latter had lost a series against arch enemy Pakistan in the 1982-83 season for which, as Indian cricket aficionados knew, there could be no pardon. The axe fell on Gavaskar and in his place rose the 24-year-old Kapil Dev as the new messiah of Indian cricket.

The fear that this reshuffle in captaincy would create a conflict between India's two main players was never substantiated, but lingered nevertheless when the team reached England for the World Cup.

In circa 1983, therefore, only the most optimistic or foolhardy would have plumped for India, and there were not many of these species around in England. But cricket has a peculiar logic that can make book form into hogwash. In less than three weeks after their arrival Kapil Dev and his merry band of cricketers scythe through the caustic criticism and cynicism to record one of the biggest upsets in sport this century. From no-hopers to champions, from the lukewarm introduction at Heathrow to the sizzling victory at Lord's, they chart out an amazing path and leave in their wake shattered rivals, befuddled spectators and chastened critics. But in fact, this astounding turnaround has its genesis in a little-discussed match played more than two months earlier.

March 29, 1983, Berbice. It is the second one day international against the West Indies and a packed house in this small ground have come to see India get walloped again by Clive Lloyd's team who have won the first match convincingly by 52 runs. But wait! There is something strange happening here. The Indians seem to have finally got over their fear and the demonic fast bowlers are actually getting thrashed. Gavaskar run out for a strokeful 90, Kapil Dev for a belligerent 72, India a formidable 282 in 47 overs. And then the fine bowling and fielding, thwarting the flurry of shots from Viv Richards and stifling the late surge from Dujon. India win by 27 runs, the first time they have beaten the West Indies in limited overs cricket. A psychological gap has been bridged.

By the time the World Cup commences this match has been forgotten, of course. Indeed, for India's first game of the tournament is against Clive Lloyd's side, which the media ignores, expecting no surprise. They are drastically wrong.

June 9, 10, Old Trafford. Intermittent rains mar the first day making batting a frustrating exercise. This is a rain-hit match which spills over into the second day. That's when India get the thrills as they stymie a spirited rearguard action from fast bowlers Andy Roberts and Joel Garner who put on 71 runs for the last wicket to enable West Indies to reach 228. But that is still 34 runs short of India's bountiful 262. Kapil Dev's men have taken a giant step towards cricketing glory.

After a victory against Zimbabwe in the next game, however, the momentum sags. India are thrashed by Australia by 162 runs, and in the return match of the league, West Indies exact sweet revenge by posting a 66 runs victory. To clinch a berth in the semi-finals, India simply have to win their next two games.

June 18, Tunbridge Wells. In the salubrious environs of this small spa town in Kent, India are off to a horrific start after being put in to bat by Zimbabwe. Gavaskar goes for a blob, two more wickets fall on 6, the fourth on 9 and the fifth on 17. Skipper Kapil Dev, who has walked in at the fall of the fourth wicket, is faced with a hopeless situation. With no frontline batsmen remaining, what should he do?

He opts to do or die, and stays on to play perhaps the most spectacular one-day innings ever. Strokes emerge from his bat in a fusillade, dispersing the field and peppering the boundary with fours (17) and sixes (6). The Zimbabweans,

Smash hit: *Srikkanth gives Andy Roberts a taste of his prowess in the final*   P Eager

Historic moment: *Michael Holding's wicket falls and Roger Binny and Yashpal Sharma swoop for souvenirs*   All Sport

cockahoop not too long ago, are now cowering under the fury of his assault. With Binny, Kapil Dev adds 60 runs for the sixth wicket, with Madan Lal 62 for the eighth and a spirited unbroken 126 runs for the ninth with Syed Kirmani. At the end of the innings, India's score reads 266 for eight, Kapil Dev, 175 not out. Under this extraordinary onslaught, Zimbabwe are demolished. India have hit the throttle.

June 20, Chelmsford. This is the last league match. Australia are riven by internecine problems but experts still reckon that upstarts India have run their course. This had to be it. Not for the first time, the experts are off the mark. Down the order, India bat well to score 247.

Then comes the bigger surprise. Roger Binny and Madan

Lal, two honest-to-goodness medium pace trundlers, bundle out the cocky Aussies with controlled swing and seam bowling that has the onlookers gasping in disbelief. Australia dismissed for 129. India, unbelievably, are in the semi-finals.

June 22, Manchester. It is a packed Old Trafford that greets Kapil Dev's team. England are strong contenders for the Cup; hear the inspirational chants and patriotic songs of the supporters who have thronged here to will their side to victory. But cricket does not respect sentiments, even less poor performance. England, put in to bat, struggle to make 213, two part-time bowlers, Kirti Azad and Mohinder Amarnath putting the brakes on their progress with some controlled seam and spin bowling. On an easy-paced wicket this is a modest target. Gavaskar and Srikkanth provide a flying start, Amarnath sensibly drops anchor to prevent hiccups, and Sandeep Patil and Yashpal Sharma come out to play rousing half-centuries that leave the English bowlers beaten and tired. In the stands, one Indian supporter holds up a banner which says that 'Kapil Dev eats Ian Botham for breakfast'. There could have been no more sumptuous summation of the match. Onward to Lord's!

June 25, Lord's. The stewards at Grace Gates cannot conceal their amazement. "So, now we have Gandhi coming to Lord's," says the wise one to which the other nods sagely. The caustic comment is both a salute to Richard Attenborough's magnum opus on the Mahatma as well as symptomatic of the gross disbelief which has accompanied India's passage into the final. The opponents here are the by-now-familiar West Indies who are in cracking form having stormed their last four matches in roaring style.

The match begins badly for India. By the time the Grace Gates have been closed, Gavaskar has been dismissed by Andy Roberts. A scintillating cameo innings from Srikkanth pumps up the adrenalin of the Indian supporters, but cannot prevent the West Indies bowlers from making regular strikes. The resolute Amarnath holds one end up for a while, but not much longer. India don't last out the overs and are bowled out for a paltry 183. It seems like a cakewalk from here for the West Indies. The final could be an anticlimax.

In the Indian dressing room during the break between innings, there is only muffled conversation. Most players believe they have blown their chance. Then skipper Kapil Dev rises from his seat and exhorts his teammates. "Let's go out and fight!"

A 'banana' inswinger from Balwinder Sandhu bamboozles Gordon Greenidge and bowls him. West Indies 5 for one, and there is now a discernible spring in the steps of the Indian players. But out strides the majestic Viv Richards to a standing ovation and soon demonstrates why he is called the king of batsmen. Boundaries explode from his bat as he unleashes his unmatched repertoire of strokes. Richards gallops to 33 in a trice and the bowling already looks helpless. Then, in a fit of misplaced arrogance, he miscues a pull off Madan Lal. The ball soars high into the sky on the on side. Kapil Dev, fielding at mid-wicket, sprints back 20 yards and holds the catch over his shoulder with nonchalant ease. In fact it is a spectacular effort. The biggest threat to India has been removed. The floodgates have been opened.

Innocuous medium pacers, Amarnath, Madan Lal, Binny and Sandhu, as they have done right through the tournament, chisel away at the batting now with regular success. The calypso beat with which the West Indies supporters had set the tempo for the match right through the day, loses rhythm and then fades into gloom as wickets tumble rapidly. When Amarnath has Michael Holding leg before wicket, there is stunned silence at Lord's. Then pandemonium. The West Indies dressing room is stricken with grief. Ten thousand miles away, from Kashmir to Kanyakumari, an entire nation has gone into delirium.

In one memorable day, India have turned the cricketing world upside down. ∎

THE KAPIL DEV STORY
All-round success

KAPIL Dev was easily the most gifted player to represent India. A natural sportsman who could have excelled at any game, he took to cricket as a teenager, then grew into becoming an outstanding player of not only his, but any era.

Kapil Dev made an immediate impact on cricket when he forced Pakistan opener Sadiq Mohammed to wear a helmet against him in the 1978 series. The Indian attack had by then got taken over completely by spinners and the arrival of this 19-year-old youngster from Haryana was like a breath of fresh air. It was also to give Indian cricket a new direction.

In the a few years after his debut, Kapil Dev blossomed into an exciting cricketer and soon honed his skills to be rated as one of the four great all-rounders who played cricket in the 1980s, the others being Imran Khan, Ian Botham and Richard Hadlee. He bowled fast medium pace with excellent control and variations, and was a brilliant striker of the ball, if a trifle impetuous.

Having quickly established himself as India's premier matchwinner, Kapil Dev became one of the pillars of the team alongwith master batsman Sunil Gavaskar. As they rewrote record after record, these two players helped raise India's stock enormously in the cricketing world.

Kapil Dev's golden hour came in the 1983 World Cup when he inspired a team that was written off before it began playing to snatch a sensational win. His own performance in that tournament was nothing short of remarkable and his 175 not out against Zimbabwe is widely regarded as perhaps the greatest one day innings ever.

Stints as captain did not weigh on his performances. Kapil Dev carried the responsibility with the nonchalance that marked his cricket. Even when he was unceremomiously dropped from the captaincy, he continued to render yeoman service to the team, bowling with unflagging zest on unhelpful wickets in India, or rising to take his place as spearhead when playing overseas. When he quit in 1994, he left a void that seems impossible to fill.

Tests 131, Runs 5248, Ave 31.05, Wkts 434, Ave 29.64
ODI 224, Runs 3783, Ave 23.79, Wkts 253, Ave 27.45

The making of
a NATION

On the go: *Kapil Dev's breath-taking 175 not out against Zimbabwe changes the course of the 1983 World Cup*
Patrick Eager

Top Indian Players 1972-1997

Gundappa Vishwanath: Stylish player with wrists of steel and a fascinating repertoire of strokes. Only 5'4, he had a big heart that enabled him stand up to fast bowlers with courage as well as play the game like a gentleman. Perhaps India's most loved cricketer ever.

    Tests 91, Runs 6080, Ave 41.93 ODI 25, Runs 439, Ave: 19.95

Mohinder Amarnath: The comeback man of Indian cricket, he played for 20 years without quite being a regular member of the team. For three of these, in the early '80s, he was rated as the top batsman in the world.

    Tests 69, Runs 4377, Ave 42.49, Wkts 32, Ave 55.68
    ODI: 85, Runs 1924, Ave 30.53, Wkts 46, Ave 42.84

Dilip Vengsarkar: Tall and elegant, he was the most versatile Indian batsman in the mid-80s. A joy to watch when in full flow, he scored three hundreds in a row at Lord's, the Mecca of cricket.

    Tests 116, Runs 6868, Ave 42.13 ODI 129, Runs 3508, Ave 34.73

Mohammed Azharuddin: Began his international career with three hundreds in three Tests, earned renown as a batsman of style and panache and brilliant fielder. Unexpectdly made captain in 1990, became the most successful ever in India's history.

    Tests 83, Runs 5011, Ave 43.95 ODI 1245, Runs 6701, Ave 36.62

Krishnamachari Srikkanth: Opening batsman whose ebullience and unpredictable strokeplay brought in spectators in droves but made his rivals into nervous wrecks. In one-day cricket, especially, he could be deadly with his uninhibited batting.

    Tests 43, Runs 2062, Ave 29.88 ODI: 146, Runs 4092, Ave 29.02

Syed Kirmani: Wicket-keeper par excellence, he earned the sobriquet Kojak after shaving his head a la Telly Savalas. Dapper and supple, Kirmani was a splendid man behind the stumps, whether standing back or up. A doughty late-order batsman too.

    Tests 88, Runs 2759, Ave 27.04, Catches 160, Stumping 38
    ODI 49, Runs 372, Ave 20.72, Catches 27, Stumping 9

Dilip Doshi : Orthodox left-arm spinner, his professorial looks hid a cunning mind and considerable skill, went out in acrimony. But in five years had done enough to make his departure regrettable.

    Tests 33, Wkts 114, Ave 30.71 ODI: 15, Wkts 22, Ave 23.81

Ravi Shastri: Hardworking cricketer whom the Indian spectators loved to hate. From left-arm spinner batting at number 10, he became all-rounder then an opening batsman of substance. Highly rated for his acumen, he could but lead India in only one match which he won.

    Tests 80, Runs 3830, Ave 35.79, Wkts 151, Ave 40.96
    ODI: 150, Runs 3108, Ave 29.04, Wkts 129, Ave 36.04

Manoj Prabhakar: A feisty and fighting cricketer, he made his mark as an all-rounder of merit. Crafty swing bowler and a gritty batsman who priced his wicket dearly. Faded out sadly in controversy and bitterness.

    Tests 36, Runs 1490, Ave 32.39, Wkts 94, Ave 36.58
    ODI: 129, Runs 1855, Ave 24.09, Wkts 157, Ave 28.88

Javagal Srinath: Perhaps the quickest bowler since Mohammed Nissar, he spent his years as apprentice to Kapil Dev learning the tricks of the trade. With him, India were able to match fire with fire and contest on even terms with opponents.

    Tests 27, Wkts 92, Ave 31.92 ODI 123, Wkts 158, Ave 28.96

Anil Kumble: Unorthodox leg-spinner, his steady line and length and steely determination helped him become one of the pillars of the team of the '90s. An intelligent man, he played within his limitations, but never ceased expanding and exploiting the scope of his talent.

    Tests 38, Runs 618, Ave 16.70, Wkts 163, Ave 27.44
    ODI 120, Runs 398, Ave 8.84, Wkts 167, Ave 26.27

Sachin Tendulkar: Took the cricket world by storm even as a schoolboy. Made his international debut at 16, his first Test hundred at 17 and was captain of the team just after his 23rd birthday. By this time, his spectacular batting had already marked him out as India's best player – perhaps of all time – and arguably the best batsman in the world in the late '90s.

    Tests 53, Runs 3617, Ave 50.23
    ODI 150, Runs 5321, Ave 39.13, Wkts 46, Ave 57.53

Sachin Tendulkar   Mohammed Azharuddin

PLAYING FOR INDIA
Memories of two wonderful tours
By Sunil Gavaskar

FIFTY years after Independence, with the fanatical following for cricket increasing everyday, the question commonly asked is why isn't India a champion cricketing nation. India has had some of the finest players in the world. And the following for the game has grown phenomenally. Cricket is popular even in villages, thanks to the far-sightedness of All India Radio in having regional commentary and now with satellite TV bringing into the living rooms, matches played as far away as in the West Indies.

But the Indian team has had sporadic wins in Tests, and even more rare series victories. In 1971, the scenario changed, for that year, under Ajit Wadekar's captaincy, India won not only one, but two series abroad. Now, winning overseas was considered a dream till then, though India had defeated New Zealand in their country in 1967-68 under Tiger Pataudi. That was an impressive victory but coming as it did on the heels of an 0-4 drubbing by the Australians it did not generate the kind of euphoria that the 1971 successes did. Of course the opposition is an important factor and New Zealand have seldom been considered one of the top teams in the world.

The West Indies on the other hand have invariably been amongst the best teams playing in any era and so to beat them in their den was a feat that brought joy to millions of cricket lovers in the country. Then, to follow it up only a few months later with a win over our erstwhile rulers, England, was like icing on the cake. Those victories were the turning point for India in Test cricket. No longer did the Indian team set out to tour already believing that they were inferior to the opposition. No longer could the opposition take the Indian team for granted. Sure there were some disasters that followed these victories, notably the 1974 tour of England, where India lost all the three Tests and that too badly; but the feeling the opposition used to have, that they just had to make an appearance on the field to win, was no longer fated.

If 1971 was the turning point for Indian cricket in Test matches, 1983 was the year the Indians began to believe they could be winners in limited overs cricket too. That was, of course, the year the third World Cup was played in England and India, against all expectations, went on to win it, beating no less than the defending champions West Indies in the final. In one-day cricket till then, India had had even rarer wins than in Tests. With that World Cup triumph the Indians began to look differently at one-day cricket which was considered more of an appendage than a proper cricket match.

It was only on the 1980-81 tour of Australia, where the Indian team played in a triangular series with New Zealand as the third team, did the Indians begin to take the one-day game seriously. Till then in most series, home or away, involved India playing a couple of one-day games at the end of the tour. And many of the top Test players did not even play in these games, preferring to rest.

All that changed in 1983, and as the one-day game became an integral part of the modern tour, the players too learnt to make adjustments to try and be successful at this level. The most difficult adjustments were in temperament. Though the belief is that a good player will play well in any form of cricket, it is truly only the good player who can make quick mental alterations and develop the approach and attitude that can succeed in both versions of the game. To many players, bought up in an era by coaches who taught the player to play risk-free cricket, it was difficult to imagine taking the kind of risks that the one-day game demands at certain stages. So they struggled, whether they were batsmen or bowlers. But today these adjustments come easily and naturally, simply because the attitude and approach to one-day cricket has changed. It no longer is a game where one just goes to play without any strategy or planning. It is no longer a 'time-pass' game as it was when it first started in international cricket.

The architects of these two turning points in Indian cricket were the captains of those teams. The 1971 victories were achieved under the leadership of Ajit Wadekar and the 1983 World Cup triumph was under Kapil Dev Nikhanj. There were never two more different personalities, but it was their individual brand of leadership that was required to make Indian cricket believe in itself in the two formats of the game.

Ajit Wadekar was appointed captain by the casting vote of the then chairman of the selection committee, Vijay Merchant. Since Wadekar had displaced Tiger Pataudi as captain, there was

Captain's choice: *Sunil Gavaskar and his first captain Ajit Wadekar beating the English weather*   Central Press Photo

a big hue and cry, with newspapers speculating that Merchant had acted so because of the differences he had had with Tiger Pataudi's father more than two decades earlier. Over the 50 years of our Independence if there is one thing that has not changed, it is the ability to 'read' the minds of those in public focus. So every action by the public figure is invariably given a non-cricketing reason by such 'mind-readers'. That Wadekar went on to win their first series as captain and then to beat England in England did not make an iota of difference to the 'mind-readers', for no credit was given to Vijay Merchant. One of India's greatest cricketers was and still continues to be maligned by people who have neither the experience nor knowledge of what happened in that meeting.

Wadekar's leadership style was low-key and he took his time to get the loyalty of those who had played under Tiger Pataudi. For the youngsters in the side, it was terrific to have a captain on whose door you could knock without any trepidation or reservation. Wadekar often gave an impression of indecisiveness on that first tour, but when he made a decision it usually turned out to be one of genius. His bringing on Salim Durrani to bowl just when the West Indians were effecting a recovery in the second Test was terrific, for Durrani got rid of Clive Lloyd and the incomparable Garfield Sobers in two consecutive deliveries to ensure that India did not have a huge target to chase for victory.

Similarly, Wadekar's bringing on Bishan Bedi for just one over to get rid of a stubborn stand between Richard Hutton and Derek Underwood was another stroke of genius. As soon as that wicket fell, Wadekar brought back Chandrashekhar who went on to dismiss the tail and set India on the road to victory.

If Wadekar's leadership style was marked by a certain self-diffidence, Kapil Dev's was flamboyant and energetic. Here was a cricketer who was born to play sport. Kapil was a natural athlete who would have excelled in any sport he concentrated on. It was Indian cricket's good fortune that he chose cricket to show his natural skills. While Wadekar seemed a trifle too thoughtful in his decision-making, Kapil was instinctive, as distinct from being impulsive. A captain who goes by his instinct is likely to be more successful then one who goes by impulse, and in 1983 Kapil Dev did nothing wrong.

He won the tosses which the team needed to win simply because then we got the choice to either set or chase a target. His bowling was incisive which meant that the opposition seldom got a good start and his batting was explosive. The 175 he scored against Zimbabwe after India were five wickets down for only 17 runs must rank as one of the greatest one-day innings ever. His bowling changes and field placing were top class and his never-say-die spirit inspired every player to fight and not give up, as was evident in the finals when India were defending a paltry score of 183.

Two wins in different formats under captains who had different personalities. To be part of those teams was a privilege as my good friend and India's world class wicket-keeper, Syed Kirmani, will verify. To be part of teams that brought about a change in the perception about Indian cricket was an honour that is rare and unforgettable. To see the Indian tricolour on top of world cricket was an achievement that still gives me goose pimples...

And reliving those special moments? Well, only those who were part of it would know the feeling!

UNHOLY VENTURE

June 3, 1984

Operation Bluestar targets militants in the Golden Temple and bruises the Sikh morale everywhere. Terrorism unleashes new horrors all over India

I am not a Guru. I am only a postman of the Guru. I read out his message to his followers.

— *Sant Jarnail Singh Bhindranwale*

BUT undoubtedly, Jarnail Singh Bhindranwale, the young Akali leader, is being modest. For thousands of Sikhs, in a Punjab looking for its rightful place in the list of nations, he is close to a messiah, his pronouncements are more important than those of a poor postman's.

In the confused world of Sikh politics in the 1980s, Bhindranwale straddles both spiritual and temporal power. His rise, it is said, was thanks to the highest powers within the Central Government and the Congress Party. But much like pets which bite the hand that feeds them, so Bhindranwale makes the transition from puppet to power centre. And he chooses for his well-armed, militant and anti-government movement Amritsar's famed Golden Temple as headquarters.

As the Akali Dal and the Congress squabble and negotiate over ending the rise of militancy in Punjab through political solutions, Bhindranwale's stockpiling in the Golden Temple continues. Taking the line of least resistance, state and Central Governments watch. Already, in Punjab and the rest of the country, the demand for Khalistan has exploded from *rasta rokos* to hijackings and shootings. Arms have been smuggled over from Pakistan, where, it is believed, extremists are being trained. Hindu passengers are pulled out of a bus and shot. Lala Jagat Narain of the *Samachar* group of newspapers, who does not support the Khalistan movement, is killed in 1981. A year later, his son, who carried on his father's line, is also murdered. In 1983, 20 Punjab Police officers are killed.

"The government has denied us our rights for the last 34 years. We are fed up. We want more rights. We want a separate place for Sikhs," says Bhindranwale.

What these acts do create is a change in the popular perception of the Sikh. From being hard-working, brave and fun-loving, prosperous people, India starts to see its turbaned Northern brethren as terrorists, men who hurt. The strong, brave Sikh warrior who was perceived as a guardian of the Indian people now becomes an enemy, someone to be protected from. It is this fear that creates perhaps more separation than even Bhindranwale and his tribe could imagine.

The fear psychosis spills into everyday life — a helpless government, a demoralised police force and an increasingly militant populace. A sacred temple over-run with arms. Hopeless as the Punjab problem seems, Indira Gandhi, Prime Minister of India, is reluctant to bring the army into the Golden Temple to flush out the terrorists. But there appears to be no alternative. The Central Reserve Police Force has already refused the job after its Director General Shiv Sarup decided the task was too messy and complicated for him. Apart from the militants housed in the temple, there are ordinary people, pilgrims and devotees. The risk is high.

Enter the army.

June 1, 1984. Major-General Kuldip Singh Brar of the 9th Infantry Division cancels his holiday in Manila after a summons from the Western Command headquarters in Shimla. He is to attend a meeting in Chandigarh. Western army commander Lieutenant-General K Sundarji and chief of staff, Lt-General Ranjit Singh Dayal brief the small audience. Operation Bluestar is launched. Brar has charge on the ground. Over 70,000 crack troops are to be brought into use. An indefinite curfew is imposed in Amritsar.

June 2, 1984. Prime Minister Indira Gandhi announces on All India Radio that the government has been trying to negotiate with the militants in Punjab, but every meeting of demands was met with fresh stipulations. It appears, she says, that the Akalis are run by extremists, pointing to the non-cooperation movement scheduled for the next day. '*Sare Jahan Se Achha*' sings the radio before she starts. And a prayer to Saraswati. An appeal to beauty, unity and wisdom?

June 3, 1984. The siege by the army begins. Will a show of military might quell the extremists into submission? The answer, after temple towers fired at one day are manned again the next, seems to be a resounding 'no!'.

June 4, 1984. The army brings into attack mountain guns and 25-pounders. The extremists retaliate with rocket-propelled grenade launchers and rockets. This is not going to be an easy battle.

June 5, 1984. Army gunners get into the act. But there are civilians in the Temple complex and the extremists have strong defences. Casualties are already heavy. Under cover of night, army commandos slip into the Temple to bring the moderates out. Other units give them covering fire. Infantrymen move in to cut off the extremists. Jawans, ordered not to fire at the Golden Temple, are killed in the cross-fire. The storming of the Temple now becomes a reality.

June 6, 1984, 7.30 am. There is no alternative but to order tanks and armoured personnel carriers into the Temple to destroy the fortifications around the holiest of holy sites — the Akal Takht and the Harminder Sahib. Bluestar can now no longer just flush out terrorists from the Golden Temple. To protect the Temple from terrorists, it must destroy part of it. As night falls, Bhindranwale and his two lieutenants, Shahbeg Singh and Amrik Singh, fight their last battle from the Akal Takht basement. They are shot in sten gun fire. The death of their leader diminishes the strength of the militant defence. It is over. In the rest of the Punjab, Operation Woodrose has cleared other gurudwaras of terrorists. The army operation has been successful.

But the damage done has been immeasurable. The government's White Paper says 4,712 killed and over 10,000 injured. The army itself loses over 1,000 men. The Akal Takht has been damaged. The lives of many innocent men, women and children trapped in the Temple during the curfew have been lost. And Bhindranwale has become a martyr.

But the greater damage could be to Sikhs everywhere. The change of perception from a position of trust to one of

The making of a NATION

(opposite) Misguided messiah: *Jarnail Singh Bhindranwale*   P Pushkarna/India Today

suspicion has already affected many of them. Now, however, the pain of an army assault on their most holy site is felt by all Sikhs — secessionist or not. If the extremist takeover of the Golden Temple was not bad enough, this seemingly brutal clean-up operation is worse.

Bluestar acts as the point from which Punjab seems to go completely out of control — starting with the assassination of Mrs Gandhi on October 31, 1984

July 24, 1985. A summer interlude as Prime Minister Rajiv Gandhi and moderate Akali leader Sant Harchand Singh Longowal sign an accord.

August 20, 1985. Longowal falls to an assassin's bullet as he leans over the Guru Granth Sahib.

August 10, 1986, General A S Vaidya, Chief of Army Staff during Bluestar, now retired, is shot dead in Pune. Later, Air-India's jumbo jet Kanishka explodes mid-air over the coast of Ireland. Acts of terrorism increase in frequency and horror. Bhindranwale rules in death with an authority he could not acquire in life. Surjit Singh Barnala, newly voted into power in September 1985, heads an Akali government riven by dissent. Weak and handicapped by breakaway factions, he cannot control the spread and threat of militancy. But he can and does attempt to revitalise the Punjab Police, now headed by Julio Ribeiro.

May 11, 1987, President's Rule is imposed on Punjab.

Yet, the almost insane spate of violence spawned by Bluestar, now gradually slows down. Partly because the police is more confident, partly because the people themselves are tired of life under the threat of militancy. Time, the great healer, works its slow cure.

By the time militants hole up in the Golden Temple again, both the authorities and the people have learned their lessons.

May 15, 1988. Operation Black Thunder has its first success as 146 militants surrender. This operation, conducted by the National Security Guard assisted by the Punjab Police, is a siege, with a strategy to combat militant thinking. The curfew is limited to the Golden Temple. The maneouvres are commando-style. The media is informed. The damage is limited. Thirty killed and none from the security forces.

The Sikh spirit is not damaged. Bhindranwale is definitely dead. ∎

The shepherd and his flock: *Bhindranwale and followers* Raghu Rai/India Today

WOUNDED PYSCHE
The need for a Sikh identity
By Rahul Singh

THE Sikh religion is the youngest major religion in the world. It was founded relatively recently in the 15th century by the first Sikh Guru, Nanak. He tried to bridge the two main religions of the time in India, Hinduism and Islam, by combining the best of both.

Guru Nanak was basically a peace-loving man, his teachings and philosophy reflecting this. However, soon after it was established, Sikhism began to face persecution at the hands of the Mughals. The pacifism of Nanak started to gradually give way to a more militant creed, largely by force of circumstance. This culminated with the last Guru, Gobind Singh, a formidable military leader who often defeated the Mughal forces sent against him and who founded the "Khalsa".

It was under Guru Gobind Singh that the distinctive Sikh identity of the turban, the uncut hair and beard was established. Thereafter, these two contrary strands of Sikhism — pacifism and militancy — were to become an integral part of the religion and explain its appeal.

The Sikhs reached their apogee under the great 18th century Sikh emperor, Ranjit Singh, whose empire covered most of undivided Punjab and Kashmir. One of his generals even tried to invade Tibet. The British, who were becoming the dominant power in India, waited till the death of Ranjit Singh before they militarily took on the Sikhs. After a series of pitched and closely-fought battles, the Sikh empire succumbed.

The British, appreciating the fighting qualities of the Sikhs, quickly incorporated them into their army by "raising" Sikh battalions, as they did with the equally formidable Gurkhas. The Sikhs served with great distinction in the British army in the two World Wars. In fact, at one time, 35 per cent of the Indian army consisted of Sikhs and 25 per cent of its officers were also Sikhs, even though only 1.5 per cent of the Indian population was Sikh.

When Partition came, the Sikhs in Punjab, where they were concentrated, threw in their lot with India, since they had been traditionally closer to the Hindus even though their monotheistic creed was really more akin to Islam. Millions of Sikhs came from what became West Pakistan, as destitute and demoralised refugees. Yet within a few years they picked themselves up, put their lives together and prospered. Punjab, which was 60 per cent Sikh, became the granary of the Sikh farmer. The Green Revolution, almost entirely the creation of the Sikhs, was one of the very few economic success stories of Independent India.

This background to the Sikhs is essential to an understanding of the trauma the community faced from the mid 1980s to the mid 1990s. After the initial glow of Independence, many Sikhs began to feel uneasy. They felt they were not being given a fair deal, considering their sacrifices to the nation (Sikhs had also played a prominent role in the movement for independence, out of all proportion to their numbers) and their role as soldiers and farmers. This feeling took the shape of the demand of a "Punjabi Suba", a Punjabi-speaking state which was, in truth, a not-so-cleverly disguised Sikh-majority state.

Jawaharlal Nehru resisted the demand but Indira Gandhi succumbed to it, in her own clever fashion. She gave the Akali Party, the party which claimed to represent the Sikhs, a Punjab shorn of much of its former glory.

Sikh alienation was further reinforced by a powerful feeling that the community was losing its identity. This had nothing to do with Indira Gandhi, it had everything to do with modernism. More and more Sikhs were casting aside their traditional symbols, the main being their long hair, turbans and beards. They were becoming "mechanised".

For quite a few Sikhs, this mechanisation was sounding the death knell of the community. Something had to be done about it. When a religion, especially a young religion, or a community, particularly a proud one, feels itself in crisis, there is usually a desperate search for a saviour. Master Tara Singh and Sant Fateh Singh tried to be such saviours in the three or four decades after Independence. They failed.

In the early 1980s, another figure arose, much more malevolent — and probably a little crazed — who was aided and abetted by the Congress Party: Jarnail Singh Bhindranwale, an obscure semi-literate preacher. The Congress thought he would come in handy against the Akalis which proved to be a terrible miscalculation. The puppet turned into a Frankenstein's monster, preaching violence, hatred of the Hindus and an independent state for Sikhs that was unacceptable.

Terrorism was Bhindranwale's main weapon. Sadly and unfortunately, he had the support of quite a few Sikhs who looked on him as a kind of modern-day Guru Gobind Singh. He was nothing of the sort, but he had many honourable Sikhs, it must be said, in his thrall.

One of them was General Shahbeg Singh, the man who had trained the Mukti Bahini, the Bangladeshi guerilla forces, in their war for independence. Shahbeg was dismissed from the Indian Army for reasons which are still not very clear. Then, Bhajan Lal, when he was chief minister of Haryana and when terrorism had started to rear its ugly head in Punjab, issued an infamous order that all Sikhs passing through his state had to be searched, no matter how important they were.

Shahbeg Singh, along with many other highly-respected Sikhs, had to undergo this humiliating experience. Shahbeg subsequently said in an interview that this was the last straw. He joined Bhindranwale and was, in fact, the man who masterminded the terrorist resistance in Amritsar's Golden Temple during the June 1984 army action: Operation Bluestar. Shahbeg and Bhindranwale were killed in the action, along with hundreds of terrorists, soldiers and innocent pilgrims caught in the crossfire (the exact figure of those killed is still not known).

Bluestar wounded the Sikh psyche as few actions had done in Sikh history. Indira Gandhi thought she could use it for her political ends, to show her firmness against terrorism and demonstrate to the nation how she stood for unity against secessionist forces. But it was a gross miscalculation (the army, in its arrogance, had apparently assured her that it would be quick action, with little loss of life). She paid for it with her life when two of her Sikh bodyguards assassinated her in her garden five months later.

But slowly the tide began to turn against the terrorists as the Punjab police got their act together. At the same time, the fraternal ties between Hindus and Sikhs, though strained, held. Above all, the Sikh community itself, which at one time had a sneaking sympathy for the terrorists because of Bluestar and the killings of Sikhs after Indira Gandhi's assassination, also turned against the terrorists.

By the beginning of 1996, except for the isolated incident, Sikh terrorism came to a virtual end. For the first time in years, Baisakhi was celebrated with gay abandon. Punjab's nightmare decade had come to an end.

Tough stance: *Militants at the Golden Temple*   India Today

TAMING THE TERROR
How the Punjab Police did it
By Julio Ribeiro

THERE is no better way of explaining terrorism than to cite the example of a man-eater. The man-eating tiger or leopard strikes unsuspecting victims miles away from the scenes of its previous kills. Nobody knows when it will strike or who it will strike. Hence everybody in the extended vicinity lives in mortal fear of instant death and this built-up fear makes life in the surrounding areas extremely uncomfortable and miserable.

The terrorist does basically that same thing. His intention being to create panic and terror, he may strike at one village in district 'A' on one day, at a town in district 'B' after a few days and then even in a crowded place in a city in district 'C' after a gap, leaving sufficient time for the effect of the terror to sink into the consciousness of the population. It is easier to do this in the nationalist form of terrorism where even law-abiding and thinking members of the community to which the terrorist belong provide the sympathy they want.

The first real test of terrorism that this country witnessed, terrorism of the nationalist variety in its classical form, was in Punjab after the death of Bhindranwale. Sikh separatists, fired by the call for a separate state of Khalistan and fed on stories of injustice against the Sikhs, both real and imagined, attacked Hindus in different places at different times with the sole purpose of creating terror and forcing the Indian state to concede to their demand. They pulled out people from buses and trains, segregated the women, then separated the men who had no beards and turbans and lined them up to shoot them with AK47 automatic weapons in cold blood. The weapons were mostly procured from across the border. When trains and buses began to be guarded, they targeted the market places where mainly Hindus gathered or the open parks in cities where the RSS organised its parades or the 'jagrans' which only Hindus attended.

If reinforcements were poured into the affected districts, the terrorists shifted their area of operations to other districts, forcing the authorities to extend their defence, thinly so as to enable them to strike at will. It was basically a cat and mouse game which could not ensure a victory for either side since it did not involve face-to-face combat. Mass migrations of Hindus from villages followed. They fled to the towns where the population of the Hindus was sizeable. Some even left the state in a desperate attempt to save their lives.

This led to immense anger against the government. The impotence and inability of the state to protect life and property was highlighted and condemned. Police officers hesitated to visit the scenes of the killings because public anger invariably translated itself into attacks on the police with stones and other missiles. The police were accused, wrongly as it was later proved, of sympathising and collaborating with the terrorists. The people made such allegations in desperation, but their only result was to demoralise the police.

One of the suggestions was to hand over the state to the army. The army, of course, resisted attempts to get involved. The army top brass knew that terrorists do not fight conventional wars with troops, tanks, artillery and mortar. They strike from behind when it is least expected, a type of war in which the army is not trained. Also, the people they are called upon to fight are not enemies but their own countrymen who have been led astray. Incidentally, the internal security forces, that is, the police and the para-military had also found themselves in a situation where they were fighting unconventional criminals who were motivated by factors other than gain or pelf.

The predominantly Sikh police force of the Punjab was confused. Terrorism was not a familiar phenomenon. The force had never confronted law-breakers who were convinced that they had a moral right to kill. They had never confronted law-breakers who when caught were not repentant and who before being caught were not afraid of losing their lives.

At the beginning, it was said that terrorism is a low-cost war. Conventional warfare requires money, an unlimited number of volunteers to fight and sophisticated weapons of destruction. When these are not available to malcontents, a ready solution can be found in terrorism, where the enemy relies on only a few brainwashed men who become the leaders and a slightly larger number of followers, who are drawn from among the ranks of ordinary criminals.

If a country neighbouring the one in which terrorism has erupted is inimical and is ready to provide training camps, sanctuaries and safe passage for arms and money, terrorist operations become easier. This has happened in Punjab and later in Kashmir, with Pakistan providing the necessary assistance.

From Pakistan's point of view, supporting terrorist activity across the border is much easier than risking a conventional war, where the outcome is bound to go against them and the economic and political costs are bound to be daunting.

The classical method of fighting the nationalist form of terrorism is to appeal to the minds and hearts of the affected community, the co-religionists of the terrorists, who form the natural constituency and recruiting ground for new volunteers. At the same time, it was necessary to identify and neutralise the brainwashed cadres of the underground network. Hence, the security forces had to concentrate on gathering information about their identity, their hide-outs, their supporters and the source of their arms and ammunition, including the places where these were stored.

In terrorist situations, the main problem faced by the police is that of obtaining information about the identity and the movements of the terrorist, their logistical support and sanctuaries. The population is either afraid to give such information for fear of reprisals or they themselves have sneaking sympathies on religious or community basis. The police are then forced to adopt unconventional methods to obtain the information they require in order to neutralise the gangs. One of these methods, which has been used from time immemorial, is to infiltrate the gangs. This is not easy because the type of individuals who would be willing to carry out this extremely risky operation have themselves to be criminally inclined besides being sufficiently bold. This is the tragedy of anti-terrorist operations. You have to rely for help on individuals who are willing to live on the edge of death, just like the terrorists themselves do.

Informers have to be recruited from among the ranks of terrorist themselves, the minor followers who after capture are willing to risk the wrath of their friends in return for their freedom. In Punjab, the local officers had devised a method of using repentant terrorists to help the police in identifying the main culprits.

A major problem faced by the police was of strict compliance with the law. It is ironic that people who do not acknowledge the legitimacy of the state and its laws, who say that such laws do not apply to them, want the police to be particular about compliance with those very same laws. The then Chief Minister of Punjab, Sardar Surjit Singh Barnala, once complained that the police had developed cold feet and were not moving out to patrol at night. He said that the terrorists ruled the countryside from dusk to dawn and that was unacceptable. Enquiries with the officers at the grass roots revealed that the policemen were reluctant to patrol in uniform. The terrorists moved in the normal garb of villagers. When challenged, they replied with their AK47s and the police were at a distinct disadvantage in such a situation. At the same time, it was not legal nor advisable for the police to open fire on a group of people who may turn out to be ordinary villagers and not terrorists at all.

Another problem was the incessant propaganda of human rights groups against what was termed as 'state terrorism'. Some of these groups were pro-terrorist, and the PHRO was, in fact, a front for the terrorists. Retired High Court Judge Ajit Singh Bains and his colleagues were more feared by senior police leaders than terrorists. By addressing and influencing real and committed human rights activists worldwide, they effectively hindered anti-terrorist operations.

Human rights propaganda usually took the form of alleging that terrorists were shot in cold blood after capture. While nobody can with conviction assert that this never happened, shooting of culprits by the police without producing them before courts of law was an age-old practice in Punjab. The Jats of Punjab are essentially tribal in their attitudes and culture, where revenge is a predominant emotion and personal vendetta took precedence over belief in courts of law. Policemen, it must not be forgotten, share the culture and attitudes of the people from whom they are drawn.

But Sikh peasants were not basically separatists and they were not in favour of living in disturbed conditions for prolonged periods. But they did have sneaking sympathies for the terrorists who they felt were fighting not for their own selfish ends, but for the community as a whole. Sacrifice has always been admired in the Indian ethos. It is more marked in the Sikh ethos.

The Sikh peasantry found two sets of predators sponging on them. One, of course, was the terrorist who wanted money, food, shelter. The second was the police who came usually during the day and threatened to arrest farmers

Under siege: *Militants surrender after Operation Black Thunder* India Today

The making *of* a NATION

and landlords for harbouring the terrorists. The question then, before the people, was which was the greater evil? Which group was more troublesome — the terrorist or the police? When it was the terrorist menace, the people turned against them. This happened especially when the criminal component from among the terrorists went beyond the demand of money and shelter to the demand for sex. When their wives and daughters were raped, the Sikh peasantry rose against the terrorists and gave them up to the police. This led to the decimation of a great many terrorist cadres.

The police forces in terrorist-affected states are driven to extra-judicial methods in their desperation. Laws like the now disbanded Terrorist and Disruptive Activities (Prevention) Act did help to correct this. It helped conscientious officers to employ enacted laws to put away terrorists who otherwise would have been released on bail if these laws did not exist. The release of brain-washed terrorists on bail inevitably results in their committing more terrorist crimes and killing more innocent civilians. The police are then doubly frustrated because they are burdened with the task of again tracing and arresting offenders whom they had once traced with considerable difficulty.

Laws like TADA become important in areas like terrorist-afflicted Punjab, where the judicial system has collapsed.

REVENGE MOST FOUL

October 31, 1984

Operation Bluestar brings no peace. Prime Minister Indira Gandhi is shot dead in her own courtyard by her own security staff. A nation is stunned

"If I die today, every drop of my blood will invigorate the country."

— Indira Gandhi, Orissa, October 30, 1984

NEW Delhi, October 31, 1984, just after 9 am. Prime Minister Indira Gandhi is walking at her usual brisk pace from her 1, Safdarjung Road residence towards the neighbouring 1, Akbar Road, a 15 second walk through a garden gate. Waiting at the other side is actor Peter Ustinov, here to interview the Prime Minister for Irish Television. Behind Mrs Gandhi, her secretaries and in front of her, security guards at the gate.

Or not, as it turns out. As Mrs Gandhi approaches the gate, Senior Inspector Beant Singh aims his service revolver at her and fires. Point blank range. She cries out and starts falling. On cue, Constable Satwant empties his carbine into the frail body of the 67-year-old woman. Five shots from the revolver and 25 from the carbine.

9.12 am. Indira Gandhi, prime minister of India, lies bleeding...

"Hamne jo karna tha kar diya. Tumhe jo karna ho kar lo." In the horrified silence before anyone can react, the two assassins throw down their weapons. They are apprehended by the other security staff and taken away. Only one other person, an assistant senior inspector, walking behind Mrs Gandhi, is injured. The assassins had aimed true. Reaction sets in. Panic breaks out. All systems break down. Daughter-in-law Sonia Gandhi rushes out of the house. The ambulance kept standing for just such emergencies is made redundant by a missing driver. Two Ambassador cars are pressed into service to take the injured Mrs Gandhi to hospital. No one remembers to call the All India

Prime Minister Indira Gandhi lies in state

Raghu Rai/India Today

Institute of Medical Sciences to inform them of the emergency. When the Ambassadors arrive, the emergency gate is locked.

9. 30 am. The doctors work desperately to revive the Prime Minister. But she has lost a lot of blood. The heart-lung machine, 38 bottles of O-ve blood, whatever can be, is used.

2. 23 pm. The Prime Minister of India is declared dead. "Wish me luck as you wave me goodbye, with a cheer, not a tear in your eye," she had quoted that old World War II song as she was led away to jail just after the Emergency was lifted. No cheers now, not even tears, as a nation is aghast and stricken dumb, numb even. Orphaned, is how some will describe it and then, hers is not the only blood that will be shed.

Outside AIIMS, though, life has not come to a standstill. In an inexplicable incident, the two assassins get into a shooting episode with the Indo-Tibetan Border Police commandoes guarding them.

10.05 am. They arrive at Ram Manohar Lohia Hospital in the ambulance that could not carry their victim. Beant Singh is declared dead on arrival, Satwant Singh is critical.

11 am. All India Radio declares that the Prime Minister has been shot and is being treated. Then the government-controlled media blanks out all news. Far away in West Bengal, Rajiv Gandhi, the Prime Minister's surviving son, hears the news on the police wireless. As he waits for an Air Force plane to take him back to Delhi, he tunes into his transistor for international broadcasts.

Through Delhi, the news spreads like wildfire. The rest of the country learns by rumour and from the BBC and foreign radio broadcasts. AIR is playing Hindi film music. But by now it is known that the assassins are Sikhs, policemen assigned to protect.

3.30 pm, Rajiv Gandhi arrives at the hospital. Around him are doctors, politicians, his family, unable to cope or even understand.

The President of India, Giani Zail Singh, rushes back from Yemen.

6 pm, All India Radio and Doordarshan announce the death of the Prime Minister, and soon after that Rajiv Gandhi is sworn in as Prime Minister by Zail Singh.

People had apparently warned Mrs Gandhi against having Sikh security men, especially after Operation Bluestar in June that year. But brought up in the secular, liberal and forgiving traditions of Mahatma Gandhi and Pandit Jawaharlal Nehru, she refused to pay attention to such petty thinking. Like her father, her concern for her personal safety was minimal, although that was no excuse for the abysmal state that the Prime Minister's security was in. Beant Singh and Satwant were neither policemen of worthy record, although Beant had been in her guard for several years. They were also obviously pawns in a well-planned conspiracy. The motive was, very clearly, revenge for the blasphemy of Blue Star.

Mahatma Gandhi's least heeded advice to this country might be its most significant. "An eye for an eye would leave the whole world blind," he had said, but it went, like so much of what he said, ignored, forgotten. Certainly, it was not heard either by the conspirators or those who would later wreak revenge on the entire Sikh community in Delhi.

Once the shock is over, the anger takes over. All over the country there are sporadic ourbursts of violence. Yet, what happens in Delhi is not sporadic, not outbursts, not unthinking

rage born of the well-spring of emotion. Planned, brutal, cold is the ravaging of the Sikhs — more horrific than the acts of Beant Singh and Satwant Singh for the sheer numbers of one community that are made to suffer for the acts of those two men.

November 1, 1984. Delhi is burning. Men are dragged out of their homes and burnt alive, women raped, children have their eyes gouged out. There is looting and burning as organised mobs terrorise the city's streets. The administration seems powerless to act. So the whispers state that the administration is in collusion with the rioters, the looters, the murderers. That

Brutal reaction: *Anti-Sikh protests at New Delhi's Bangla Sahib* Bhawan Singh/India Today

the Congress party has organised this form of revenge. The rumours are not all wrong. As part of a nation weeps, another takes advantage of weakness and tries to turn the situation around to its benefit — property worth crores is destroyed. Many just pick up their own and run for their lives. Over 3,000 Sikhs in the capital pay the extreme price for the actions of a few misguided, or even criminally-minded men. The sins of sinners must be suffered by the community as a whole. There is no logic or reason in mob thinking. Or even, any justification. And then, justice, which will take more than 10 years to trickle in.

November 3, 1984. The mortal remains of India's fourth prime minister are consigned to the flames. Outside, the flames of calculated anger are still being smothered by an apparently inefficient police force. There are wounds all around. Of violence, of loss, of anger, of pain.

The conspirators: *Satwant Singh, Kehar Singh and Beant Singh*

November 15, 1984, Satwant Singh signs a confession, as the investigation shifts from the Delhi Police to a Special Investigation Team. But political delays make their presence felt here as well.

July 1988, Satwant Singh and a conspirator, Kehar Singh, are found guilty and hanged. Balbir Singh is freed by the Supreme Court. Rajiv Gandhi withdraws the cases against the other accused unilaterally.

The Thakkar Commission finds, in 1985, that the security lapses in the Prime Minister's Guard were deplorable. Culpability lies not just with the police but her advisers. Too late.

Whether Indira Gandhi's blood invigorated this country or not, whether she had a premonition of death when she said those words, whether history will judge her harshly or kindly, her death, by violence, by any means, meant the end of an epoch of contemporary Indian history. Her son has now risen and will write his own pattern on the waters.

But the two losses felt by the country on October 31 — of a prime minister and sanity — make their own tears in the fabric of the nation. ∎

Innocent targets: *Victims of Delhi's anti-Sikh riots*

D Reddy/India Today

Deaths following Indira Gandhi's Assassination

Delhi	1,000	Bihar	200
Uttar Pradesh	117	Madhya Pradesh	87
Haryana	60	Maharashtra	15

Eight committed suicide in Madras; 200 men, women and children shaved their heads.
Saris worth Rs 15 crore were dumped in the famous Paranthewali Gali and set ablaze.

BEWITCHING PRESENCE
Impressions of Indira Gandhi
By Dom Moraes

It must have been in 1959 that I first met Indira Gandhi. I was then 21 and had come to India from London to write a book. For this purpose I interviewed the prime minister, Jawaharlal Nehru. He afterwards asked me to tea at his house, and I noticed a prim lady in a pastel sari flitting about at some distance from the proceedings. I later asked my father, then a prominent editor, who she might have been. He said, "Oh, that's nobody. That's his daughter Indira. She acts as a kind of housekeeper and hostess for the old man." After some reflection, he added, "She must be very tough to be able to put up with him."

By 1966 that "nobody" had succeeded her father as the Indian prime minister. A year later, some London paper asked me to write an article on the occasion of her 50th birthday. I knew nothing about her. I called up my father and other friends in India.

On the strength of what they said (and none of them was unreservedly ecstatic about her) I wrote the article, which was not a favourable one. My father called me from Delhi later, saying that an opposition member in the Lok Sabha had asked a question about this article. Mrs Gandhi had replied, majestically, "Dom Moraes is a very immature young man."

For this reason, when I returned to India a year later to write another book, and had to interview her for it, I felt rather nervous. But, sitting quietly in a pastel sari under a portrait of her father, she gave me an hour and a half of her time. She was gracious, charming, even witty. She dimpled when she smiled; naturally, I liked her. My work kept me in Delhi for some months, and I met her off and on and liked her more.

This was not only because I thought she was a gentle and honest person, in which judgment I was gravely mistaken. It was because she seemed so out of place as a politician. In this I was also mistaken. I wrote of her for *The New York Times,* and this very lengthy profile included a description of her seated in the Lok Sabha between Y B Chavan and Jagjivan Ram. I said that she "looked like a gazelle between two gorillas". The gazelle later destroyed both the gorillas. Years passed. In 1977 Mrs Gandhi fell from power. At this point I was in India, and my English and American publishers suggested that I write a biography of her. I approached her. She agreed, saying she could give me a great deal of her time, since she had retired from politics. Contracts were signed, and I started to work. Two weeks later she phoned and said the country needed her.

In case I didn't fully understand her, she explained that she could not now give me much time for the long conversations she had agreed to earlier. She had decided to

Charismatic: *Indira Gandhi with Cuban President Fidel Castro*   India Today

return to politics. What should have taken six months to finish therefore took two years. At the end of it I did not know anything about her. I knew less than I thought I had known when I started.

I watched her in many moods. Very often she was grumpy in manner. Grumpy is the exact word. Deep lines formed themselves between her eyebrows; she would never look directly at me, but stared into the distance, or at the floor; she answered questions in monosyllables, after long and depressing silences. In this she somewhat resembled her father. She also resembled him in that, for no perceptible reason, she would suddenly turn on her charm, the charisma which had captured the minds of millions.

It is very difficult to define what this charisma or charm was. But, simply speaking, it was as though you had suddenly become the only other person in her world, as though she was deeply interested in what you said and thought, and you were the only one to whom she could tell her innermost feelings. It was when she was in this (rare) mood that I suggested to her that according to what she had said there had been three important influences in her life, all men: her grandfather, Motilal, her father Jawaharlal, and her husband Feroze Gandhi. Which had been the most important? I had expected her to say her father, to my utter amazement, she said, "My husband." She had more or less abandoned Feroze to look after her father, and had taken their children with her. She said, "After Feroze died, all my physical processes were changed." I did not understand her.

But in 1977 there certainly were two men in her life, her two children, Rajiv and Sanjay. By the time I started to write my biography she had already brought Sanjay, the younger one, into politics. He had been one of the major

causes of her downfall in the 1977 elections, because of the brutal thoughtlessness with which he enforced a sterilisation programme in north India. "I watched my father betrayed, time after time, by those who said they were his friends," she once told me. "He brought me into politics because I was the only person he could trust. That is why I have brought my younger son into politics. Sanjay is a doer. Rajiv is a thinker." What Sanjay did undid Mrs Gandhi in 1977: Rajiv was not in politics when I finished my book, but what he thought may not have been what his mother thought he thought.

I had some long conversations with the two sons. Once, when I was looking for a flat in Delhi, Sanjay advised me to settle in Vasant Vihar, "because the rents are much higher but the price of brinjals is much lower." To say I was surprised by this remark would be putting it very mildly, but it was seriously meant. Mrs Gandhi did not seem to like his wife Maneka; but neither did she like Rajiv's wife. This is not a point that the Congress party, which is full of devotess of Sonia Gandhi two decades later, seems to have considered. Rajiv said to me, "We hate living with my mother because the atmosphere is so tense and the place is always full of politicians. It's bad for the children. But we can't move out. First of all, my mother lost the elections. If we left her house now, it would look as if we were abandoning her when she most needs us." This seemed a laudable sentiment, but he concluded, "And anyway we can't afford the rent of another house."

All three of them, the mother and her sons, died violently. Indira and Rajiv Gandhi were assassinated, Sanjay's death may not have been as accidental as it seemed. By the time I had finished the book Mrs Gandhi had withdrawn her help because she said I had told lies in it about Sanjay. At that point the book was still in manuscript and only the publishers had read it. Though I have no very high opinion of Ian Jack as a literary critic, one remark which he made when he reviewed it in *The Sunday Times* seemed to me perceptive. He said that parts of it read as though I was in love with Mrs Gandhi. Certainly, part of the time she bewitched me, when she chose to exercise her charisma. I can only say in my own defence that millions of people were similarly bewitched, and that for all of them it turned out to be a rather malefic spell which was cast upon their minds.

Of the people: *Indira Gandhi in costume*   India Today

POOR MAINTENANCE, HIGH COST

1978 onwards

*Shah Bano's search for justice from her husband exposes Muslim paranoia and
a government unwilling to act*

SHE is a 73-year-old woman, divorced by her husband of over 40 years. All she wanted was something more than the Rs 25 a month maintenance money awarded her by the provisions of Muslim Personal Law. Perhaps the Rs 500 allowed in the Indian Criminal Procedure Code. Just enough to live on.

What she achieved instead was a country in turmoil, an always-fragile religious unity threatened, a debate over the role of the judiciary in public life, the interpretation of the Constitution questioned and a cry of Islam in peril.

And she never got her Rs 500.

April, 1978. Shah Bano, married since 1932, and thrown out of her matrimonial home in 1975 by her husband Ahmed Khan, moves the courts in Indore for maintenance.

November 6, 1978, Khan divorces Shah Bano.

August, 1979. The magistrate rules that she get Rs 25 a month. An elderly woman, married for 43 years, five children and recently abandoned, perhaps she feels she deserves a little more each month than what the Supreme Court will later sarcastically call a "princely sum". Shah Bano appeals.

July 1, 1980. The Madhya Pradesh High Court increases the amount to Rs 179.20 a month.

April 23, 1985. The Supreme Court rules in favour of Shah Bano. Under Article 125 of the Criminal Procedure Act, she should get Rs 500 a month maintenance money from her husband.

The amount of money is still small, the woman is certainly old and insignificant. But suddenly there is an unimaginable threat to India's communal fabric and legal system. Fundamentalist Muslim groups all over the country are up in arms claiming that the Supreme Court has undermined Muslim Personal Law by superseding its provisions. After divorce, a woman gets back the money given as *mehr,* and that's that. The onus for looking after her now falls on her natural family — father, brothers, uncles. The husband has terminated his contract and his responsibility.

But the question that churns the issue is not just of maintenance money and the rights of the husband. It goes back into India's religious and cultural history. Back to the bridges built to bring ancient and medieval laws in sync with the 20th century. It goes back to a Constituent Assembly which sidestepped the issue of a uniform civil code for India because it was too contentious.

Fundamentalist Muslim groups see the Supreme Court judgment as a direct attack against Muslim Personal Law, based on the Shariat. Personal law is dependent on religion in India for all minority communities. How can the Supreme Court step in and overwrite the word of God?

Ranged against the Muslim fundamentalists are women's groups who see the backlash as one against women. From men who do not want to face their responsibilities. Men who do not want to pay for the crimes, and hide behind their religious beliefs. Liberal Muslim thinkers are equally appalled at this reactionary call against the judgment. Lurking in the background are Hindu fundamentalists. Of all India's religious communities it is only Hindus who have to follow a personal law based on the ideals, morals and ethics of the 20th century, without a religious backing. This could be a chance for them to insist that all communities follow one law. Or that they go back to their old laws.

But ultimately, the Shah Bano case is a political battle. After two years as prime minister, Rajiv Gandhi is losing his lustre as the visionary of 21st century India. His promise of providing clean government is collecting dirt at the edges. His young and professional colleagues, picked from close friends and associates, have failed to live up to their potential. The Congress Party's stalwarts, condemned once for their corrupt and conniving ways, are coming back to power.

One of the first nails in the coffin of this government comes via this old woman from Indore. The old leaders are quick to raise the red flags. They point away from progressive thinking to clear threat: the loss of Muslim vote banks. For the Congress, with its image of the party that gave India independence disintegrating, this loss, they say, might be fatal. It is too early for India to enter the 21st century with new laws that disturb the peace. In this round of progress, the victory is not to the most innovative, but the most enduring. Rajiv Gandhi must do something to staunch this wound. Can the rights of one woman be allowed to destroy a party-voter relationship nurtured over decades?

There is reason for fear too. Across the country, there are riots and demonstrations. Images of brutality and reactionary thinking are flashed and relayed. Pressure is put on the old, divorced woman too. The judgment, she is told, goes against the Shariat.

November 15, 1985, Indore. Shah Bano asks the Supreme Court to withdraw the verdict in her favour.

November 20, 1985, Bombay. Over 500,000 Muslims demonstrate against the judgment. Effigies of former Supreme Court chief justice, Y V Chandrachud, who authored the judgment, are burnt. Hindu fundamentalists, never far behind, burn effigies of Maulana Ziaur Rahman Ansari, union minister of state for the environment, in retaliation. Ansari leads the fundamentalist pressure group within the Congress.

One of the strongest critics of the judgment outside the Congress is Syed Shahabuddin of the Janata Party. "Ours is not a

Hysterical: *Syed Shahabuddin*   Principled: *Arif Mohammed Khan*

Pramod Pushkarna/India Today

communal fight," he thunders, "It only amounts to resisting the inexorable process of assimilation. We want to keep our religious identity at all costs." His decibel level drowns out the arguments of scholars and theologians who find no threat to Islam in the Supreme Court's decision. They become both impotent and ultimately, immaterial in this battle.

But there is another statement Shahabuddin makes that is far more significant and telling on his political opponents: "The Humpty-Dumpty of the Congress (I)'s vote banks has come crashing down and never again can all the king's horses and all the king's men put it back again."

On the face of it, panic within the Congress is in order. Shahabuddin himself wins, in December 1985, a by-election with a 70,000 vote margin. The constituency is Kishanganj in Bihar, where, the year before, the Congress had got a 1.3 lakh margin victory from the Bengali Muslim peasants in the area. The lights are clearly flashing red for danger.

Across the country, in various electoral categories, the Congress is losing elections in Muslim-dominated areas. What voice of reason can prevail where religious identity is threatened? And worse, when political supremacy is shaken. Rajiv Gandhi sees one answer. A new bill that will amend the law making the Supreme Court judgment invalid. The solution being that the onus for maintenance be passed on to local wakf boards. No Rs 500 for Shah Bano. Not at this cost.

There is one strong voice within the Congress though. Arif Mohammed Khan, minister of state for power. He defends the judgment in Parliament. He sees the controversy is "much ado about nothing... these people are trying to take a short-cut to heaven by making this world hell for our poor and illiterate women."

If Khan means the fundamentalist clergy by "these people", he will soon have to include his Congress colleagues in his definition. And ultimately, the president of the Congress and Prime Minister Rajiv Gandhi himself.

February 25, 1986. The Government introduces the Muslim Women Protection of Rights on Divorce Bill in the Lok Sabha.

February 26, 1986. Arif Mohammed Khan resigns. The bill, he says, is gross injustice to divorced Muslim women.

His gesture may be understandable, but it is eventually futile. There are few voices that can be heard in the clamour of victory. One such voice tries to make a last-ditch appeal for social justice.

February 28, 1986. Justice V R Krishna Iyer (retd) of the Supreme Court writes an open letter to the prime minister. He appeals against the passing of the bill: "May I entreat you not stand on prestige, which is a poor defence in crisis, but to base yourself on human rights and social justice so that principled politics may overpower communal politicking?"

But if the Lok Sabha passes the bill, Shah Bano still cannot accept her fate. Her personal marital problems may have shaken the nation, but she is still worried that she has not got justice.

March 9, 1986. Shah Bano goes back to the Supreme Court claiming a *mehr* of 3,000 silver coins from her former husband, rejecting the Rs 3,000 he has deposited with the courts.

"My religious leaders forced me not to accept maintenance because, according to them, it is against the Shariat. But now I have decided that I will not leave this matter just like that."

The making *of* a NATION

Long struggle, no avail: *Shah Bano*   India Today

Indomitable will in an impossible situation?

For the country, the consequences of Rajiv Gandhi's bill are not just limited to one woman's fight for justice. Iyer had warned of "the terrible danger of Hindu communalism being whipped up". In the government's lack of vision and political courage in the Shah Bano case lie the seeds of a Hindu backlash. The bogey of appeasement is raised — and with a clear example of injustice. The bricks are now ready for Ayodhya. ■

WOMEN AND JUSTICE
The inequities of India's Personal Laws
By Indira Jaising

THE roots of the divide and rule policy, when it comes to women, were sown into the Indian Constitution itself. When it comes to personal laws, Muslims, Hindus, Christians and all other religious communities are governed by the law of the religion to which they belong. Personal laws govern rights on marriage, divorce, child custody, inheritance, adoption, all other family matters. They are therefore the laws which affect women most. The potential to divide women along religious lines is therefore universal. Almost all of them contain provisions which are highly discriminatory against women. None of them are gender-just. Therefore, instead of being a celebration of difference and diversity, they have all ended up being instruments of oppression and divisionaries.

Article 44 of the Constitution says that the state must start to introduce a uniform civil code on family law 50 years after Independence. We are very far from that goal, and government after government takes pride in reiterating — as if it were an honourable thing to do — that they will not "interfere" with personal laws. As the experience of the Shah Bano case indicates, it is politically dangerous to "reform". Hindu law must be held up as the model of all that is good for the women of the nation, also for political gain. In all this, women are the casualty.

Let us look a little more closely at the laws governing women. In none of the laws are women entitled to matrimonial property rights. On the breakdown of a marriage, a husband can just tell his wife he owes her nothing, and her contribution to building up his career and assets and home counts for nothing. Alimony, a periodic monthly dole, is at the discretion of the judge. Muslim women are not even entitled to that — only three months maintenance during the period of *iddat*.

Women are not the natural guardians of their children, it is the father who is. This means that all decisions relating to the property of the minor are taken by the father alone. In one case, Geeta Hariharan, who wished to make a deposit in the name of her minor son was refused acceptance by the Reserve Bank of India on the ground that only the natural guardian, the father, could make the deposit and operate the account. She challenged the order in the Supreme Court. If the attitude of the bank was not bad enough, two senior judges of the Supreme Court asked during the hearing, "what is the discrimination here?". Under Hindu law, a daughter is not a coparcener and joint family property still passes from father to son, excluding the daughter.

Not all communities have the right to adopt. Christian women find it impossible to get a divorce as to do so they must prove adultery coupled with cruelty or desertion. Muslim women can still be unilaterally divorced in an out-of-court

procedure. These are some of the more discriminatory provisions of personal laws. There is no civil law against domestic violence, a phenomenon that is fairly widespread in our society, cutting across caste and class.

The few advances that have been made, are in the field of criminal law. Section 498 A of the Criminal Procedure Code enables a woman to lodge a complaint with the police, if her husband or his family have treated her with cruelty. Dowry death is treated as a separate offence and dealt with in a more expeditious manner. The procedures dealing with the offence of rape have been made more gender-sensitive, making it possible for a woman to prove that she did not consent to sexual intercourse. However, a victim of rape still suffers character assassination in court and is often for that reason, reluctant to depose.

Yet, despite this seemingly dismal picture, there have been major changes relating to women in our legal and political system. A National Commission for Women has been set up, giving women and their problems national visibility and a forum through which to ventilate their grievances.

The 73rd Constitutional amendment, introduced reservation for women in panchayat, district and municipal bodies. Thanks to this amendment, no less than 10 lakh women have been elected all over the country to local bodies. This one single change is likely to improve the status of women as never before. It is only through their participation in political fora that women can seize the initiative and change the reality of their own lives. It is another matter that the bill reserving seats in Parliament and the Assemblies has not yet been passed. Yet the training ground provided by the panchayats is bound to create women leaders who will play a constructive role in national life.

The balance sheet after 50 years of Independence is not so dismal after all. Laws may not have kept pace with women's changing roles but the self-confidence of today's woman, her participation in economic life has made it possible for her to emerge from the shadow of being wife, mother and daughter and become fully human.

Indian women: *Shackled by society, ignored by law*   Gopal Shetty/Mid-Day

DEATH Inc.

December 2, 1984

Poisonous fumes stalk the still, wintry night air and Bhopal wakes up to the nightmare of the world's worst industrial disaster

FROM *Saptahik Report,* September 17, 1982: 'Save, please save this city.'

October 1: 'Bhopal on the mouth of a volcano.'

October 8: 'If you don't understand, you will be wiped out.'

No one understood what journalist Raajkumar Keswani was saying.

From a Union Carbide report, presented in 1982, by visiting American experts:

"The plant represented either a higher potential for a serious accident or more serious consequences if an accident should occur."

The Union Carbide factory in Bhopal uses Methyl Isocyanate, familiarly called MIC, one of the most hazardous chemicals known to man, to manufacture the pesticide sold as Sevin. The words of the three men who prepared the report on the Bhopal plant would be blissfully prophetic if they had been heeded. Instead, they only underline the negligence behind the awful grimness that engulfs the North Indian town of Bhopal late into the night of December 2, 1984.

Children, adults, animals, wake up, coughing, blinded, panic-stricken, helpless, as a silent gas creeps over their city,

meaning death. But the horror of this story starts before that. It could start in 1982, when the report by the three experts was presented, detailing steps that must be taken to avoid just such an accident. It could start in 1969, when the plant was commissioned using apparently obsolete technology, from Union Carbide's MIC plant in Danbury, Connecticut, USA. It could hop a few years later to the mid-70s when the company's West Virginia MIC plant was given a computerised safety system not introduced in the Indian subsidiary.

But from the realm of speculation and what-might-have-been to the facts of the night themselves. They are terrifying enough.

December 2, 10.15 pm. Union Carbide India Limited, Bhopal. About half an hour before the night shift change, the supervisor asks for a length of piping near the MIC reactor, tank 610, to be washed. A laborious process because it must be thorough, it also requires the tube being washed to be separated from the rest of the system by a metal shield called a slip blind. MIC does not like water. Was the slip blind there at all?

10.45 pm. The shift changes.

11 pm. The pressure in tank 610 rises, as the MIC becomes volatile. The new shift believes, that like in

Chemical carnage: *Victims of the gas tragedy*

India Today

The making *of* a NATION

the neighbouring tank 611, the pressure in tank 610 has also been deliberately increased to move MIC to the pesticide unit, by the earlier shift.

11.30 pm. Workers in the utility area feel a little irritation in the eyes, put it down to a not unusual minor gas leak.

"My eyes were burning as if someone was burning chillies to ward off the evil eye."

2400 hours, between December 2 and 3. Workers near MIC unit also feel an irritation and report to the production assistant. At the same time, the MIC control room operator informs the production assistant that the pressure in tank 610 is high.

Minutes into December 3. A check reveals that the rupture disc in tank 610 has burst and the safety valve has popped.

00.30 am. The water washing the tubes is turned off. Already, too late.

"We were choking and our eyes were burning. We could barely see the road through the fog, and sirens were blaring. We didn't know which way to run."

1.00 am. MIC vapour escapes from the atmosphere vent. Target: Bhopal.

"It was Kafkaesque. People running all over, chappals and shards of glass on the road."

3.00 am. All 40 tonnes of MIC have escaped into the atmosphere. No plugs, only a search for loopholes.

There is, in fact, nowhere to run. The gas comes from all sides. People running away from the factory meet the suffocating fumes carried in the opposite direction by the wind. There are 700,000 people in Bhopal. Enough fodder for a gas that is familiar to chemical warfare. The MIC at Union Carbide is also mixed with the equally deadly phosgene — a killer word to those thousands of young men who died from poison gas in World War I. This is India, 70 years since that war started.

It might as well be 70 years ago, for all that the authorities have in modern communications and disaster management techniques. Blasted by the worst industrial disaster in the world, Bhopal flounders. Like the city's people, the government has nowhere to run either. Blinded by the gas, by ignorance, by heartlessness, by inefficiency, by callousness, by greed.

MIC does not, however, only blind. It also ultimately, and fatally, causes pulmonary oedema. Death by drowning. In your own lungs. At first count there are 2,500 dead, thousands affected. Hospitals and doctors, blundering in the dark against an unknown enemy, can only effect emergency measures. There is not enough information available about the effects of MIC on humans and animals. Even a fortnight later, a patient is admitted to a Bhopal hospital suffering from the effects of the gas every minute. Finally, 5.23 lakh people file cases against Union Carbide.

As investigations begin, it becomes clear that the first mistake was in the omission of the slip blind when the washing of the pipes began. But that was only the first of the horrors to be revealed. Of the five fail-safe methods in the factory to contain MIC, three were out of commission, one was not used in time and the other not used at all. Three earlier gas-leaks — in 1978, 1982 and 1983 — had been covered up, even though a worker died after exposure to phosgene. The plant had also been

consistently cutting back on experienced and expert manpower, apart from ignoring the '82 report of the American experts. Making and selling Sevin is expensive. Human life is cheap. And in multinational land, Third World human life is cheaper.

Spare a curse for Tara Singh Viyogi, Madhya Pradesh labour minister. He told the MP Assembly on December 21, '82, after doubts were expressed about the plant's safety: "It is not as if a great danger is posed to Bhopal by the factory. It is a Rs 25 crore investment. It is not a small stone that can be picked up from one place and put in another." Official collusion and apathy are the final culprits here, holding human life even cheaper than western corporate marauders. Lack of curiosity in the inherent dangers of MIC and the lack of an environmental safety policy mean that a Rs 25 crore plant is a rogue landslide with the right to crush anything that crosses its path.

If there are heroes in this story, they come from the people of Bhopal themselves. Even before the official machinery started working, private operators used their cars, trucks, vans, autorickshaws to ferry people to safety, doctors worked till they were spitting blood, and then some more, volunteers went from house to house looking for victims. The Army also stepped in faster than any other official agency.

December 6, 1984. Warren Anderson, Union Carbide chairman, is arrested when he arrives in India, along with Keshub Mahindra, Union Carbide India Limited's chairman and Managing Director V P Gokhale.

Hours later, Anderson is out on bail. He points out that maintenance of the plant's safety measures was incumbent on the Indian management. Responsibility absolved.

Waiving responsibility: *Union Carbide Chairman Warren Anderson*   India Today

Prime Minister Rajiv Gandhi visits Bhopal. Announces a meagre compensation. Responsibility absolved.

December 12, 1984. A statement is released that the plant will be in operation again. Meanwhile, the lawyers like Melvin Belli have descended, like vultures or saviours, depending on perspective.

It's business as usual. Except for those for whom the nightmare will never end.   ∎

(opposite) The grim face of death in Bhopal   Raghu Rai/India Today

GLOBAL WARNING
The perils of liberalisation
By Dr Vandana Shiva

SINCE the Earth Summit took place in Rio de Janeiro in 1992, countries have been more preoccupied with implementing the trade-liberalisation agenda emerging from the structural adjustment programmes of the World Bank and the Uruguay Round of General Agreement on Trade and Tariff Talks, than with implementing Agenda 21 and the Biodiversity Climate Change Conventions. These agendas for globalisation are conditionalities on the Third World, demanded by the International Monetary Fund and the World Bank.

In the 1990s, Third World governments are not as conscious as they used to be of the conditionalities inherent to trade liberalisation policies imposed by international institutions like the International Monetary Fund and the World Bank. They only refer to the new attempts by Northern governments to impose social and environmental conditionalities on the Third World as social and environmental clauses in free trade treaties.

Five years after the Earth Summit at Rio de Janeiro in 1992, the real assessment that needs to be made is about the environmental costs of globalisation, trade liberalisation, and the conditionalities associated with trade liberalisation that force countries to destroy their environment, or prevent them from taking steps to regulate environmental threats.

One example of countries being forced to destroy the environment is by trade liberalisation measures in the undoing of land reforms and the removal of land ceilings which is destroying the ecologically managed small farms, and converting agricultural land into non-sustainable large export oriented farms. The states of Maharashtra, Karnataka, Madhya Pradesh and Gujarat have changed their land legislation since the new economic policies were introduced in India in 1991 to make the conversion of land from agriculture to industry easier, and to remove ownership limits on land for export production.

An example of countries being prevented from taking steps to protect the environment is the imposing of intellectual property rights in biodiversity and patents on life-forms which undermine community rights and hence undermine the conservation of biodiversity.

The destruction of ecosystems and livelihoods as a result of trade liberalisation is a major environmental and social subsidy to global trade and commerce and those who control it. The main mantra of globalisation is "international competitiveness". In the context of the environment this translates into the largest corporations competing for the natural resources that the poor people in the Third World need for their survival. This competition is highly unequal not only because the corporations are powerful and the poor are not, but because the rules of free trade allow corporations to use the machinery of the nation state to appropriate resources from the people, and prevent people from asserting and exercising their rights.

It is often argued that globalisation will create more trade, trade will create growth and growth will remove poverty. What is overlooked in this myth is that globalisation and liberalised trade and investment creates growth by destruction of the environment and local, sustainable livelihoods. It therefore, creates poverty instead of removing it. The new globalisation policies have accelerated and expanded environmental destruction and displaced millions of people from their homes and their sustenance base.

The focus of the past 50 years of Independence was basic needs. Plans and policies focused on food, health and education. It is another matter that the means used to fulfil these basic needs were non-sustainable. The Green Revolution promoted chemical agriculture. Health care was focused on western allopathic medicine ignoring our rich, indigenous medical systems. Education promoted colonial learning and colonial ignorance.

New social and environmental movements are emerging as a response to the widespread destruction being caused by the resource demands for the new investments based on a major environmental subsidy to global corporations.

The Enron and Cogentrix projects are still being resisted by local communities which will be displaced either directly by the project or by its resultant environmental destruction.

The fish farms and the shrimp industry promoted by the new policy, and financed by the World Bank, has already created ecological and social havoc along India's 7,500 km coastline. Industrial fish farming has destroyed mangroves and fertile agricultural land, created salination of ground water and thus a drinking water scarcity, and polluted the sea. The Supreme Court even passed an order on the basis of a Public Interest Litigation to destroy farms within the Coastal Regulation Zone (CRZ) and regular farms outside the CRZ.

The focus on meat production and meat exports in the New Livestock Policy is in fact an export of our ecological capital in the form of animal wealth. It has led to a mushrooming of slaughter houses. The decrease in livestock populations had created many problems for farmers, and especially for small farmers. Due to the illegal buying of cattle from shandees by slaughter house agents, their cost has tripled, and become unaffordable for most farmers. The decrease in cattle populations has led to a decrease of dung available for manure on farmers' fields, a shortage of dung cakes for cooking, and the closure of biogas plants.

These trends have resulted in the growing indebtedness of farmers who now purchase chemical fertilisers, fuelwood and hire tractor or bullocks to plough their fields. Most farmers complained that the chemical fertilisers that they were using were becoming ineffective, and that they were causing health problems and environmental degradation. In addition, some farmers have become landless after borrowing of money to purchase these external inputs, making the entire process of agriculture unsustainable. It is in this ecological context that a livestock policy guided by trade in meat products needs to be assessed. Communal forces undermine the sustainability discussion of conserving our cattle wealth. Anti-communal

Awakening: *Protestors with an effigy of Warren Anderson at the Union Carbide factory a year after the gas leak*

forces avoid the livestock issue. The protection of Indian agriculture requires a non-communal, ecological approach to the conservation of our cattle wealth.

Five years after trade-liberalisation policies were introduced in 1991, the United Front government came to power in 1996 on the basis of an anti-reform electoral agenda. However, the UF government has continued the reform policies put in place by the Congress government.

It can be predicted that the trade-liberalisation policies will continue unchanged no matter which government comes to power since the primary impact of globalisation is to reduce the capacity of democratically elected national governments to make national policy. These policies are shaped and determined by the World Bank, the IMF, the WTO and the Transnational Corporations.

In Maharashtra, the political parties that made resistance to the Enron project their main election campaign issue, have rushed its clearance through after coming to power. When the Cogentrix project was challenged because it did not have an environmental clearance from the Ministry of Environment, the central clearances were bypassed and decisions left to the state, which does not have any environmental appraisal capacity. In effect, this move makes power projects free of environment appraisal and regulation.

On December 24, 1996, the Provision of the Panchayats (Extension to the Scheduled Areas, Act 1996) was passed. This act is based on a reversal of the logic of a centralised state of the Nehruvian era and centralised TNC control in the globalisation era. The new law is based on the premise that the community is the basic building block of the national system. A formal national system does not exclude the possibility of local self-rule. In fact, the only way to protect the national interest in a period of globalisation is by decentralising decision-making, ownership and control over natural resources.

The Act states that every Gram Sabha shall be competent to safeguard and preserve the traditions and customs of the people, their cultural identity, community resources and the customary mode of dispute resolution.

This is the first concrete step in independent India to realise Mahatma Gandhi's dream of Gram Swaraj.

The movement for Community Rights to Biodiversity and Indigenous Knowledge is another building block in shaping a decentralised democracy based on people's rights and resisting the privatisation of life and living processes through patents and other forms of "intellectual property rights".

These steps in establishing local control over natural resources are necessary for creating environmental and social responsibility and responsibility in government as well as in corporations. They are steps to a future based on protection of people and the environment in place of the "state protectionism" of the Nehruvian era and of the "corporate protectionism" of the globalisation era.

ONLY AMBANI

1982

Arriving from Aden with a few thousand rupees in his pocket, Dhirubhai Ambani and Reliance climb the slippery slope to success

To have success traditionally, you require education or money or family background. I didn't have education. I didn't have money. I didn't have a family background. It is due to my own sheer efforts that my company has become a unique one.

— Dhirubhai Ambani

APRIL 30, 1982. Settlement day at the Bombay Stock Exchange. Day of reckoning for Dhirubhai Ambani. Day of disaster for his detractors and hidden enemies.

Since March 18, a group of bears on the stock market have been giving Ambani's Reliance shares a battering on the BSE, and correspondingly sending all blue-chip prices crashing. By short-selling Reliance Textile Industries, the bear syndicate has pushed the price down by Rs 10, off-loading 350,000 shares on to the market.

Short-selling is simple — sell shares you don't have and then pick them up when the price falls, making a profit. Short-selling works if no one else picks up the shares when you sell them. So who was going to challenge the powerful bears as they sell 1.1 million Reliance shares worth over Rs 160 million?

Who indeed? Ambani is still a yarn trader, not yet the industrialist he is fast becoming. But he does understand the market.

From the time the assault started, Ambani brokers have been hard at work buying up Reliance shares. The quickly-formed Friends of Reliance Association — managements cannot buy their own shares, say the rules — picks up 857,000 of the bears' 1.1 million shares. Ambani, however, is waiting for his day. Every alternate Friday is delivery day at the stock market. Brokers must either deliver the fortnight's dealings, or postpone transactions by buying time, known as *badla*.

April 30, 1982 arrives. Friends of Reliance demands delivery. The bears don't have the goods. Transactions will only be postponed, say the brokers, on a hefty Rs 50 badla charge.

The result is chaos. The bears run helter-skelter to pick up Reliance, the price skyrockets, the BSE is closed down for three days in the ensuing melee.

May 10, 1982. The bears have been burnt and India's markets have a new hero.

It was in 1977 that Dhirubhai Ambani, who started out as a petrol pump clerk in Aden at 17, first went to the stock markets for capital. Indian markets were relatively small then, and businessmen usually went to banks for their money, not to the people. Reliance got 58,000 investors then. In '89, the figure went up to 1.5 million. Five years later, over 3.7 million. By the late '80s, Reliance was holding its annual general meetings in football stadiums. Reliance was the scrip that decided the mood of the stock market. Only a fool would have underestimated

Dhirubhai Ambani: *From merchant to magnate*

Namas Bhojani

Ambani's knowledge of the Indian investor and the Indian investment system, as the bears discovered in '82.

Or indeed, his ability to strike where opportunity lies, taking risks, but covering his weaknesses. This is clear, right from where his story starts.

December 31, 1958. Dhirubhai Ambani lands back on Indian soil with a few thousand rupees. He sets up Reliance Commercial Corporation, with a capital of Rs 15,000 and a bank loan. Exporting spices, oil and yarn, initially to Aden.

But this is a man with a burning hunger. Walking the streets of Bombay's crowded Bhuleshwar area, travelling the country, he saw the future for him — man-made fibres.

February 1966, in Naroda, Gujarat, Ambani starts Reliance Textile Industries, a powerloom unit with a paid-up capital of Rs 150,000. Powerlooms, however, just make unfinished grey fabric, sold unbranded to the wholesale trade. Ambani dreamed of backward integration, a new concept in India that was to become a family business motto. Reliance grew slowly but surely, adding machines one by one — warp-knitting, dyeing, offering more than the average powerloom. By 1977, when it went public, Reliance was making neat profits.

The focus now shifted to establishing Vimal as a brand name. When dealers were reluctant to stock Vimal — not suited to the common man's lifestyle — Ambani travelled indefatigably all over the country, offering franchises to shareholders. He targeted the smaller cities and towns, opening up new profit centres. Enormous advertising campaigns ensured that 'Only Vimal' was synonymous with Reliance.

By 1983, Reliance was India's largest composite textile mill. Getting the best technology was important. It kept one ahead of the competition, important in a country where textile mills were getting defunct faster than yesterday's news. It took Bombay Dyeing, one of India's most respected textile houses, a hundred years to reach a turnover of Rs one billion. Reliance did it in under 12. The arriviste had arrived.

Ambani was also joined by his two sons, Mukesh and Anil. Unlike their father, they had studied at the best American business schools. Like their father, they understood his unmatchable grasp of Indian business methods and opportunities.

But wrapped into Ambani's uncanny knack of getting under the skin of Indian laws and ways of thinking, is the unmistakable mark of a man who is willing to change things to suit him — no matter how. This is an India where Indian business is tightly ruled and controlled by the mandarins in Delhi. No progress is possible, it is said, without 'unofficial' official help.

July 26, 1983, questions are asked in the Rajya Sabha about Non-Resident Indian investment in Indian companies, a new scheme. The questions are probably aimed at London-based industrialist Swraj Paul and his takeover bids for DCM and Escorts. The target shifts when Finance Minister Pranab Mukherjee names 11 companies which have put Rs 225 million in Reliance between April 82 and March 83.

In the glare of public scrutiny it turns out that many of these companies are registered in the Isle of Man, known as a tax haven. They have names like Fiasco and Crocodile Investments. Newspapers reveal that many of the companies were registered only after Mukherjee's statement in Parliament. Most of the investments seem to have been made during Ambani's 1982

Advantage Reliance: *Ambani addresses a stockholders' meeting*   Mukesh Parpiani

squeeze on the bulls. Nothing can be proved, and the subject dies down. A fiasco averted for the moment.

Meanwhile, work is on at Patalganga, a polyester filament yarn plant close to Bombay. Foreign collaborations with Dupont, government licences and regulations that are in their favour, import laws that are changed seemingly to help them and the Ambanis are in big business like never before. On the sidelines is Bombay Dyeing's Nusli Wadia, who has fallen out with the Rajiv Gandhi government and now has to watch Ambani eat the profits of his own inability to buck the system.

But fiascos are waiting for Ambani too. A strike at the Naroda factory. Patalganga takes longer than scheduled to complete. Policy changes do not seem to go in their favour. Costs escalate. The clearance for a debenture issue comes late.

February 9, 1986, Dhirubhai Ambani suffers a paralytic stroke. Now 53, he will start handing over to his sons, keeping his razor-sharp mind in the background. The first test comes in June '86 with the anti-Ambani media blitz that is started by Nusli Wadia's friend, Ramnath Goenka of *The Indian Express.* Every licence change in the government, every seemingly favourable coincidence in the corridors of power is examined. The image of Reliance from a company that is all get-up and go shifts slightly to one willing to pay for the way it goes. Neither Wadia nor *Indian Express* come out clean, but the mud sticks nonetheless. Reliance is stricken, but carries on. Patalganga does get going in 1987, and soon filament yarn will overtake textiles as the company's biggest money-spinner.

A big storm rises a year later, and from then on, Reliance pays the price for being a high-profile company, always in the public eye.

It is revealed in 1988, that Reliance has steadily been buying up shares of Larsen & Toubro, a respected, professionally run, engineering firm. These transactions, helped by financial institutions, had been furtive, not in keeping with transparency requirements. L&T's board does not want to be taken over by a family-run company. Its shareholders do not want to be run by Reliance. They fight back.

This war is carried out in the press, in public, and in boardrooms. Every murky detail about Reliance's past is paraded for eager public consumption. The game gets dirty once again, as Ambani's sons try and get back at *The Indian Express's* anti-Reliance campaign by targeting Wadia — for holding a British passport, being anti-national. By 1991, the Ambanis have bought *The Sunday Observer*, and its daily avatar, *The Business and Political Observer*, tries to take on the might of the *Express*. Charges are traded, allegations made. Matters reach a head when an anonymous attempt is made on Wadia's life. Investigations only reveal the involvement of an orchestra conductor, but the invisible hand of Reliance is gossiped about.

But the battle has always been about business interests and what emerges, eventually, is that Reliance was always clever to skirt the law, without actually breaking it. Like the Fiasco fiasco, the L&T and Wadia dramas also die down. In a few years, the licence raj will be dismantled, remaking the norms of the Indian economy.

Ambani, however, will remain a name to be remembered.■

Bete noire: *Nusli Wadia*

Dinodia Picture Agency

RETARDED DEVELOPMENT
How the licence raj stunted economic growth
Dr Kirit S Parikh

TILL the economic reforms initiated in June 1991, we followed one development strategy. The roots of Indian economic development go back to the debates and discussions in the pre-independence era. There was a surprising degree of consensus among various plans put forward by different groups on the objective of planning. Thus, the National Planning Committee constituted in 1938 under the Chairmanship of Pandit Jawaharlal Nehru, the plan put forward by the doyen of Indian engineers, M Visveswaraya (1934), the People's Plan published in 1944 by the Post-war Reconstruction Committee of the Indian Federation of Labour, or the Bombay Plan by a group of businessmen, Thakurdas et al in 1944, all desired a doubling of per capita income in 10 to 15 years, elimination of poverty, minimum caloric intake targets, removal of illiteracy and provision of medical care (none of which, incidentally, we have met even by 1992).

While the National Planning Committee and Visveswaraya strongly stressed industrialisation, with particular emphasis on heavy and capital goods industries, and equated development with industrialisation, the People's Plan called for stress on agriculture. The Bombay Plan asked for a more balanced development, recognised the importance of heavy and basic industries but also cautioned against excessive emphasis on them.

From the vantage point of the late 1940s, our strategy seemed sensible. If one had looked back then, at the historical experience, one would have noticed the following:

(a) World trade had stagnated for the two decades of 30s and 40s; (b) During World War II, both UK and USA had used price control and production planning; and (c) With central planning, the Soviet Union had become over a short period of 30 years, a world power.

Thus, a development strategy based on planning and export pessimism (that is, import substitution) seemed a logical one. Also, import substitution, self-reliance and the dominant role of state and public sector were clearly articulated in the plans referred to above. One may also note that there was a consensus on this strategy among nearly all economists in India and even abroad.

Yet on the eve of economic reforms in June 1991, after nearly 45 years of following this strategy, one would have noticed that the Indian economy had not performed as well as it could have.

The signs were there for all to see. In spite of 40 years of planning, more than 200 million persons were (and still are) below the poverty line, adult literacy was only 44 per cent, fully 43 per cent of population did not have access to safe water, and the under-five mortality rate was 145 per 1000. Our economic performance was also inadequate. For the first three decades, in spite of fairly high rates of savings, the economy grew only at 3.5 per cent per annum. While the growth rate during the '80s was 5.5 per cent, we faced many problems. Our external debt steadily increased and by June '91 posed a serious balance of payments crisis. Mounting budgetary deficits threatened to push us into an inflationary spiral. Most of our industries, though diversified, were not internationally competitive due to high cost and poor quality. Even the improved industrial growth over the '80s had not led to a corresponding increase in regular employment. Our performance looked pale when compared to what many developing countries of East Asia had achieved. So what went wrong?

The inefficient, slow-growth economy is the result of the strategy of development that we have followed, which has, for the most part, been an import substitution-based growth strategy arising out of export pessimism. A corollary of export pessimism is that foreign exchange is a scarce commodity. Similarly, self-reliance implies that investible capital will be in short supply. Thus both foreign exchange and capital have to be efficiently allocated. To do this, import licensing and industrial permits were introduced. They soon became all-pervasive and the evils of the permit-quota raj infected every part of our economy.

The strategy for industrialisation was based on a 'heavy industry first' strategy. To further self-reliance, technology imports were restricted to only one time, followed by assimilation of the imported technology. Thus, reduction in import content rather than the domestic resource cost of production became the guiding parameter in the drive towards self-reliance. This strategy led to a number of problems. Heavy industries involved lumpy investment with high capital output ratios and long gestation lags. They also required large imports of capital goods. Inadequate infrastructure, lack of experience and the necessity to learn by doing, further stretched the period of gestation. The costs increased and cascaded into all industries using these inputs. To protect the high cost of domestic industry against foreign imports, trade was restricted and protection through tariffs and quotas was provided. To stimulate investment in spite of the high costs of domestically produced capital goods, capital was subsidised through cheap credit and factor prices got distorted. This resulted in the choice of more capital-intensive techniques than would have been appropriate, given the abundance of labour in the country.

Were such a strategy to be properly implemented, even then a capital-intensive slow-growth economy was bound to result. Given the tremendous scope it provided for affecting what economists call rent-seeking activities, influencing government policies or bureaucratic decisions in one's favour to make windfall gains to industrialists, traders, bureaucrats and politicians, it was much more profitable to seek these rents rather than increase the efficiency of domestic production or improve the functioning of the domestic economy.

Domestic industry, which was already protected from foreign competition through import restrictions against any domestically available product, and from domestic competition through industrial licensing, had thus no incentive to be efficient. The plethora of controls, procedures, permits and bureaucratic restrictions have created such a maze that the net effects of these policies were not at all obvious. While the nominal tariffs remained extremely high, averaging 117 per cent in 1989-90, a World Bank study in a review of 16 sub-sectors, found that effective protection rate ranged from 16 per cent to 162 per cent. In another study, a detailed review of 60 projects showed that half the firms studied received negative protection. It was, then, not a

case of the right hand not knowing what the left hand does, but of the right hand not knowing what the right hand does!

The public sector played a dominant role in India and its impact on the economy and consequently on poverty cannot be neglected. The public sector was developed for a variety of reasons. To reduce concentration of economic power in private hands, it was to reach the commanding heights of the economy. It was expected to provide a means to balance industrial development across regions. In the initial phase of development, it was seen as the only way to start large projects requiring heavy investments which private entrepreneurs in India were unwilling to make or were considered incapable of making. It was to generate increasing surpluses and profits, all of which would be available to the state for reinvestment so that investment rates could go on increasing without raising tax rates on private incomes. It was also to be a model employer.

Roughly 50 per cent of the capital formation in the Indian economy between 1965-66 and 1990-91 was in the public sector. It has reached the "commanding heights" in the sense that it generates more than two-thirds of the employment in the organised sector, and around 55 per cent of the value added in the organised sector. Unfortunately, the public sector has failed miserably in generating surpluses and its gross savings have been less than 40 per cent of the investment in it between 1950 to 1985. The reforms initiated in June '91 have led the economy to a higher growth path of 6 per cent to 7 per cent. Yet, we need to shed a lot of excess weight from our past ill-judged socialist policies. This needs to be done fast to help us reach a laudable socialist objective.

The making *of* a NATION

Top 25 Indian Companies

		Mkt Cap 1996	Mkt Cap 1997
1	Oil & Natural Gas Corporation Limited	Mar-96 30229.50	16950.08
2	Indian Oil Corporation Limited	Mar-96 29193.75	22188.00
3	Steel Authority of India Limited	Mar-96 11358.60	13552.00
4	State Bank of India	Mar-96 11269.59	8343.00
5	Tata Engineering & Locomotive Company	Mar-96 11026.99	5751.00
6	Mahanagar Telephone Nigam Limited	Mar-96 10680.00	10350.00
7	Hindustan Lever Limited	Dec-95 10354.64	8167.00
8	Videsh Sanchar Nigam Limited	Mar-96 9600.00	5680.00
9	Reliance Industries Limited	Mar-96 9531.18	11909.00
10	Tata Iron and Steel Company	Mar-96 7271.15	7201.00
11	Industrial Development Bank of India	Mar-96 7069.52	–
12	Bajaj Auto Limited	Mar-96 6478.63	5532.00
13	Hindustan Petroleum Corporation	Mar-96 6415.45	6224.00
14	Larsen & Toubro Limited	Mar-96 6012.97	5949.00
15	Hindalco Industries	Mar-96 5660.10	4273.00
16	ITC Ltd	Mar-96 5570.81	6921.00
17	Bharat Petroleum Corporation	Mar-96 4350.00	4350.00
18	Grasim Industries	Mar-96 4049.36	4194.00
19	Indian Petroleum Corporation	Mar-96 3908.52	3732.00
20	Brooke Bond Lipton India Limited	Dec-95 3879.46	3976.00
21	Hindustan Development Finance Corpn.	Mar-96 3859.16	2025.00
22	Tata Chemicals Limited	Mar-96 3812.56	3923.00
23	Colgate-Palmolive (India) Limited	Mar-96 3562.94	5406.00
24	Indian Hotels Company Limited	Mar-96 3216.70	2275.00
25	National Aluminium Company Limited	Mar-96 3203.52	2964.00

Sourcce: *Balance Sheets*

LOOSE CANNON

1986 —

When the scandal over the purchase of the Bofors gun breaks, charges of corruption boom through the country. And a government falls...

JANUARY 22, 1986, Swedish Prime Minister Olof Palme tells Indian Prime Minister Rajiv Gandhi that there are no middlemen being used in the deal to sell howitzer guns made by the Swedish arms manufacturer, Bofors, to India.

February 28, 1986, Olof Palme is assassinated.

March 24, 1986, the contract between Bofors and India is signed.

April 16, 1987, Swedish national radio's news programme, *Dagens Eko* reveals that Bofors paid 32 million kroner to the account Lotus in connection with the Indian deal.

"Met Bob Wilson at the Sergel Plaza Hotel 09.00. He understood that I could be forced to tell the whole story. One did not care about the consequences for N, however Q involvement was a problem because he came close connection with R. There are no demands... W promised to find out what was said between P and R."

Dangerous recoil: *The Bofors howitzer causes turmoil in the nation*

— From the diary of Martin Ardbo, former managing director, Bofors, dated September 2, 1987.

"O what a tangled web we weave
When we first practice to deceive"

— William Shakespeare, *As You Like It*, 1564-1616

As events unfold over the curious deal between the Government of India and the Swedish arms manufacturer, it seems clear that Shakespeare was uncommonly farseeing. But literary criticism has no place here. Rather, the joy is in the unravelling of a mystery. If Q is who we think it is, can R and P be anyone other than the obvious? And what about the role of N?

These are questions which will hold a country in thrall and disgust for now and for some years to come as revelations stumble out of closets and more and more webs are woven. But first, the setting of the stage. The government of Rajiv 'Mr Clean' Gandhi is in its fourth year when *Dagens Eko* makes its damaging claim. But negotiations to buy howitzers for the Indian Army have started some years before that, and the Swedes have won over the French, the British, the Austrian. The first choice of army generals, apparently, is the French. The first skein in the web.

Arms deals are notorious for the commissions and kickbacks paid and received. Hence the keenness of Gandhi's administration to remove all shadows of doubt. The Bofors deal with India is important to Sweden. Hence the eagerness of the Swedish prime minister to come to India and dispel all doubts. Note: R can stand for Rajiv, P for Palme. And Rajiv means lotus in Sanskrit.

The Bofors deal is worth Rs 1,700 crore. The amount of the kickback apparently paid to the unknown Lotus is Rs 64 crore. Peanuts or the principle of the thing? But as denials and assurances fly around Parliament, India and Sweden after *Dagens Eko's* revelations, one thing is sure: Mr Clean is looking dirty at the edges.

The Bofors gun explodes at a bad time for Rajiv Gandhi's government. He has not had a happy relationship with President Giani Zail Singh, soon to be replaced by C Venkataraman. The star of his Cabinet, V P Singh, has been in the news for appointing a foreign agency, Fairfax, to investigate FERA violations by high people in high places. Then he resigns, after ordering a probe into a shady submarine deal.

Whispers about those involved in the Bofors deal include the Bachchan brothers, film star and Rajiv's close friend Amitabh and Ajitabh, the Non-Resident Indian business family, the Hindujas, Ottavio Quattrochi, Italian businessman and close friend of Rajiv amd Sonia Gandhi, international arms dealer Adnan Khashoggi, godman Chandraswami and Bofors agent in India, Win Chaddha.

Then there are others, whose involvement led them to move away from the deal — close friend and minister of state for defence, Arun Singh, cousin and part of the initial negotiations, Arun Nehru. But all this is still speculation. As newspapers and

Friends to foes: *Rajiv Gandhi and V P Singh*

Namas Bhojani/India Today   Pramod Pushkarna/India Today

Chief opponent: *General K Sundarji votes against Bofors but to no avail*   India Today

87, Martin Ardbo's diaries are confiscated. An entry made in September claims, "Palme's involvement, should it become known, will probably bring down the Swedish government."

As investigations continue, those involved become more and more tightlipped. Two Indian newspapers play a vital role in bringing information to the public: The Hindu from Madras, and the Indian Express. The Government of India is not happy. Nor are those whose names are bandied about. Hardly surprising.

What the Government of India is not able to realise is that the more it obfuscates on the Bofors deal, the worse the repercussions will be. A government that promised openness and new breezes in official procedures is not easy to forgive when it hides behind traditional and musty defences. The newly formed opposition headed by V P Singh is not slow to take advantage of this classic ostrich defence. As Rajiv Gandhi's head is buried in the sand, his opponents gain political and electoral ground.

Whatever actions the government may take, Bofors is not forgotten. Information trickles in, and each time there is an uproar. Perhaps one that attacks the credibility of the Government most is when in September 1989, former chief of army staff, General K Sundarji (retd) reveals in a press interview that he was bulldozed into approving the Bofors gun over the others. And that he had wanted to cancel the contract.

Two months later, the country goes to the polls in the general elections. Rajiv Gandhi, damaged in the recoil of a Swedish howitzer, loses. V P Singh, the new Mr Clean, is the new prime minister.

But the affair of the Bofors gun is far from over. It ceases to be an electoral issue, but the questions have not been answered. The Swiss courts take over the case for the next 10 years as the Indian authorities fumble and bumble through permissions and letters rogotaries, all marked by their incredibly incompetent attention to detail and the requirements of international law.

Olof Palme's assassination is never explained. The man arrested and tried for it — a petty criminal — is acquitted. Amitabh Bachchan wins a defamation suit against the Swedish newspaper *Dagens Nyheter* for involving him in the case. Ten years later, India and Sweden are still looking for the answers. ∎

the Opposition start baying for action, it is necessary to show that something is being done.

Fear makes strange judgments and the result is that dissenters and the suspicious are moved away. By August 1987, Arun Singh has resigned, Arun Nehru has been expelled from the Congress (I), Amitabh Bachchan has resigned from the Lok Sabha, a probe has been ordered into Ajitabh's foreign holdings...

Yet in the streets, the voices shout, *"Gali gali mein shor hai, Rajiv Gandhi chor hai,"* and *"Mr Clean, Mr Clean, gandi kyon hai tope machine".* There are no answers forthcoming from a beleagured government, desperately trying to hold up the image with pep rallies outside the prime minister's residence.

The action is already shifting to a new Mr Clean. "V P Singh sangharsh karo, hum tumhare saath hai", and *"V P Singh aur bhanda phoro, aur bhanda phoro"* : these are the new sounds sweeping across the country. With Singh on his sweepingly successful campaign are Arun Nehru, Arif Mohammed Khan who had resigned in protest when the government had passed the Muslim Women's Bill (in 1986) going against the Supreme Court judgment in the Shah Bano case, Satyapal Malik and Ram Dhan. All former Rajiv men.

Concerned by the boom generated by the Bofors deal, the Indian Parliament decides in August 1987, that a Joint Parliamentary Committee should investigate it. The Swedish government has already ordered its own enquiries. In Stockholm, as much as in India, a cover up seems essential. But in November

India's Defence Expenditure

Year	Def Ex bns in Rs. ($ bn)	GDP bns in Rs. ($ bn)	Armed Forces 1000	Population million	Def Ex/ GDP %	Per Capita Def Ex/ (US $)	Soldiers/ 1000 citizens
1988	133.41 ($9.58)	3957.79 ($284.96)	1362.0	812.0	3.37	11.8	1.69
1989	144.16 ($8.94)	4568.20 ($283.22)	1260.0	825.0	3.17	10.7	1.56
1990	154.26 ($8.79)	5355.34 ($303.25)	1200.0	843.0	2.88	10.4	1.42
1991	163.47 ($6.53)	6167.99 ($252.41)	1200.0	858.0	2.65	7.61	1.39
1992	174.10 ($6.70)	7053.28 ($272.20)	1150.0	877.0	2.49	7.63	1.31
1993	215.00 ($7.00)	8010.32 ($290.00)	1100.0	892.0	2.68	7.84	1.23
1994	230.00 ($7.37)	9456.00 ($301.00)	1100.0	910.0	2.43	7.89	1.20
1995	279.00 ($8.30)	10700.00 ($330.00)	1145.0	934.2	2.45	8.73	1.22
1996	287.00 ($8.10)	–	1050.0 +300 ®	950.6	–	8.52	1.10

One US $ =	1992 Rs 28.75	1993 Rs 31.25
	1994 Rs 31.25	1995 Rs 31.25
	1996 Rs 35.40	

Source: Asian Strategic Review, 1996

PRESSING CHARGES
Uncovering an explosive scandal
By Chitra Subramaniam

IN 1997, *l' affaire* Bofors was 10 years old.

In many ways, this arms-for-bribes story is more than the tale of corruption in high places. It is the story of betrayal of faith by a prime minister, a system, a government. It is also the story of betrayal of faith by Sweden, whose Prime Minister Olof Palme was seen as the conscience-keeper of the world, a messiah of peace and solidarity.

There have been other scandals before and after Bofors. But what has made Bofors different is not only the fact that the money and sleaze trail washed up around prime minister Rajiv Gandhi, but that after the evidence was established, I don't think that at any other time methods have been adopted that so thoroughly and systematically undermined institutions whose primary task was to safeguard democracy and ensure its responsibility. The prime minister's office, the Parliament, the bureaucracy, the army and the Central Bureau of Investigation were made to buckle to save one man's skin. People, processes, and precedents were destroyed or tarnished in a massive cover-up that was launched in New Delhi and Stockholm. This is a lot of damage to carry into our 50th year of Independence.

There was a cover-up then. There is a cover-up now. For 10 years, successive Indian governments have tried to scuttle the investigation, the reasons are not far to see. Most of our politicians have little or large 'Bofors' in their closets. Even when V P Singh launched the first serious investigation in India and Switzerland into the payoffs in 1990, there were senior ministers in his cabinet seeking to destroy his work. If the story has come this far and Rajiv Gandhi has been named in a chargesheet as being among the people who conspired to lie to the country, it is because the press in India has kept up the pressure by doing its job. When my former employers, the Hindu, under political pressure from New Delhi, stopped the Bofors story, 42 Indian newspapers and magazines offered to help me take the story through its logcal conclusion. There are not many democracies in the world where the press has shown such solidarity.

Sting was my principal source. There was no doubt in Sting's mind that Indian politicians had been bribed and Sweden, taking instructions from New Delhi, was a key player in the

cover-up. He knew this in 1987. I will never forget the day I walked into his room in early to collect the first set of documents that destroyed the official Indian "no bribes, no middleman" stand. There were papers all over the room — 300 of them, or was it 700? Every document showed that when Bofors, India and Sweden said in unison that the Howitzer deal was a clean one, they were putting out a clumsily orchestrated lie.

"These papers will show you how, where, to whom and when the bribes were paid ... study them carefully," Sting said as he handed me several files beginning in 1988 and through the autumn of 1989. He passed on several documents that blew the bottom out of India's stand. Among the documents were payment slips, forged and genuine contracts with names of recipients, diaries of former Bofors executives and hand-written notes that talked in detail about the illegal payments and the cover-up. They showed how Bofors had used three tracks of payments — one linked to the Hindujas, one to former Bofors agent in India Win Chadha and the third to a front company called A E Services— to take the Howitzer contract home despite an Indian government requirement that middlemen be kept out of the deal. "A E services is the political payoff," Sting had said in 1988.

That paper trail led to Ottavio Quattrocchi, an Italian businessman based in Delhi with close links to Rajiv Gandhi, in particular his Italian-born wife Sonia Gandhi. The evidence was sensational. Martin Ardbo, the man from Bofors who negotiated the contract with India, had noted in his diaries that he was very concerned about the evidence surrounding "Q" because of his closeness to "R". Quattrocchi's name in diaries of Bofors officials explained the cover-up.

In early 1997, the Swiss government sent the first batch of secret Swiss Bank documents that show the bribe trail. Another set is expected soon and that will complete the Swiss chapter of the Bofors story, a chapter full of legal battles, delays on the part of India, the Solanki episode and more. With all the papers in hand, India can begin sending people to jail. "Sooner or later the truth will come out... politicians have to be made responsible for their actions," Sting told me recently.

At a time when India says it is liberalising and introducing more transparency into its processes, we will have to wait and see if our leaders rise to the challenge thrown up by l'affaire Bofors. Indeed there have been similar scandals in other countries and when prime ministers have been caught they have been suitably punished or sent out. If we want the world to respect us, we have to begin by respecting our institutions.

The making *of* a NATION

The Players: *(left to right) Ottavio Quattrochi, Sonia Gandhi, Arun Nehru and Arun Singh*

Pramod Pushkarna/India Today

HAPPENINGS

1977-1986

February 11
President Fakhruddin Ali Ahmed dies in New Delhi

February 25
The country's second satellite earth station is commissioned at Dehra Dun, to improve overseas telecommunication facilities

March 2
Over 100 people die in Ahmedabad after drinking spurious liquor

March 8
Kishan Chander, noted Urdu writer, dies in Bombay

April 30
Nearly 250 notorious smugglers including Yusuf Patel, Haji Mastan and Sukarnarain Bakhia, pledge before Jayaprakash Narayan in Bombay their intention to renounce smuggling

May 30
46 persons killed and over 100 injured in a train accident at Kalabari, about 100 km from Gauhati.

May 31
Mount Kanchenjunga is conquered by two members of an Indian Army expedition, Major Prem Chand and Naik N D Sherpa

June 3
13 harijans are burnt alive by an armed gang in Belchhi village in Patna district.

Fakhruddin Ali Ahmed

January 16
Currency notes of denominations of Rs 1,000, Rs 5,000 and Rs 10,000 are demonetised

February 2
The Indian National Congress (I) is recognised as a national party and allotted the hand as an election symbol

January 6
Rohini - 200, the first monsoon experiment rocket, is launched from Thumba

Feb 11
The Cellular Jail in the Andaman and Nicobar Islands is declared a national memorial

June 3
The Soviets launch India's second satellite, Bhaskara

January 20
India wins the Madras Test against Pakistan to win the series 2-0, their first series win against Pakistan since 1952-53. Kapil Dev takes 7 wickets for 56 runs in the second innings, Sunil Gavaskar makes 166 runs in the first innings

February 19
England beats India in the Golden Jubilee Test Match, held to celebrate 50 years of the Indian Cricket Control Board. The match is noted for India captain G R Vishwanath's sporting gesture of calling back England's Bob Taylor who was given out, caught behind. Taylor and Ian Botham team up for a match-winning partnership of 171 runs. Botham, with 113 runs and 13 wickets, is man of the match

G R Vishwanath

April 24
Nirankari chief Baba Gurbachan Singh is assassinated and his son takes over as the new chief.

June 23
Sanjay Gandhi, younger son of Prime Minister Indira Gandhi, dies in a plane crash in New Delhi. He is survived by his wife, Maneka and son, Feroze Varun. Gandhi was flying his latest passion, a new aircraft acquired by the Delhi Flying Club. Apparently, he had been making loops and flying dangerously low when the plane suddenly nose-dived and crashed. Despite his questionable role in the Emergency and the Maruti car deal, Mrs Gandhi had nominated Sanjay as her successor. He was given a state funeral and the void caused by his death was later filled in by his elder brother Rajiv.

V V Giri

June 24
Former president V V Giri dies

January 17
Central government offers full statehood to Mizoram

January 26
Vayudoot, India's third nationalised airline, inaugurated

1977   1978   1979   1980   1981

August 25
Sir Edmund Hillary's 'Ocean to the Sky' expedition, up the Ganga from the Bay of Bengal, sets off

September 26
Famous dancer and choreographer Uday Shankar, dies in Calcutta

October 4
Hindi is heard for the first time in the UN General Assembly during External Affairs Minister A B Vajpayee's address

November 6
At the 24th National Film Festival awards, Mrinal Sen's Mrigaya picks up the Swarna Kamal for the best feature film of 1976, as well as an award of best actor for Mithun Chakraborty. The best actress of the year award goes to Lakshmi for the Tamil film Sila Nerangalil Sila Manithargal. Kanan Devi gets the Dadasaheb Phalke award

October 16
India play cricket with Pakistan after 16 years, and loses the series 0-2

Indian National Congress (I)

August 12
Damburst floods at Morvi and Lilapur in Gujarat, claim over 4,000 lives

August 31
M Hidayatullah is consensus choice of political parties as Vice-President of India

October 2
Operation (Milk) Flood - II launched

October 17
The Supreme Court stays the execution of all death sentences

December
Unemployment jumps from 19 lakh in 1970 to 110 lakh. The price of an Ambassador car moves from Rs 20,000 to Rs 50,000

July 31
Hindi film playback singer Mohammed Rafi dies. Versatile and popular, Rafi's voice covered a range of musical genres from classical to pop

July 18
The SLV-3 Rocket puts the Rohini satellite into orbit

November
The country is shocked by revelations in Sunday magazine that since March, 31 under-trial prisoners have been blinded by the police in Bhagalpur. Their eyes had been gouged out and then acid poured into the sockets to deliberately blind them. As voices are raised against torture in police custody, the defence put forward is that this was a measure to deal with the crime situation. After an investigation, the Central Bureau of Investigation, 76 policemen and medical officers were held guilty on various charges

December 8
Soviet President Leonid Brezhnev visits New Delhi

M Hidayatullah

Sanjay Gandhi

Mohammed Rafi

January 18
Trade Union leader Dr Datta Samant leads 2.5 lakh workers in a strike that cripples 60 textile mills in Bombay. The strike sounds a death knell for Bombay's textile industry and represents a landmark in labour-management conflicts. Samant's supporters put tremendous faith in his abilities but when the strike lasts more than a year, faith flags. Ultimately, the blow to both labour and industry is immeasurable

January 19
The Bombay High Court finds allegations against Maharashtra Chief Minister A R Antulay justified.Antulay resigns. The chief minister of Maharashtra is hounded out of office by media exposure for his role in the sale of adulterated cement in the state, as well as various public trusts he had set up, notably the Indira Pratisthan Trust. Three months of wrangling finally leads to his resignation.
"I am the chief minister only legally; morally I am not the chief minister. How can I be when the Governor has my resignation?" he says, after resigning. Other people had other opinions — Bhupesh Gupta of the CPI calls him "a political cowboy running amuck on a wild horse". Arun Shourie of the Indian Express, who exposed Antulay's shenanigans, says, "Just a few revelations and Antulay, the self-righteous sultan of Bombay is on the run.... the man has made a commerce of not just Mrs Gandhi's name but of everything else." Babasaheb Bhosale replaces him as CM.

A R Antulay

February 17,
Prime Minister Indira Gandhi dissolves nine state Assemblies

March 21
N T Rama Rao forms the Telugu Desam party in Andhra Pradesh

March 23
Maneka Gandhi and Feroze, widow of the late Sanjay Gandhi, storms out of Prime Minister Indira Gandhi's house with her son, luggage and dogs after a family squabble. Maneka alleges that her mother-in-law asked her to get out in front of the staff and had her luggage searched. The reason for this fall-out in what was never a very happy relationship, is said to be the fact that Mrs Gandhi had chosen Rajiv over her widowed daughter-in-law as political successor to Sanjay.

April 10
Insat 1A placed in orbit. Snag detected

June 22
19 killed and 25 injured as an Air India Boeing 707 crashes at Bombay

February 4
India lose 0-3 in a six-Test cricket series in an away tour. Kapil Dev replaces Sunil Gavaskar as captain

April 12
Richard Attenborough's Gandhi wins 8 Oscars, including Best Actor for Ben Kingsley in the title role

Squadron leader Rakesh Sharma

April 5
Squadron leader Rakesh Sharma becomes India's first spaceman when he is launched aboard Soyuz T -11 of the Soviet Union

May 9
Phu Dorjee conquers Mount Everest without oxygen

Charles Sobhraj

Jan 10
Pakistan decides to lift an 8-year-old ban on private trade with India

February 1
Pope John Paul II arrives in New Delhi

March 16
Dreaded murderer and conman, Charles Sobhraj, and six other criminals escape from the high-security Tihar Jail

April 7
Charles Sobhraj and associate David Hall are nabbed at Mapusa in Goa

May 9
Tenzing Norkay, who scaled Mount Everest with Edmund Hillary 33 years ago, dies in Darjeeling

May 16
Noted film-maker V Shantaram chosen for Dadasaheb Phalke award

June 9
First Acquired Immunity Defiency Syndrome death reported in a private hospital in Bombay. The victim was a businessman who had had a blood transfusion for a bypass heart surgery in 1980

March 10
India wins the World Championship of Cricket in Melbourne, with an 5-0 unbeaten record, led by Sunil Gavaskar playing his last series as captain. India beat Pakistan in the final. Ravi Shastri makes his third consecutive 50 in the tournament, and with his bowling figures of 8 for 166, win the Champion of Champions trophy and an Audi car.

June 23
All 329 persons on board are killed when the Air-India Boeing 747, Kanishka, from Toronto to Bombay, crashes into the North Atlantic over the coast of Ireland. The crash is caused by a bomb planted by Khalistan extremists, signifying one of the more horrific outcomes of the Punjab separatist movement

1983   1984   1985   1986

September 7
eikh Mohammed Abdullah, e of the Chinar, leader of the National Conference and riously, prime minister and ef minister of Kashmir, dies

October 15
R D Tata flies in a 1930s Leopard Moth on the old mail route from Bombay to Karachi to Bombay via medabad, on the 50th anniversary he launch of civil aviation in India with his 1932 flight

December 14
The first Maruti cars roll out from the company's Faridabad factory, changing forever the look of Indian roads and Indian motoring lifestyles

Air India Boeing 707

Dr Datta Samant

July 6
Veteran Congress leader Jagjivan Ram dies

July 8
India draw the third Test against England but win the series 2-0, the first overseas win since 1971

July 20
India withdraws from the Commonwealth Games in Edinburgh

October 2
Prime Minister Rajiv Gandhi escapes an attempt on his life at a ceremony at New Delhi's Rajghat

November 29
The Sharad Pawar group of Congress (S) decides to join Congress (I)

December 13
Smita Patil, one of India's most talented actresses started as a newscaster. Her roles in Bhumika, Manthan and Mirch Masala were memorable. She dies at 31 in childbirth

Smita Patil

R D Tata

"By honest means, if you can, but by any means make money."
— Horace, Epistles, 1, 1, 66

The collapse of Communism throws the world into confusion and disorder. Mikhail Gorbachev introduces *glasnost* and *perestroika* and destroys 40 years of well-crafted checks and balances. The Cold War ends as if it never existed and in the new system everyone is brought closer by technology and awareness.

For the most part, this awareness is economic. The swashbuckling colonial marauders of the 15th and 16th centuries are replaced by people in suits and ties, carrying briefcases full of contracts. Where once Christopher Columbus sailed the world for Queen Isabella, men now do so for Coca-Cola.

These new waves lap at India's shores. The call of the pocketbook cannot be ignored. Communism may be dead but the  understanding of the monthly budget is paramount. Together with this economic resurgence is the hard fact of economic want. Between the two, greed raises its ugly head, and the nation realises that there is a price to be paid for getting too much, too soon.

Then, in a shattering experience, India's hard-won secular nature is torn apart by the demolition of the Babri Masjid. Years of work towards unity seems to lie among the rubble, bringing the country to the brink of total disaster. India, however, steps back to assess the damage and then starts towards the necessary re-casting. In the dust of the past must lie the bricks of the future.

The narrowing distances between the countries of the world at the end of the century make all happenings that much more significant, and that much less. Awareness takes hold of people, and from there, the future looks more secure. Knowledge is power, and everybody comes to accept that there is no future without being part of the global process. Even more certainly, now, there is no future without democracy.

1987 1996

FIRES, FISSURES, FEARS

1989

The National Front comes to power on a promise of hope and leaves on a note of despair.
Will India break?

SEPTEMBER 19, 1990. Rajiv Goswami, 19, a student at Delhi University, sets himself on fire. The flames from his body spread to towns across northern India, as too many young people follow his lead. The common enemy: V P Singh. The common cause: a protest against the implementation of the Mandal Commission.

Of all the fissures that have the power to break Indian society, caste is perhaps the most insidious. Over 5,000 years old, its wounds run deep. So too does its effect on people. In a modern society, where each is pitted against each in a struggle for success, old angers are quick to rise to the surface. The Mandal Commission attempts to set right thousands of years of injustice to Hinduism's untouchable and backward peoples. But to India's upper castes, no longer universally rich and powerful, more reservations means less chance for their own progress.

Says Chhatarpal Singh, 18, a Faridabad student, two days before he dies of his self-inflicted burns: "I am against reservations. No one in my family or in the family of my uncles has a government job. We barely eke out an existence... Some time ago, they were recruiting people for government service. People with less marks than I got in; I was left out. I was angry. And now, again, they have increased the number of reserved seats. I burnt myself this way to show what it feels like to be left out."

Hindsight will show that many of the arguments against the implementation of the Mandal Commission are irrational and unsustainable. But in the second half of 1990, this is a crisis of overwhelming proportions, social, political, administrative. Through these levels is revealed a series of games played by politicians with each other and with the electorate.

The Mandal story is over 20 years old, when the commission was appointed to identify India's myriad backward castes and communities, not included in the existing schedule of castes and tribes. Caste lines cut across religion and Mandal is an attempt to set right the wrongs of history. The implementation of the commission's report is part of the National Front Government's election manifesto.

But the timing of its implementation is political. When V P Singh comes to power on December 2, 1989, it is on the roar of the Bofors gun. He is the new 'Mr Clean', having wrested the title from his former colleague, patron and predecessor as prime minister, Rajiv Gandhi. But his coalition government, supported by the communal Bharatiya Janata Party is always fragile. So too is the fabric of Indian society. Progress has meant new power groups bursting through the warp and weft, grabbing at their share of the Great Indian Pie. Singh must prove to them that he has something concrete to offer. The implementation of the Mandal Commission is that gift.

Waiting in the wings, waiting for Singh to trip up are two men within his coalition — the Tao of Haryana, Devi Lal, and the Young Turk from Bihar, Chandra Shekhar. Both saw their ambitions vanish before their eyes when Singh was made prime minister after four days of hectic negotiation in December 1989. The manipulator's clock turns back to July 3, 1990. Devi

Lal's son Om Prakash Chautala is sworn in as chief minister of Haryana. Central Cabinet Ministers Arif Mohammed Khan and Arun Nehru resign in protest — Chautala is a hooligan who won through violence. Singh also offers to resign. Finally, Chautala goes, but Devi Lal is waiting even more eagerly. He resigns from the Cabinet. A massive farmer's rally is planned to showt the strength that Tauji wields.

August 7, 1990. The first day of the monsoon session of Parliament. Prime Minister V P Singh announces 27 per cent job reservations in the Central Government for Other Backward Classes, as identified in the Mandal Commission, taking the wind out of Devi Lal's sails.

August 15, 1990. V P Singh repeats the Mandal pledge from the ramparts of the Red Fort. He evokes the spirit of B R Ambedkar, champion of India's deprived castes. He declares that Prophet Mohammed's birthday is now a holiday. To the victor belong the spoils of caste and religious groups.

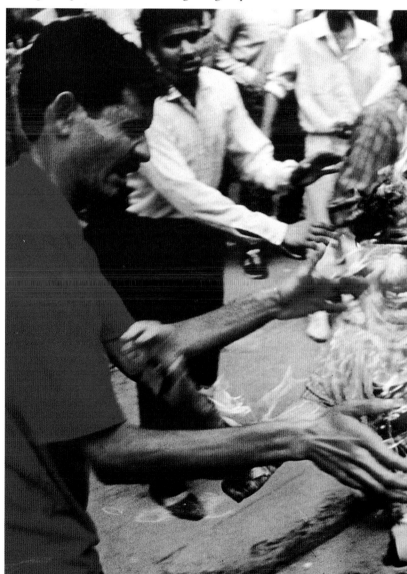

Burning issue: *Rajiv Goswami's self immolation bid sets India on fire*

But events through the months of August and September show that all victory is malignant as an embittered middle class loses its young and promising in the aftermath. The official reaction to the Mandal protests is harsh and brutal. Student protests are put down without mercy. A nation watches horrified as self-immolation becomes the new credo — satyagraha turned on itself with unrelenting savagery. The backward classes themselves are confused and hurt. The displaced, the rootless, the misguided of Indian society are ready for any conflagration that will burn through their miseries, any cause that will effect a solution.

The answer comes for some, indeed for many, from the BJP.

As much as Devi Lal and Chandra Shekhar have been waiting for the position of power, so have L K Advani, Murli Manohar Joshi and the Vishwa Hindu Parishad. Simmering under the surface has been the resurgent demand for the Ram Janmabhoomi Temple at Ayodhya, at the site of the Babri Masjid. Hemmed in by Singh's move over Mandal — no one can afford to offend the Dalits, whom the report most benefits — Hindutva becomes the best political alternative for the BJP.

Hindutva is an attempt to forge a pan-Hindu feeling, breaking through barriers of the various sects, cults, beliefs,

Rallying force: *V P Singh* Prashant Panjiar/India Today

religions, contradictions, regional differences that make up India's pluralistic, pantheistic society. The binding force is to be a journey across the country. From Somnath in Gujarat to Ayodhya in Uttar Pradesh. A distance of 10,000 km to be crossed by Advani to meet the thousands of kar sevaks who will be collecting at the Ram Jamnabhoomi site on October 30, for a Vishwa Hindu Parishad-organised puja. The Hindu face of the BJP is now clearly revealed. The repercussions will be political, social, religious.

September 25, 1990. The small town of Prabhas Patan in Saurashtra. The magnificent Somnath Temple in the background. Two converted Toyota vans start slowly, majestically, crushing a carpet of bright golden marigold flowers. The Rath Yatra has started. A juggernaut that will crush beneath its wheels both sense and sensitivity. But from the BJP's point of view, this is a political journey, and will yield political gains. Certainly, it enables the BJP to wield the whip that controls Hindu passions.

The Yatra passes through the country. Picking up along the way both jubilation and tribulation. The country's Muslims are aghast at this show of strength. So too are Hindus who are not comfortable with BJP philosophy. The Government, rent apart as it is by internal tensions, dithers.

October 20, 1990. The President of India, R Venkataraman, promulgates an ordinance to acquire the disputed land at Ayodhya. Desperate measures by desperate politicians.

Sporadic violence, thundering speeches, and unfettered intoxication accompany the BJP's version of a sacred journey.

But everything is not sacred to everyone.

In Bihar, Chief Minister Laloo Prasad Yadav has no sympathy for this saffron wave.

October 23, 1990. Yadav stops the yatra in Samastipur. Advani is arrested. Communal fires must be stopped from being stoked any further. What Yadav does stoke is a political crisis.

The BJP withdraws support to the National Front Government. V P Singh rushes to the President to try and get his Ayodhya ordinance withdrawn.

In Uttar Pradesh, there is chaos as thousands of kar sevaks await their messiah's chariot. In the rest of the country, Advani's arrest has a backlash effect. Tensions rise even further.

October 30, 1990. The appointed day. Devotthan Ekadashi. Auspicious for temple-building. Enthusiastic kar sevaks storm the Babri mosque and hoist saffron flags on the middle dome. But the paramilitary forces are waiting. Chief Minister Mulayam

AFP/India Today

The making *of* a NATION

Singh Yadav is even more determined than his Bihar counterpart to counter communalism. Sevaks battle bullets, teargas shells and lathi-charges through the lanes of Ayodhya. The holy city is cleared of holy volunteers. But at a price, that will have to be paid later. For now, instant martyrdom is the result.

November 5, 1990. The Janata Dal splits. Chandra Shekhar has 58 crucial MPs with him.

November 7, 1990. Singh loses the vote of confidence in Parliament.

After just 11 months, India has a new prime minister.

From party non grata, the Congress rises in esteem. It is the BJP that has become the political pariah. Chandra Shekhar becomes prime minister with the support of Rajiv Gandhi, the very man Singh had sought to remove from power 15 months before. Prime Minister Chandra Shekhar tries his best at fire-fighting. Advani is released and allowed to complete his yatra. Chandra Shekhar brings the VHP and the Babri Masjid Action Committee face to face to sort out their differences. Well-meant,

Deadly juggernaut: *L K Advani's modern-day chariot crushes marigolds and communal harmony*

but ineffective, as the Prime Minister has his own differences to sort out. Not least with Rajiv Gandhi, who wakes up one morning and finds plainclothesmen of the Haryana Police outside his house.

March 6, 1991. The Congress withdraws support to the 16-month-old National Front Government.

March 13, 1991. The Lok Sabha is dissolved. Elections are called.

But the animosities that have sprouted in these 16 months are growing fast. Fires, fissures, fears. India awaits them. ■

Prashant Panjiar/India Today

FACTS, MYTHS, LEGENDS
The Babri Masjid Conflict
By K N Panikkar

NO other event in independent India has so visibly symbolised two contending forces —communalism and secularism — as the dispute over the Babri Masjid, built in 1528 by Mir Baqi, one of the nobles of Mughal emperor Babur. The dispute, when it began in the second half of the 19th century had no such connotations. It became a communal issue only in the last decade when the Vishwa Hindu Parishad, supported by its allies in the Sangh Parivar, mounted a campaign for its possession and the construction of a temple at its site.

Claiming, though without any historical evidence, that the masjid was built at the birthplace of the legendary king Rama after demolishing a temple, the Sangh Parivar mobilised the Hindus through a series of well-orchestrated programmes to achieve their aim. Supported by the government in Uttar Pradesh, then headed by the Bharatiya Janata Party, and encouraged by the dithering attitude of the Central Government, a group of Hindu fanatics pulled down the mosque on December 6, 1992. And in its place erected a temporary structure to house the idol of Rama. This criminal act, perpetrated in the presence of the national leaders of the BJP and publicly celebrated by them has long-term adverse implications for the secular-democratic polity of India.

The dispute over the mosque evolved over three distinctly discernible phases. The first covers the period from 1857 to 1947, the second from 1947 to 1979 and the third from 1980 to 1992 and onwards. The first phase was mainly confined to legal claims over the proprietorship of land. The second witnessed a slow communalisation of the issue. In the third, the masjid was brought to the centre-stage of an aggressive communal mobilisation.

Ayodhya abounds in myths, including the one about the birthplace of Rama. But a myth of recent origin is about the long history of conflicts between the Hindus and Muslims — 77 well-fought battles, according to some accounts of the VHP — over the Babri Masjid. In fact, there was hardly any before 1855. And the one in 1855 was not about Babri at all, as wrongly stated by some historians and romanticised by Hindu communal ideologues. It was about Hanumangarhi temple, located near the masjid, which a Sunni leader, Shah Gulam Hussain, claimed had supplanted a mosque which existed there earlier. In the conflict that ensued, the Bairagis of the temple defeated the Muslims and killed those who had taken shelter in the masjid. They entered the masjid but did not occupy it. Instead, they almost immediately returned to the temple. Obviousy they had not laid any claim to it as the birthplace of Rama. Since this incident has been misrepresented as a conflict over the mosque, it may be stated that voluminous records about this

The making *of* a NATION

incident, including the proceedings of an enquiry instituted by the Nawab of Oudh, is lodged in the National Archives of India.

This dispute began immediately after 1857, possibly because of the rather unsettled conditions after the revolt. The mahant of Hanumangarhi, peeved by the action of Gulam Hussain, took over a part of the compound of the masjid and constructed a chabutra on it. The local Muslims and the maulavi of the masjid objected to it and petitioned the magistrate for its removal. Since the government did not take any action, the complaint was repeated several times, without any result. The mahant, on his part, went on the offensive by filing a suit in 1885 for legal title to the land and for permission to construct a temple on the chabutra. The court, on the basis of existing evidence, found his claims untenable. Yet, by the end of the century, the land on which the masjid stood had become a disputed area.

Although the claim of the mahant to the land was not based on its association with the birthplace of Rama, such a construction was made by British officials in the second half of the 19th century. The earlier texts, both Persian and Hindi, though referred to Ayodhya, did not mention the existence of a temple. Nor did a temple at the Janmasthan figure in the Hindu pilgrimage literature. The British official publications were the first to establish a connection between the temple and the masjid. Even they had no proof to profer, except "locally affirmed" information and "the well-known Mahomedan principle of enforcing their religion on all those whom they conquered".

By the time H R Neville wrote the *Gazetteer of Faizabad* in 1905, the British officials had given considerable credence and currency to the association between the masjid and the temple. Yet, there was not much of a tension between the two communities in the area. The only exception was the riots of 1934 in which a part of the masjid was damaged. It, however, was not caused by the dispute over the masjid, but was triggered off by the slaughter of a cow.

The dispute took an altogether different turn in the post-Independence period. It no more remained a legal issue between the mahant and the maulvi, but slowly changed into a communal problem. The first sign of this transformation was manifested in December 1949. In the communal atmosphere prevailing in the country as a whole, a group of Hindus broke into the mosque in the night of December 22 and installed an idol of Rama. The Hindu devotees and later the VHP claimed that the idol had miraculously appeared in the mosque. The local administration appeared to be privy to this criminal trespass. Neither the police nor the district magistrate took any action. Nehru and Patel were quite exercised by the incident. The former counselled the chief minister to undo the harm. Patel, though he termed it an act of "aggression and coercion", was cautious. He recognised the "sentiment behind the move which has taken place" and advocated a peaceful and amicable settlement without allowing the accomplished facts to stand in the way. Yet, the government did nothing to undo the outrage; the conversion

Religion on a rampage: *Artificial distinctions*   D Ravinder Reddy/India Today

of the masjid into a mandir by use of force was accepted as a fait accompli. What happened in 1949 was to be a forerunner of later events.

Despite the assertion of the Hindus and the reluctance of the state to intervene the dispute had remained dormant and localised till the beginning of the 1980s. During this interregnum the Hindu communal forces had grown, but were yet a marginal force in Indian polity. The post-Emergency period had opened up a political space: the Congress lost its legitimacy and the Left was unable to make any substantial advance. The Hindu communal forces sensed the possibilities inherent in this situation. They opted for a populist movement which would yield immediate results. The mandir-masjid controversy then came to the centre-stage.

The movement collectively generated by the Sangh Parivar led to unprecedented mobilisation of the Hindus. The campaign sought to indentify the mandir with the religious faith and interests of the Hindus and the masjid with their collective humiliation and defeat. The demolition of the masjid did not resolve the dispute; it only enlarged its arena to a struggle between secularism and communalism; between democracy and authoritarianism, between coercion and tolerance. The Babri Masjid has forced Indian society to make the choice.

While making the choice, an introspection is in order. Why was a local dispute transformed into a national calamity, undermining the fundamental principles of the Republic! Scholars and political leaders have offered a plethora of explanations. Among them, one reason needs to be restated: the wilful acceptance and appeasement of the sentiments of the majority. Particularly by the state. As in 1949, in 1992 also the state did not go beyond anti-communal rhetoric. It remained passive, vacillatory and compromising. Not the state alone, even intellectuals and political parties, at least some of them. Ramsay Macdonald the prime minister of Britain, had learnt to his dismay that all his attempts to appease the Nazis only helped to add fuel to the fire. That is a lesson worth recalling in India.

GARLAND OF DEATH

May 21, 1991

A former Prime Minister meets a gruesome, shocking death. The loss of Rajiv Gandhi is compounded by the stealth of his assassins

"Simon Cormack died of massive explosive damage to spine and abdomen, caused by a detonation of small but concentrated effect near the base of his back. At the time he was carrying the bomb on his person...

The bomb Simon Cormack had been carrying was concealed in the broad leather belt he wore around his waist and which had been given him by his abductors to hold up the denim jeans...

The explosive had been a two-ounce wafer of Semtex, composed of 45 per cent Pentra Tetro Ether Nitrate (or PETN), 45 per cent RDX and 10 per cent plasticiser... Buried within the plastic explosive had been a miniature detonator, or minidet..."

— *From The Negotiator by Frederick Forsyth, published 1989*

IT is a hot summer in 1991, and not just because of the weather. The country has just seen a coalition headed by the Janata Dal fall. The burning summer breezes have brought with them the seeds of change. India goes into the whirlwind of a mid-term general election.

Across the country, there is, it seems, one hero. Deposed from prime ministership two years ago, an effect of the recoil of the Bofors gun, Rajiv Gandhi is poised to return. A tireless and fearless campaigner, he travels the country, shaking hands, hugging his followers, accepting their tributes, laughing with their joys, sharing their sorrows. The prince is back. Perhaps more flawed than before, but more mature as well. Like his mother and grandfather before him, Rajiv Gandhi is scornful of too much security. Every so often, he breaks through the cordons and reaches out to the people. It makes him that much more lovable. It makes him that much more vulnerable.

May 21, 1991, 9.30 pm. The atmosphere is electric with anticipation in Sriperumbudur, a small town in Tamil Nadu. Rajiv Gandhi is due at any moment. Amidst the throng of fans, followers, party workers is anxious, eager, 15-year-old Kokila Kannan. She is going to recite a poem she has written in Hindi for Rajiv.

Kokila, perhaps, is still innocent of the undercurrents of political motivations moving around her. Not quite so innocent, but possibly equally anxious, is the group headed by Sivarajan, standing quite close to the young girl. There is Dhanu, garland in hand, for Rajiv. There is Haribabu, a freelance photographer, ready to record the historic moment. Elsewhere in the crowd are

Last greeting: *Rajiv Gandhi at Sriperumbudur moments before his death*

M A Parthasarathy/India Today

Gory end: *The remains of Rajiv Gandhi*   M A Parthasarthy/India Today

their friends Nalini and Murugun. All waiting.

10 pm. Rajiv Gandhi arrives to a tumultuous welcome. The crowd surges forward, with gifts, outstretched hands, poems to be read, garlands. Rajiv's security men get pushed back by the thrusts of the throng.

10.15 pm. Rajiv reaches Kokila and readies himself to listen to her poem.

10.19 pm. As Haribabu clicks, Dhanu moves forward for her turn. She garlands Rajiv and then bends down towards his feet.

10.20 pm. A gigantic explosion rips the tent.

Taking in its wake, Rajiv, Dhanu, the young Kokila, Haribabu...

Dhanu's garland was innocent enough. But not her belt of plastic explosives, triggered off when she bent down.

Amidst the chaos and the horrifying spectacle of gore, stunned security forces swing into action. But Dhanu's co-conspirators have already fled for Madras. What is left behind is a roll of film — Haribabu's chronicle of the hour, on his borrowed automatic Canon.

Like the security forces at the site, the nation is stunned. Thoughts immediately rush back to Rajiv's mother's death at the hand of assassins. The price that the Nehru-Gandhi family pays for serving the nation seems heavy, almost too heavy. But just as Indira Gandhi was killed for her role in Operation Bluestar, the military storming of the Golden Temple in Amritsar, so Rajiv's death also seems linked to violence. No group takes credit for this daring and despicable murder, unusual in the world of terrorism.

May 22, 1991. The Central Government, under the prime ministership of Chandra Shekhar, hands the Rajiv Gandhi assassination case over to the Central Bureau of Investigation. A Special Investigation Team is immediately constituted.

May 24, 1991. The Hindu newspaper publishes the photographs from Haribabu's roll. There, caught in unerring detail are Dhanu, Sivarajan, Nalini and Murugan. These, it appears, are the conspirators in the murder. Even Haribabu himself, it seems, was no innocent. But the publishing of these pictures unmasks not just the killers but the lack of coordination between the local police, who gave the roll to the newspaper, and the special team, which should have got the roll immediately.

Although crucial time has been lost, it seems apparent that the assassins are part of the Tamil separatist movement of Sri Lanka. The most obvious suspect is the Liberation Tigers of Tamil Eelam, the strongest of the Sri Lankan Tamil groups. Rajiv Gandhi's crime must have been his decision to send in an Indian Peace-keeping Force to Sri Lanka in 1987, after an accord with the then Sri Lankan President, Junius Jayewardene. The methodology of this bomb attack, at any rate, points to the committed and single-minded LTTE.

But while the investigation must continue, find probable cause and even try and get to Jaffna, India must answer other crucial questions. Even if the operation carried out by the killers was daring and innovative — inspired, perhaps, by a thriller novel — why was security so lax? Rajiv Gandhi, as former prime minister, was inevitably on several hit lists. Yet, Indian intelligence appeared to have had no clue of this plot.

The Government appoints the Verma Commission to find some answers. The former judge is given a novel brief — he may not inquire into the cause of the killing but only into the security lapses.

Apart from the personal tragedy of the Gandhi family, there is the tragedy of the Congress Party. Rajiv's new-found popularity had meant a resurgence of the party's fortunes. Would his untimely death affect the outcome of the polls. But as the heat sweeps the country in May 1991, so does a sympathy wave for the Congress, in memory of its lost leader. Ultimately, India would have a new Congress government. In death, as sure as it seemed imminent in life, Rajiv Gandhi triumphs.

Investigators, meanwhile, are unravelling a trail that spreads across South India. Local sympathy for the Tamil movement in Sri Lanka is widespread. No foreign team of assassins, no matter how organised or committed, could have pulled off such a stunt without local help. To galvanise the people, for there are sympathisers for Rajiv Gandhi too, photographs of the conspirators are released to the press. Large rewards are offered for information about their whereabouts. It emerges that Forsyth's fictional belt-bomb was indeed an inspiration. In that light, it seems almost comically horrifying that Sivarajan, leader of the group, is also known as One-Eyed Jack. Comparisons between him and the dreaded international hitman, Carlos, are made. Strangely, Frederick Forsyth had based an earlier thriller on Carlos...

The breakthroughs that come for the investigators,

however are not quite so thrilling. Progress is slow, as associates and helpers are picked up for questioning. The trail finally stops at a house in Konankunte, an area on the outskirts of Bangalore.

August 18, 1991. Rajiv Gandhi has been dead for 90 days. Information says that the conspirators are hiding in this house. The police surround the area. The owner of the house and his wife are picked up by the police as they try to flee. Confirmation.

But this is not going to be an easy arrest. The assassination squad, if they are of the LTTE as is now almost a certainty, will not give up without a fight. More chillingly, it will not be without its regular issue, cyanide capsules. For the Indian authorities, if they are to get to the source of the plot, the squad must be taken alive.

Is it already too late, as the house is shrouded in silence?

Then, at sunset, a burst of AK-47 gunfire comes from a window. The over-2,000-strong security force is jolted out of its complacency. The return fire and the militant reply goes on for half an hour. Then again, silence. Are the conspirators trying to test the weaponry of their opponents to see if escape is possible?

As the assassination squad waits, so do the security forces. The strategy to take the assassins is still to be worked out. To wear them down is one option. To stealthily take the house in a commando-style operation is another.

But the questions take too long to find answers. The importance of timing, of the self-sacrificing nature of the culprits are seemingly forgotten.

August 20, 1991. After two days of silent waiting, the decision is to enter the house. But the cyanide has not waited. Sivarajan, One-Eyed Jack, the leader of the group, has taken no chances. He has also shot himself. In those two, now vital days, bodies have started decomposing. Now, dead terrorists will tell no tales.

August 20, 1991. Rajiv Gandhi's birthday. ∎

Still in grief: *Priyanka, Rahul and Sonia Gandhi at Rajiv Gandhi's samadhi a year later*
Pramod Pushkarna/India Today

LOVING THY NEIGHBOUR
Why South Asian cooperation has to work
By J N Dixit

NEARLY 26 years ago, in the introduction to his three volume classic on Asian development, *Asian Drama - An enquiry into the poverty of nations*, Dr Gunnar Myrdal wrote: "Many of the concepts and theories regarding South Asian relations analysing the problems of South Asia broke down when examined in terms of their adequacy to realities." This is a succinct description of the underlying characteristics of India's relations with its South Asian neighbours.

The bitter heritage of the partition of British India in 1947 and the subsequent role that India played in assisting Bangladesh to break away from Pakistan have profoundly affected India's relations with these two countries. In addition, a number of problems have afflicted our relations with these neighbours because of the contradiction resulting from the fragmentation of what was a naturally unified geo-political region. This statement is made only in terms of a generic value judgment and not arguing for any reversal of the processes of history suggesting any reunification of Bangladesh or Pakistan with India. This is neither desirable nor possible. In fact, India should consciously avoid any such prospect. The problems of Kashmir, the demarcation of certain sections of the boundary between India and Pakistan, the fundamental difference of opinion between India and Pakistan about the two nation theory and a number of other minor issues have affected Indo-Pakistan relations over the last 50 years.

Despite India having supported Bangladesh's liberation, the apprehension of the Muslim majority population of Bangladesh about the possible revival of Hindu domination remains a factor in Indo-Bangladesh relations. The issue of Farakka, massive migration of Bangladeshis to India, the mutual difficulties of India and Bangladesh in granting each other full transit facilities for trade purposes, and the adverse balance of trade which Bangladesh has with India, are matters which have to be resolved if Indo-Bangladesh relations have to be stable and have to contribute to durable friendship between the two countries.

India's smaller neighbours like Nepal and Bhutan have incipient apprehensions about India's cultural, religious and ethnic linkages with them resulting in cultural and socio-economic hegemony, even if it is not direct political domination. The crises which affected Indo-Nepalese relations in the late 1980s and Indo-Sri Lanka relations between 1983 and 1990 reflected this phenomenon. India has to acknowledge this perception even if in reality India has no negative intentions towards its neighbours (which in fact is the reality in Indian policies).

It is in this context that we have to assess the prospects of India structuring better relations with neighbours and contributing to an integrated process of cooperation in the

The making *of* a NATION

South Asian region. Paradoxically, it is the very commonality of ethno-cultural and religious heritage which has created problems of national political identity among India's neighbours, especially in Pakistan and more recently in Bangladesh. Despite this shared inheritance, the assertion of a separate political identity necessitates — and results in — countries of the region pulling back from processes of economic and socio-cultural interaction. South Asia has to strive towards such cohesion, although there is some distance still to be covered before the objective can be realised.

At the time of South Asian Assoication for Regional Cooperation's inception, member states were a disparate group in these respects. There were two monarchies (Nepal and Bhutan), two military dictatorships pretending to be democracies (Pakistan and Bangladesh) and three democracies (the Maldives, Sri Lanka and India). At that time one of the democracies was, in essence, a one party state (Sri Lanka). Since 1989, however, the landscape has changed. Notwithstanding tensions and uncertainties, all SAARC countries have democratic governments with elected legislatures and ministries conducting affairs of state, though new difficulties have emerged in Pakistan. This is a positive trend which should encourage regional cooperation. Having said this, one would expect elected governments to be subjected to increasing domestic political tensions, if the choice is between ensuring the survival of the government in power and contributing to regional cooperation. However noble the latter objective may be, it is the former objective which will often find favour. It is therefore only the stabilisation of democratic institutions which will overcome this interim hindrance.

India's approach until 1991 was to steer SAARC towards projects and programmes which were practical, feasible and devoid of political controversy. It was also opposed to SAARC expanding its activities to areas which would create political problems, or which would encourage extraneous non-regional interference and presence in regional affairs. While India's basic stance remains the same, its position became somewhat more nuanced in November 1991. It decided and conveyed to other member countries that it would join cooperative efforts at the level, extent and tempo acceptable to other members. It also reiterated that it would not oppose the Secretariat's efforts to initiate contacts with other regional groupings and countries so as to explore possibilities for additional resources and information inputs for SAARC activities, provided that these conformed with the stipulations of the Charter, and that the external inputs, so sought and obtained, did not contradict the terms of reference of cooperation within the region. The poverty alleviation programmes and the establishment of South Asia Preferential Trade Arrangement (SAPTA) were the products of this policy stance.

As for Pakistan, its substantive interest in SAARC is related to the Indian presence. In terms of political ethos Pakistan has, since the partition of the subcontinent, sought to establish for itself a West Asian, Arab-Persian Muslim identity. Its attempts to associate with the Gulf regional grouping and more recently its intensified efforts to consolidate the Economic Cooperation Organisation with Iran and Turkey (and the Central Asian Republics) indicate that Pakistan's participation in SAARC is

attributable mainly to Indophobic political motivations. Indicative of this tendency is its soft-pedalling of the SAPTA arrangement and lukewarm participation in SAARC activities across the board. Pakistan's present political orientation is north-westward in regional terms. Therefore of late Indo-Pak cooperation in SAARC has improved.

Since Sri Lanka assumed the chairmanship of SAARC in 1991, it has shown a greater interest in it. Its participation in SAARC proceedings from 1985 to 1990, however, has been subject to the ups and downs of Indo-Sri Lankan relations. Sri Lanka could not and did not view SAARC as an instrumentality which could overcome its bilateral political problems with India. It should also be recalled that in the early 1980s the Sri Lankan government made a determined effort to become a full-fledged member of ASEAN. Only after it realised that the proposition was a non-starter did it turn its attention to SAARC. Its desire to join ASEAN was both natural and logical at that time in the context of the liberalised market economy and its links with ASEAN countries like Singapore and Malaysia. It should be mentioned in passing that India was an aspirant for ASEAN membership in the late 1970s, early 1980s, and that it too failed in this respect. Here also things have changed for the better in relation to ASEAN since 1995.

Despite being the originator of the SAARC idea, even Bangladesh had incipient hopes of organising some sort of a regional arrangement incorporating the Islamic countries of East Asia. Sheikh Mujib-ur-Rehman articulated such views as early as 1974 after participating in the OIC summit in London. The point to be noted is that four out of the seven member countries of SAARC decided to join the organisation for reasons other than enthusiastic endorsement of mutual interests. Perhaps SAARC was and is the option chosen, but only as a second-best alternative. This contradiction must be removed if SAARC is to emerge as a purposeful and effective instrument for regional cooperation. The origin and content of this contradiction of India's neighbours looking elsewhere to other regional groupings or countries lies basically in the geopolitical asymmetry between India and its neighbours in terms of territory, population, and resources.

There is also the difficulty posed by the identity crisis facing India's neighbours, because the more significant components of their collective persona are derived from their old Indian connections. As mentioned before, geography underlines this predicament, as India's land and sea borders abut on all the other six countries of SAARC, while none of them is a direct neighbour of any of the others. The solution lies in a conscious, continuous, even repetitious assertion and emphasis by India on the separate political identity of all its neighbours, along with the communication of formal assurances, as often as is necessary, that India does not aspire to reintegrate them into any contrived or centralised 'Indian subcontinental political system'.

On such issues as Siachen, Sir Creek, Farakka, trade disputes and illegal migration, India has the capacity to accommodate and find a middle way, provided public opinion is educated, mindsets are changed, and a national consensus is developed, giving structure and strength to the political resolve and decision-making processes of the government.

AERIAL INVASION
1991

Non-stop telecast of the Gulf War on CNN hooks India on to satellite television. And then,
enslavement by entertainment

Spellbinding: *Live images of the Gulf War on CNN*

India Today

January 20, 1991. Saddam Hussein of Iraq takes a military walk through Kuwait, deciding he likes the little kingdom's oil fields for himself. The Gulf War begins.

January 20, 1991. India wakes up to a new life and freedom — the slavery of television.

Ted Turner is an unlikely messiah. Few Indians have even heard of him. Yet the Indian television revolution starts with Turner's Cable News Network and its coverage of Saddam Hussein's exploits. From out there in the Middle Eastern desert, Scud missiles and Patriots whizz through the air and straight into Indian drawing rooms. Terrestial television, what's that? Welcome to the world of the local cable operator and the dish antenna. Welcome to the world of television.

Across the country, people are scrambling to get CNN. Cable operators are scrambling to buy dish antennae. Hotel bars start charging a premium for the crowds who rush in to watch CNN. Doordarshan and All India Radio, the state's broadcasters, limp sadly, a poor last choice against the barrage of instant, constant coverage of this exciting event. Never before have Indians watched, live — except perhaps with sports coverage — reporters speaking with bombs exploding

behind them. Never before have such images of carnage and courage been shown so directly. This is not fiction, this is real life, and it is both exhilirating and frightening at the same time.

The newest invasion in India has come from the skies and the bombardment is here to stay. For too long dependent on state-run, state-controlled and state-determined television, the India of the '90s is experiencing the fruits of liberalisation — free choice and what a choice.

Soon, after the explosions of the Gulf War have died down, comes the deluge. The first break is made by a Hong Kong-based company called Hutchvision. Satellite Television Asian Region starts its first tentative satellite transmissions over Asia in April, 1991. The programmes are mainly in English, mainly re-runs of old American serials. Over the next few months, STAR will offer a choice of channels — Prime Sports, the American music video network MTV, the BBC and the re-constituted Star Plus. News, music, sports and entertainment — a perfect mix.

One year later, and the government is forced to sit up and take notice of the STAR phenomenon. Numbers are still small, but growing. Cable operators — so far limited to running movie channels for the nieghbourhood — are now big business. Advertisers are finding the STAR offer attractive — niche markets of upper-income western oriented viewers hooked to constant news and English entertainment. And at Rs 25,200 for a 10-second slot, considerably cheaper than Doordarshan's Rs 90,000.

February 22, 1992. The World Cup series opens in Australia and Prime Sports is covering 24 of the 39 matches live, Doordarshan only 11. A shop in Bombay's Lamington Road, the electronics market wholesale area, sells at least 30 dishes a month, most in the fortnight preceding the World Cup. At between Rs 25,000 to Rs 1.25 lakh a system, he's not doing too badly either. Even the buying frenzy is tied up with an event, it only demonstrated the power of the medium.

Numbers are still, however, small. The tremendous reach of Doordarshan is hard to beat, and few are able. But between February and June 1992, the number of STAR-households has jumped from four lakh to over 12 lakh, and growing. The government finds it impossible to legislate air waves telecast from satellites that are not even above Indian air space. It tries, desperately, to give Doordarshan a fillip with a revamped Metro channel, more sponsored programmes, more choice.

October 1, 1992, 7 pm. Zee TV starts a three-hour transmission of song and dance. The satellite invasion is ready to move into a new dimension. Zee is the Hindi channel of the STAR network. The language of the people, with programming that will unhindered by bureaucratic ideas of what's good for the people.

Now there is no looking back. Zee jumps from success to success, Rupert Murdoch, the world's most aggressive media businessman, buys out STAR and new channels fight for every last available bit of satellite space. ATN, Jain, BITV, Sony, Home TV, Discovery, TNT, ESPN and more will arrive. Some will burn out faster than asteroids in the atmosphere, others will limp along, still others will start slow to build big.

In a quiet sidelight, urban radio sees a resurgence with the privatisation of the frequency modulation wave. Programmes, run mainly by media houses like Times of India and Mid-Day, cater to varying tastes and styles, and display not a modicum of government control. Across India, FM radio becomes a fad, and then an accepted reality.

With this total takeover, come the inevitable fears — is Indian culture losing its hold, when everyone has abandoned the *National Programme of Music and Dance* for the soap opera *Tara?* Will this incessant exposure to other attitudes and lifestyles create impossible desires and schisms? Should the government regulate what people can and cannot watch? It is possible that all these fears are justified, but the past is over. India has jumped headfirst into the global village, and people are revelling in talking about their private problems in public with each successive chat show. Or singing tunelessly on singing shows. Or watching hundreds of similar Hindi film countdown shows, soap operas, game shows on different channels, 24 hours a day.

If there is an answer, the government tries to find it in a proposed broadcasting bill. Prasar Bharati will give autonomy to Doordarshan and All India Radio, it will magnanimously allow private telecast (although it could not stop it if it wanted), but it will still try and keep some power with the authorities. The winds of privatisation, however, balk at government control and the battle continues. Meanwhile, so does the television takeover of India.

SOAPS, SUDS AND SPONSORS
Commercial television looks for direction
By Bhaskar Ghose

THE first sponsored programme on Doordarshan was the serial *Hum Log*, which was aired between 1984 and 1985. It rapidly gathered an enormous audience, limited only by the availability of television sets. It was watched in many homes, particularly in the lower middle class levels of society, not only by the family but by assorted neighbours who came in just for the serial. Soon the characters in the serial — Rijjak Ram, Bhagwanti, Badki, Chutki and the rest — became household names and every week, for 156 weeks, people across the country were riveted by the fortunes of the families in the serial.

One has to remember, though, that this was 1984, when Doordarshan was the only television channel one could see, and that this was the only sponsored serial being shown. In a sense it was, therefore, a captive audience. But then, had the serial been dull and boring it would not have had the enormous viewership it got. The audience would have drifted away. But *Hum Log* worked. As Sevanti Ninan says in her book *Through the Magic Window*, "By the time it ended, its viewers were hooked, and the food product being promoted through its sponsors — Maggi 2-Minute Noodles — also became a huge commercial success."

Hum Log was followed by some very successful serials, each cashing in on the newly awakened hunger for such entertainment: *Khandaan, Buniyaad* and Nukkad drew very large, rapt audiences. Clearly these programmes had a very great impact on viewers. The glitter of *Khandaan* brought to thousands a lifestyle they saw only in the cinema, and here it was available right in their homes. *Buniyaad* and *Nukkad*, on the other hand, brought to them characters and situations they related to and that made them extremely popular.

What was the effect of these sponsored serials on viewers? Going by surveys conducted at that time, very considerable. The social habits of people changed; they tended to avoid visitors or engagements around the time when the serials were telecast, to cite one instance. The message of family planning which was built into *Hum Log*, was found to have gone home to as many as 71 per cent of its viewers according to a study by researchers Arvind Singhal and Everett M Rogers.

Later, sponsored serials like *Ramayan* and *Mahabharat* had an even greater impact. It was common knowledge that younger viewers adopted the archaic styles of greeting that the serials popularised. Both were telecast during my tenure as Director General of Doordarshan, and I was told by a leading eye specialist of Bombay that the number of cases of youngsters being injured in the eyes by arrows increased significantly. Other surveys revealed a sharp rise in the demand for bows and arrows as presents for boys, and there are some who maintain that the rise in Hindu fundamentalism is linked to the telecast of these two serials. The last may or may not be true, but one has to admit that the rise did come about just after the two serials had been shown over the period 1987 to 1988.

The most noticeable impact was, of course, the advertising of products by the sponsors of these serials. That sales went sharply up was evident from the enormous amounts that began to be spent on television advertising, on mythological texts, like *Ramayan* and *Mahabharat*.

More concern is expressed in some quarters about the effect of the advertising the serials carry: All those lovely household items, textiles and the rest give rise, according to them, to an undesirable craving for what is called consumerism. This again is a simplistic view, and assumes that the television viewer is more gullible than he or she actually is.

It is basically a question of choice, and this is exercised with a degree of caution even now. A comprehensive study conducted in the mid-80s by the Karve Institute of Social Sciences in Pune discovered that in rural areas the family structure was stronger than the induced consumerism such as it was. A child wanting a chocolate bar, or some sweet, after seeing an advertisement for one, was told he could not have it by the mother, and this was accepted without demur.

Channel serfs: *Watching TV is the new fix*
Dinodia Picture Agency

Top 10 TV grossers

1	Mahabharat
2	Ramayan
3	Sri Krishna
4	Chandrakanta
5	Rangoli
6	Close-up Antakshari
7	Superhit Muqabla
8	Philips Top 10
9	All The Best
10	Sponsored feature films

In any event, serials on television have been swamped by films and film-based programmes. There was a time when only one or two films were shown every week on Doordarshan. That changed by the early 1990s as sponsorship came to films, and now there are a large number of films, on all channels, not to mention the satellite channels, some of which are exclusively film channels. The impact on audiences is now more that of films than serials.

Not that the popularity of serials has waned. It may have, slightly, but they are still widely watched. While serial makers are still about levels of violence and explicit scenes of sex, a new phenomenon which has again attracted the ire of some opinion groups to be undesirable is that of fathers with mistresses, wives having affairs and so on.

But the concern appears to be misplaced. The viewer is now no longer the wide-eyed, open-mouthed newcomer to television; besides he has a choice of several serials, and each has some sets of relationships, so he or she is not really going to be influenced by the depiction of an affair with a married woman or something similar. And, usually, the producers end up asserting the folly of such ways, and the virtue of being a wholesome family. But one thing is certain; in terms of content most serials are mediocre. Stereotypes, hackneyed situations, exaggerated acting and poor scripts make them a pain to watch. But then obviously a fair number do, and find them interesting which is why they are kept on.

This is the real danger and the one factor that deserves to be viewed with concern. Tastes are slowly being vulgarised by the quality of serials, much as they have been in the United States. Since television in India has been pushed into commercialism by the government, it has to take the blame. Had they been wiser, and more far-sighted, they could have developed television serials on the lines of the BBC — well-written, carefully crafted and acted by the finest actors — they could have set standards and moulded tastes to a level of sensitivity which would, in time, influence other programmes as well.

But that opportunity has, sadly, been put aside, and commercial television will inevitably follow the path it has taken in the United States. One can only hope for at least one channel which will try to provide some worthwhile fare. But it appears that will be a long wait.

The making *of* a NATION

GOING GLOBAL
1992

A new budget takes the country out of Nehruvian socialism and into economic liberalisation

March to globalisation: *Finance Minister Dr Manmohan Singh outside Parliament, on his way to deliver his historic budget speech*   Pramod Pushkarna/ India Today

"Our nation will remain eternally grateful to Jawaharlal Nehru for his vision and insistence that the social and economic transformation of India had to take place in the framework of an open society, committed to Parliamentary democracy and the rule of law... This budget represents a contribution to the successful implementation of this great national enterprise, of building an India free from the fear of war, want and exploitation, an India worthy of the dreams of the founding fathers of our republic."

— Finance Minister Dr. Manmohan Singh

FEBRUARY 28, 1992. With these stirring words, Manmohan Singh, Union Minister for Finance, commends his budget to the august Lower House of Parliament. It is a budget, however, that will turn around on its head Nehru's Fabian vision of a socialist India. It is a budget that will set India on a course that, for the first time in 45 years, moves away from government control towards a free-market economy. But as it opens India out to the world, and even invites the world in, this budget will also open India to a host of new problems. Questions, economic and ethical, will demand answering as the world's largest democracy with the world's second largest population attempts to balance a welfare ideal with a *laissez-faire* goal.

March 2, 1992. For the moment, though, only the excitement. Noted budget analyst, Nani Palkhivala, who has long criticised the government's protectionist policies, says, at a mammoth meeting at Bombay's Cricket Club of India grounds,

"This is a watershed budget which is not for the greedy but paid for the needy." He praises it for ending a 45-year affair with socialism and opening the doors to liberalisation. Indeed, Palkhivala will, over the coming years, stop giving his much-awaited budget speeches. With the government on the right track, his incisive comments and trenchant criticism are unnecessary. India has twigged on to the magic mantra.

The new buzzword is liberalisation. A word that will mean as much in India as *perestroika* and *glasnost* meant in Mikhail Gorbachev's Russia a few years before. It is a word that has the potential to make India an economic and industrial giant, an Asian tiger that is springing to take its place among the smaller nations of the continent who all aspire to or have already acquired that sobriquet. It is also a word that will put fear into the hearts of leftist economists, of Indian industries and businesses accustomed to living in a protected environment, of socialists who see the divisive potential of a policy that will widen, initially at least, the disparity between India's poor and rich.

But even those who fear it will see that India has no option. The portents for the 1992-93 budget are to be found in the provisional July 1991 budget, when the new Congress government came to power to a country verging on economic collapse. Too many years of government protection have stultified the economy, have led to an enormous foreign debt that is on verge of crippling India. For too long have bureaucrats, with little economic sense, dictated economic policies that ultimately seem to serve only their sense of power. For too long have huge public sector industrial enterprises run like wasteful government departments, draining the exchequer. For too long have politicians decided when and where licences should be distributed, for their own personal gain. For too long has the parallel economy ruled, and the corruption of 'black money' corroded all spheres of Indian life.

Cleaning up the polity, however, is not Dr Singh's only imperative. Even before he was made finance minister by a forward-thinking prime minister, P V Narasimha Rao, the winds of liberalisation were howling at the closed windows of India's economy. Everyone heard them but no one had the courage to open the windows. Dr Singh, gentle, erudite, soft-spoken, a former bureaucrat himself, appears to be no Hercules orSamson either. But the sheer burden of India's debt to the International Monetary Fund, and her dwindling foreign exchange reserves called for these drastic measures. And Dr Singh is the man in the hot seat.

In 1992, the interest on India's foreign borrowings stand at Rs 32,000 crore. The message from the IMF has been clear — Singh has to reduce that and change the negative growth trend of the economy. He says in his budget speech that it is not true that he has been dictated to by the IMF, but that he has implemented policies that are in the national interest. They also, interestingly enough, happen to be in line with IMF thinking. The union deficit has been brought down to 5 per cent of the Gross Domestic Product, from 6.5 per cent. Tax reforms have broadened the tax base and lowered import duties, support to public sector enterprises has gone down, the rupee has been made partially convertible against the dollar, public sector disinvestment is on.

For some, there is fear that India is moving too fast, for others, not fast enough. Palkhivala has no truck with Marxist critics. The fear that India will be run by multinationals is entertained "only by those whose critical perceptions do not exceed 40 watts and who are under the illusion that they are still fighting the East India Company."

Indian business is, for the most part, equally gung-ho. Aditya Birla, part of one of India's largest industrial family calls this the most outstanding budget seen so far. " The finance minister is a man of vision. Posterity will remember him as a man who changed the destiny of India."

Birla could have been prescient. The next few year will show that India can only move inexorably forward. And the credit and blame for all changes lie here. In a budget that took India's gigantic monolithic economy structure and started shaking it towards rationalisation. That shake-up is an on-going process.

As Dr Singh put it himself, " We are travelling through difficult and uncharted terrain, where no action is without attendant risks and success will not always be immediate. We need patience, perseverance and national cohesion if we are to succeed."

The gauntlet for a new India had been thrown down. ∎

Top 5 Multinational companies in India

Rank	Name	Current Mkt Cap (Rs crore)	Industry
1	Hindustan Lever	14569.42	Personal care
2	ITC	10135.43	Diversified
3	Brooke Bond Lipton	5240.88	Diversified
4	Colgate Palmolive	4310.88	Personal care
5	Castrol India	2821.98	Lubricants

NO EASY SURRENDER
The other view of liberalisation
By Rahul Bajaj

BEFORE 1991, India by and large, followed the policy of a mixed economy and during the 1960s, 1970s and 1980s we had a protected economy. However, there was a positive side to this situation. Due to its policy of import substitution at that time, the nation developed a manufacturing base unlike industries in certain south Asian countries that were mainly screwdriver technology driven.

But since we operated in a protected environment till 1991, none of India's industries were truly internationally competitive. Costs were high, quality low and technology obsolete. In industry there is only one guru who teaches you to be efficient and that is not any business school but a buzzword called competition. Without competition, industry will not be competitive and if not competitive we will perish-leave alone prosper.

By the early seventies the black chapter for Indian industry had started. During the seventies, apart from old existing agreements, hardly any new technology agreements were signed in the private sector industry.

Indian industry greeted the process of liberalisation, started by PV Narasimha Rao, Manmohan Singh and P Chidambaram. Between 1991-94, the pace of liberalisation was so fast that Indian industry was pleasantly surprised.

The process of liberalisation slowed down considerably after 1994 due to political reasons.

Some industrialists did not realise the full implications of this liberalisation.

Industry, which had functioned under controls for decades, was suddenly exposed to both internal and external competition.

The controls were perhaps justified till the end of the sixties, but subsequently they started having a detrimental effect on industry.

It is in this background that the liberalisation process from 1991 onwards was welcomed in the areas of trade and industrial policy, taxation, exchange rate reform etc. The world too had changed by that time with Communism and the old economic policies existing only in North Korea and Cuba.

However, after 1994, there were some weaknesses in the policies pursued by both the Rao and Deve Gowda governments, though the 1997 budget was outstanding.

In case there is any misunderstanding, let me clarify, that we still need a lot more liberalisation.

Let the government not privatise defence related areas and we may not privatise the railways like in some countries.

But there are over a hundred companies in the public sector which can be privatised and disinvestment can take place so that the governments' holding dips to less than 50

The making of a NATION

per cent. But there is not consensus. If the government maintains its more than 50 per cent ownerships the Controller and Auditor general comes into the picture which means the bureaucrats and ministers still interfere claiming that they have to answer to Parliament. In case the government holding is brought down to below 50 per cent we would have eliminated this problem but political expediency rules this out at least for the moment.

The fiscal deficit for 1996-97 was 5.5 per cent of the GDP and we want to bring it down to 4.5 per cent for 1996-98. But we knew for a fact that it was not 5.5 per cent even in 1996-97. If we add the state government' deficits and the PSUs deficits and the total would be more like 9 to 10 per cent. To reduce this deficit, subsidies that do not reach the real poor should be eliminated.

Another major problem is our labour policy. We do not want to throw labour out of jobs and one cannot annoy labour and progress. But we must have a flexible policy which favours more employment. Today we are scared to employ people. Moreover, to improve quality and productivity there has to be a flexible labour policy and the possibility that if some one does not work properly he might lose his job. Another area that needs liberalisation is the financial sector including insurance, banks, stock markets and the financial institutions. If Indian industry is to be competitive many more reforms are required in these sectors.

Now to the so called Bombay Club. People have been given the wrong impression that the Bombay Club is protectionist and wants the reforms process to be rolled back. Let me clarify that there is no such thing as Bombay Club. But since I am perceived as a spokesperson for this club I believe that almost all the big Indian companies in future should not become foreign controlled. Should we not have in the top 200 companies in the country, at least a 100 Indian owned companies? Every country in the world, including the developed countries, supports its domestic industries. In India we are some times told that industry is important and not the industrialist. I am not saying the Indian industrialist should be protected. And the day we become one World I will not worry. However, today there are 185 countries in the UN. If, for example, an Indian wants to settle in the US he is not allowed to do so. Hence, each country has to support not only its industries but its nationals.

In India we require foreign capital and technology. Certain technologies are in the hands of only a few corporates in the world and these companies will not part with it unless they have a majority stake in the company in India. So we should readily offer them this equity because otherwise we will not get such technology. Similarly, in certain infrastructure projects where the capital required is very large we should welcome MNCs as Indian companies may not be able to raise the required resources.

In sectors such as cement, sugar, textile, steel amongst others there is not reason why we should offer MNCs above 26 or 40 per cent equity. For instance, Bajaj Auto, which has no foreign equity is still the leader in the

Laissez-faire: *MNC might through a hoarding*   Dinodia Picture Agency

Indian two-wheeler industry.

Let's have a level playing field with our foreign competitors. We should create some Indian MNCs. Pepsi Cola, Coca-Cola or Ford Motors are welcome. But can you call a Pepsi or a Coca-Cola an Indian MNC? If it exports Coke from India, that's good. But it's far more prestigious that we export a Tata, Godrej or a Bajaj product.

Are there a large number of foreign companies in Japan or South Korea? A great majority of their top companies are Japanese and Korean .

We need foreign technology and capital. We also want to be a respected member of the international Community. I am also conscious that we cannot, without adequate reason, flout the regulations of the World Trade Organisation. This, however, does not mean that we don't argue for and, if necessary, fight for our interests.

Nowadays, we are continuously reminded about the interests of the consumers. No one can argue against this. Companies that do not satisfy their customers, will not survive. However, there is also a thing called national interests and national pride. In the past, this was sometimes, in certain countries, including India, taken to an extreme. Nowadays, it is appears that we are completely forgetting this. Most other countries, whether developing or developed, continue to be very conscious of the need to support local industries.

The more developed a country, naturally, the more open it can afford to be. We in India should follow a balanced policy which on the one hand encourages and welcomes the entry of foreign capital and technology while at the same time ensures the creation of a large number of Indian owend and controlled MNCs in the next 15 to 20 years.

If we follow the right policies and have the right work ethic, I have no doubt that by the year 2020, India will take its rightful place among the leading economic powers of the world. It is this vision of India that inspires and motivates me to do what I am doing.

THE DARKEST HOUR

December 6, 1992

The militant rise of Hindu fundamentalism and its political manifestation leads to the destruction of the Babri Masjid at Ayodhya — with tragic consequences

The fact of the matter is that for all our boasts, we have shown ourselves as a backward people, totally lacking in the elements of culture as any country understands them. It is only those who lack all understanding of culture, who talk so much about it.

—*April 17, 1950, Prime Minister Jawaharlal Nehru to Govind Ballabh Pant, chief minister of Uttar Pradesh.*

WHEN idols of Rama "mysteriously manifest" themselves in the Babri Masjid at Ayodhya on the night of December 22, 1949, there is little inkling of the repercussions of the event. The Prime Minister is, understandably for a man of his thinking, horrified, and appeals to the chief minister to take action. Union Home Minister Sardar Vallabhbhai Patel tells Chief Minister Pant that, "If peaceful and persuasive methods are to be followed, any unilateral action based on an attitude of aggression or coercion cannot be countenanced."

Yet, the Central Government takes no direct action and the Uttar Pradesh government allows the matter to drift. Ultimately, in a number of court judgments, the Babri Masjid is no longer open to Muslims for prayer. Instead, Hindus are allowed limited *darshan* of the miraculous idols.

But the battle for the Babri Masjid is far from over. In fact, it has only just begun. As Indian politics gets more and more factionalised over the coming decades, marginal interests get louder. So, in the late 1980s, the Hindu communal voice emerges as a roar to be reckoned with. From the fringes, the fundamentalists in the majority community are ready to take their place in the sun. The heat they generate will not be easy to cool down.

In the confusions and complexities of Indian politics, it is never easy to discern whether an issue is only religion or community or minority identity or caste or just plain politics. What is clear, however, is that as matters rise to a head, all ancient rivalries come to the fore, all old wounds start festering, all once-perceived wrongs scream out to be righted. So, with the Babri Masjid-Ram Janmabhoomi conflict, there are no easy answers. Sometimes, there is no answer at all, just a thread of connectivity.

November 9, 1989, Rajiv Gandhi, as prime minister of India, allows a prayer to bricks — Shilanyas — outside the Babri Masjid, at the spot where the Ram Chabutra is to be built. *Kar sevaks,* or religious workers, pour in from all over the country for this prayer. Although this concept of praying to bricks is new to Hinduism, it is sanctified by a resurgent priesthood, anxious to gather new lambs to the fold. The demand for the brick *puja* is

The making of a NATION

Vitriolic rhetoric: *Vishwa Hindu Parishad's Sadhvi Rithambara raising fundamentalist crowds to a frenzy at New Delhi Boat Club*

Sharad Saxena/India Today

masterly; the government permission to it perhaps not quite so.

But by November 1989, a beleaguered Rajiv Gandhi is far removed from his anguished grandfather of 1950. It is not an understanding of culture that compels Gandhi to do this, it is a desire to save his own skin and that of his party. The 1986 fiasco over the Shah Bano case ranged Muslim and Hindu fundamentalists against each other and the Congress lost both substantial Muslim and Hindu vote banks. If that had not been bad enough, his personal popularity started waning. Scandals like the Fairfax investigation and a submarine deal did not help either. And finally, the Bofors gun was threatening to explode with mighty consequences. Allowing a few Hindu fundamentalists to worship a few bricks could even be seen as the act of a drowning man grasping at any available votes.

But as the force of the gathered crowd grows too strong for the Shilanyas in Ayodhya, UP Chief Minister, Mulayam Singh Yadav, proves he is no Govind Ballabh Pant either. He uses a show of strength to disperse the *kar sevaks*. Victory, for the family of Hindu fundamentalist parties, is deferred to later.

October 23, 1990. L K Advani's Rath Yatra reaches Samastipur in Bihar, on the way to Ayodhya for a grand finale and *puja* on October 30. But Advani has reckoned without Laloo Prasad Yadav, chief minister of Bihar, Like his namesake in UP, Yadav arrests Advani and halts the Yatra. But the crowds of holy men and priests and believers have already gathered at Ayodhya awaiting the arrival of the Bharatiya Janata Party leader. Violence erupts once again, and once again, Mulayam Singh Yadav has no truck with fundamentalists.

This elusive desire for Hindu 'victory' is complicated not only by politics and expediency, but also from within the Hindu sense of belief and history. As the clamour for the Ram temple at the site of the Babri Masjid becomes louder, so do the cries from

Between Advani's Rath Yatra and the day of reckoning in 1992, two governments fall, a former prime minister is assassinated on the campaign trail, the country goes to the polls, the Congress wins an election on a sympathy vote. But the demand for the Ram temple at Ayodhya is not forgotten. The BJP has made substantial electoral gains on this promise.

The appointed day for the beginning of the construction of the *chabutra* on which the temple would be built is December 6, 1992. Thousands of saffron-clad religious workers converge towards Ayodhya.

December 3, 1992. Prime Minister P V Narasimha Rao meets leaders of the Sangh Parivar and various sants and mahants. He is given an assurance that the building of the *chabutra*, or foundation platform, will be peaceful. There is no chance of any damage to the Babri Masjid. The prime minister believes what he hears.

The Union Minister for Home Affairs S B Chavan assures the nation that nothing will go wrong. In any event, para-military forces will be waiting close by — just in case. It appears that most of the nation believes the home minister.

December 5, 1992. The air is electric at the Babri Masjid Complex. Thousands of *kar sevaks* have already arrived, waiting for their big moment. But by the afternoon, leaders announce that there will only be a symbolic *kar seva*. The charge changes subtly, perhaps from negative to positive. Says Harcharan Singh from Haryana, "After all this if the leaders do not allow *kar seva*, they will face our *maar seva*." The portents are becoming clearer.

December 6, 1992, morning. Eager workers wait for their leaders to arrive, for the ceremonies to begin. Full of zest, enthusiastic *sevaks* break through the security cordon around the area. They are successfully pushed back into place.

11.30 am. The *puja* is about to start. The crowd breaks

Key Players: *(left to right): Kalyan Singh, Mulayam Singh Yadav, P V Narasimha Rao and S B Chavan*

India Today

the historians and archaeologists that Ram's connection to this Ayodhya are tenuous at best. Historically, there is no record that this is the Ayodhya where Ram was born. Indeed, there is no history of such worship in the place, much less of a Ram temple where the Babri Masjid now stands.

It emerges that history and fact are immaterial before the citadel of faith. Further, the Sangh Parivar, the family of Hindu fundamentalist groups, has a political agenda here. Ram is a symbol with which to woo Hindu vote banks, to deflect attention from mundane problems by uniting the dissatisfied with a common goal. The Hindu *per se* has never been wooed as a vote bank and the BJP is quick to seize the opportunity. The BJP gives voice to the silent Hindu, and then provides him with a focus — a Ram temple at Ayodhya. A common goal often needs a common enemy, and the "children of Babur" are the target.

free of all restrictions. Armed, not with coconuts and marigold garlands but pick axes, crow bars, iron rods. The security forces are helpless against this barrage. The destination, indeed the intention of this crowd is clear — the domes of the Babri Masjid.

As the domes begin to fall, observers are turned to stone. The media, the police, the leaders of the Sangh Parivar watch, some with horror, some with amazement, still others perhaps with hidden glee. Because what is falling is not just a 400-year-old mosque, till recently of no great significance. It is the edifice of Indian tolerance, brotherhood, peace and spiritual enlightenment. But that is the larger picture, with repercussions which will be slow to fully develop. What is immediately clear is that the Central government was completely unprepared for such an eventuality, leading to a crisis of leadership and decision.Not just the Central government, but even the BJP leadership.

(facing page) Forces of destruction: *Kar sevaks reducing the 400-year-old Babri Masjid to rubble*

D Ravinder Reddy/India Today

A dismayed Advani turns to his BJP colleague Uma Bharati, "As the time for the *kar seva* has passed, I appeal to the Ram bhakts to listen to their leaders and come back."

Down in the field, the BJP's Sadhvi Rithambara is exultant and frenzied: *"Ek dhakka aur do, Babri Masjid tor do."*

Whose voice should a manic mob heed? Whose voice could it hear?

By 5 pm, the voice of reason has been ignored and the Babri Masjid is rubble, part of the history it came from.

The VHP takes out a victory procession even before the dust settles.

But the greatest shame is not here. It is in Delhi, where a Central Government watches helplessly as UP Chief Minister Kalyan Singh of the BJP prevents paramilitary forces from stopping the demolition. After 5 pm, when it is all over, the government's machinery rolls in. Too much, too late.

The backlash in the country is predictable, and swift. Almost an entire nation seems under curfew as Hindu-Muslim riots break out all over. For those who can remember, the fury is like that of Partition. Neighbours become mortal enemies, social and economic injustices get confused with faith and belief. The intelligentsia takes hope from the stories of inter-community solidarity and there are some of those. But more than anything, there is shock. At the brash daring of the act, of the lack of official action, of the apparent crumbling of a social fabric, bought through hardship and blood, but perhaps not paid for with enough hard work and dedication.

"The fact of the matter is that for all our boasts, we have shown ourselves as a backward people, totally lacking in the elements of culture as any country understands them."

— *Jawaharlal Nehru, 1950* ■

The aftermath: *Bombay burns in the post-Babri Masjid demolition mayhem*   Mukesh Parpiani

Post-Demolition Riot Casualties

Gujarat: 246 dead	Kerala: 12 dead.
Madhya Pradesh: 120 dead	Andhra Pradesh: 12 dead
Maharashtra: 259 dead	Karnataka: 60 dead
Assam: 100 dead	Tamil Nadu: 2 dead
Punjab & Haryana: Two towns affected, put under curfew.	

PATTERNS IN THE SAND
Rising Hindutva tries to capture the initiative from Hinduism. But can it survive?
By Ashis Nandy

THE demolition of the Babri Masjid Ayodhya on December 6, 1992, was a watershed in the culture of Indian politics. Yet, the intelligentsia and the press behaved after the event as if they knew all along what had precipitated the event and what could have been done about it, as if they had nothing to learn from the fact that the Ayodhya events could take place despite their formulaic slogans, their closeness to the Indian state during the previous five decades, and their use of the state to ram their message down the throat of the population.

The Hindu nationalists, on the other hand, saw December 6 as a red-letter day in the history of 'resurgent Hinduism'; they were convinced that their political 'success' had at last confirmed their reading of the Indian politics and culture. So apparently nothing much changed in the intellectual climate of India. Yet, there is now a new and bitter divide in the Indian bourgeoisie, specially the intellectuals on the event. First a word on that divide.

Including Ayodhya, there have been till now four nodal points or archetypal episodes in the political culture of independent India. The others are: the assassination of M K Gandhi, the Emergency imposed in the mid-70s, and the anti-Sikh riots. It is an indicator of things that three out of the four involve religion-based nationalism. Each of these episodes has continued to divide, emotionally and morally, friends, families and colleagues long after the political possibilities of the episode have been exhausted.

Much can be said about the factors precipitating the earlier episodes — security lapses in the case of Gandhi's assassination in 1948, wrong advice given by scheming factotums to prime minister Indira Gandhi who imposed the Emergency or mounted the army operation at the Golden Temple, so on. Yet, in the long run, no one has gone by objective criteria or empirical data. Everyone has taken position, at least among that section of the middle class that sets the tone of Indian public life. As a result, what a person or a group did or did not do during the episodes have remained embossed on public consciousness.

Even the Hindu nationalists who assassinated Gandhi and were involved in two earlier attempts to kill him, have now added his name to their pantheon. Not only is Gandhi remembered in the daily prayers of the Rashtriya Swayamsevak Sangh, the Bharatiya Janata Party, has fought two general elections on the platform of Gandhian socialism. It is pretty certain that, years later, the Indians will continue to judge each other by the positions they took on the vandalism on December 6 at Ayodhya and will look back upon the instigators of the event the same way they have looked upon the killers of Gandhi, the anti-heroes of the

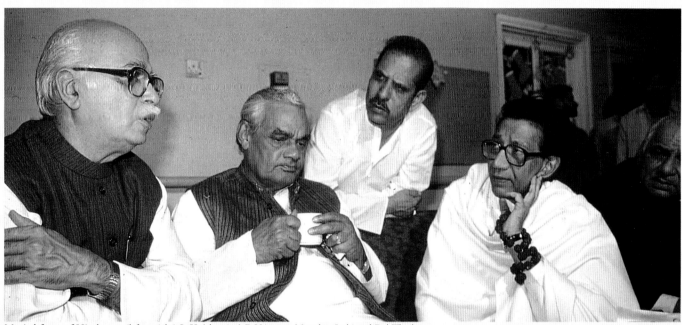

Myriad faces of Hindutva: *(left to right) L K Advani, A B Vajpayee, Manohar Joshi and Bal Thackeray*   Ashesh Shah/India Today

Emergency, or the sponsors of the anti-Sikh pogrom in 1984. This is because each of the episodes involved a vital issue that was political and moral, though at the beginning it looked purely political. Each of them, when it happened, seduced many to believe that their response would be judged only tactically and, many persons aside, it would be too much to avoid.

They were proved wrong. For not merely the self-interests but the very selfhood of their compatriots was intertwined with the issues. Against the background of this divide, I venture a few propositions about the changing nature and present status of religious nationalism in India. To start with the politically concrete, the internal politics of Sangh Parivar has changed in the course of the Ramjanmabhoomi movement. One indicator of change is the marginalisation of the Akhil Bharatiya Vidyarthi Parishad, the student wing of the BJP. It is now a pale copy of its old self. In its place, the Bajrang Dal seems to have emerged as the 'true' youth wing of the parivar. And the Dal owes allegiance not to the BJP but the VHP, which raised the Dal as its fighting arm.

The stalwarts of the RSS may think the Dal to be only a necessary evil, a collection of hot-headed youth and local toughs for a good cause, but politically the Dal can no longer be held in leash by the political kinds within the parivar. Likewise, the status of the BJP has declined in comparison to that of the VHP. The VHP now has better access to and clout with the upper rungs of the RSS and the locus of financial power in the family has shifted towards the VHP, which reportedly collected in millions of dollars world-wide for the Ramjanmabhoomi movement. To this money the BJP has no access, it has to fend for itself as the other parties do.

After Ayodhya, the sadhus and sants in the front too are flexing their political muscle in ways that cannot but unnerve the serious politicians in the BJP. Some of the recent statements of the VHP-sponsored Hindu religious figures — on issues such as the Constitution and the fate of Delhi's Jama Masjid — show that these figures are now trying to set the political agenda of the parivar independently of the BJP; BJP is

mainly responding to such initiatives, sometimes without much self-confidence. In other words, the BJP as a political party has emerged, however odd this may sound, weaker from the events of December 6. It looks increasingly like a parliamentary wing of a front.

The other parties have sensed this decline and they have begun to handle the BJP differently. Knowing BJP's expanding support base and diminishing manoeuvrability, they are trying to reduce it to a 'normal' political force.

Their future as individual politicians now seems as bright as that of the leaders of the 'ultra-Hindu' Shiv Sena of Mumbai constantly being accused of living off bribes, extortion, smuggling, and protection rackets, directly or indirectly. As for the stigma of playing communal politics, if the Congress-I can be seen today as a party standing for inter-religious amity after presiding over the state-sanctioned anti-Sikh riots in which about 5000 Sikhs were killed, the BJP also can whitewash its sins. Only it will have to be prepared to pay a price for it. My suspicion is that the BJP will pay the price and other parties will accept it gleefully, since they have their own pasts to rewrite.

Secondly, there is the new social sector from which the Sangh Parivar has begun to get support, in addition to the support it usually gets from urban trading communities and politically dispossessed upper-castes. Democratic elections being a game of numbers, over the last two decades the India's urban, modernising middle class has consistently lost power. The changing composition of Parliament and the state legislatures and the changing culture of Indian politics reflect this.

Paradoxically, this class is now trying to regain a part of its lost power by moving closer to the centres of power in the name of professional expertise, skill in modern management, and especially modern media. The parivar has won the battle for the mind of a sizeable section of this class. There are many reasons for this. The most important of them is that old-style secularists never had much of a clue to the ways of thinking of a large majority of Indians. Their secularism was built around a borrowed version of statism, backed by commitment to a centralised political economy and mega-technology and by a nationalism that idealised a direct relationship between the state and the individual unmediated by any cultural or community ties.

Once this ideology caught on among the modernised Indians, the parivar could push it to its logical conclusion. After all, the ideology of Hindutva is only an edited version of the post-Independence official ideology of the Indian state and pre-war European nationalism. That is why, in recent years, the anti-Muslim stance of the parivar has increasingly sought legitimacy among the middle classes not on religious but secular grounds (such as the alleged Muslim hostility to family planning, unified civil code, monogamy and women's rights).

On the other hand, the 'imperfect' secularists who define secularism to mean equal respect for others' faiths and, therefore, take seriously the different religious traditions of India may not have lost the battle of minds entirely. For they have a more restricted faith in the ideology of the nation-state and European-style monocultural nationalism; they are willing to alter and adapt the ideas of the state and governance to the South Asian cultural and social environment. Unfortunately, among India's political ultra-elite, this species is now endangered.

Fortunately, there is still the forgotten majority that has traditionally based its religious tolerance on faiths and local cultures. All one can hope is that this section, taking advantage of the still-open Indian polity, will throw up a new set of leaders to give political voice to their values. The declining ability of the Congress party and the Left to relate to the Hindus *qua* Hindus has created a vacuum that is being quickly filled by a variety of political Hinduism, some of them clearly belonging to the lunatic fringe, the others closer to mainstream politics and capable of tapping a new vote bank taking shape in India. This vote bank comprises a new middle class, partly decultured and massified, looking for a new, pan-Indian Hinduism suited to modern living and competitive mass politics.

Let me spell this out. The *kar sevaks* who assembled at Ayodhya on December 6 included many villagers, traditional religious leaders and a sizeable contingent of women volunteers. However, a large majority of them were urban, partly modernised, educated young men. These youth, who seemed to be looking for a cause and solidarity that life had denied them, represented neither a cross-section of Indian society nor Indian traditions. They were mostly the massified, abandoned children of modern India, thrown up by the quickening processes of social change and development. Most of their political leaders, too, were not orthodox Hindus; many of them drew inspiration from the 19th-century reform movements that tried to unify and modernise Hinduism and the Hindus. Many of these leaders were anti-idolatrous.

The others were non-believers or belonged to sects that did not grant the divinity of Ram. Ram was neither their personal god nor the subject of their spiritual veneration. They openly talked of him as a national hero. Their goal was nothing less than to build a monocultural nation out of martialised, politically organised Hindus. The model for most Hindu nationalists is not the European fascism of the 1930s, but the modern European nation-states battling their real or imaginary enemies and steam-rolling their minorities into conformity. Afraid of the strongly anarchist, non-statist, culturally plural features of Hinduism — of the kind Mohandas Karamchand Gandhi deployed so creatively — the ideal of the Hindu nationalists has remained the White Man, seen as strutting around the world on the basis of the qualities the parivar, as a faithful foot soldier of the modern West, is trying to instill in the Hindus.

The Muslim becomes the other not only as an enemy of Hinduism, but as one who has rejected this ideal. The enmity is sharpened by the fact that while as a counter-modernist the Muslim is the rejected self of the Hindu nationalist, Islam as a monotheistic, prophetic creed having a Semitic connection-and inhabiting the liminal world between the colonial construction of Hinduism and Christianity-is part of the Hindu nationalist's cultural ideal. Hence the ideology of Hindutva, the ersatz Hinduism the Parivar has popularised in urban India and, predictably, among the expatriate Indians in the first world.

Hindutva seeks to retool the Hindus into a single ethnic category or nationality, according to the 19th-century European concepts of nationality and national culture. Modern nation-states always find nationalities of the kind the Parivar is trying to build on the basis of a house-broken Hinduism, much more palatable than the open-ended, fuzzy cultural reality that everyday Hinduism has traditionally been. It is the same colonial anthropology of Hinduism that once allowed the RSS to play footsie with British colonialism and to swallow hook, line and sinker the line that cultural reforms had to have priority over political action to enable the Hindus to learn state craft and citizenship under the Raj. (That is why whatever else the RSS might or might not have, it has no record of anti-imperialist activism.)

The future of this clash between faith and ideology is uncertain. However, two possibilities seem open. First, as the colonial Hinduism of the Parivar has no genuine place for everyday faith and rejects the traditional self-definition of the Hindus, in the battle between Hinduism and Hindutva, the former may find new partisans among the new generations of Indian less burdened by memories of colonialism and embarrassed by Hinduism as it is. The self-hatred and self-doubt that produced the ideology of the Parivar may diminish with the death of the first generation of post-colonial Indians who have lived in awe of the achievements of Europe.

There is also, however, the possibility that, with more Indians entering the modern sector and being exposed to the standardised definition of faith and the official enthusiasm for the 'high culture' of Hinduism and fear of its popular local versions, the 'natural' constituency of Hindutva has expanded. I suspect, though, that the future of Hinduism, as opposed to that of Hindutva, is not as bleak as many believe. After all, Hinduism is the faith of a large majority of Hindus rooted in their culture and confident of it; Hindutva is the ideology of Hindus partly uprooted from their culture and massified.

It is doubtful if the faith of this minority will prevail against the proven resilience of Hinduism. Fortunately, Ayodhya has forced a fraction of politically aware Indians to tacitly admit that a potent set of cultural symbols need not have been handed over on a platter to the Parivar for monopolistic use.

ALL BULL

1992

Harshad Mehta takes the stock market and the country by storm. Only to be blown away by a financial scandal bigger than his dreams — or nightmares

Stylebhai: *Harshad Mehta posing with his Lexus at the peak of his bull run*

Namas Bhojani/India Today

"India is a turnaround scrip in the world market."

— Harshad Mehta, February 28, 1992, on Doordarshan, after being raided by the IT authorities

HARSHAD Mehta, Big Bull. The man who single-handedly shook the Indian stock markets out of their legendary sloth and set them on a roller-coaster ride.

Harshad Mehta. The man who single-handedly exposed the best-kept secret of the Indian banking world — that it was the worst-kept business in the country.

Harshad Mehta, son of a seller of yarn, is now a giant seller of yarns, peddler of dreams.

The biggest yarn is the one everyone wanted to believe the most. That it's possible to make lots of money out of nothing. As the Bombay Stock Exchange's sensitive index rises to a dizzying 4387 — quadrupling in the span of one year, as Mehta takes his favourite scrip, ACC, from Rs 500 to Rs 10,000, there is no end to the yarns people will believe, dreams they will buy.

And indeed, they do buy. "Buy! Buy! Buy!" goes the scream at the stock market as Mehta picks up any scrip he likes and turns it around. Indian companies are undervalued, he says, which is why the stock market is under-priced. The bears try to bring down the scales, but to no avail. Who's listening? When the Big Bull talks, everyone else is shouted down.

But someone, somewhere is curious. And someone, somewhere is looking for something else. After a query from the Reserve Bank of India, the State Bank of India is looking into its accounts. One is the country's central banking authority, the other is the biggest bank in the land. The accounts are not of personal savings or merchant activities. These have to do with the statutory liquidity ratio — the minimum percentage that banks are supposed to invest in approved securities, or central and state loans. Someone, somewhere has found a discrepancy in the State Bank of India's subsidiary general ledger. The discrepancy seems to be connected with the Big Bull stock market and securities broker Harshad Mehta.

April 23, 1992. An item in the *Times of India* states that Mehta has been asked to clear Rs 500 crore worth of irregularities. The dice are rolling.

April 26, 1992. The Sensex has already dropped by 1,077 points. What is going to happen to the Amitabh Bachchan of the stock market? Or should he be called the Einstein, as one of his fans insist? It is still not absolutely clear what has gone wrong. Mehta himself says he was "breaking the monopoly of foreign

Hero's welcome: *In spite of the fall-out of the scam, Harshad Mehta is fêted by fans on his release from jail*   Mukesh

banks as market makers in the securities market". As the market goes into free fall, it becomes clear that the Mehta's great run on the stock exchange was fuelled by funds got in a novel manner. Government securities that were supposed to be moving from bank to bank were, instead, finding their way into Mehta's private accounts in the form of cash. The State Bank of India, the Reserve Bank of India subsidiary, the National Housing Bank and ANZ Grindlays Bank were definitely part of Mehta's little game. The game to break the monopoly of market makers in the securities market. Mehta is the flashiest fish in the official net. But he is not the only one.

April 29, 1992. Finance Minister Manmohan Singh announces in Parliament that the Reserve Bank of India will probe the irregularities. The Central Bureau of Investigation is called in.

But the RBI, surprisingly to many, has already been on the job. The fantastic high prices on the country's stock exchanges have astounded even this high-caste body, want to look down its impressive nose at the ants which people Dalal Street, the country's commercial heartbeat. In all Bombay's crowded streets, Dalal Street with its sky-scraping Jeejeebhoy Towers and million other brokerage firms, is truly paved with gold. Too much gold and much too shiny suspects the RBI.

Where is all that money coming from?

April 30, 1992. The *Indian Express* carries a report stating that the UCO Bank allowed Harshad Mehta to use over Rs 50 crore by discounting its bill

This is, clearly, not an ordinary stock market broker. Or even an ordinary stock market illegality. Not even an ordinary financial irregularity. It is a full-blown fiscal crisis, where the norms of the banking industry are exposed as being as weighty as dandelion seeds in a strong wind.

Harshad Mehta is only one player in a deep and devious game. He's just the newest boy in town and the one with the biggest mouth. He's just the catalyst, not the cause. As he gets all the public attention, it becomes clear to those working behind the scenes that large Indian and foreign banks and mutual funds have been working together to defraud the system and maximise profits. Like those proverbial dominoes, bank employees, from chairmen to clerks, fall before the collected evidence. But no one, not even the whispered suicide of former NHB chairman M J Pherwani, owner of the Big Bull title before it was usurped, captures the public imagination like Harshad Mehta.

June 4, 1992. Harshad Mehta is arrested. The stock market he created has crashed around his ears and so have his dreams. So have the dreams of millions of small investors who followed his lead blindly, unthinkingly. For many, the rise and fall of Harshad Mehta point to the perils of liberalisation, of opening up a market to a people not used to its spoils. But The Scam, as it will now be known, also points to an Indian financial market that is governed by toothless, blind and deaf bodies, too dumb to see what is happening around them. From insider trading to false entries, every financial crime is committed with impunity. When the Sensex is down to less than 3,000 points, the time has come to give regularity bodies a good dose of the five senses and then some, if small investors are to be safeguarded from sharks and even from their gullible selves.

September 22, 1992. Harshad Mehta is released from jail. The amount of money involved in this scam is put at Rs 6,000 crore by conservative estimates. Apart from Grindlays, foreign banks like Standard Chartered and Citibank are involved. The Bank of Karad has been liquidated. The once-respected broker Bhupen Dalal has lost his credibility and so have too many of his colleagues. The frenzy that once ruled the Indian stock markets seems to be over.

Not for Mehta, though. "I burn inside. I can't stop burning big," he says in October 1992. The young boy who bribed a man to pretend to be his father to soothe an irate teacher, the college dropout, jobber who lost Rs 2,000 on his first transactions now sits in his 15,000 square foot south Bombay flat, having lost his Rs 1,000 crore fortune, his fleet of cars including his beloved red-brown Toyota Lexus waiting to be auctioned. He may have lost it all, but his legend continues. ■

Lowkey: *Harshad Mehta in a post-release chastened mood*   Hemant Pithwa/India Today

Landmarks of the Bombay Stock Exchange Sensitive Index

Date	Sensex	Reasons
19.08.1979	100	Index launched with 100 basis points
30.11.1984	300	Rajiv Gandhi takes over as Prime Minister with a young team, promising economic reform
28.02.1986	664.53	Rajiv Gandhi's Finance Minister V P Singh unveils the new economic policy that pledges to open out the economy, allowing multinational entry and foreign investment
03.03.1988	440	V P Singh is shifted by Rajiv Gandhi from Finance to Defence, parts with the Congress over the Bofors scam to join the Opposition
09.01.1989	658	Market moves on buying support from local mututal funds
25.07.1990	1007	Good monsoon coupled with good corporate reserves pushes the sensex up
30.07.1990	1098	Government announces concession in industrial policy
09.01.1991	947	The Sensex dips as the Gulf War breaks out and an embargo imposed on Iraq by Western allies sets off an international oil crisis
28.02.1992	3049	Dr Manmohan Singh's budget finally puts on to paper past promises. Dr Singh is hailed as the father of liberalisation and the sensex shoots up
02.04.1992	4546	Harshad Mehta's share market manipulations sends the sensex zooming to unprecedented levels as bull operators jump on the bandwagon
30.04.1993	1980	Harshad's scam is out. The bubble bursts. Scam has nationwide implications with even the country's biggest bank, State Bank of India, being involved
04.03.1994	4299	After the crash, the sensex makes a remarkable recovery on promising Union Budget announcements
10.05.1994	3694	Sensex dips as the BSE bans badla
11.09.1994	4643	Hectic buying by Foreign Institutional Investors (FIIs)
25.12.1995	2991	With elections to the Lok Sabha imminent, Congress slows down its reforms push. And with the prospects of Congress being voted out looming large with doubts about a stable alternative government, economic outlook turns gloomy, reflected in the sensex
28.06.1996	4133	P Chidambaram's appointment as Finance Minister of the 13-party United Front coalition government with the support of the Congress, sparks off another rally as the new finance minister projects a more dynamic image than his predecessor Dr Manmohan Singh
05.12.1996	2991	Cut in government spending and an all-pervasive liquidity crisis results in an economic slowdown. Many fear a recession
12.12.1996	2713	FIIs selling to book profits at year's end
01.04.1997	3360	Congress withdraws support to United Front government
01.07.1997	4300	FIIs on a buying spree. Like their Indian counterparts, they too start buying low and selling high, booking short-term returns
02.07.1997	4333	Heavy buying from FIIs continues

(Source: Bombay Stock Exchange)

The making *of* a NATION

THE COLOUR OF BLOOD

January 1993

*Bombay flows red as the city becomes a gruesome spectacle of
senseless bloodlust and contrived fury*

JANUARY 5, 1993. Two *mathadi* workers are killed in a clash in Dongri, after being attacked by eight unidentified men carrying choppers. Two others are injured. The police are investigating the attack. The cause is not yet clear.

January 6, 1993. Exactly a month to the day that the Babri Masjid in Ayodhya was demolished by Hindu fundamentalists. In December, as the country burned, cosmopolitan, commercial Bombay saw some of the worst riots — 273 dead — in its history. Or so the city thought.

January 6, 1993. The Hindu fundamentalist Shiv Sena in Bombay has promised a series of *maha artis* to celebrate the first month of life without the Babri Masjid. As the Sena's fiery leader Bal Thackeray has declared, "The Shiv Sainiks did play their role

dislocate normal life and exacerbate raw feelings.

January 6, 1993, midnight. Riots break out in Bhendi Bazaar, Mohammed Ali Road, Mahim, Crawford Market and Dongri, all known to be "Muslim" areas. At least 12 people are feared killed, 54 buses burnt. Curfew is imposed, relaxed at 6 am. Is this rioting a reaction to the maha artis? Is it a well-planned attack against Muslim establishments? Is it just temporary madness? The killing of the sturdy Maratha loaders working in the Bombay docks is seen as the catalyst. The police believe that this incident could have been an inter-union killing, since it carries all the marks of a gangland operation. The rumour mill believes otherwise.

January 7, 1993. Close to midnight. The Bane family of

Daggers drawn: *Bombay attacks itself during the January '93 riots*

in the demolition of the mosque, but I am not saying this as a matter of pride. It was a holy task."

The *maha arti* is also a holy task, and perhaps, like the Babri demolition, its intentions are not bathed in purity. This is a novel form of worship, where hundreds congregate outside a temple so that the evening prayers are conducted practically on the street. If the Muslims can hold their namaz prayers on the streets, why not the Hindus? Have not the Hindus and other communities put up with the resultant discomfort for years?

January 6, 1993 and people do not quite know what to expect. The tension is palpable and sporadic incidents of violence break out in areas dubbed to be "communally sensitive". The *maha artis* achieve their less apparent object — to

seven and frightened neighbours are huddled into their home in the Gandhi Chawl in Jogeshwari East, an area known for its Hindu-Muslim problems. When the knock comes, it is from armed men, looking for trouble. The family begs for mercy. The men leave and come back with cans of kerosene. A lit match is thrown in. The only escape route is through the tiny kitchen window. Four die in the fire, trapped. Naina Bane lies bandaged in hospital. She has lost her father, her family, friends and more in the fire. "Our Muslim neighbours helped pour water on our wounds," she says. For her, the crime was committed by outsiders. The cause — the *maha arti* held that evening.

For the mobs that will now overtake the city without mind or mercy, Naina Bane's beliefs are immaterial. A family of

Maharashtrian Hindus has been attacked by some Muslims. The target from now on is all Muslims. Bombay becomes a city under siege from itself, as neighbour seems to turn against neighbour, friend against friend. Systematically, Muslim businesses, shops, godowns are targeted, smashed, ransacked, burnt. Manohar Joshi, first lieutenant of the Shiv Sena's Bal Thackeray, says, "The attack on Hindu families and property on January 6 and 7 was a pre-arranged conspiracy. So naturally there was a Hindu response. Shiv Sainiks have spontaneously attacked them all over Bombay. But other Hindus are also retaliating. Criminals too are taking part in the attacks, but that happens in every riot."

Across the city there are cries of the Sena mobs, armed with swords and sticks, attacking buildings, asking for Muslim families. The evening sky in Bandra and Mahim burns red as the setting sun is diminished in the glare of timber yards, owned by Muslims, on fire. Attempts at retaliation are practically swamped by the deluge. Across the city are stories of the police standing

Silent witness: *Death stalks the streets*   Sherwin Crasto

easy to control. Bombay's citizens now know that these riots are not to do so much with religion, but with social injustice, with urban aggression, with the angst of the displaced, with a search for identity, with the sheer bloodlust of mob fury. The army moves into the city, and achieves through intimidatory presence alone what the police cannot through action.

Although the role of the Shiv Sena in these riots is not disputed — Sena leader Madhukar Sarpotdar is caught by the army carrying arms and ammunition in his car — the Congress government is reluctant to take action against it.

If Bombay finds its spirit again, it is not in the crazed rumours that all packet milk has been poisoned. Instead, it is in noted cricketer Sunil Gavaskar watching from his balcony in Worli, a mob attacking a family of terrified Bohra Muslims. He runs down, remonstrates with the mob, and drives them away. It is of Hindu neighbours sheltering their Muslim friends, it is of Armani-suited and chiffon sari-ed residents of the city's posh environs — targeted for the first time in such riots — wandering into areas that had never sullied their feet before, pleading for peace.

The making of a NATION

Still, there are thousands fleeing the city of gold. Their dreams turned to ashes, they pack up to go home to their distant villages, cries of "Hindu ja Musalman" ringing in their ears. Bombay is no longer a haven, but closer to hell. Is it surprising that when Prime Minister P V Narasimha Rao makes a tour of the city on January 15, he does not even get out of his car?

As the city waits for the inner call to find out what happened, attempts must be made. The government appoints a commission headed by Justice B N Srikrishna to probe the riots in January '93. The Shiv Sena and Bharatiya Janata Party come to power in April '95 and the inquiry is cancelled. The ostensible reason is that raking up old wounds would just be too painful for all concerned — the riots are over and should be forgotten. But the connection between the damning evidence against the Sena and the winding up of the commission is too glaring to be ignored. The Bharatiya Janata Party comes to power at the Centre for a few days in 1996 and the commission resumes its hearings. In 1997, the results are still awaited. But for the city that is waiting to forget the riots, 1993 has more tragedy in store.   ∎

Sherwin Crasto

by, as mobs burn, kill, loot. Hurt by the criticism after the December riots, where they were accused of targeting Muslims, Bombay's famed policemen are now reluctant to shoot at all. The state Government, headed by Sudhakarrao Naik, appears to do little. The city's Police Commissioner, Shrikant Bapat, seems similarly afflicted. Union Defence Minister Sharad Pawar, not so long ago chief minister of Maharashtra, flies in. On the streets, the battle is of supremacy. In the upper echelons of government, it is also of supremacy — political rather than social.

January 9, 1993 and the Shiv Sena's mouthpiece, *Saamna*, declares that enough is enough, "the bigots have been taught a lesson". The violence abates slightly, but mobs are not always

SINISTER SERIAL

March 12, 1993

Barely recovered from numbing violence, Bombay is shattered by a succession of bomb explosions. But the spirit of the city survives

MARCH 12, 1993, 1.26 pm. Trading at the Bombay Stock Exchange, the commercial hub of India, is almost coming to an end. Then, what seems like a "million times more than a Diwali atom bomb" goes off. The blast destroys the high-rise building's parking lot. Outside on the crowded Dalal Street, it feels like an earthquake. Inside, there is blood and panic as brokers and sub-brokers scramble to get out. Help from passers-by is immediate. Ambulances, the police, the fire brigade are called into service.

But even as Jeejeebhoy Towers shudders from the impact, more explosions tear Bombay apart. Between 1.26 pm and 3.54 pm, the city experiences the worst serial blasts in the world: the Air-India building in the corporate district of Nariman Point, two Air-India owned hotels in Santa Cruz and Juhu, Zaveri Bazaar, a petrol pump behind the Shiv Sena's headquarters, two cinema halls in Central Bombay, a bus-stop close to Century Bazaar in Worli and the Sea-Rock Hotel in Bandra. Over 300 dead, over 1,000 injured.

Born in the riots of December '92 and January '93, this calamity attacks not just selected areas or communities but randomly targets the city's most visible aspect — its commercial character. The destruction is aimed at nobody in particular and everyone in general. If it is revenge for the devastation of the riots, it is peculiar in that it hurts those it seeks to avenge as much as those perceived as perpetrators. Were the blasts revenge for the destruction that the riots wrought on Bombay's Muslims? Revenge for the destruction of Bombay's famed underworld by former chief minister Sudhakarrao Naik? An attempt to destabilise the city's economy so that ganglords could regain lost ground? An ISI show of strength?

But the reasons come later. First Bombay, stunned, shell-shocked, hurt and bloody, must deal with the immediate damage. And Bombay stands up, to the last citizen, and faces the challenge. Strangers take people to hospital, donate blood, work to clear the debris. The fire brigade, hard-pressed for tenders and men, works round the clock, the police get down to picking up clues right away. This is not an attack to be taken lying down. There is no official dithering, no public apathy or paralysis.

The use of Research and Defence Explosive — RDX — the military precision of the operation, the fact that no militant organisation takes credit for the serial blasts lead the police to believe that the 'foreign hand', usually just a convenient scapegoat, cannot be ruled out. Paksitan's Inter-Services Intelligence — the omnipresent ISI — is one immediate suspect. But there are flaws in the bombers' modus operandi too. On March 12 itself, the police find a maroon Maruti van parked near the Worli-Century Bazaar bomb site. The van contains four hand-grenades, seven new AK-56 rifles, 14 magazines, two plastic prayer beads, two small plastic bottles filled with water and labelled holy water in Arabic.

The van is traced to one Yakub Memon, a chartered accountant, who left the city for Dubai just hours before the blasts began. His family have gone on ahead. The police have their one big breakthrough. The next few months and Yakub and his family will become India's most wanted people. As the story emerges, it is clear that the mastermind is Yakub's brother Ibrahim. Or Tiger Memon, an underworld gangster, closely associated with the dreaded Dubai-based don, Dawood Ibrahim. The Central Bureau of Investigation and the Intelligence Bureau get into the act, Interpol and international intelligence agencies are alerted. After reports that the Memons may be in Pakistan, Prime Minister Nawaz Sharif promises to return them gift-wrapped.

Before that happens, however, police are able to piece together a story where revenge for the demolition of the Babri Masjid was planned one dark December night in 1992. The January '93 riots in Bombay only served, apparently, to heighten resolve and avenge the deaths of hundreds of Muslims. Almost immediately, large quantities of RDX were being off-loaded onto the coast of Western India. Tiger Memon and his friends were putting their plan into operation.

While the Memons are still somewhere between Dubai and Pakistan, the police start rounding up their suspects. Minor gangsters, junior criminals, even dubious film financiers are picked up in their dragnet. Including one very big fish — film star Sanjay Dutt. Between April 26 and May 3, '93, Dutt is questioned for storing AK-56 rifles and hand-grenades as favours for two fellow accused and filmi friends — Samir Hingora and Hanif Kadawala. Dutt confesses to the storage. He is released on interim bail on May 3, and gets back to shooting films. Is he guilty or just plain stupid? If that is to be determined, the time is not yet. In any case, by the time the trial starts, Dutt is back in jail, his bail cancelled on July 4.

July 14, 1994. The blasts trial starts at the designated court of Judge J H Patel. The chargesheet for the case is one of the longest ever — it runs into 10,000 pages. The number of accused is also one of the largest ever — 189. Of that, 43 are absconding. The rest are being held under an act that will come up for a lot of criticism over the coming years — the Terrorist and Destructive Activities (Prevention) Act. Bail, the presumption of innocence, all these are taboo in TADA.

July 24, 1994. A man is detained at Kathmandu airport for having both Indian and Pakistani passports. Four days later, he is handed over to the Indian authorities. Yakub Memon has landed in India. And he wants to hand himself over to the Indian legal system. The Memon family, he contends, had little to do with Tiger's plots — they just left the country according to his instructions. Living in Pakistan, even under the care of the ISI, had no thrill for the Memons. Legal advice apparently told them that their chances were good in India, and, at any rate, a short jail sentence at home was better than permanent exile in Pakistan.

August 25, 1994. Six more of the Memon family arrive in Delhi on an Air-India flight from Dubai, and go straight into the custody of the Central Bureau of Investigation.

Yakub has in the briefcase he carries with him, a number of false documents and a microcassette. This purports to be of a secret conversation in Pakistan on May 19 between Tiger, Taufiq

(opposite) Utter destruction: *The damage to life and property is severe* Namas Bhojani/TT

Wanted: *Underworld don Dawood Ibrahim and associate Tiger Memon*   IT

Jaliawala, a smuggler who helped the ISI in the blasts conspiracy,and three other Memon brothers — Yakub, Suleiman and Ayub. The tape makes it clear that Dawood Ibrahim and the ISI are both involved. Dawood, however, denies his role in the serial blasts. It is all Tiger's show, he says.

Tiger remains elusive. The blasts trial progresses, slowly, as over 3,500 witnesses are questioned. Many of the accused have played so small a role in the conspiracy as to be insignificant. Yet, they are booked under TADA. Some who are more important are not charged — like additional customs collector S N Thapa, who is supposed to have known about the smuggling of the RDX . Ultimately, TADA itself is repealed and many of the accused — including Dutt — are let out on bail.

By this time, Bombay has long picked itself up and gone on with life. If the riots tore at the heart of the city, the blasts shocked it back into ticking. The answer could not lie in attacking each other, it had to be in standing united in adversity.   ∎

Bomb Blasts factfile

Date of occurence: March 12, 1993

Total number of blasts: 12

Buildings and places affected:

Bombay Stock Exchange	1.26 pm	84	217	Rs 5 crore
Katha (Satta) Bazaar	2.15 pm	04	21	Rs 40 lakh
Sena Bhavan	2.30 pm	04	50	Rs 21.2 lakh
Century Bazar	2.45 pm	113	227	Rs 2.5 crore
Mahim Causeway	2.45 pm	03	06	Rs 50,000 ★
Air-India building	2.45 pm	20	87	Rs 2 crore
Zaveri Bazaar	3.05 pm	17	57	Rs 2 crore
Hotel Searock	3.10 pm	—	—	Rs 9 crore
Plaza Theatre	3.13 pm	10	37	Rs 85 lakh
Juhu Centaur Hotel	3.20 pm	—	03	Rs 2.1 crore
Sahar Airport	3.30 pm	—	—	— ★
Airport Centaur Hotel	3.40 pm	02	08	Rs 2 crore

★ No bombs, but hand grenades thrown

Unexploded bombs found at: Naigaum Cross Road and Dhanji Street

Casualties: 257 killed, 713 injured.

Property lost: Around Rs 27 crore (according to government estimates)

Type of explosives used: Over 100 kg of RDX. This is a legal explosive produced only by the army's ordinance factories.

Number of charge-sheets filed: Four. One by the Bombay Police and three by CBI

(figures of casualties and injuries from official figures)

SS RISING
Bal Thackeray's Shiv Sena and its contentious ideology
By Y D Phadke

SIX years after the creation of a separate state of Maharashtra, the Shiv Sena emerged in June 1966 as a militant communal organisation. Its founder, Bal Thackeray, a leading cartoonist and the editor of *Marmik*, a weekly which was started on August 13, 1960, continues to enjoy an unchallenged position in the party for more than three decades. Except for his association with the Rashtriya Swayamsevak Sangh from 1940 to 1943, the Shiv Sena chief had kept away from politics till 1965 and had been a spectator rather than an active political worker.

It is significant that the Shiv Sena emerged first in Greater Bombay and at present, Metropolitan Bombay comprising Greater Bombay, Thane and New Bombay is tightly controlled by the Sena. The Shiv Sena supremo began his political career by vociferously articulating the feelings of anger and frustration of the Marathi-speaking sons of the soil (Bhumiputras) against outsiders migrating from other parts of India. Greater Bombay's population was 40 lakh in 1961 and now it is more than a crore and ten lakhs In this megacity, more than half the population consists of pavement-dwellers. Bombay, now known as Mumbai, has swollen rather than grown. Life in the Metropolitan region has become, for most people a daily nightmare with a feeling of being lost in a jungle of cement. The skyscrapers, stinking slums and shanty colonies have made the congestion worse, leading to more transport bottlenecks, polluted air and water, and tremendous strain on water supply and sewage systems.

The Congress, with its governing rural elites, neglected the metropolitan region's need for planned development. The non-Congress alliance of 13 opposition parties known as the Samyukta Maharashtra Samiti had started disintegrating on the eve of the formation of the Maharashtra State and by 1967 had become a spent political force. The declining population of Marathi-speaking people in the metropolitan region felt forlorn and deserted. Thackeray successfully projected his image as the saviour of Marathi-speaking people who felt increasingly insecure after May 1, 1960. Through a network of Sthaniya Lokadhikar Samitis, the Shiv Sena demanded special preference for local lads in both private and public sector jobs.

For more than a decade, the Shiv Sena operated as a pressure group rather than a political party. It was skilfully used by Congress chief ministers of Maharashtra, including Vasantrao Naik and Vasantdada Patil, in their tussle with the Congress High Command over the still-pending boundary dispute with Karnataka. The State government connived at the activities of the Sena which was often dubbed the 'Vasant Sena'.

Aggressive posture: *Bal Thackeray*   Namas Bhojani/India Today

As early as 1948, the future of Bombay appeared gloomy and grim to a perceptive economist such as D R Gadgil, a staunch supporter of the demand for Samyukta Maharashtra including Bombay city. In 1948 as well as in 1965, Gadgil recommended to both Union and state governments that they should deny permission for setting up new industries and expanding existing industries in Greater Bombay. He favoured dispersal and shifting of industries to less developed areas of the state.

Despite repeated warnings from Gadgil and other economists during 1960-1982, the Union Government granted 4,052 new licences to industries in Maharashtra. Of these, 1,772 or 43.7 per cent were issued in Greater Bombay. The influx of migrants continued unchecked leading to a change in the composition of population of the metropolitan region. The Hindi-speaking migrants now constitute the second largest linguistic group in the region.

So long as Thackeray was concentrating only on improving the position of Marathi-speaking people, his hold over the region was not very strong. In the 1980s he began openly asserting his identity as a Hindu and instead of South Indians, the Muslim minority became his main target. With the increasing influence of the Bharatiya Janata Party, the Vishwa Hindu Parishad and other militant Hindu organisations in the Hindi-speaking states of Northern and Western India, the Shiv Sena could easily enter into an alliance with them. In view of the changing political situation, his love for the Marathi language was relegated to a subordinate position. There had long been, from time to time, an outburst of anti-Muslim feelings leading to communal riots at Bhiwandi, Mahad, Jalgaon, Mumbai and other cities in Maharashtra. The Madan Commission of Enquiry held the Shiv Sena branches in Bhiwandi and Mahad responsible for the communal riots in 1970.

When Thackeray began proudly asserting his identity as a Hindu from 1984 onwards, other linguistic groups such as the Tamilians, Gujratis, Sindhis and Punjabis who also practised Hindu religion rallied behind him. His wider support was reflected in the state Assembly elections of 1990 and 1995. The Sena had only one member in the Assembly in 1972. It captured 52 seats in 1990 and 73 in 1995. In its uneasy alliance with the BJP at present, the Shiv Sena is evidently a dominant partner and the Sena chief does not conceal his remote control of the state Government. The Maratha-Kunbi caste cluster, which for so many years solidly supported the Congress, is now divided. It is significant that 40 Maratha-Kumbi candidates won the 1995 elections as Shiv Sena candidates. Even among the 18 reserved constituencies for scheduled castes, the Sena won four seats and captured three constituencies reserved for the scheduled tribes. The Shiv Sena-BJP alliance did not win a clear majority in the Assembly elections of 1995 but it succeeded in securing the support of a majority of 'independent' members, especially Congress rebels. There is no immediate threat to the stability of the state Government which is likely to complete its five-year term.

Since the 1995 victory, despite allegations of widespread corruption and dynastic rule, Thackeray and his Sena have acquired more strength as is evident from results of recent elections to local bodies and by-elections to the Assembly. People get the government they deserve. Thackeray is no longer regarded as a mere regional satrap or a subhedar and evokes a sense of awe and admiration from Hindus in other states of India. Even a notorious underworld don such as Arun Gawli, a former Shiv Sainik, feels his life is in danger because of Thackeray's hold over the rival gangsters. Senior administrators and police officers, along with journalists and writers, are afraid to incur his wrath and often chose to remain silent even if he humiliates them in public and lashes them with his foul and abusive language and ridicules them with ribald jokes.

In January 1993, *Time* magazine published his answers to the questions asked by its representative Anita Pratap. Mentioning his idols whom he worships, he stated that in politics, it is Shivaji the great Marathi hero who fought for Swarajya in the 17th century; while in religion it is god Shiva who, according to a legend, destroys everything by opening his third eye. This self-proclaimed Hindu Hridaya Samrat declares that there is nothing wrong if his followers extort protection money from those who can pay, as his party always needs funds.

He denounces liberal democracy and hates socialism and Communism. He condemns secularism and glorifies aggressive nationalism. He wants to follow Hitler and as the latter hated the Jews and drove them out of Germany, Thackeray declares openly that if Muslims do not leave India voluntarily, they should be kicked out. Though the Indian Constitution refers to India as Bharat, Thackeray prefers to call it Hindustan. He has already stated publicly his desire to become the Prime Minister of India provided he is unanimously requested to accept the post. In future, if he gets that coveted post, instead of amending the present Constitution, he will certainly put an end to it and treat the entire country as his personal property which he would like to bequeath to his son. He loves to describe the present alliance government in Maharashtra as Shiv Shahi which is, in reality, a 20th century caricature of the original enlightened rule of that fearless Maratha hero of spotless character.

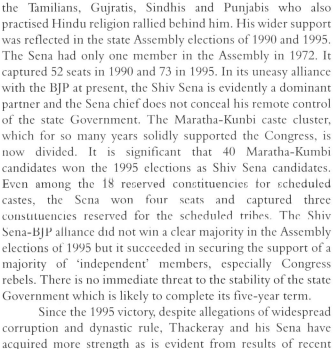

BEAUTY AND THE BOUNTY

1994

Sushmita Sen and Aishwarya Rai win international pageants and modelling becomes the career of the year

A woman is one who shows a man what love and sharing and caring is all about. That is the essence of a woman.

—Sushmita Sen before winning Miss Universe

MAY 20, 1994, Manila. Sushmita Sen's winning words take her to the top. And the 18-year-old becomes Miss Universe. For the first time since Rita Farya became Miss World in 1966, an Indian woman has taken centre-stage in the global stakes for physical beauty, charm, grace and the presence of mind to come up with convincing banalities at short notice. Says her fulfilled mother, who was watching in the audience, "My tears had curtained from my sight the most important moment of my life."

Like Shubra Sen, India is proud. The long hand of the media now stretches into unaccountable homes. Sen is a national heroine. Not only does she understand the essence of a woman, she also appears to know her onions. For an 18-year-old, she is remarkably self-possessed and assured, a girl guaranteed to do her country proud.

So it had been earlier in the year, when the smart-talking Sen beat the favourite Aishwarya Rai in a close battle for the Miss India crown. The beauty pageant organised by a leading woman's magazine now had its dividends paid — for the first time one of its contestants had starred internationally.

Sen, now, is flavour of the month. On a whistle-stop to India before she is set up in Los Angeles to fulfil her Miss Universe duties, Sen is all spun-sugar and sass. The press eats out of her hand. A beauty who can actually talk! Every second of her due 15 minutes of fame are accorded her. The influence, though, that Sen will wield goes beyond clever words, fancy hairstyles and a charming smile. In some way, after this, many Indian women will never be the same.

November 19, 1994. The pretty and delicate Aishwarya Rai, Miss India World, is already a feted figure in South Africa and its Sun City, where the pageant is situated. Her quiet fragility is endearing. India cannot expect two of its women to stun the world with their beauty, yet Rai's victory is almost no surprise. As the 22-year-old architecture student mimics Sen's winning gesture of hands to incredulous mouth in her moment of glory, India is jubilant once again. At last, Indian beauty is appreciated and lauded. And worth considerable sums of money. "We did it!" Rai mother and Rai daughter say to each other when they meet at the Miss World coronation ball.

But what Sen and Rai have really done is to open Indian women out to a new dimension. Shallow and self-obsessed, some will remark scornfully, and undoubtedly they are right. But that is also a narrow-minded view. With the titles of Miss Universe and Miss World in their grasp, the Indian beauty business explodes. All over the country, aspiring pageant winners strut their stuff, parading their pulchritude.

Every second street now has a beauty contest named after it. Colleges, schools, mahila mandals, women under 60, girls under 10, they all have their own stages to set them on the road to glory. Men aren't far behind either. Suits and swimsuits,

Victory parade: *Sushmita Sen as Miss Universe*   Pramod Pushkarna/India Today

ripped jeans and sexily torn T-shirts, they wear and strut them. Indian culture, the purists scream, isn't built for this. Nor was it, perhaps, built for satellite TV, but that's another story.

The bottomline to all this, of course, is not a curvaceous derrière. It is, simply, money. There is tremendous money to be made from people's vanity. There is also tremendous money to be made in a life of glamour. Television and advertising, and television advertising, and the ever-present world of films beckon with promise of great riches and rewards. Few parts of the world have adequate defences against these, few want to.

A few years later, mid-1996 brings with it the promise of excitement. After four years, the Miss World pageant leaves Sun City and heads towards India via the Amitabh Bachchan Corporation Limited. The Indian superstar's new corporate identity is to be enhanced by association with world-class glitzy events. And India's image is to be enhanced by world-wide exposure. India has a new prime minister in 1996, H D Deve Gowda, till recently, chief minister of Karnataka. He may live in Delhi, but the prime minister is never far from Bangalore. It seems a smart move to pick Bangalore as the venue for the Miss World competition. Clean, up-and-coming and keen, Bangalore is supposed to be India's fastest growing city.

But also the city where the populace have fought the entry

Winning smile: *Aishwarya Rai charms the world*   Dinodia Picture Agency

COSMETIC HEAVEN
Indian women get a change of face
By Shobha Dé

THERE is something big happening in the beauty business world-wide and India is obviously at the centre of it. I do believe it was no coincidence that two Indian contestants, Sushmita Sen and Aishwarya Rai, managed a twin win at international beauty pageants in the very same year. There was strategy at work there, and a method behind what appeared like madness to some sceptics. Method, that spelt money. Mucho Moolah. We have the market. They have the products. It's a marriage made in cosmetics' heaven. Only a blinkered fool would ignore the obvious. Cosmetic giants sensed India was ready for the onslaught. It was time to go for it — the looks you always wanted, the figure you were ready to kill for, the breaks you sought. It cost. But then what doesn't?

Before Sushmita and Aishwarya strutted their stuff and raked it in, beauty contests were nothing more than obligatory entertainment shows staged by two leading women's magazines, for the benefit of fat-cat advertisers and influential government officials. They were glamorous PR exercises — nothing more. The stakes were low and so were the hemlines. Clumsy, tacky and amateurish, these annual cattle parades attracted ambitious young women who had nothing to lose but their adolescent acne. The prize money was as paltry as the response it generated. The actual marketing of beauty was considered an add-on to the main event — the image of the magazine. The bi-annual crowning of the queens did cause minor flutters in the media for sure, but it didn't exactly compete with the top news stories.

Today it's another ball game altogether — and not just in India. Naomi Campbell, the world's first officially recognised black beauty, made headlines across the globe when she reportedly consumed an overdose of sleeping pills after an argument with her boyfriend. Hourly health bulletins were issued — and amazingly enough carried on the front pages by mainstream publications, including our very own Times of India. Ten years ago, the only people who'd heard of the feline-looking supermodel and been sufficiently interested in her fluctuating pulse rate, would have been a select coterie of fashion followers —those whose careers depended on such momentous developments. Miss Campbell's precarious condition was as avidly monitored as Mother Teresa's. Why? Because a great deal of money was riding on it. Had Campbell conked it, with her would have died about a dozen brands. It wasn't concern over her state that prompted the attention, it was anxiety over the millions invested in her. Finally, it was all about money. And the mobile calculators (otherwise known as supermodels floating around, whether here in India or abroad), know it.

Eleven year-old Ruchika is like any other urban pre-

The making of a NATION

of the American fast-food chain, Kentucky Fried Chicken, hard and long. The objection is not to the menu but to the concomitant dangers of western eating habits to the lives of Karnataka's farmers. If the theme of the moment is Indian, then Miss World's parades and pouts have little place in Bangalore. Women's groups, activists, even the farmers, get into the anti-Miss World act. Immolations are threatened and carried out. A simple beauty contest becomes a matter of prestige — for both sides.

A bemused Daskins sees off his protesters against his pageant, but the dice seem to be loaded against him. If the protests were not bad enough, the Karnataka High Court restricts the state Government from providing him with too much assistance. Miss World may parade India to the world, but it has to be a private enterprise. A glamorous, if innocuous, event has now become full of patriotism, gender sensitivity, economic sense — or nonsense — and more. Unfortunately for the organisers, as media coverage increases, public interest seems to decrease. The swimsuit contest is held in Seychelles to appease the protesters, Karnataka superstar Rajkumar declines to lend his support.

November 23, 1996. The morning of the pageant dawns with rain, as if everything else were not bad enough. Later, though the weather may clear up, the evening is something of a washout. By the time Miss Greece takes the tiara, Miss World excitement is well and truly over.

Missed world, as it were.

∎

Ugly backlash: *Amitabh Bachchan faces the wrath of protestors in Bangalore as the beauty pageant charm fades in India by 1996*

Mukesh Parpiani

teen — enthusiastic, energetic and ambitious... Except that this 11-year-old has weekly appointments at a local parlour where her regular beautician waxes, threads, bleaches and steams the requisite areas of her body to young Ruchika's mother's satisfaction. "It's important for both my daughter and me to feel good about ourselves. I decided to start her off early because she wants to compete in beauty contests, model and maybe join films later. It's so competitive these days. If you haven't made it by 20, forget it." While this may sound over-the-top to those outside the circuit, I'd say it's a pretty realistic assessment.

And Ruchika's is not an isolated example. Countless young things across India are spending more time and money on grooming than on grades. They see it as a valid investment — one with attractive returns, whether or not the children decide to enter the glamour industry later. This is no longer an upper-middle class phenomenon. Walk through any slum colony and chances are there will be at least one beauty parlour offering a wide variety of services at cut-rate prices. In affluent residential areas, appearance-conscious maids don't have to resort to do-it-yourself beauty kits. Special salons catering to their specific needs are run by canny beauticians who streak, snip, soak and shampoo for a modest amount.

It isn't just women who are primping and preening these days. A visit to any swanky five-star parlour shows that the cabins and chairs are equally divided between the sexes. Make-up artists (an unknown breed 20 years ago) are booked round the year by as many men as women interested in major makeovers designed to bring out their best features. No shame in that. But when cosmetic gurus insist they get exasperated by looks-conscious bridegrooms who demand as much pancake on their faces as their brides', it's time to review the whole business of beauty and the enormous pressure exerted on consumers to conform to any given season's well-defined "look".

For a lot of under-20s, Sushmita and Aishwarya represent sex-appeal and success at their snazziest. Their titles are more than mere symbols of beauty. Rather, they are an affirmation of what is achievable with a bit of help from god, the gene pool and glitter dust. No longer do little girls lisp, "I want to be a nurse when I grow up." The goals have changed dramatically. So have middle class aspirations. It's nothing less than a very determined, "I want to be Miss Universe." Cosmetic firms, particularly the overseas giants, haven't wasted too much time exploiting the current, beauty-worshipping mood. Newer and pricier products show up on crowded shelves at the rate of seven a week and there's obviously no dearth of buyers. Working women dedicate a generous slice of their earnings to beautifying themselves without suffering guilt pangs as a previous generation might have. If the choice was miserably limited a decade ago, today is bewildering. Market analysts are keenly monitoring the money-spending pattern of middle income housewives who don't think twice before putting down Rs 200 on a cream that convinces them it has a secret anti-ageing ingredient blended into it.

The beauty cult has its band of faithful followers all over India. What was once an urban phenomenon has managed to penetrate into smaller towns with satellite television beaming seductive images of Khoobsoorti all day. Once upon a time there used to be a solitary cake of soap endorsed by leading film stars claiming it to be their secret of beauty. Everybody believed them. They are still peddling the same soap but the credibility gap has widened. The definition of what constitutes beauty itself has changed to the point it's no longer possible to categorise it. Yesterday's generation would've dismissed Sushmita for being too tall, too gangly, too thin, too dusky. And yet she walked away with the coveted crown at a fiercely competitive international contest. Self-help books, CD's, videos, live demos, workshops, full-fledged courses — you name it, you've got it. Ads galore announce the arrival of latest miracle-products which, if nothing else, do a lot for flagging morale while disingenuously promising to thin those flabby thighs.

Twenty-something smoke, starve, skip and sweat to gain entry into the hallowed Anorexics Anonymous club. Role models may vary, but a random campus survey is likely to throw up the names of top mannequins and TV anchors. History is just that, history. Of no relevance or interest to people who determinedly live in the "now". And perhaps for the first time since the advent of the talkies movie stars have taken a back seat to supermodels.

Since consumerism is no longer a dirty word in the new India, it is hardly surprising that the beauty business too is boom-boom-booming. People want to look good. And they're willing to pay for the privilege. Pay big. It's debatable whether the Sush-Ash titles have performed a service or otherwise in a nation that had hitherto placed the pursuit of beauty at the bottom of its priorities. What cannot be denied is the fact that more and more teenagers are willing to shell out more and more lolly to look more and more like these two winners. Which only goes to show that beauty no longer lies in the eyes of the beholder. It has been relocated in the consumer's deep pocket. At what price beauty did you ask? The sky is the upper limit but a few down-to-earth lakhs wisely invested on cosmetic enhancements may not be a bad way to begin, given that the quickest route to easy money and fame is a short catwalk away. Who's complaining? India needs a nice face.

Total makeover: *The beauty boom*   Dinodia Picture Agency

PARADISE REGAINED?

1995

After years of living under the shadow of the gun,
the Kashmir Valley makes a valiant attempt for peace

Caught in the crossfire: *The town of Charar-e-Shareef becomes a battleground for the army and militants*   Prashant Penjiar/India Today

**"When a voter loses faith in the ballot, the next step is the
bullet. People at the helm of affairs should learn from history."**

— Abdul Qayoom, Janata Dal politician from Charar-e-Shareef

IT is not easy, though, to maintain the right balance between the ballot and the bullet. In fact, once the bullet establishes itself, getting back to the ballot can be an impossible dream, a thankless effort. The long and hard journey back to democracy — when it is undertaken at all — is made worse by local disillusionment compounded by official negligence and short-sightedness. For too long has Kashmir suffered both.

December 1994. The town of Charar-e-Shareef in Kashmir's Badgam district is known for the shrine of the Sufi Noor-ud-din Noorani, Kashmir's most revered saint. It is visited by the faithful from all over. Including by Mast Gul, leader of the Harkut-Al-Ansar. Mast Gul, however, is no ordinary pilgrim. Pro-Pakistani and decidedly militant, Gul's visit to Charar-e-Shareef

bears marked resemblance to a similar stopover made by a self-styled Sikh saviour to the Golden Temple in Amritsar more than 10 years ago. Then, the government acted with precipitate haste, leading to disastrous consequences.

March 5, 1995. The Government, as it did in Hazratbal in 1993, has been trying to ignore Mast Gul's presence in Charar-e-Shareef. In an act of apparently calculated provocation, two Border Security Force men are killed near the shrine. Immediately, the army is sent in.

March 11. Most residents of the town leave, for fear of the impending clash between the Indian Army and militants. No amount of protests from the authorities that they do not intend to take the shrine by storm to flush out the militants is consolation. Indeed, it is not believed. Nor do the militants take up the government's offer of safe passage to Pakistan.

March 13. The Valley of Kashmir observes a bandh to protest against the proliferation of army checkposts.

Terror from Pakistan: *Mast Gul eludes the Indian authorities*   PTI/IT

March 21. The media is prevented from entering the town.

April 5. The All Party Hurriyat Conference starts on a march to Charar-e-Shareef, but is stopped. Students in Srinagar, 35 km away, demand a lifting of the army siege on the town.

May 8. A huge fire engulfs the town. Most of the 15,000 houses are gutted. With few witnesses and local inhabitants left, the army and militants trade charges.

May 10. Almost the entire town is burnt. Except the shrine.

May 11. The destruction is complete. The shrine is gone. Mast Gul escapes and is given a hero's welcome in Pakistan. The people of Kashmir look at the Indian Army with horror, dismay, rage. Was this destruction necessary? "There are hundreds of so-called foreign mercenaries under the noses of security forces. Did they have to destroy an entire town and our holy shrine to catch a few militants?" asks Yasin Malik of the Jammu and Kashmir Liberation Front.

Of the 30 people dead in the fire, only 10 are supposed to be militants. The most important of all got away. Few Kashmiris are willing to accept the government position. Was it really Pakistan who ordered that the shrine be set on fire? The Army was present, and the Army is not popular.

In fact, since 1988, after the dismissal of the Farooq Abdullah government in 1987, India has not been very popular in Kashmir. Militancy has taken over perhaps because all else seemed to have failed. The see-saw game between Delhi and Srinagar, started between Sheikh Abdullah and Jawaharlal Nehru 40 years before, is continued by their successors. The role of Pakistan becomes more strident. The welfare of the people remains neglected. If the 1987 elections were said to have been rigged by the National Conference, then perhaps the time was ripe for the ballot to be replaced by the bullet: incidences of terrorist violence went up from 390 in 1988 to 2154 in 1989. The kidnapping of Rubaiya Sayeed, daughter of then Home Minister Mufti Mohammed Sayeed in 1989 is followed by a series of attacks on banks and security officers. The Jammu and Kashmir police go on strike, so do the state's IAS officers. Lassa Kaul, station director of Doordarshan in Srinagar is killed. K Doraiswamy, an executive of the Indian Oil Corporation is kidnapped. Meanwhile, there are reports of army excesses, there are militants caught and militants who escape, there are bomb attacks on police stations. Kashmir itself seems to be in a state of siege. Each negotiation with militants is marked by official dithering and insecurity, each subsequent event leads to more ammunition for the terrorists' gun. Governments come and go in Delhi. Each change brings more anxiety because each change is accompanied by a political will to undo what the last administration has done. If the controversial Governor Jagmohan is removed, those who come after him hardly cover themselves with glory. Kashmir has been called a paradise on Earth. It is not much in evidence now.

Mast Gul, however, did not have to take his inspiration only from Sant Bhindranwale. He could even have looked closer to home and the siege of Hazratbal. In 1993, militants take position in the Hazratbal shrine, no stranger to the vagaries of Kashmiri politics. The government turns its customary blind eye. It then plays the game that has typified its stand — an initial hard-line topped by total capitulation. It is this attitude more than anything that has lost the Indian Government its respect, from people and militants both. After long negotiations, firings, strikes and processions, the militants surrender. In six months, the Hazratbal incident has been turned into a crisis. The ground for Charar-e-Shareef had been well-laid.

But even with the Hazratbal siege, Kashmir is realising that life has no meaning under the shadow of the gun. Militants

The making of
a NATION

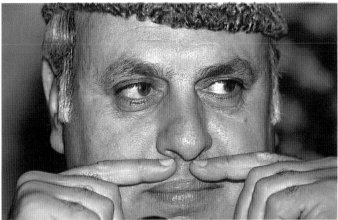

Democratic solution: *Farooq Abdullah, Chief Minister*   Mukesh Parpiani

Losing all hope: *A Kashmiri outside his blasted home*   Meraj-ud-din/India Today

are losing their idealistic edge, and the people are becoming tired of living in fear. They have lost their livelihood to prolonged militancy, now they are losing hope. The government cannot take responsibility here — in most cases, it has only enhanced the despondency. Charar-e-Shareef brings Kashmir to the cross-roads. A protest march called to the shrine two weeks after the fire musters barely 3,000 people.

The Centre, eager to take advantage, calls for elections. There is widespread disbelief. The electoral process has failed Kashmir too many times before. The militants, especially those with allegiances in Pakistan, certainly do not want an election. Stepping out of the shadows, biding his time, is Farooq Abdullah. His National Conference may have lost some of its lustre, but it is still the party that most of Kashmir trusts. "How do you tell the world we are a democracy? Not by Governor's rule, but by people's rule," he declares.

The people do not seem to be ready in 1995, though. But beginnings have been made. The militants bring no small disrepute to themselves by a spate of kidnapping of foreign tourists. While kidnappings are not new to Kashmir, the savage beheading of the Norwegian Hans Christian Ostro, his body found on August 12, 1995, shocks the ordinary man. Militancy or not, what is left of the tourist trade is important to Kashmir's thin economic lifeline. Ostro's body has Al-Faran carved on its

chest. Negotiations start with this new group, which has taken four other foreigners. The international community, long critical of India's atrocities and human rights abuses on militants, sees Kashmir terrorism and the role of Pakistan in a slightly different light now. The tourists, however, are not found, despite long negotiations.

1996. When the whole country goes to the polls, so does Kashmir. There are allegations that the security forces coerced people into voting. But amidst the suspicion is the undoubted fact that Kashmir now has an elected government. Farooq Abdullah starts on a promise to scrub militancy out of the Valley. Well begun is half done?   ∎

Violence in Kashmir, 1990 to 1996	
Explosions	6,551
Rocket attacks	547
Crossfire cases	9,570
Crossfire deaths	2,308
Abductions	2,466
Civilians killed by militants	5,035
Civilians injured by militants	6,854
Security men killed	2,236
Security men injured	4,326
Militants killed	7,371
Militants surrendered	2,217

Source: India Today

WHAT WENT WRONG
Solving the Kashmir problem
By Ved Marwah

THE last eight years of terrorism in the state of Jammu and Kashmir have only brought misery to the people of the state. They have been the years of unmitigated disaster. The people in the Valley have suffered much more than in the other parts of the state. There is hardly a family left in the Valley which has not suffered serious loss. Many have lost their near and dear ones. Everyone has been hit economically. With industry and tourism in total disarray, incomes have shrunk; but the cost of living has been constantly going up, thanks to the frequent bandhs and civil curfews imposed by the militants.

Students have been badly hit. They have lost precious years because of frequent closure of schools and colleges for days, sometimes weeks at a stretch. Women had to bear the burden of the reforming zeal of the fundamentalists. Their social reform programme has meant more restrictions on women's education and employment. They had to wear burqa and were strictly prohibited from making friends with the opposite sex. A few of the young girls accused of having love affairs were brutally killed, one by exploding like a live human bomb, to understand the horrible consequences of disobeying their commands. Life for most people had become a drudgery, as all places of entertainment like cinemas and restaurants etc, were closed under the militants' orders.

Who has gained? Really, no one! Not even the militants and their sponsors, Pakistan. The average life of a militant is very short, and they have suffered heavy casualties. Pakistan is no longer a loved country. The government in New Delhi may not be their favourite, but the Pakistani government is hated more today than at any time since Independence. All these years, political life had been brought to a standstill by the terrorist violence. Political leaders of all mainstream political parties have been special targets of the terrorists. Veteran leaders, some of whom were in their late 60s and 70s, were brutally killed.

But the Kashmiri Pundits have been the worst sufferers. Over 150,000 of them were forced to flee from their homes in the Valley and migrate to Jammu and other parts in India. They have become refugees in their own country. No one leaves his hearth and home unless he becomes absolutely desperate. All these allegations of Jagmohan hatching a conspiracy for the migration of the Kashmiri Pundits during his second tenure as the governor of J&K are without any substance. It is only when the Kashmiri Pundits were being systematically targeted for assassination by the militants in the end of 1989 and the beginning of 1990 that they started leaving the Valley. In any case, if there was any truth in the allegations, they would have come back after Jagmohan's departure from the state in May 1990. Jagmohan's second tenure as the governor lasted a little over four months.

Kidnapped!: *Hostages held by Kashmir militants*   Meraj-ud-din/India Today

How is that even after the restoration of Farooq Abdullah's government in 1996, the pundits have still not returned to their homes in the Valley. The answer is obvious. It is because they still suffer from a sense of insecurity. Not many will come back till the security environment considerably improves in the Valley. And that is going to take some time, notwithstanding the serious efforts made by the successive governments in J&K.

How did the security environment deteriorate so rapidly in the Valley, even though the Kashmiri people are known to be very peace-loving people? One of the major factor responsible for the rapid growth of terrorist violence in the state was the systematic demoralisation of the state police. Till the middle of 1989, the J&K Police was in the forefront of the battle against terrorism. It had some major successes to its credit. But towards the end of 1989, it was becoming increasingly obvious to the police that neither the state nor the Central Government was going to support them in this thankless task. Why then should they risk their lives, is the question they asked themselves. The assassination of the station house officer of Massuma Police station, not very far from the seat of the state government, and complete indifference on the part of the administration to respond effectively, turned out to be a watershed in this tragic decline of the state police. After this incident, the state police soon becomes nonfunctional, and the role of fighting terrorism had to be entrusted to the para-military forces and the army.

Intelligence is the key to control terrorism, and that input can only be provided effectively by the local police. In the absence of local knowledge, not only about the identity of the terrorists and their plans, but also about the local customs and politics, the armed forces have got sucked into this quagmire more as foes than friends of the people. Terrorism cannot be successfully tackled without active support of the people. The allegations of excesses and illegal acts have made their task more difficult. The police and the armed forces cannot be treated as above the rule of law. The Farooq Abdullah government will have to remedy this, otherwise the situation will continue to drift and the state will be in for a long period of uncertainty and violence.

LEFT NOT RIGHT AT CENTRE

1996

Jyoti Basu does not make it as prime minister. But the Left's unmatchable record in West Bengal makes it an essential part of any political configuration in Delhi

ACCORDING to Jyoti Basu, it was a historic blunder. Rather than allow him to become Prime Minister of a United Front government at the Centre, the Communist Party of India (Marxist) decides that it will support the government from the outside. The 1996 general elections have left no party the clear winner. If the Congress has been practically trounced, and the Bharatiya Janata Party too far away from the winning post to make it, then who's left? A motley group of parties, of which Jyoti Basu and the Left are one.

But who is Jyoti Basu anyway? From a national perspective, he is one of India's oldest statesmen, matched in age and experience and wisdom perhaps only by Biju Patnaik of Orissa. He belongs to the old mould of the Jawaharlal Nehru and Sardar Patel type of politician, who looked at ideology and principles before political skullduggery. He has also been, for almost 20 years, Chief Minister of West Bengal,

a feat unparalleled so far in Indian history. And he looks set to take the Left Front in Bengal flying past its fifth assembly election in 1997.

The year is 1977. The Emergency has just been lifted and the country is looking forward to freedom from repression. But if the oppressive atmosphere has been difficult in the rest of India, it has been close to intolerable in West Bengal. The Congress Government, headed by Siddhartha Shankar Ray, has been putting its detractors through a regime of terror and violence. The Naxalite Movement has been crushed with ruthless brutality. The elections of 1972 were said to have been openly rigged in the Congress's favour; the voice of the people to have been kept firmly out. But the Emergency has weakened the Congress and strengthened the Opposition. The mistakes of the past will not be repeated in 1977.

Rigging and violence notwithstanding, the Left Front,

Building bridges: *(left to right) Sheikh Hasina of Bangladesh, H D Deve Gowda, Jyoti Basu and I K Gujral sign a water-sharing agreement*   Frontline

Leading from the front: *Jyoti Basu's early days as Chief Minister*   The Statesman

headed by the Communist Party of India (Marxist) routs the Congress and its ally, the Communist Party of India, and sweeps the polls. If it is said that a new dawn has broken in West Bengal, the time for sunset is not yet foreseen. This is not, however, the CPM's first foray into power. Exactly 10 years before, a United Front government, with Ajoy Mukherjee as chief minister and Jyoti Basu as deputy chief minister. But 1967 is also the year that the Naxalite Movement breaks out, and the government cannot stand strong in the wake of that fury.

But in that defeat lie the secrets of today's strengths. The strong-arm tactics of the Congress at that time have cost it dearly now. The Naxalites — offshoots from the CPM — were fighting for land reforms. That need still remains. Thirty years of Independence has left India's peasantry much as it was when it started — only, the rich have got richer, the gaps have widened.

Chief Minister Jyoti Basu heads a coalition government of committed Marxists and Leftists. The Communist states of China and the USSR are still strong, and the call of Mao's

Back in power again... and again: *Basu demonstrates his oratory at the Maidan*   The Statesman

peasant revolution still echoes in Bengal's comrades' years. So too does the proletariat outbursts of Russia's industrial workers. Basu himself has strong trade union roots. Despite his middle class upbringing, encounters with Rajani Palme Dutt in London in the late '30s found him entranced by communism. Together with Feroze Gandhi, Mulk Raj Anand, Mohan Dharia, Rajni Patel. From then on, a political career as a communist was perhaps only to be expected.

So the Left Front government turns its back on the pundits in urban Calcutta and builds its base in the countryside. Disciplined cadres, well-entrenched in the grass-roots, full of the arrogant triumph of victory, take West Bengal into a seeming downspin. Trade union movements grow strong and loud and belligerent; industry flees. The government focuses on panchayat systems, on land reforms for equitable distribution, on food for work programmes; power generation suffers. Calcutta, to the outsider, is a city filled with Mother Teresa's dying and destitute, it is a dying city, if there is joy it is only by tremendous figurative sleights of speech.

But election after election, the Left Front is returned to power. Much as the intelligentsia in Calcutta, indeed the rest of the country, looks on with horror and amazement, West Bengal marches to its chosen drummer. The death of Pramode Dasgupta, general secretary of the CPM, in 1982 leaves Basu as the party's most senior leader. Now, in the administration and the party, he is the last word. Long years in power take their toll and charges of corruption, of inefficiency, even of rigging start becoming louder. But the endurance of Basu and the Left Front is such that mere carping cannot curb it. Besides, outside the winds of change are blowing and West Bengal cannot be unaffected. The introduction of glasnost and perestroika by Mikhail Gorbachev in Russia, China's Deng Zhao Ping's leanings towards foreign investment, are looked at askance by die-hard Communists in India, still found in large numbers in West Bengal and Kerala. Were revolutions fought and lives lost so that power could be taken away from the people and the party and handed over to outsiders and foreigners?

Yet, in the confusion, Basu sees the sense. Having established the foundation of the Left Front through the state's villages, he now turns his attention to trade and industry. Trade unions are told, strictly, brooking no argument, that unceasing confrontation with management leads only to disaster. The chief minister now actively woos foreign investment, outside investment in West Bengal. Even as P V Narasimha Rao and Dr Manmohan Singh embark on their journey towards liberalisation, Basu is a step ahead.

There are many who will claim, perhaps with some justification, that Basu's brand of communism is not communism at all. That he has jettisoned principles for practicality. The word Basu himself might prefer is pragmatic. And, after close to 20 years in power, the Left Front in Bengal is still one of the country's least corrupt administrations. Somewhere, ideology has stuck fast. The goal is apparently still a classless society, but the means of getting there have changed somewhat. Rather than bring

Economic resurgence: *new industry in West Bengal*   The Statesman

everyone down to the level of the lowest common denominator, the effort must be to lift the lowest standard. Brave ideals, but backed up by hard work, there may even be a measure of success somewhere.

The Opposition Congress struggles to get some foothold, but as the situation in Calcutta improves, the infighting becomes worse. Industry slowly trickles back into Bengal. Big names like Goenka and Tata, who once practically scrabbled to get out, now come back. Hurt by rising uncertainty in other parts of the country, investors look at West Bengal with new eyes.

Communist-run West Bengal offers the country one more advantage. As communal and sectarian fever runs high all over India, only a few pockets remain calm. The demolition of the Babri Masjid in Ayodhya on December 6, 1992 sets a nation on fire. If any part of Calcutta burns, it is swiftly squashed. "I will not let Calcutta become another Bombay," says the chief minister with his firm, bhadralok manner. And he keeps his word.

If nothing else, Basu's longevity catapults him to centre-stage. Every time the Congress loses power at the Centre, Basu's advice is sought. The 1990s bring regional parties to the forefront of national politics, and clearly, he is the most senior statesman among them. His failure to make it to the country's top post is then, perhaps, countered by the advantages it brings to his home state. The Centre's loss is still Bengal's gain?   ■

STAYING WITH COMMUNISM
Why the Left ideology continues to appeal in Bengal
By Dr Ashok Mitra

NOTIONS are often the offspring of prejudices. It is taken for granted, by many, that a Communist Party is incapable of mustering majority support from free people: are not Communists vermin, how could decent human beings choose them as rulers? The prejudice dies hard, which is why there are so many 'oohs' and 'aahs' at the spectacle of a Communist-led government being continuously in power in the state of West Bengal. West Bengal may appear to be a unique illustration of communists coming to power via free elections; in case it is so, it is on account of determined resistance on the part of so-called believers in freedom entrenched in the Western countries, not to permit communist parties to participate in government in 'open' societies.

The North Atlantic Treaty Organisation alliance conspired to prevent the Italian Communist Party from winning the 1948 elections in that country. It is only last year that the conspiracy against the Communists collapsed and Communists entered the administration in Italy. The Communist Party was again the leading political entity in France for at least a quarter of a century, following the Second World War; it was not once given the first chance to form the government. Even in post-1991 Russia, despite all the tall talk about freedom being restored to the Russian people, consequent to the collapse of the Soviet Union, the experience the citizens have gone through over the past six years of free-wheeling capitalism has ensured the return of their loyalty to the Communist Party, which has emerged as the nation's premier political party. It is a different matter that it will nonetheless be kept out of power by the votaries of free democracy.

There need, therefore, be no particular surprise if the Left Front regime led by the Communist Party of India (Marxist) continues to win democratic elections one after another for another 20 years or thereabouts. It is not simply that the Communists have the best-knit organisation among all the parties operating in the state, taking pride in the capital stock of thousands of dedicated workers in town and country. In the rural areas, its position appears to be nearly unassailable, given the remarkable things that have been accomplished through the three-tier panchayat systems, the devolution of 50 per cent of developmental funds to the panchayats, the strong symbiotic link established between the peasant movement and the panchayat functionaries and the secular effects of the rapid spread of elementary education in the course of the past two decades.

Forget every other little or big accomplishment, the toiling sections in the state will remain steadfast in their loyalty to the Left Front not merely because it has provided them a solid material base for at least a modestly better living standard. What is vastly more significant, it has endowed them with the awareness of the dignity of living, which was missing in the state in the past, and which continues to be missing in the relationship between the rulers and the ruled in the rest of the country.

The Left Front's successes in the urban sphere have been much more restricted. It has been grappling with the massive problems created by the de-industrialisation that ensued in the 1950s and continued over the next quarter of a century. There was the added burden of the influx of 7 to 8 million refugees from what was then East Pakistan. It has been a tough situation, even as industry after industry closed down and thousands were thrown out of employment, central investment almost dried up. Liberalisation has rendered things much worse.

The kind of industrial revival the present government is hankering after calls for massive public investments which are clearly beyond the capability of a state administration. Much of the urban distress in the state is the outcome of perverse policies pursued by New Delhi and the persistent reluctance on the part of public financial institutions and banks to allocate resources proportionate to the state's population. Now, of course, the uncertainties which liberalisation has contributed to the nation's industrial picture has aggravated the problems West Bengal has been facing. It is a tribute to the skill and imagination with which the Left Front government has been tackling these issues that, despite all the difficulties, West Bengal remains a haven of tranquility in the midst of the social chaos that has descended upon the rest of the country, or at least large chunks of it.

There is this final desideratum then which will fortify the prospects of the Left Front in the state. When things are falling apart in the rest of the country, only West Bengal promises stability. It is altogether possible that a wobbly political regime at the Centre will seek support from the Left Front government. Already there is a general impression, which is not without basis, that without the sobering influence of the Communists, the so-called United Front in the nation's capital would have come apart many months ago. The Left Front will survive and attain new pinnacles of glory if it stays true to its commitments to the people.

The making *of* a NATION

SCAM AFTER SCAM AFTER...

1996

The Congress loses the Centre. Nobody wins. And political skeletons keep tumbling out of cupboards. What a year!

JULY 9, 1996. P V Narasimha Rao is issued a summons to appear before the court of New Delhi Chief Metropolitan Magistrate. Rao is no ordinary Indian citizen. Till three months ago he was Prime Minister of India. He is still President of the Congress, the country's oldest party, the one that fought and won Independence. Rao, who was not even expected to last a couple of years when he assumed leadership of the country in 1991, completed a full term. He headed some of the most momentous changes and shattering events that the country would experience. He was called a Machiavelli, a Chanakya, India's best prime minister, India's worst.

Today he is called the man who brought the worst shame upon the high office he once held. Rao is the first Indian prime

Corruption is rarely far away from public life. But never has the underbelly so taken over the whole body, never has Indian polity so resembled a carcass. In 1947, V K Krishna Menon, then high commissioner in Britain, was slightly touched by the Jeep scandal. In 1957, Finance Minister T T Krishnamachari had to resign over the Mundhra case, where the Life Insurance Corporation lent Haridas Mundhra Rs one crore and then bought shares in his company to boost prices. In 1964, the Chief Minister of Punjab, Pratap Singh Kairon resigned after the Dass Commission indicted him of allowing his family to his position to acquire wealth. But from a scandal every 10 years, from 1987, it seems that India has a scandal every year. By 1996, there are revelations almost every month.

Rao's rows: *The former prime minister in the dock*

Mid-day

minister, former or present, to be summoned in a criminal case. He has been accused of taking a bribe from Lakhubhai Pathak, a pickle maker and then not coming through with the required licences. Rao, indeed, has fallen prey to the one malady of Indian public life that seems to have exploded in 1996: corruption. Never before in Independent India's history have so many politicians been accused of so many cases of corruption, bribery, financial impropriety and illegality. Most of the accused are Congressmen, most of the cases seem to involve Rao. There are many who cheer at his downfall, but they are all tainted by the same curse.

After the alienation of Muslims over the government inaction during the Babri Masjid demolition and the disparate gains of liberalisation come a barrage of cases against politicians. Skeletons locked tightly into cupboards for years come bursting out. It is hardly surprising that Rao and the Congress have lost the general elections of May. Nor is it surprising that no party has managed a clear majority in Parliament, required to form a government. Who is the Indian voter to trust?

For Rao himself, there are indictments in a shady foreign exchange transaction case, involving the Jain brothers in 1995, an alleged involvement in the St Kitts forgery affair, a shameful case invented by Rajiv Gandhi's acolytes years earlier to discredit V P Singh after the Bofors probe in 1989, an accusation of bribing MPs of the Jharkhand Mukti Morcha to vote with the Congress during a no-trust vote in June 1993.

The irony for many is that it is during Rao's tenure that P Chidambaram is made to resign as commerce minister for having some connection with the Harshad Mehta-fired stock market scandal in 1992. That Kalpnath Rai is made to resign as food supplies minister over the sugar scam in 1994. That Madhavrao Scindia and Arjun Singh are expelled from the party over their involvement in the hawala scam. Now Rao himself is in the dock.

The reason for this explosion of scandals is a sudden desire to return probity to polity. The Indian judiciary, unfortunately used by the executive in the past, wakes up to the importance of addressing the disgust of the common man with corrupt leaders. The Supreme Court sets the pace and the others follow. The new phrase is judicial activism. Public interest litigations bring corruption to the fore, the courts direct the Central Bureau of Investigation to do its job without fear or favour. The Very Important Person status of the Indian politician is being shaken to the core. As every big name is called out in disgrace, more people cheer. Even the apparently less corrupt members of the Bharatiya Janata Party like L K Advani are caught in the net. So is the Janata Dal's Laloo Prasad Yadav, chief minister of Bihar. No one is too great or too important to be caught. And so, says the voice of the people, it should be.

So it has been proved in the general elections of May 1996. The message of the electorate has been negative and the result is a hung Parliament. The Congress, in spite of completing a full term in office, loses ignominiously with 136 seats. Realising that the vote has gone against it, the wily Rao does not make a bid to form a government. But the Bharatiya Janata Party, which has done marginally better with 161 seats, stakes its claim. The president gives the party two weeks to prove

Bittersweet: *L K Advani and A B Vajpayee's temporary glee*   Sharad Saxena /India Today

its majority on the floor of the House.

May 16, 1996. Atal Behari Vajpayee is sworn in as India's 11th Prime Minister. His government lasts all of 13 days.

May 31, the BJP is unable to get the required 269 seats in the Lok Sabha. The country is back to being headless.

But champing at the bit, waiting for its turn, is a collection of diverse political parties united in strange ways. They are all anti-BJP and very strongly secularist. Most of them have very solid regional bases. The biggest party is the Janata Dal, descendant of the first Janata Party from which the BJP was also born. The Left Front is the next most powerful member. The United Front is made up of 13 parties, many in power in India's states. Apart they are powerless, together they have dreams of power. The Congress, anxious to see the BJP fail at the Centre, is willing to help. H D Deve Gowda, Chief Minister of Karnataka, is the consensus candidate for Prime Minister. Even before Vajpayee's vote of confidence, the Front has picked Gowda on May 24. It is now only a matter of time.

Gowda is an unknown quantity when he becomes Prime Minister. His best credentials are symptomatic of the strange exigencies that dictate Indian politics: he comes from a low caste, is a South Indian and appears to be the most suitable and least objectionable after Jyoti Basu of Bengal, former Prime Minister V P Singh and G K Moopanar have turned down the honour.

But Gowda's lack of experience and lack of national stature make him all the more vulnerable. Shrewd and canny, he must not only keep his shaky coalition firm and stable, he must also ensure that he contains the threat from within. Soon, Gowda's greatest preoccupation appears to be keeping potential rivals at bay. The ideal weapon for this seems to be the CBI and the unending

The making *of* a NATION

Futile bid: *Sharad Pawar*   Hemant Pithwa/India Today

exposure of scams and keeping the Congress happy.

The Lakhubhai Pathak case puts paid to any ambitions Rao may have had of remaining at the centrestage of Indian politics. Within the Congress, there are moves to remove him from power. Sharad Pawar, former defence minister and chief minister of Maharashtra, is ready to take his chances for Congress President. So is the younger and more rebellious Rajesh Pilot. And, more ominously, for them, is the Old Guard. Rao had not only turned the economy away from Nehruvian socialism, he has also turned the party away from Nehru's descendants. More exactly, the widow of Rajiv Gandhi, Sonia. Trapped by its own corrupt past and desperate for a charismatic name to bring some glory back to the party, sidelined Congressmen work to despatch Rao to pasture. Amidst all the challengers, it is Sitaram Kesri, Gandhi loyalist, who wins. The Congress is now anti-liberalisation, pro-socialism and most important, anti-Deve Gowda.

The scams, meanwhile, do not stop. Former tele-communications minister Sukh Ram's house is raided in connection with suspect orders in 1993 lead to the discovery of inordinately large sums of money. The courts indict Sheila Kaul, former housing minister, for out-of-turn allotments and ask for personal compensation to be paid. Former petroleum minister Satish Sharma is indicted for out-of-turn petrol pump alignments. Past misdemeanours have awful present consequences.

Deve Gowda's government is also threatened by a scandal from the past. The Bofors deal led to the fall of a government in 1989. It comes back now, almost 10 years since it first surfaced, with more ammunition than ever before. And straight in its line of fire is the name of the one man that the Congress now wants to use to get back some glitter. Rajiv Gandhi may be dead, but his home still wields some power. Who in the Congress would now risk the disgrace of Rajiv Gandhi, when it is a party bereft of honour, ideology and a strong presence with the voter?

India ends the year in a state of confusion. These shenanigans in Delhi only serve to accentuate public disgust. Now, more than ever, the courts are looked upon as the only means to a cleaner government. The stage is set for 1997. ∎

Party Positions in the 1996 Lok Sabha

United Front		186	Samata Party	5
Janata Dal	44		Akali Dal	8
CPM	32		Congress	140
CPI	13		Others	26
RSP	5		BSP	11
Forward Bloc	3		SJP	2
TDP	17		MIM	1
DMK	17		JMM	1
TMC	20		Muslim League	2
SP	17		Kerala Congress (M)	1
AGP	5			
Cong (T)	1		Independents and	
BKKP	1		unattached members	
Independents and others	9		(including the speaker)	4
BJP and allies		193	Nominated	2
BJP	162		Vacancies	2
Shiv Sena	15		**Total**	**545**
HVP	3			

(figures as on March 3, 1997)

WHITHER CONGRESS?
A story of steady decline
By Janardan Thakur

IF a 112-year-old organisation has become a tottering monument, and looks more grotesque with every coat of paint that it applies to itself, it should not be much of a surprise. This may well have been one of the reasons why the Mahatma wanted the party to disband itself when the country gained her freedom. Had Gandhi's followers taken his advice, the new party that Jawaharlal Nehru, Sardar Patel, Rajendra Prasad and others had then floated would now have been just so, in the prime of life. But then Gandhi was always a bit of a utopian and though his acolytes touched his feet, parroted his words, shed tears when he fasted, they did very much what they wished to do. They were the pragmatists, who wanted immediate returns for their long struggle: power. Never mind if it ripped the country apart or left trails of blood and tears all over.

Nobody knew better than that astute leader in loincloth the stuff his followers were made of. Gandhi must have known how soon the rot would set in, and in pain he cut himself adrift in the very hour of his triumph. He preferred to trudge the blood-stained lanes and bylanes of Calcutta while his men rejoiced. Gandhi's own "tryst with destiny" was so very poignant he even talked of settling down in Pakistan!

But the pragmatists of the Congress had little time to ponder. Their agenda was very different. They had to take over the reins of power, they had to prove Churchill wrong. Nothing wrong with that, for after all the vacuum had to be filled up and the band of people in the Congress would have been very much the same, even under a different nomenclature. Except that Gandhi did not want the name of the party that had gained freedom to be soiled and besmirched in the muck of power, as he was certain it would be sooner or later.

It all stemmed, perhaps, from the deep-seated dichotomy of the new rulers of India, whose public faces and private faces began going different ways a bit too soon. It took some years for the decay to show because of the comparative purity and idealism of the upper crust of leaders who had been strongly imbued in the Gandhian spirit.

Even the best and the brightest of the lot had their Achilles' heels. Writing under a pseudonym years before freedom, the great democrat Jawaharlal Nehru had confessed how close his inclinations were to becoming a dictator. In a way he couldn't help that trait showing up: consider the way he got Purushottam Das Tandon hounded out of the party. How close and "brotherly" Nehru was to Jayaprakash Narayan, and yet in his own way he ensured that JP did not become his successor. Many Nehruvians would consider it a blasphemy, but there is much evidence to show that he often went out of his way to groom his daughter for the succession, and if his soul blessed the anointing of his 'little sepoy' Lal Bahadur, it must have been

Keeper of the faith?: *Sitaram Kesri with Sonia Gandhi*

Sharad Saxena /India Today

so only because it was to be such a brief interregnum.

Nehru was a man of great charm, and a great visionary and thinker, a leader untouched by personal greed. Pettiness he hated, and corruption he hated even more, to the point that he often talked of hanging the corrupt by the nearest lamp-posts, and yet his court became the breeding ground for the corrupt and the petty. When his own son-in-law raised his sword against corruption, Nehru got impatient and said too much talk about corruption only vitiates the atmosphere!

Within years of coming to power, Congressmen were getting caught between two stools, lost and confused between two idioms. On the one hand they swore by the Gandhian idiom, on the other they were eager to get on in life and were getting embroiled in machine politics, and all that goes with brazen quest for power The 'Syndicate' and the Tammany Hail bosses had begun to tighten their grips over the Congress within years of Indepedence. For long they did not have the guts to stand up to Nehru, but by the late '50s they had started raising their heads. In his later years, Nehru was a mere shadow of himself, as pained and concerned about the toboggan slide all around him as about the slowing down of his own body. There was little he could do to stem the decay that had overtaken the Congress and the government. One of his constant refrains, according to some who were close to him, had become: "What will happen to Indu (Indira Gandhi)."

"Indu" was to do much better for herself than her father could ever have imagined. Starting as a *"goongi gudiya"* (dumb doll), she slashed down all the veterans one by one until she became the "only man" in the Congress. A great player of the political game, she manoeuvred and manipulated everything to her advantage, till she had the hubris to declare that while her

father was "only a statesman", she herself was a "much better politician." As a lonely little girl in the feudal Nehru household at Allahabad, she had been used to 'making monkeys' of the big band of retainers. That was her Vanar Sena. In later years she was to do the same not only with members of her own captive party, but with all the institutions within her purview. She achieved great personal heights, became the unquestioned Boss of the party and the government, the "Empress of India", but she failed to see that Indira Gandhi could never become India.

She was falling even as she rose. Her stunning defeat in 1977 was more than just the result of the Emergency; it was the fall of a great party gone to seed. An unputdownable fighter, Indira Gandhi rose from the ashes, but by then she had become a goongi gudiya in the hands of her overbearing son, Sanjay, who would surely have elbowed her aside and taken over the Congress, but for his sudden end. After Sanjay, Indira Gandhi's "only hope" was Rajiv, and so hell bent was she on foisting him on the party — and the government — that all other considerations became secondary. By then the old and tottering party had become putty in the hands of the Gandhis, transformed into a shouting brigade of personal standard-bearers, a large body of spineless men and women, mistakenly called leaders, whose only compensation for crawling at court was an office or an opportunity to fill up their coffers on the side, for which there was evergrowing scope all around.

The Congress story is the story of a great decline. The decline goes on. Instead of the great titans of yesteryears the party now has only the puny pygmies struggling to rise again — on the shoulders of a widow with a Gandhi title. It's like trying to go up a greasy pole.

ORDER, ORDER
Or why judicial activism needs to be supported in spite of the criticism
By A H Ahmadi

SINCE the last couple of years, there has been a raging debate about the role of the country's judiciary as one of the organs of the country's democratic set-up, particularly in regard to certain pronouncements made by different courts in what has come to be known as Public Interest Litigation (PIL). A lot has been said in the media and from the public platform by persons belonging to different hues. There have emerged two schools of thought, one which favours, what is called the court's activist role, the other which has been critical of it. The criticism could have been stronger but for the fear of contempt of court action.

This debate generally revolves around certain pro–nouncements made by courts at different levels in cases involving prominent personalities. Some of these pro–nouncements have been welcomed by the people and the media, whereas the political entities and bureaucracy have been critical of the activist mantle donned by the judiciary. But merely because the criticism comes from those at the receiving end of court orders is no ground to reject it out of hand.

The popular interest these decisions generated was only to be expected because of the people's wrath or disenchantment for the political and executive wings of the government. While this response may not be indicative of the correctness or propriety of some of the pronouncements, it certainly puts one to enquire about the reason for the people's wrath. More than any one else, it is for those against whom it is directed to introspect and come up with answers.

Personally I feel that the people's enchantment with those in power is essentially on account of their indifference and insensitivity towards the expectations of the people and large scale corruption. To put it differently, the administrative apparatus that has developed since independence has not been people-friendly and service-oriented. Since independence the administrative machinery has so developed that people feel scared approaching it. In fact they feel insecure in approaching those in power and authority.

Corruption has been eating into the vitals of the entire system and has made it inaccessible for a vast majority of the people. Our political system has ceased to be value-based and has degenerated further from the criminalisation of politics– which was bad enough – to the politicisation of criminals. Caste and communal politics has been injected, regardless of the toll it takes of human lives, to garner votes to acquire power, the lack of ethics is all pervading and disturbing stories, which cannot be brushed under the carpet, hit the headlines regularly.

This is the hard reality. I wish it were not so. It is because of this background that both the media and the people applaud court pronouncements which target these groups, and one can sense the element of vendetta therein. It is therefore

necessary that those in power, and those aspiring to be in power should search and consult their conscience to find ways and means to restore ethical norms in the governance of the country; if not for ourselves, at least for posterity. Let bygones be bygones, let us start a fresh chapter. This golden opportunity to remove the cancerous growth should not be missed in this golden jubilee year of our independence.

A word of caution for the judiciary. While the praise showered by the media on court pronouncements may be pleasing to the ears and the headline may raise a twinkle or two, it is exactly the situation to guard against as the publicity and the euphoria may cloud decision-making. Press publicity or press hostility can both be dangerous and may affect the judgment of those who are not strong enough to resist this. Judges, no doubt, are trained to maintain their cool and examine the evidence dispassionately, without fear or favour, affection or ill will, but when aberrations creep in doubts are raised. It is therefore advisable to couch orders in dignified language; moderation is a virtue and not a weakness.

But the question is how far is criticism levelled against pronouncements in PIL justified? How far is the criticism that the judiciary has invaded the fields reserved for the legislature and the executive well-founded? Since the judiciary does not go in search of litigation — it has sufficient, nay more than sufficient to deal with — why do people rush to court for relief? It is true that there are certain courtbirds who seek cheap publicity, there are others who want to satisfy their whims, but there are also a few who put in considerable industry and research before approaching the court.

A large number of PILs are rejected by courts but they do not attract media attention for obvious reasons. Only a few are entertained on the court being satisfied that public interest is involved. I would like to make it clear that no one has a right to contend that his PIL must be entertained. It is entirely the court's discretion to decide whether or not the 'locus standi' rule should be waived in favour of the petitioner.

I may now briefly deal with the role of the judiciary in such cases. The constitution of India has conferred a very wide jurisdiction on the Supreme Court of India. It shows that the Constitution-makers placed great confidence in the sagacity and wisdom of those who were to exercise such enormous powers. It necessarily follows that the court must excercise that jurisdiction with utmost care and caution. When power is conferred on a constitutional functionary, its is always to be understood by the functionary as a duty; others may view it as power.

When the functionary is a judicial officer, he must be extra-careful, lest he may appear to be carried away by emotion or bias. Self-imposed discipline and judicial restraint should be his armament, otherwise there is the fear that he may not be viewed as impartial. It is difficult to draw the 'lakshman rekha' but one can say, without fear of contradiction, that the power must be exercised with restraint and should not appear to be an immature impulse.

The judge's task is particularly difficult in the field of Public Interest Litigation. That is because in a large number of such cases, the material is wanting, and whatever little material is placed, is unfiltered. The entire proceeding tends to become

INDIA
50
1987 1996

inquisitorial in character with the Judge, or Judges, playing a more active, participatory role. The role of the judiciary is extremely delicate in such cases because it must not appear to be playing to the gallery or playing a role which may be described as being partisan. It must also be realised that the position of the opposite party in such cases is precarious, in that, it has to meet with allegations which are incomplete and often half-truths. In the absence of properly drawn up pleadings, it is always difficult to counter the charge levelled against the opposite party.

Certain flashy orders which are against the establishment do make headlines and the media may blow them up, which at times, may draw instant applause but if they cannot be carried to their logical end, may cause embarrassment. In the past, the Supreme Court has had to face such embarrassment of its orders and directions not being implemented in a few cases. There are cases where the implementing authorities have pleaded their inability to enforce the Court's order, on account of various difficulties faced at the ground level. This may give rise to a perception amongst certain sections of the people that the Court is becoming a paper tiger, prone to emitting moralising roars, to which a deaf ear can be turned with impunity, by the enforcing authorities on account of their inherently unenforceable nature.

Not being armed by either the purse or the sword, the Court is uniquely dependant upon the power of legitimacy for the compliance of its orders. Therefore, to ensure the continuance of this legitimacy, the Court should issue directions only after assessing the ground realities, and analysing the prospects of their being successfully implemented. Only orders which are judicially manageable ought to be passed so that their execution is guaranteed. One factor which must nearly always be considered is the fiscal aspect – whether the enforcing authority has the material resources to spare to be able to carry the directions of the Court to their logical end.

The Supreme Court is regarded by the people as the greatest institutional watchdog of people's fundamental rights and the most assertive organ that the nation possesses. This perception of the people has caused a spate of politico-legal issues to come to court for adjudication. These mainly come through the pipeline of public interest litigations. Not all are genuine cases, many come to court with half-baked material or on unconfirmed reports of the press or media. Some are essentially to settle scores or to gain publicity. Such abuse means the court is burdened with avoidable work.

But notwithstanding these abuses, there are some genuine public interest litigation cases, brought to court by informed citizens, which the court unhesitatingly entertains and examines. These petitions can do a lot of good to the people and the society. The remedy by way of the public interest litigation is, therefore, a very valuable weapon and my appeal to all concerned is not to blunt this valuable weapon by abusing it. It would be apposite to recall the words of wisdom of justice H R Khanna when he said, in his article 'Dilemmas and Dangers before the Indian judiciary':

"Resort to public interest litigation has undoubtably highlighted some of the unsavoury and pernicious matters in the field of the administration and has resulted in remedial measures being provided to rectify them. At the same time it needs to be mentioned that the opening of the door too wide for such litigation has also led to filing of many frivolous petitions..."

While I would forcefully defend the need to retain such discretionary jurisdiction, it should be made clear to those that abuse the process that they are harming the extremely potent weapon which can, in the right type of cases be of great service to the society. It is understandable that because of the awareness brought about by the media as regards the role of Supreme Court more and more people tend to bring public causes to court and hence the court must be wary in the excercise of its jurisdiction. We all know that when invented, penicillin was considered a wonder drug, the queen of drugs – but its indiscriminate use saw people dying of anaphylactic shock forcing the medical world to abandon it. Let not such a fate fall on the people-friendly jurisdiction exercised in public interest.

Therefore, to uphold and maintain the public interest jurisdiction, the Supreme Court as also the High Courts must exercise it with restraint and circumspection, more so, in cases where they are sorely tempted to intervene to remedy grave defects, if it senses that any orders issued by them may be difficult to enforce.

In the ultimate analysis the endeavour must be to ensure that the Rule of Law prevails no matter who the actors are. This responsibility under our constitution rests on all the three organs of government. There is no vertical hierarchy so far as these three organs are concerned. Even so by training the judiciary gives sufficient time and opportunity to the other two organs to act. If they fail to act and the court's are moved they are left with no alternative but to act.

Take corruption, which raised its ugly head when the Mundhra chapter surfaced but it has increased with galloping speed and has reached a stage when people have become so insensitive that they have almost accepted corruption as a way of life. Almost resigned to the fate and have given up the will to fight. Unless we restore probity in public life, inculcate discipline and respect for the Rule of Law, introduce an administrative machinery, including the police force, that is people-friendly and respect Human Rights, abhor considerations of caste, creed and communities, we shall not be able to build up a society worth living in. Adherence to rule of law is the first priority because without it there will be no liberty, no equality, no respect for human dignity and in the ultimate, the responsibility for upholding the Rule of Law will fall on the judiciary if the other two organs fail.

Is it not a good contribution by the judiciary that it has awakened the people and generated a debate on values which is still making the rounds and should do so till the goal is achieved. I am an optimist, I carry that eternal hope in my heart, I have that dream for a better India. Unlike others who say they are ashamed to call themselves Indians, I am proud to say I am an Indian and look forward to better days ahead.

HAPPENINGS

1987-1996

Charan Singh

January 27
P T Usha nominated as Asian Athlete of the Year of 1986 by the US Sports Academy

February 20
Arunachal Pradesh becomes India's 24th state

March 7
Sunil Gavaskar becomes the first man to score 10,000 runs in Test cricket at Ahmedabad against Pakistan

March 24
India's first new generation rocket ASLV plunges within two minutes and 40 seconds of its launching.

March 29
Former Prime Minister Charan Singh dies. The leader of Haryana's 10 million Jats, he was prime minister for just five months and 15 days after the collapse of the Morarji Desai government in the 1977-80 Janata Party stint

March 30
Goa becomes India's 25th state

Khan Abdul Gaffar Khan

January 20
Frontier Gandhi Khan Abdul Gaffar Khan dies

January 21
Kiran Bedi's alleged lathi charge on lawyers in Delhi and then her apparent order for the police to turn to stone when lawyers are attacked by a mob brings the courts to a standstill. A judicial committee is appointed and Bedi is transferred out of her post as DCP, Delhi, North district

February 25
Sachin Tendulkar, 14, and Vinod Kambli, 15, put on a world record 664-runs third wicket partnership in the Harris Shield

April 30
Raj Kapoor gets the Dadasaheb Phalke Award

June 2 1988
The Showman, Raj Kapoor, dies. The Indian Charlie Chaplin made bittersweet films with social themes and then, total blockbusters. Bobby succeeded where Mera Naam Joker failed

Ashok Kumar

February 2
France's highest civilian award, Legion d' Honour, is conferred upon director Satyajit Ray in Calcutta

March 1
Vasantrao Patil, Governor of Rajasthan and former Maharashtra chief minister, dies

April 14
Actor Ashok Kumar gets the Dadasaheb Phalke Award

January 2
Nivedita Bhasin, 26, becomes the youngest woman pilot in world aviation history to command a jet aircraft

January 19
Godman and philosopher Osho dies in Pune. The controversial godman returned to India after a sojourn in Oregon ended when the American authorities forced him to leave, on allegations of financial irregularities. Formerly known as Zorba the Buddha and Bhagwan Rajneesh. His free sex, feel-good philosophy found ready followers outside India, but he struggled to find acceptance in his homeland. He was credited with writing over 650 books

Osho

February 14
Over 90 people killed in an Indian Airlines Airbus crash at Bangalore. The accident created a controversy over the purchase of the computer-run A320 aircraft

April 8
A 285-kmph cyclone lashes the Andhra Pradesh coast, causing heavy losses to life and property

June 24
Defence scientists successfully test fire country's first third generation anti-tank missile 'NAG'

January 11
Former prime minister Morarji Desai is awarded the Bharat Ratna

March 25
1991 census report released; India has 844 million people

June 9
Civil service prelimina exams cancelled after th question paper leaks

June 17
Rajiv Gandhi and Sardar Vallabhbhai Patel are awarded the Bharat Ratna posthumously

| 1987 | 1988 | 1989 | 1990 | 1991 |

July 17
R Venkataraman elected president of India

August 2
Vishwanathan Anand becomes the first Asian to win the World Junior Chess Championship

September 4
18-year-old Roop Kanwar commits sati on her husband's funeral pyre, in the town of Deorala in Rajasthan. Although sati has been abolished in India for almost two centuries, it is still surreptitiously practised and the ideal of the sati revered. Kanwar's suicide is watched by almost 5,000 people, who do nothing to stop it. The government makes half-hearted attempts to nab the abettors

October 12
Unceasingly versatile and endlessly entertaining singer, film-maker and comedian Kishore Kumar dies

December 24
Tamil Nadu Chief Minister and former actor M G Ramachandran, 70, dies

December
Industrial production falls by 10 per cent, agricultural production rises by 8 per cent, the Gross National Product rises by 2 per cent and prices by 10 per cent. The 1987 monsoon is the worst recorded since Independence

July 8
More than 100 people are killed when Bangalore-Trivandrum Island Express jumps rails and falls into Ashtamudi Lake in Kerala's Quilon district

July 28
National badminton champ Syed Modi is shot dead. Suspected are his wife, Ameeta Modi nee Kulkarni, and politician and friend Sanjay Singh. The case gets political implications, as Singh is the nephew of V P Singh. Both suspects are finally exonerated of the murder charge and get married to each other

July 31
The 26 Down from Bangalore to Trivandrum is crossing the Perumon Bridge near Quilon at 80 kmph when nine coaches plunge into the river. Villagers put on a marvellous resuce effort, but 100 die

September 28
A day without newspapers in the country as the newspaper industry protests against the proposed Defamation Bill

December 18
Rajiv Gandhi visits China — the first visit to China in 34 years by an Indian prime minister

July 15
Rajiv Gandhi arrives in Pakistan, the first visit by an Indian prime minister in 30 years

August 6
Top Indian cricketers — Dilip Vengsarkar, Kapil Dev, Kiran More, Arun Lal, Mohammed Azharuddin — are banned for one year by the Board of Control for Cricket in India over an unofficial tour to America. The ban is revoked soon after, when the Supreme Court ruled for the players

October 21
Sukhdev Singh alias Sukha and Harminder Singh alias Jinda sentenced to death for the murder of former Army chief General A K Vaidya. The general was killed for his role in Operation Bluestar

August 1
Deputy prime minister Devi Lal is dropped from the Union Cabinet following charges he made against colleagues, replete with unsavoury language, in an interview with The Illustrated Weekly of India

September 16
Air-India establishes a world record by evacuating more than one lakh people in eight weeks from Kuwait and Iraq, as the two countries prepare for war

October 16
Nelson Mandela, South African leader, is awarded the Bharat Ratna, the highest civilian honour, during his visit to India

October 28
Veteran film-maker V Shantaram, 80, dies. One of the mughals of the film industry, Shantaram's films always contained a soical message. Memorable: Dr Kotnis Ki Amar Kahani, about the China war and Do Aankhen Barah Haath, about prison reforms

December 1
Former US ambassador and sister of Jawaharlal Nehru, Vijayalakshmi Pandit, 90, dies

December 20
India and Pakistan agree not to attack each other's nuclear installations

December
India makes 948 films, to remain at the top of the world. The last high was 912 in 1985

August 3
About 280 kg of gold ornaments valued at $ 15 million which had been deposited in the Portuguese bank in Goa by Goans is flown back to India

August 7
India successfully launches the Prithvi III ground-to-air missile from Sriharikota

September 22
Film actress Durga Khote, 86, dies

October 5
Ramnath Goenka, 87, founder chairman of the Indian Express Group of Newspapers, dies

October 20
About 1,000 people perish in an earthquake that rocks three northern districts of UP

November 26
Romanian diplomat Liviu Radu released by Sikh militants after 48 days in captivity

R Venkataraman

Syed Modi

Raj Kapoor

Kiran Bedi

N T Rama Rao

Shiv Sena comes to power

S L Kirloskar

January 8
Maharashtra Government clears the controversial Enron Dabhol Power Project at a tariff of Rs 1.86 per unit

January 16
Union cabinet minister V C Shukla, Balram Jakhar, Madhavrao Scindia and others including L K Advani, Arjun Singh and Devi Lal are chargesheeted in the hawala case

January 18
Andhra Pradesh Chief Minister and former superstar N T Rama Rao dies in Hyderabad

January 24
H K L Bhagat, senior Congress politician and former minister, is arrested in connection with the 1984 anti-Sikh riot case

January 31
Asia's first sports university is inaugurated in Pune

February 2
Gold zooms to an all-time price high of Rs 5,600 per 10 gm

March 18
Sri Lanka wins the Wills World Cup beating Australia in Lahore. The India-Sri Lanka semi-final in Calcutta on March 13 had to be abandoned because of unruly crowds and rioting when India was facing defeat

March 22
Amritsar's Golden temple is renamed Harmandir Sahib, its original name, meaning abode of God

April 18
Train mishap at Gorakhpur kills 100

April 20
Massive bomb explosion kills 17 in Paharganj Guest House in New Delhi

May 21
Powerful explosion in Delhi's Lajpatnagar market kills 25

June 1
Former President Neelam Sanjeeva Reddy dies. Veteran Congressman who shifted loyalties after falling out with Indira Gandhi. Spent his retirement years in oblivion

January 8
ONGC's oil rig blows out at Pasalpudi site in Andhra Pradesh

January 26
Nelson Mandela attends India's 46th Republic Day celebrations as a national guest

March 14
The Shiv Sena and Bharatiya Janata Party form a coalition government in Maharashtra, after the Congress loses the state for the first time since Independence. Manohar Joshi of the Sena is made chief minister, while the BJP gets the post of deputy chief minister for Gopinath Munde. Bal Thackeray gives himself the title of remote control

April 10
Former Prime Minister, Morarji Desai, 99, dies, belying the hopes of his supporters that he would live to be 100. Desai was twice done out of the Prime Minister's post — once, after Nehru's death in 1964 and then after Lal Bahadur Shastri's death in 1966, when Indira Gandhi became Prime Minister. He finally made the post in 1977, when the Janata Party came to power after the Emergency, but lost it to Charan Singh in 1979. A strong disciplinarian and often too outspoken for his colleagues, Desai was also chief minister of Bombay State during the language riots of the late 1950s

June 30
CNN launches a 24-houram news channel in partnership with Doordarshan

January 4
Music director R D Burman, 56, dies. Son of S D Burman, husband of singer Asha Bhosale, Rahul Dev was known for his catchy, innovative tunes

January 15
Bandh and violence in Marathwada in Maharashtra after the Shiv Sena protests against the renaming of Marathwada University after B R Ambedkar

March 1
Popular film-maker Manmohan Desai, 58, falls off his balcony and dies. Insiders allege that the depressed Desai committed suicide

March 9
The first lady of the Indian screen, Devika Rani Roerich, 87, dies in Bangalore

March 20
Pakistan closes down its consulate in Bombay

April 24
Industrial magnate S L Kirloskar, 91, dies in Pune

January 2
Posthumous Bharat Ratnas for Netaji Subhas Chandra Bose and Maulana Abul Kalam Azad

January 25
Bharat Ratna for JRD Tata

March 11
Dr Anita Bose-Pfaff, daughter of Subhas Chandra Bose, declines to accept the Bharat Ratna conferred on her father

March 16
Satyajit Ray is presented an honorary Oscar award by a three-member Oscar committee at a Calcutta nursing home. Four days later he is awarded the Bharat Ratna

May 5
Prithvi, India's medium range surface-to-surface missile is successfully launched

May 9
Adulterated, illicit liquor kills 175 in Orissa

April 25
IA plane hijacker shot dead by commandoes, all persons rescued

April 26
IA plane crashes at Aurangabad, killing 55 passengers

June 7
Godman Satya Sai Baba escapes attempt on life. Four assailants and two bodyguards are killed

1993   1994   1995   1996

July 10
The first Indian-made satellite, Insat 2A, is shot into space from Kourore

September 18
Former Vice-President M Hidayatullah, 87, dies

October 3
Geet Sethi beats holder Mike Russell of Britain to become the first Indian to claim the World Professional Billiard Championship in Bombay

November 21
7 killed in bomb blast engineered by Bodo extremists in a bus in Assam

November 27
Sachin Tendulkar at 19 years and 22 days becomes the youngest cricketer to make 1,000 Test runs while playing against South Africa in Johannesburg

Sachin Tendulkar

July 19
India beats France 3-2 in the Davis Cup tie to enter the semi-finals

September 30
An earthquake obiliterates about 40 villages in Latur and Osmanabad districts of Maharashtra and Andhra Pradesh. The damage to life and property is extensive and the tremors are felt in a radius of up to 400 km

July 4
India's most famous policewoman, Kiran Bedi, wins the Ramon Magsaysay Award for public service, particularly for her work in re-organising the Indian prison system to make it more humane.

December 25
Former president Giani Zail Singh, 78, dies. An Indira Gandhi loyalist, he held many ministerial posts before becoming President. He then fell out with Rajiv Gandhi and was reportedly behind a conspiracy to oust Rajiv from the prime ministership

Giani Zail Singh

August 20
208 persons killed and 230 injured in a train accident in Ferozabad, Uttar Pradesh, when the Kalindi Express and Purushottam Express collide

August 23
India's first-ever cellular phone service begins in Calcutta

August 31
Punjab Chief Minister Beant Singh and 14 others killed in a suicide car bomb explosion in Chandigarh

October 26
The Reserve Bank of India boosts the rupee, which had plunged to an all-time low of Rs 35.85 per dollar, by selling several million dollars

December 23
400 persons, mostly children and their parents, die in a fire during the annual day celebrations of DAV Public School that breaks out probably due to a short-circuit in Mandi Dabvali, Haryana

December 31
Punjab Director General of Police, KPS Gill, retires. Gill had taken over from Julio Ribeiro and is said to have broken the backbone of terrorism in Punjab. He was also involved in an unsavoury courtcase over the molestation of a female IAS office. His tenure as President of the Indian Hockey Federation was not without its share of controversy

Leander Paes

July 8
Chief Election Commissioner T N Seshan gets the Ramon Magsaysay award

August 3
Leander Paes wins a bronze medal at the Atlanta Olympics. Paes is the first Indian to get an individual medal after K D Jadhav won the bronze for wrestling in the 1952 Helsinki Olympics

August 9
Sachin Tendulkar becomes skipper of India, replacing Mohammed Azharuddin. He is the second-youngest captain of India after Mansur Ali Khan Pataudi

August 25
Severe cold weather kills 194 pilgrims to the Cave temples of Amarnath

September 2
Grandmaster Vishwanathan Anand beats Garry Kasparov in a rapid chess tournament in Geneva

September 23
Sitaram Kesri is elected president of the Congress

October 2
Mother Teresa is made an honorary US citizen

October 30
Pop star Michael Jackson arrives in Mumbai. His concert is spectacular but touched by controversy over allegations of financial skullduggery

November 6
India wins the Titan Cup beating South Africa in Mumbai

November 7
Cyclonic storm hits Andhra Pradesh, over 1,000 people die

November 12
Over 350 people die in a mid-air collision between a Saudi Airlines commercial craft and a Kazhakistan cargo plane waiting to land at Delhi airport. The debris lands in the village of Charkhi Dadri in Haryana

INDIA AT 50: THE MAKING OF A NATION
1997

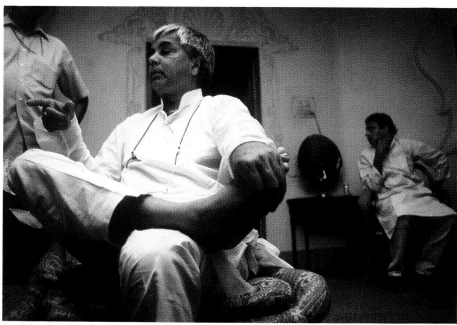

Food for thought: *The arrogance of Laloo Prasad Yadav*   Saibal Das/India Today

Uneasy lies the head: *H D Deve Gowda* Sharad Saxena/india Today

A nation, perhaps, gets made in the making. It stumbles, falls, picks itself up again, it travels to the brink of disintegration and then pulls back. It pats itself on the back over its triumphs, but learns from its failures. India is 50, but has it made a nation?

The year opens and a great-grandson gets permission to rescue his great-grandfather's ashes from a bank vault where they have lain since he was killed and then cremated in 1948. Is there any significance in the fact that Mahatma Gandhi's ashes should reach the news after lying dormant, forgotten, forlorn for so long, in the 50th year of India's Independence? A nudge, perhaps, in the right direction?

Direction is sorely needed, as uncertainty looms over the choice of candidate for Congress President, after P V Narasimha Rao resigns. Sharad Pawar and Rajesh Pilot are beaten to the post by the wily Sitaram Kesri. The political scenario gets fuzzy and flimsy simultaneously. Immediately, the future of the shaky United Front coalition government is thrown open to question. The fear is fulfilled on March 30 when the Congress withdraws support to the Government and H D Deve Gowda is no longer Prime Minister and Kesri says he wants to be.

The Bharatiya Janata Party and Bahujan Samaj Party put aside all ideological differences in Uttar Pradesh and form a coalition government with a unique power-sharing equation. The chief minister alternates from each party every six months. Former enmities are buried to stay on top.

Meanwhile, in Bihar, Chief Minister Laloo Prasad Yadav refuses to take any responsibility for the Rs 950 crore animal fodder scam in his state, which dogs him as a leftover from the year before. He rails against the Central Bureau of Investigation and hints at dark conspiracies. The United

Taking India forward: *Prime Minister I K Gujral*

Front Government seems helpless but forced to protect the President of the Janata Dal.

Yadav is finally removed from the post as President. But when a warrant is issued for his arrest in the case, he throws the dust in everyone's eyes. He breaks away and forms a new party. When arrest is imminent, in a masterly sleight of hand, he relinquishes charge. To his wife, the politically innocent housewife, Rabri Devi.

Elsewhere, the Indian cricket team is haunted by bad performance and worse selection, compounded by allegations of betting by players to fix matches. The biggest disgrace comes when Sri Lanka thrash a whopping 952 for 7, a world record, against Sachin Tendulkar's hapless side.

And the underworld shows its complete clout over the film industry by picking off errant producers and directors, pointing to the recurring woes of disorganisation in a money-making sector. If small films do surprisingly well, spectacular films do spectacularly badly. Amitabh Bachchan's *Mrityudand* being a case in point.

And, DГ B ГГ АГНООЦГГАГ Г ГРОГ ГРАНГ are removed from courtrooms, causing some small upheavals. The worst comes when a garland of slippers is found on a statue of the architect of the Indian Constitution. Protests from Dalits lead to an unfortunate and uncalled-for police firing, and 12 deaths in Mumbai. The reaction is sharp and violent, and latent caste angers emerge.

And, Parliament and all political parties insist that something must be done about uplifting the status and numbers of women in politics. The Bill that reserves 33 per cent seats for women in legislatures, however, never gets passed. The Prime Minister tries to make amends by inducting four women into his Cabinet, limiting them, however, to domestic portfolios — welfare, health,

women's issues rather than defence, external affairs, finance, home.

And yet.

The year 1997 has more to offer.

No communal clashes for instance.

An abiding interest in cleaning up Indian political life.

The Supreme Court still looking out for the interests of the common man.

Moreover, the Gujral Doctrine from Prime Minister I K Gujral which makes a concerted and genuine effort to mend bridges with Pakistan and try and build a relationship on mutual trust and understanding.

And, in the race to become President of India, the two personalities pitted against each other have some worth — they are not just political stooges.

And, if K R Narayanan, scholar, diplomat and former vice-president wins, it is because he is the better man, and not a Dalit.

And, if former Chief Election Commissioner T N Seshan, who revolutionised and cleaned up the Indian electoral system and told a few home truths about corruption, loses, it may be ГРГ ГГ ГГ ГГГ ГГГ ГГГ ГГГ ГГГ ГГГ ГГГ ГГ get the appropriate support.

August 15, 1997, just after midnight. Another tryst with destiny.

President K R Narayanan talks about how corruption, communalism, casteism and criminalisation have ruined the country.

Appropriate words for a vital retrospective on how the past 50 years have treated India? Indeed, on how Indians have treated their hard-won freedom?

But perhaps the fears of fragmentation and disintegration are misplaced. To approach the future, the past needs to be scrutinised. Not just 50 years, but 5,000, to know why India will survive.

The only way now is ahead.

The making *of* a NATION

INDIA: VITAL SIGNS

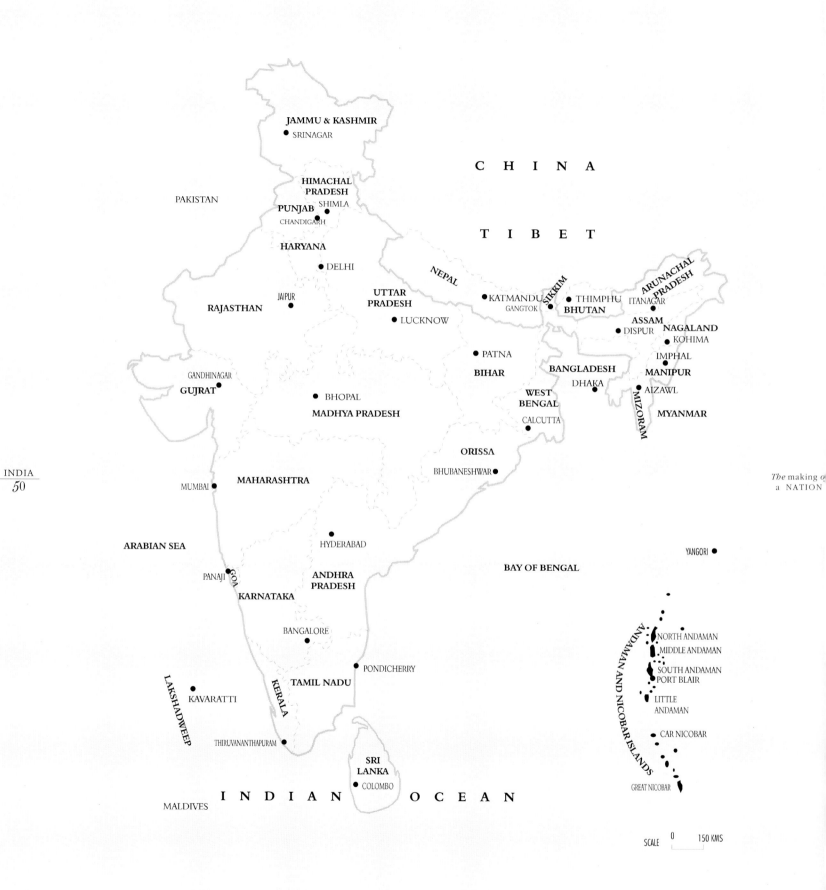

*The making of
a NATION*

INDIA: VITAL SIGNS

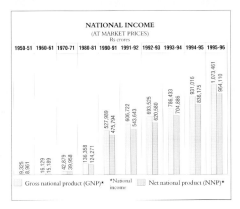

NATIONAL INCOME
(AT MARKET PRICES)
Rs crores

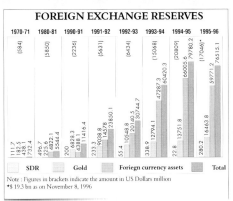

FOREIGN EXCHANGE RESERVES

Note : Figures in brackets indicate the amount in US Dollars million
*$ 19.3 bn as on November 8, 1996

SDR · Gold · Foriegn currency assets · Total

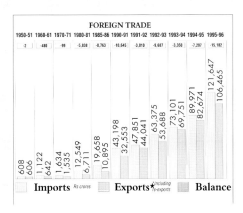

FOREIGN TRADE

Imports *Rs crores* · Exports *(including re-exports)* · Balance

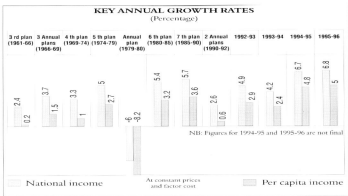

KEY ANNUAL GROWTH RATES
(Percentage)

NB: Figures for 1994-95 and 1995-96 are not final

National income · At constant prices and factor cost · Per capita income

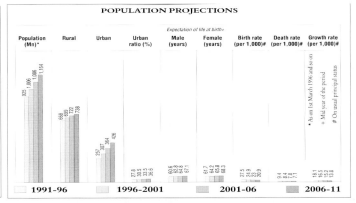

POPULATION PROJECTIONS

Expectation of life at birth+

* As on 1st March 1996 and so on
+ Mid year of the period
# On usual principal status

1991-96 · 1996-2001 · 2001-06 · 2006-11

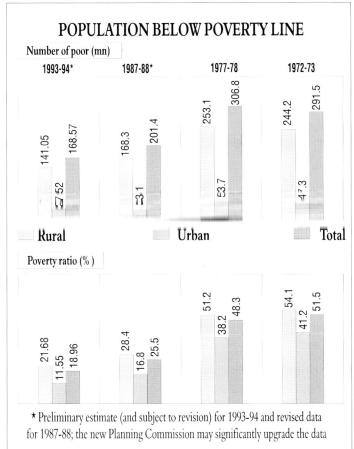

POPULATION BELOW POVERTY LINE

Number of poor (mn)

1993-94* · 1987-88* · 1977-78 · 1972-73

Rural · Urban · Total

Poverty ratio (%)

* Preliminary estimate (and subject to revision) for 1993-94 and revised data
for 1987-88; the new Planning Commission may significantly upgrade the data

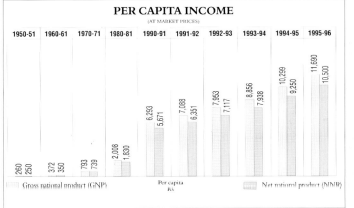

PER CAPITA INCOME
(AT MARKET PRICES)

Gross national product (GNP) · Per capita Rs · Net national product (NNP)

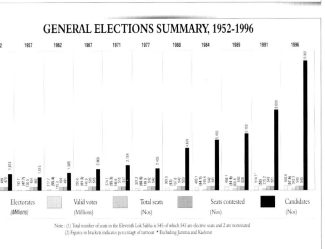

GENERAL ELECTIONS SUMMARY, 1952-1996

Electorates *(Millions)* · Valid votes *(Millions)* · Total seats *(Nos)* · Seats contested *(Nos)* · Candidates *(Nos)*

Note : (1) Total number of seats in the Eleventh Lok Sabha is 545 of which 543 are elective seats and 2 are nominated
(2) Figures in brackets indicates percentage of turnout * Excluding Jammu and Kashmir

Source: Statistical Outline of India, 1996-97, Tata Services Limited

CONTRIBUTORS

A H Ahmadi
Retired Chief Justice of the Supreme Court, known for his role in bringing judicial activism to the forefront

Ali Sardar Jafri
Poet and writer, in both Urdu and English. Founder member of Progressive Writers' Group and freedom fighter

Anil Shastri
Son of India's second Prime Minister Lal Bahadur Shastri, he was minister for Economic Affairs in 1989

Ashis Nandy
Reputed political and social psychologist and commentator. Books include *The Intimate Enemy: Loss and Recovery of Self Under Colonialism*

Dr Ashok Mitra
Reputed economist. Was professor of economics at IIM and Finance Minister with the Government of West Bengal

B K Karanjia
Respected film critic and author. Former editor of Screen and Filmfare. Was chairman of the NFDC

Bhaskar Ghose
Television personality and columnist. Former director general of Doordarshan

Chitra Subramaniam
Eminent journalist. Noted for her role in exposing the Bofors scandal. Has written *Bofors: The Story Behind the Good News*

Dom Moraes
Noted poet, writer and columnist. Author of several books of poetry, as well his famous autobiography, *My Son's Father*

Dr Farooq Abdullah
Currently Chief Minister of Jammu and Kashmir, Has held this post several times since the death of his father, Sheikh Abdullah

Dr Gita Piramal
Free-lance journalist. Author of *Business Maharajas,* and working on a prequel, *Business Legends*

Indira Jaising
Distinguished Supreme Court lawyer, known for her espousal of social causes and women's issues

Gopal Godse
Younger brother of Nathuram Godse. Knew about the conspiracy to kill Mahatma Gandhi

Iqbal Masud
Respected film critic. Started as an income tax officer and became Commissioner. Was part of a United Nations deputation to the Middle East

J N Dixit
Political commentator and columnist. As a diplomat, was Ambassador to Afghanistan, Sri Lanka and Pakistan

Janardan Thakur
Political commentator. Currently editor of *Free Press Journal,* Mumbai

Jasjit Singh
Director of the Institute for Defence Studies and Analyses, New Delhi.

Julio Ribeiro
Was police commissioner of Bombay, Director General of Police, Punjab and Ambassador to Roumania

K N Pannikar
Professor of Modern History at Jawaharlal Nehru University, specialising in intellectual and cultural history

K N Prabhu
Noted cricket writer and columnist, known for his lyrical prose. Former sports editor of *The Times of India*

Dr Kirit S Parikh
Founding Director of the Indira Gandhi Institute for Development Research, Mumbai

K F Rustamji
Columnist, particularly on security matters. Former Director of the Border Security Force

CONTRIBUTORS

Khushwant Singh
Noted author and journalist. His works include *Train to Pakistan* and translations of Urdu poetry. Was editor of *The Illustrated Weekly of India*

Dr Rudrangshu Mukherjee
Editor, Editorial Pages, *The Telegraph,* Calcutta. Visiting fellow at Princeton and Manchester Universities. Edited *The Gandhi Reader*

Dr Vandana Shiva
Noted environmentalist. Director of the Research Foundation for Science Technology and Natural Resource Policy in Dehra Dun

M M Somaiya
Sturdy half-back and former India Hockey captain

Sunil Gavaskar
Sports writer and commentator. Former Cricket Captain and India's greatest batsman. Scored 34 centuries, a world record

Urvashi Butalia
Feminist and publisher. Co-founder of Kali For Women, a social work organisation and publishing house which specialises in women's issues

Michael Ferreira
Billiards player and sports writer. Twice World Amateur Billiards Champion and World Open Champion

Shobha Dé
Noted author and columnist. Her books include *Socialite Evenings*. First editor of *Stardust, Society* and *Celebrity* magazines

Vir Sanghvi
Political commentator and television personality. Currently consulting editor to Ananda Bazar Patrika Group

Mushirul Hasan
Acting Vice-Chancellor at Jamia Milia University. An eminent historian. His books include *The Legacy of a Divided India*

Shyam Benegal
Noted film-maker His best works include Ankur and Making of the Mahatma, and Bharat Ek Khoj, based on Nehru's Discovery of India

Vara Vara Rao
Revolutionary poet. Joined Naxalite Movement in the late '60s. Was jailed several times for his writings

Mulk Raj Anand
Founder member of the Progressive Writers' Group. His novels include *The Bubble*. Chairman of the Lalit Kala Akademi from 1955 to '70

S Ramakrishnan
Director of Bharatiya Vidya Bhavan, Mumbai and founder editor of *Bhavan's Journal*. Was private secretary to Vallabhbhai Patel

Ved Marwah
Research professor at the Centre for Policy Research, New Delhi. Was advisor to governor of Jammu & Kashmir Has written *Uncivil Wars*

Natwar Singh
Political commentator, particularly on India's foreign policy and role in the South Asian region. Former External Affairs Minister

Soli Sorabjee
Supreme Court lawyer and columnist. Former Advocate General of India

V P Singh
Former Prime Minister of India. Was also Chief Minister of Uttar Pradesh and Union Defence Minister and Finance Minister

Rahul Bajaj
Noted industrialist. An MBA from Harvard, has been Chief Executive Officer of Bajaj Auto since 1968

Dr Teotonio R de Souza
Fellow of Portuguese Academy of History and Professor of Economic and Social History, Universidade Lusofona, Lisbon

Y D Phadke
Was professor of social studies at Tata Institute of Social Sciences, specialising in political science and public administration

Rahul Singh
Former editor-in-chief of *Reader's Digest* and *Sunday Observer,* and resident editor of *Indian Express*. Noted columnist

The making of a NATION

BIBLIOGRAPHY

BOOKS

Freedom at Midnight,
Larry Collins and Dominique Lapierre

Partition and Independence,
Manmath Nath Das

Mountbatten and the Partition of India,
S Hashim Raza

Assassination of Mahatma Gandhi,
K L Gauba

Dalit Movement in India and Its Leaders,
R K Kshirsagar

The Constitution of India,
P B Gajendragadkar

Bhoodan Movement,
B R Misra

Lal Bahadur Shastri,
Mankekar

The Role of the Opposition in Indian
Politics,
Renu Saksena

The Problem of Transition,
Shah

Split in a Predominant Party - The Indian
National Congress in 1969,
Mahendra Singh

My Truth,
Indira Gandhi

Mrs Gandhi,
Dom Moraes

That Woman,
K A Abbas

The New Cambridge History of India,
The Politics of India since Independence,
Paul Brass

Business Maharajas,
Gita Piramal

Towards Total Revolution,
Jayaprakash Narayan

The Nehrus and the Gandhis: An Indian
Dynasty,
Tariq Ali

The Good Boatman,
Rajmohan Gandhi

Indian Judiciary, A Tribute,
Poornima Advani

The Penguin Gandhi Reader,
Rudrangshu Mukherjee

Surrender at Dacca, Birth of a Nation,
Lt Gen JFR Jacob

The Sikh People,
K S Duggal

Uncivil Wars,
Ved Marwah

India: The Siege Within,
M J Akbar

My Years With Nehru, The Chinese
Betrayal,
B N Mullick

Himalayan Blunder,
Brigadier J P Dalvi

India's China War,
Neville Maxwell

I, Phoolan Devi, with
Marie-Therese Cuny and Paul Rambali

Forever Nehru,
Alanka Shankar

The Indian Army,
Lt Gen S L Menezes

An Advanced History of India,
*R C Majumdar, H C Raychaudhuri and
Kalikinkar Datta*

Jawaharlal Nehru,
Frank Moraes

Modern India,
Manohar R Wadhwani

Battle Honours of the Indian Army,
Major Sarbans Singh

Confrontation with Pakistan,
B M Kaul

Modern Indian History,
V D Mahajan

Selected Works of Jawaharlal Nehru,
Edited by S Gopal

A History of India,
Percival Spear

India, A Modern History,
T G P Spear

Jawaharlal Nehru, A Biography,
Sarvepalli Gopal

Bofors, The Story Behind the News,
Chitra Subramaniam

Classified, The Political Cover-up of the Bofors Sacndal.
Henrik Westander

Ethnicity and Equality, The Shiv Sena Party and Preferential Policies in Bombay,
Mary Fansoid Katzenstein

India-China and Panchsheel, edited by
Jasjit Singh

Mother Teresa, A Simple Path,
Lucinda Vardey

The Creation of Wealth,
R M Lala

A Rare Legacy, Memoirs of B K Birla

Integration of Indian States,
V P Menon

The Transfer of Power in India,
V P Menon

Sholay, A Cultural Reading,
Wimal Dissanayake and Malti Sahai

Kashmir, Behind the Vale,
M J Akbar

The Scam: Who Won, Who Lost, Who Got Away,
Debashis Basu, Sucheta Dalal

25 Years of Indian Independence, edited by
Jag Mohan

The Advent of Advani,
Atmaram Kulkarni

India's Bandit Queen,
Mala Sen

The Discovery of Bangladesh,
Prabhat Srivastava

Anatomy of a Confrontation, The Babri Masjid-Ram Janmabhumi Issue, edited by
S Gopal

Communalism in India,
Asghar Ali Engineer

My Years with Nehru, Kashmir,
B N Mullick

The Missionary Position,
Christopher Hitchens

Love of Christ, Mother Teresa, edited by
Georges Goree and Jean Barbier

The New Cambridge History of India, Peasant Labour and Colonial Capital,
Sugata Bose

New Approach, Jyoti Basu, edited by
Sekhar Basu Roy

The History and Culture of the Indian People, edited by
R C Majumdar

History of India,
A N Banerjee

Bangladesh, Emergence of a Nation,
A M A Muhith

Rediscovery of India: A New Subcontinent,
Ansar Hussain Khan

Who's Who of Cricket,
Christopher Martin-Jenkins

Portraits of Indian Test Cricketers,
L N Mathur

Sunny Days,
Sunil Gavaskar

My Cricketing Years,
Ajit Wadekar

Kapil Dev: A Triumph of the Spirit,
Romi Dev

Wills Book of Excellence - Cricket,
Mudar Patherya

The Olympic Games, 1896-1984,
Peter Arnold

Wills Book of Excellence - One-day Cricket,
Ayaz Memon

Wills Book of Excellence - Hockey,
Ron Hendricks

100 Luminaries,
Dinesh Raheja

Raj Kapoor,
Bunny Rueben

So Many Cinemas,
B D Garga

Journal of Art and Ideas, 'Shifting Codes, Dissolving Identities',
Ravi Vasudevan

Sunil Gavaskar: Portrait if a Hero,
Clifford Narinesingh

Barclay's World of Cricket

Limca Book of Records

My Days,
R K Narayan

R K Narayan, The Early Years,
Susan and N Ram

The Joy of Achievement,
R M Lala

PERIODICALS AND JOURNALS

India Today
The Illustrated Weekly of India
Sunday
Frontline
Outlook
Bombay The City Magazine
Probe
Onlooker
Economic and Political Weekly
Foreign Affairs
Femina
Time Magazine
Sportstar
Sportsweek

NEWSPAPERS

The Times of India
The Indian Express
The Hindustan Times
The Statesman
The Telegraph
The Hindu
The Deccan Herald
The Sunday Observer
The Business and Political Observer
The Economic Times
Asiad Chronicle